General History of Africa · VI

Africa in the Nineteenth Century until the 1880s

Abridged Edition

UNESCO General History of Africa

Volume I   *Methodology and African Prehistory*
             Editor **J. Ki-Zerbo**

Volume II   *Ancient Civilizations of Africa*
             Editor **G. Mokhtar**

Volume III   *Africa from the Seventh to the Eleventh Century*
             Editor **I. Hrbek**

Volume IV   *Africa from the Twelfth to Sixteenth Century*
             Editors **J. Ki-Zerbo and D. T. Niane**

Volume V   *Africa from the Sixteenth to Eighteenth Century*★
             Editor **B. A. Ogot**

Volume VI   *Africa in the Nineteenth Century until the 1880s*
             Editor **J. F. Ade Ajayi**

Volume VII   *Africa under Foreign Domination 1880–1935*
             Editor **A. Adu Boahen**

Volume VIII *Africa since 1935*★
             Editor **A. A. Mazrui**

             ★forthcoming

The abridged edition of
THE UNESCO GENERAL HISTORY OF AFRICA
is published by the following publishers

In Ghana, Sierra Leone,
the Gambia and Cameroon by
Ott-Attafua
P.O. Box 2692
Osu-Accra, Ghana
In Kenya by
EAEP
P.O. Box 45314
Nairobi, Kenya
In Nigeria by
Heinemann Nigeria
P.O. Box 6205
Ibadan, Nigeria
In South Africa, Namibia, Botswana,
Lesotho and Swaziland by
David Philip Publishers
P.O. Box 23408
Claremont 7735, South Africa
In Tanzania by
Tanzania Publishing House
P.O. Box 2138
Dar es Salaam, Tanzania
In Uganda by
Fountain Publishers
P.O. Box 488
Kampala, Uganda
In Zambia by
UNZA Press
P.O. Box 32379
Lusaka, Zambia
In Zimbabwe,
Botswana, Swaziland and Malawi by
Baobab Books
P.O. Box 1559
Harare, Zimbabwe
In the United States of America
and Canada by
The University of California Press
2120 Berkeley Way
Berkeley, California 94720
And in the United Kingdom, Europe
and the rest of the world by
James Currey Publishers   and
73 Botley Road   UNESCO Publishing
Oxford OX2 0BS   7 Place de Fontenoy, 75700, Paris

International Scientific Committee for the Drafting of a General History of Africa (UNESCO)

General History of Africa · VI

Africa in the Nineteenth Century until the 1880s

EDITOR J. F ADE AJAYI

Abridged Edition

JAMES CURREY · CALIFORNIA · UNESCO

First published 1998 by the
United Nations Educational, Scientific
and Cultural Organization
7 Place de Fontenoy, 75700, Paris

James Currey Ltd
73 Botley Road
Oxford OX2 0BS

and

University of California Press
2120 Berkeley Way, Berkeley
California 94720, United States of America

©UNESCO 1988 and 1998
ISBN (UNESCO): 92-3-102498-1
ISBN (UC Press): 0-520-06701-0

British Library Cataloguing in Publication Data
UNESCO general history of Africa. – Abridged ed.
  6: Africa in the nineteenth century until the 1880s.
  1. Africa – History – 19th century
  I. Ajayi, J. F. Ade (Jacob Festus Ade), 1929– II. UNESCO
  III. General history of Africa
  960.2'3
  ISBN 0-85255-096-0

Typeset in Bembo by Exe Valley Dataset Ltd, Exeter, UK,
and printed in Britain by Villiers Publications, London N3

Contents

Preface by Amadou-Mahtar M'Bow, former Director-General of
UNESCO (1974–87)   vii

Description of the Project by B. A. Ogot, President of the International
Scientific Committee for the Drafting of a General History of Africa
(1978–83)   xiii

Note on chronology   xv

Acknowledgements for plates   xvi

Members of the International Scientific Committee for the Drafting of
a General History of Africa   xix

Biographies of the authors who contributed to the main edition   xxi

1   Africa at the beginning of the nineteenth century:
    issues and prospects   1

2   Africa and the world-economy   10

3   New trends and processes in Africa in the nineteenth
    century   15

4   The abolition of the slave trade   27

5   The Mfecane and the rise of new African states   39

6   The impact of the Mfecane on the Cape Colony   50

7   The British, Boers and Africans in South Africa,
    1850–80   59

8   The countries of the Zambezi basin   68

9   The East African coast and hinterland, 1800–45   79

10   The East African coast and hinterland, 1845–80   88

11   Peoples and states of the Great Lakes region   100

12   The Congo Basin and Angola   112

13   The renaissance of Egypt, 1805–81   129

14   The Sudan in the nineteenth century   140

15   Ethiopia and Somalia   150

16   Madagascar 1800–80   164

17   New trends in the Maghrib: Algeria, Tunisia and Libya   176

18   Morocco from the beginning of the nineteenth
     century to 1880   189

19   New patterns of European intervention in the Maghrib   199

20   The Sahara in the nineteenth century   209

21   The nineteenth-century Islamic revolutions in West Africa   218

22   The Sokoto caliphate and Borno   225

23   Massina and the Torodbe (Tukuloor) empire until 1878   239

24   States and peoples of Senegambia and Upper Guinea   252

25   States and peoples of the Niger Bend and the Volta   262

26   Dahomey, Yorubaland, Borgu and Benin in the
     nineteenth century   279

27   The Niger delta and the Cameroon region   292

28   The African diaspora   305

29   Conclusion: Africa on the eve of the European conquest   315

Bibliography   323

Index   347

Preface

AMADOU-MAHTAR M'BOW

Former Director-General of UNESCO (1974–87)

For a long time, all kinds of myths and prejudices concealed the true history of Africa from the world at large. African societies were looked upon as societies that could have no history. In spite of important work done by such pioneers as Leo Frobenius, Maurice Delafosse and Arturo Labriola, as early as the first decades of this century, a great many non-African experts could not rid themselves of certain preconceptions and argued that the lack of written sources and documents made it impossible to engage in any scientific study of such sciences.

Although the *Iliad* and *Odyssey* were rightly regarded as essential sources for the history of ancient Greece, African oral tradition, the collective memory of peoples that holds the thread of many events marking their lives, was rejected as worthless. In writing the history of a large part of Africa, the only sources used were from outside the continent, and the final product gave a picture not so much of the paths actually taken by the African peoples as of those that the authors thought they must have taken. Since the European Middle Ages were often used as a yardstick, modes of production, social relations and political institutions were visualized only by reference to the European past.

In fact, there was a refusal to see Africans as the creators of original cultures which flowered and survived over the centuries in patterns of their own making and which historians are unable to grasp unless they forgo their prejudices and rethink their approach.

Furthermore, the continent of Africa was hardly ever looked upon as a historical entity. On the contrary, emphasis was laid on everything likely to lend credence to the idea that a split had existed, from time immemorial, between a 'white Africa' and a 'black Africa', each unaware of the other's existence. The Sahara was often presented as an impenetrable space preventing any intermingling of ethnic groups and peoples or any exchange of goods, beliefs, customs and ideas between the societies that had grown up on either side of the desert. Hermetic frontiers were drawn between the civilizations of Ancient Egypt and Nubia and those of the people of the Sahara.

It is true that the history of Africa north of the Sahara has been more closely linked with that of the Mediterranean basin than has the history of sub-Saharan Africa, but it is now widely recognized that the various civilizations of the African continent, for all their differing languages and cultures, represent, to a greater or lesser degree, the historical offshoots of a set of peoples and societies united by bonds centuries old.

Another phenomenon that did great disservice to the objective study of the African past was the appearance, with the slave trade and colonization, of racial stereotypes that bred contempt and lack of understanding and became so deep-rooted that they distorted even the basic concepts of historiography. From the time when the notions of 'white' and 'black' were used as generic labels by the colonialists, who were regarded as superior, the colonized Africans had to struggle against both economic and psychological enslavement. Africans were identifiable by the colour of their skin, they had become a kind of merchandise, they were earmarked for hard labour and eventually, in the minds of those dominating them, they came to symbolize an imaginary and allegedly inferior _Negro_ race. This pattern of spurious identification relegated the history of the African peoples in many minds to the rank of ethno-history, in which appreciation of the historical and cultural facts was bound to be warped.

The situation has changed significantly since the end of the Second World War and in particular since the African countries became independent and began to take an active part in the life of the international community and in the mutual exchanges that are its _raison d'être_. An increasing number of historians have endeavoured to tackle the study of Africa with a more rigorous, objective and open-minded outlook by using – with all due precautions – actual African sources. In exercising their right to take the historical initiative, Africans themselves have felt a deep-seated need to re-establish the historical authenticity of their societies on solid foundations.

In this context, the importance of the eight-volume _General History of Africa_, which UNESCO is publishing, speaks for itself.

The experts from many countries working on this project began by laying down the theoretical and methodological basis for the _History_. They have been at pains to call into question the over-simplification arising from a linear and restrictive conception of world history and to re-establish the true facts wherever necessary and possible. They have endeavoured to highlight the historical data that give a clearer picture of the evolution of the different peoples of Africa in their specific socio-cultural setting.

To tackle this huge task, made all the more complex and difficult by the vast range of sources and the fact that documents were widely scattered, UNESCO has had to proceed by stages. The first stage, from 1965 to 1969, was devoted to gathering documentation and planning the work. Operational assignments were conducted in the field and included campaigns to collect oral traditions, the creation of regional documentation centres for oral traditions, the collection of unpublished manuscripts in Arabic and Ajami (African languages written in Arabic script), the compilation of archival inventories and the preparation of a _Guide to the Sources of the History of Africa_, culled from the archives and libraries of the countries of Europe and later published in eleven volumes. In addition, meetings were organized to enable experts from Africa and other continents to discuss questions of methodology and lay down the broad lines for the project after careful examination of the available sources.

The second stage, which lasted from 1969 to 1971, was devoted to shaping the _History_ and linking its different parts. The purpose of the international meetings of experts held in Paris in 1969 and Addis Ababa in 1970 was to study and define the problems involved in drafting and publishing the _History_; presentation in eight volumes, the principal edition in English, French and Arabic, translation into African languages such as Kiswahili, Hausa, Fulfulde, Yoruba or Lingala, prospective versions in German, Russian, Portuguese, Spanish and Chinese, as well as abridged editions designed for a wide African and international public.

The third stage has involved actual drafting and publication. This began with the appointment of the 39-member International Scientific Committee, two-thirds African and one-third non-African, which assumes intellectual responsibility for the *History*.

The method used is interdisciplinary and is based on a multi-faceted approach and a wide variety of sources. The first among these is archaeology, which holds many of the keys to the history of African cultures and civilizations. Thanks to archaeology, it is now acknowledged that Africa was very probably the cradle of humankind and the scene – in the neolithic period – of one of the first technological revolutions in history. Archaeology has also shown that Egypt was the setting for one of the most brilliant ancient civilizations of the world. But another very important source is oral tradition, which, after being long despised, has now emerged as an invaluable instrument for discovering the history of Africa, making it possible to follow the movements of its different peoples in both space and time, to understand the African vision of the world from the inside and to grasp the original features of the values on which the cultures and institutions of the continent are based.

We are indebted to the International Scientific Committee in charge of this *General History of Africa*, and to its Rapporteur and the editors and authors of the various volumes and chapters, for having shed a new light on the African past in its authentic and all-encompassing form and for having avoided any dogmatism in the study of essential issues. Among these issues we might cite: the slave trade, that 'endlessly bleeding wound', which was responsible for one of the cruellest mass deportations in the history of mankind, which sapped the African continent of its life-blood while contributing significantly to the economic and commercial expansion of Europe; colonization, with all the effects it had on population, economics, psychology and culture; relations between Africa south of the Sahara and the Arab world; and, finally, the process of decolonization and nation-building which mobilized the intelligence and passion of people still alive and sometimes still active today. All these issues have been broached with a concern for honesty and rigour which is not the least of the *History*'s merits. By taking stock of our knowledge of Africa, putting forward a variety of viewpoints on African cultures and offering a new reading of history, the *History* has the signal advantage of showing up the light and shade and of openly portraying the differences of opinion that may exist between scholars.

By demonstrating the inadequacy of the methodological approaches which have long been used in research on Africa, this *History* calls for a new and careful study of the twofold problem areas of historiography and cultural identity, which are united by links of reciprocity. Like any historical work of value, the *History* paves the way for a great deal of further research on a variety of topics.

It is for this reason that the International Scientific Committee, in close collaboration with UNESCO, decided to embark on additional studies in an attempt to go deeper into a number of issues that will permit a clearer understanding of certain aspects of the African past. The findings being published in the series 'UNESCO Studies and

Documents – General History of Africa'[1] will prove a useful supplement to the *History*, as will the works planned on aspects of national or subregional history.

The *General History* sheds light both on the historical unity of Africa and also its relations with the other continents, particularly the Americas and the Caribbean. For a long time, the creative manifestations of the descendants of Africans in the Americas were lumped together by some historians as a heterogeneous collection of *Africanisms*. Needless to say, this is not the attitude of the authors of the *History*, in which the resistance of the slaves shipped to America, the constant and massive participation of the descendants of Africans in the struggles for the initial independence of America and in national liberation movements, are rightly perceived for what they were: vigorous assertions of identity, which helped forge the universal concept of humankind. Although the phenomenon may vary in different places, it is now quite clear that ways of feeling, thinking, dreaming and acting in certain nations of the western hemisphere have been marked by their African heritage. The cultural inheritance of Africa is visible everywhere, from the southern United States to northern Brazil, across the Caribbean and on the Pacific seaboard. In certain places it even underpins the cultural identity of some of the most important elements of the population.

The *History* also clearly brings out Africa's relations with southern Asia across the Indian Ocean and the African contributions to other civilizations through mutual exchanges.

I am convinced that the efforts of the peoples of Africa to conquer or strengthen their independence, secure their development and assert their cultural characteristics must be rooted in historical awareness renewed, keenly felt and taken up by each succeeding generation.

My own background, the experience I gained as a teacher and as chairperson, from the early days of independence, of the first commission set up to reform history and geography curricula in some of the countries of West and Central Africa, taught me how necessary it was for the education of young people and for the information of the public at large to have a history book produced by scholars with inside knowledge of the problems and hopes of Africa and with the ability to apprehend the continent in its entirety.

For all these reasons, UNESCO's goal will be to ensure that this *General History of Africa* is widely disseminated in a large number of languages and is used as a basis for producing children's books, school textbooks and radio and television programmes. Young people, whether schoolchildren or students and adults in Africa and elsewhere will thus be able to form a truer picture of the African continent's past and the factors that explain it, as well as a fairer understanding of its cultural heritage and its

1. The following 12 volumes have already been published in this series:
The peopling of ancient Egypt and the deciphering of Meroitic script; The African slave trade from the fifteenth to the nineteenth century; Historical relations across the Indian Ocean; The historiography of Southern Africa; The decolonization of Africa; Southern Africa and the Horn of Africa; African ethnonyms and toponyms; Historical and socio-cultural relations between black Africa and the Arab world from 1935 to the present; The methodology of contemporary African history; Africa and the Second World War; The educational process and historiography in Africa; Libya Antiqua; The role of African Student Movements in the political and social evolution of Africa from 1900 to 1975.

contribution to the general progress of humankind. The *History* should thus contribute to improved international co-operation and stronger solidarity among peoples in their aspirations to justice, progress and peace. This is, at least, my most cherished hope.

It remains for me to express my deep gratitude to the members of the International Scientific Committee, the Rapporteur, the different volume editors, the authors and all those who have collaborated in this tremendous undertaking. The work they have accomplished and the contribution they have made plainly go to show how people from different backgrounds, but all imbued with the same spirit of goodwill and enthusiasm in the service of universal truth can, within the international framework provided by UNESCO, bring to fruition a project of considerable scientific and cultural import. My thanks also go to the organizations and governments whose generosity has made it possible for UNESCO to publish this *History* in different languages and thus ensure that it will have the worldwide impact it deserves and thereby serve the international community as a whole.

Description of the Project

B. A. OGOT[1]
Former President, International Scientific Committee
for the Drafting of a General History of Africa

The General Conference of UNESCO at its 16th Session instructed the Director-General to undertake the drafting of a *General History of Africa*. The enormous task of implementing the project was entrusted to an International Scientific Committee which was established by the Executive Board in 1970. This Committee, under the Statutes adopted by the Executive Board of UNESCO in 1971, is composed of 39 members (two-thirds of whom are African and one-third non-African) serving in their personal capacity and appointed by the Director-General of UNESCO for the duration of the Committee's mandate.

The first task of the Committee was to define the principal characteristics of the work. These were defined at the first session of the Committee as follows:

(a)   Although aiming at the highest possible scientific level, the history does not seek to be exhaustive and is a work of synthesis avoiding dogmatism. In many respects, it is a statement of problems showing the present state of knowledge and the main trends in research, and it does not hesitate to show divergencies of views where these exist. In this way, it prepares the ground for future work.

(b)   Africa is considered in this work as a totality. The aim is to show the historical relationships between the various parts of the continent, too frequently sub-divided in works published to date. Africa's historical connections with the other continents receive due attention, these connections being analysed in terms of mutual exchanges and multilateral influences, bringing out, in its appropriate light, Africa's contribution to the history of mankind.

(c)   The *General History of Africa* is, in particular, a history of ideas and civilizations, societies and institutions. It is based on a wide variety of sources, including oral tradition and art forms.

(d)   The *History* is viewed essentially from the inside. Although a scholarly work, it is also, in large measure, a faithful reflection of the way in which African authors view their own civilization. While prepared in an international framework and drawing to the full on the present stock of scientific knowledge, it should also be a vitally important element in the recognition of the African heritage and should bring out the factors making for unity in the continent. This effort to view things

---

1. During the Sixth Plenary Session of the International Scientific Committee for the Drafting of a General History of Africa (Brazzaville, August 1983), an election of the new Bureau was held and Professor Ogot was replaced by Professor Albert Adu Boahen.

from within is the novel feature of the project and should, in addition to its scientific quality, give it great topical significance. By showing the true face of Africa, the *History* could, in an era absorbed in economic and technical struggles, offer a particular conception of human values.

The Committee has decided to present the work covering over three million years of African history in eight volumes, each containing about 800 pages of text with illustrations, photographs, maps and line drawings.

A chief editor, assisted if necessary by one or two assistant editors, is responsible for the preparation of each volume. The editors are elected by the Committee either from among its members or from outside by a two-thirds majority. They are responsible for preparing the volume in accordance with the decisions and plans adopted by the Committee. On scientific matters, they are accountable to the Committee or, between two sessions of the Committee, to its Bureau for the contents of the volumes, the final version of the texts, the illustrations and, in general, for all scientific and technical aspects of the *History*. The Bureau ultimately approves the final manuscript. When it considers the manuscript ready for publication, it transmits it to the Director-General of UNESCO. Thus the Committee, or the Bureau between committee sessions, remains fully in charge of the project.

Each volume consists of some 30 chapters. Each chapter is the work of a principal author assisted, if necessary, by one or two collaborators. The authors are selected by the Committee on the basis of their *curricula vitae*. Preferences is given to African authors, provided they have requisite qualifications. Special effort is made to ensure, as far as possible, that all regions of the continent, as well as other regions having historical or cultural ties with Africa, are equitably represented among the authors.

When the editor of a volume has approved texts of chapters, they are then sent to all members of the Committee for criticism. In addition, the text of the volume editor is submitted for examination to a Reading Committee, set up within the International Scientific Committee on the basis of the members' fields of competence. The Reading Committee analyses the chapters from the standpoint of both substance and form. The Bureau then gives final approval to the manuscripts.

Such a seemingly long and involved procedure has proved necessary, since it provides the best possible guarantee of the scientific objectivity of the *General History of Africa*. There have, in fact, been instances when the Bureau has rejected manuscripts or insisted on major revisions or even reassigned the drafting of a chapter to another author. Occasionally, specialists in a particular period of history or in a particular question are consulted to put the finishing touches to a volume.

The work will be published first in a hard-cover edition in English, French and Arabic, and later in paperback editions in the same languages. An abridged version in English and French will serve as a basis for translation into African languages. The Committee has chosen Kiswahili and Hausa as the first African languages into which the work will be translated.

Also, every effort will be made to ensure publication of the *General History of Africa* in other languages of wide international currency such as Chinese, Portuguese, Russian, German, Italian, Spanish, Japanese, etc.

It is thus evident that this is a gigantic task which constitutes an immense challenge to African historians and to the scholarly community at large, as well as to UNESCO under whose auspices the work is being done. For the writing of a continental history of Africa, covering the last three million years, using the highest canons of scholarship and involving, as it must do, scholars drawn from diverse countries, cultures, ideologies and historical traditions, is surely a complex undertaking. It constitutes a continental, international and interdisciplinary project of great proportions.

In conclusion, I would like to underline the significance of this work for Africa and for the world. At a time when the peoples of Africa are striving towards unity and greater co-operation in shaping their individual destinies, a proper understanding of Africa's past, with an awareness of common ties among Africans and between Africa and other continents, should not only be a major contribution towards mutual understanding among the people of the earth, but also a source of knowledge of a cultural heritage that belongs to all humankind.

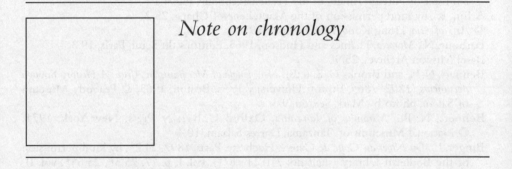

Note on chronology

It has been agreed to adopt the following method for writing dates. With regard to prehistory, dates may be written in two different ways.

One way is by reference to the present era, that is, dates BP (before present), the reference year being +1950; all dates are negative in relation to +1950.

The other way is by reference to the beginning of the Christian era. Dates are represented in relation to the Christian era by a simple + or − sign before the date. When referring to centuries, the terms BC and AD are replaced by 'before the Christian era' and 'of the Christian era'.

Some examples are as follows:
(i)   2300 BP = −350
(ii)   2900 BC = −2900
        AD 1800 = +1800
(iii) Fifth century BC = Fifth century before the Christian era
        Third century AD = Third century of the Christian era.

Acknowledgements for plates

Allen and Thompson, *Narrative of an Expedition*, London, 1848, 27.4★

al-Refei, Abdel-Rahman., *Açr Mohammad 'Alī*, Dar al-Nahdal al-Micriyyah, Cairo, 1930, 13.3 (4th edn.), 1982, Dar el-Maaref, Cairo, © Judge Helmy Shahin, 13.4

Archives du Ministère des Affaires éstrangères, Paris, by kind permission of H. Exc. the Minister of Foreign Affairs of the French Republic, Fig. 4.1

Arhin, K., by kind permission of the Asantehene of Ghana, 25.2

© *Arts of Asia*, Hong Kong, March–April 1978, p. 89, 28.1

Barbour, N., *Morocco*, Thames and Hudson, 1965, Editions du Seuil, Paris, 19.3

Basel Mission Archives, 25.9

Bennett, N. R. and Brooks G. E. (eds), *New England Merchants in Africa: A History through documents, 1802–1865*, Boston University Press, Boston, 1965, © Peabody Museum of Salem, photo by Mark Sexton, 9.3

Bennett, N. R., *Mirambo of Tanzania*, Oxford University Press, New York, 1971, © National Museums of Tanzania, Dar es Salaam, 10.4

Binger, L., *Du Niger au Golfe de Guinée*, Hachette, Paris, 1892, 24.2★, by kind permission of the Bodleian Library (shelf no: 710.11.s.8/1), vol. I, p. 17, 25.5★, 25.6★★, vol. II, 25.7★

Bowdich, T. E., *A Mission From Cape Coast Castle to Ashantee*, John Murray, London, 1819, 25.3★

Burton, R., *The Lake Region of Central Africa*, Longman, Green Longman and Roberts, London, 1860, vol. II, p. 80 and 278, © Royal Geographical Society, London, 10.2, 10.3

Burton, R., *First Footsteps in East Africa*, Routledge and Kegan Paul Ltd, London, 1894, photo reproduced by Sasor Publisher, London, 15.4

Cameron, V. L., *Across Africa*, Daldy, Isbister and Co., London, 1877, vol. I, p. 352, 12.2★

Church Missionary Gleaner, 1855, 26.3★

Collection Bibliothèque Générale et Archives, Rabat 18.3

de Chassiron, Ch., *Aperçu pittoresque de la Régence de Tunis*, Imprimerie de Bénard, Paris, 1849, 17.4★★

Denham, Clapperton and Oudney, *Narrative of Travels and Discoveries in Northern and Central Africa*, London, 1826, 22.3★

Nigerian Information Service Centre, Embassy of Nigeria, Paris, 27.3

Omer-Cooper, J., *The Zulu Aftermath*, Longman, London, 1966 (original from Gardiner, A. F., *Narrative of a Journey to the Zoolu country*, London, 1836), © Slide Centre Ltd, 1.1 (original from Livingstone, D. and C., *Narrative of an Expedition to the Zambezi*, John Murray Publishers, London, 1865), 8.3*

Photothèque, Musée de l'Homme, Paris, © 26.6

Pogge, P., *Im Reiche des Muata Jamvo*, Berlin, 1880, 12.11*

Porter, A. T., *Creoledom*, Oxford University Press, Oxford, 1963, by kind permission of the Foreign and Commonwealth Office Library, 3.3

Raison-Jourde, F., *Les Souverains de Madagascar*, Karthala, Paris, 1983, Fonds Grandidier du Musée des Collections scientifiques. Tsimbazaza, Antananarivo, 16.5

Rassam, H., *Narrative of a British Mission to Theodore, King of Abyssinia*, Murray, London, 1869, photos reproduced by Sasor Publisher, London, 15.5, 15.6

Roger Viollet, H., © Harlingue-Viollet, Paris, 28.3

Rohlfs, G., *Meine Mission nach Abessinien*, Leipzig, 1882, photo reproduced by Sasor Publisher, London, 15.8

Saunders, C., *Black Leaders in African History*, Heinemann, London, 1978 (original from John Aitken Chalmers, *Tiyo Soga, A Page of South African Mission Work* (1st edn), 1877), 3.2

Schweinfurth, G., *The Heart of Africa*, Sampson, Low, Marston, Low and Searle, London, 1873, vol. I, frontispiece, 12.5*, 14.4*

Snouk Hurgronje, C., *Mekka in the latter part of the nineteenth century: daily life, customs and learning: the Muslims of the East-Indian Archipelago*, E. J. Brill, Leiden, 1970, © E. J. Brill, 28.2*

Stanley, H. M., *Through the Dark Continent*, Sampson, Low, Marston, Low and Searle, London, 1878, vol. I, p. 89, 11.2*, 11.3*, p. 474, 11.4*, p. 322, 11.5*

Sullivan, G. L., *Dhow chasing in Zanzibar Waters*, Frank Cass Publishers, London, 1873, © Frank Cass Publishers, 4.1*

© The Tate Gallery, London, 13.2

Vansina, J., *Art History in Africa*, Longman, London, 1984, © Staatl. Museum für Völkerkunde, Munich, 6.1, © Photo Institut des Musées Nationaux du Zaire (IMNZ), no. 73.381.1, 73.381.2, 70.8.2 (left to right), 12.3, © The Walters Art Gallery, Baltimore, 12.9, © Museum für Völkerkunde, Berlin, 12.10, © Werner Forman Archive, London, 20.2, © Frobenius Institut, 25.4

* by kind permission of the Syndics of Cambridge University Library.
** by kind permission of the Bibliothèque Nationale, Paris.

We regret that we have been unable to trace the copyright holders of plates 27.5, 27.6 and would welcome any information enabling us to do so.

Members of the International Scientific Committee for the Drafting of a General History of Africa

The dates cited below refer to dates of membership.

Professor J. F. Ade Ajayi
(Nigeria), from 1971
Editor Volume VI

Professor F. A. Albuquerque Mourão
(Brazil), from 1975

Professor D. Birmingham
(UK), from 1985

Professor A. Adu Boahen
(Ghana), from 1971
Editor Volume VII

The late H. E. Boubou Hama
(Niger), 1971–8 (resigned in 1978);
deceased 1982

Dr (Mrs) Mutumba M. Bull
(Zambia), from 1971

The late Professor D. Chanaiwa
(Zimbabwe), from 1975;
deceased 1993

Professor P. D. Curtin
(USA), from 1975

Professor J. Devisse
(France), from 1971

Professor M. Difuila
(Angola), from 1978

The late Professor Cheikh Anta Diop
(Senegal), 1971–86; deceased 1986

Professor H. Djait
(Tunisia), from 1975

The late H. E. M. El Fasi
(Morocco), from 1971; deceased 1991
Editor Volume III

Professor J. D. Fage
(UK), 1971–81 (resigned)

The late Professor J. L. Franco
(Cuba), from 1971; deceased 1989

The late Mr M. H. I. Galaal
(Somalia), 1971–81; deceased 1981

Professor Dr V. L. Grottanelli
(Italy), from 1971

The late Professor E. Haberland
(Germany), from 1971;
deceased 1992

Dr Aklilu Habte
(Ethiopia), from 1971

The late H. E. A. Hampâté Bâ
(Mali), 1971–8 (resigned); deceased 1991

Dr I. S. El-Hareir
(Libya), from 1978

The late Dr I. Hrbek
(Czech Republic), from 1971;
deceased 1993
Assistant Editor Volume III

Dr (Mrs) A. Jones
(Liberia), from 1971

The late Abbé Alexis Kagame
(Rwanda), 1971–81; deceased 1981

Professor I. N. Kimambo
(Tanzania), from 1971

Professor J. Ki–Zerbo
(Burkina Faso), from 1971
Editor Volume I and IV

Mr D. Laya
(Niger), from 1979

Dr A. Letnev
(USSR), from 1971

Dr G. Mokhtar
(Egypt), from 1971
Editor Volume II

Professor P. Mutibwa
(Uganda), from 1975

Professor L. D. Ngcongco
(Botswana), from 1971

Professor D. T. Niane
(Guinea), from 1971
Editor Volume IV

Professor T. Obenga
(People's Republic of the Congo),
from 1975

Professor Bethwell A. Ogot
(Kenya), from 1971
Editor Volume V

Professor C. Ravoajanahary
(Madagascar), from 1971

The late Professor W. Rodney
(Guyana), 1979–80; deceased 1980

The late Professor M. Shibeika
(Sudan), 1971–80; deceased 1980

Professor Y. A. Talib
(Singapore), from 1975

The late Professor A. Teixeira da Mota
(Portugal), 1978–82; deceased 1982

Mgr T. Tshibangu
(Zaire), from 1971

Professor J. Vansina
(Belgium), from 1971

The late Rt Hon. Dr E. Williams
(Trinidad and Tobago), 1976–8;
resigned 1978; deceased 1980

Professor Ali A. Mazrui
(Kenya)
Editor Volume VIII,
not a member of the Committee

Professor C. Wondji
(Côte d'Ivoire)
Assistant Editor Volume VIII,
not a member of the Committee

*Secretariat of the International
Scientific Committee*
Division of International Cultural
Co-operation, Preservation and Enrichment
of Cultural Identities
UNESCO
1, rue Miollis, 75015 Paris

Biographies
of the authors who contributed
to the main edition

*The abridged version was prepared from the texts
of the main version written
by the following authors:*

CHAPTER 1   J. J. Ade Ajayi (Nigeria): specialist in nineteenth century West African history; author
of numerous publications and journal articles on African history; former Vice-
Chancellor, University of Lagos; Emeritus Professor, History Department, University
of Ibadan.

CHAPTER 2   I. Wallerstein (USA): specialist in African sociology and world-economic systems;
author of various publications and articles; formerly Professor of Sociology,
University College of Dar es Salaam, Columbia University, New York and McGill
University, Montreal; Director of the Fernand Braudel Center for the Study of
Economies, Historical Systems, and Civilizations, SUNY, Binghamton.

CHAPTER 3   A. Adu Boahen (Ghana): specialist in West African colonial history; author of
numerous publications and articles on African history; former Professor and Head of
the Department of History, University of Ghana.

CHAPTER 4   S. Daget (France): specialist in the African slave trade in the nineteenth century;
author of numerous publications and articles on the African slave trade; Professor of
History, University of Nantes; deceased.

CHAPTER 5   L. D. Ngcongco (Botswana): specialist in Southern African history; has published
various studies on Botswana in pre-colonial times; formerly Director, National
Institute of Development, Research and Documentation; Professor and Head,
Department of History, University of Botswana.

CHAPTER 6   E. K. Mashingaidze (Zimbabwe): specialist in Southern African history; former
lecturer, National University of Lesotho and former Zimbabwean Ambassador to the
United Nations; Permanent Secretary in Harare.

CHAPTER 7   N. M. Bhebe (Zimbabwe): specialist in Southern African history; author of various
works on the Ndebele; former lecturer, University of Swaziland; Senior lecturer,
University of Zimbabwe.

CHAPTER 8   A. F. Isaacman (USA): specialist in African history; author of several works on the
social history of Mozambique in the nineteenth- and twentieth-centuries; Professor
of History, University of Minnesota.

CHAPTER 9   A. I. Salim (Kenya): specialist in East African history; author of many articles on the
Swahili-speaking peoples; Professor and currently Chairman, Department of History,
University of Nairobi.

CHAPTER 10   I. N. Kimambo (Tanzania): specialist in East African history; author of several
publications on the pre-colonial history of Tanzanian peoples; formerly Chief
Academic Officer, currently Professor, Department of History, University of Dar es
Salaam.

CHAPTER 11   D. W. Cohen (USA): specialist in African historical anthropology applying the techniques of anthropology and social history to explore historical problems of the Lakes Region in the nineteenth century; with interest in the anthropologies and histories which Africans have themselves produced outside the academic guilds; Professor of History and Anthropology, The Johns Hopkins University, Baltimore.

CHAPTER 12   J. L. Vellut (Belgium): specialist in Central African history; author of several publications and articles on Congo, Zaire and Angola; Professor of History, University of Louvain.

CHAPTER 13   A. Abdel-Malek (Egypt): specialist in Arab-world sociology and social philosophy; author of numerous publications and articles on the Arab and Afro-Asian world, political and social theory; Directeur de recherche, Centre National de la Recherche Scientifique, Paris; Project Coordinator, now General Editor (SCA-NNST), the United Nations University, Tokyo; writer and columnist, Cairo.

CHAPTER 14   H. A. Ibrahim (Sudan): specialist in nineteenth and twentieth century history of Egypt and the Sudan; author of numerous publications and articles; Professor of History and Dean, Faculty of Arts, University of Khartoum.

              B. A. Ogot (Kenya): specialist in African history, pioneer in the techniques of oral history; author of many publications on East African history; former Director of the International Louis Leakey Memorial Institute; Professor of History, Kenyatta University, Nairobi.

CHAPTER 15   R. Pankhurst (UK): specialist in Ethiopian history; author of several publications on Ethiopian history and culture; former Director of the Institute of Ethiopian Studies, Addis Ababa; Professor of Ethiopian Studies, Institute of Ethiopian Studies, Addis Ababa.

CHAPTER 16   P. W. Mutibwa (Uganda): specialist and author of several publications on the history of Madagascar in the nineteenth century; Research Professor of History, Makerere University, Kampala.

              F. V. Esoavelomandroso (Madagascar): specialist in the eighteenth and nineteenth century history of Madagascar; Professor of History, Faculté des lettres, University of Antananarivo.

CHAPTER 17   M. H. Cherif (Tunisia): specialist in North African social and political history; author of several articles on North African history; University Professor and Dean, Faculté des sciences humaines et sociales, Tunis.

CHAPTER 18   A. Laroui (Morocco): specialist in the history of the Maghrib: author of several works on the history of Morocco and on nineteenth-century history of North Africa; Professor of Contemporary History, University of Rabat.

CHAPTER 19   N. A. Ivanov (USSR): specialist in mediaeval and contemporary North African history; author of several publications on contemporary North African history; Chargé de recherches, Institute of Oriental Studies, USSR Academy of Sciences, Moscow.

CHAPTER 20   S. Baier (USA): specialist in West African economic history and in particular the history of the Sahel in West Africa; author of many publications on the Sahelian economies; formerly Assistant Director of the Boston University African Studies Center; currently Senior Software Engineer at Access Technology, Natick, Massachusetts.

CHAPTER 21   A. A. Batran (Sudan): specialist in the history of Islam in Africa; author of works and articles on Religious Brotherhoods, Sufism and the Evolution of Scholarship in West and North Africa; Professor of African History, Howard University, Washington DC.

CHAPTER 22   M. Last (UK): specialist in African history and sociology; author of several works on the history and culture of the Hausa, and intellectual life in the Western Sudan; Reader in Social Anthropology, University College, London.

CHAPTER 23   M. Ly-Tall (Mali): specialist in the history of Mali; has published works on the Mali Empire and life of al-Hadjdj Umar Tall: Former Permanent Delegate of Mali to Unesco. Maître-Assistant, IFAN, University of Dakar.

CHAPTER 24   Y. Person (France): specialist in the history of Africa, particularly the Mandingo world; has published many works on the history of Africa; Professor of History, University of Paris I, Panthéon-Sorbonne; deceased.

CHAPTER 25   K. Arhin (Ghana): specialist in social anthropology, especially the history and culture of the Akan; has published many works on the Asante; Professor of African Studies, Institute of African Studies, University of Ghana.

J. Ki-Zerbo (Burkina Faso): specialist in African history and methodology; author of a number of works dealing with Black Africa and its history; former Professor of History, University of Dakar. Professor of History and Member of Parliament, Burkina Faso.

CHAPTER 26   A. I. Asiwaju (Nigeria): specialist in African history; author of several works on the Yoruba- and Aja-speaking peoples and the impact of colonial boundaries on African peoples; Professor of History, University of Lagos.

CHAPTER 27   E. J. Alagoa (Nigeria): specialist in African history and methodology; author of various studies of the Ijo, the techniques of oral history and archaeology; Professor of History, University of Port Harcourt.

L. Z. Elango (Cameroon): specialist in the history of Cameroon; Lecturer, Department of History, University of Yaoundé.

M. Metegue N'Nah (Gabon): specialist in the history of Central Africa; Head, Department of History, University of Libreville.

CHAPTER 28   F. W. Knight (Jamaica): specialist in the history of the African Diaspora; author of several publications on Cuba, the Slave society and the African Diaspora; Professor of History, The Johns Hopkins University, Baltimore.

Y. A. Talib (Singapore): specialist in Islam, the Malay world and the Middle East, particularly South-West Arabia; author of several works on the subject; Head, Department of Malay Studies, National University of Singapore.

P. D. Curtin (USA): specialist and author of numerous publications on African history and the history of the slave trade; Professor of History, The Johns Hopkins University, Baltimore.

CHAPTER 29   J. F. Ade Ajayi (Nigeria).

1

Africa at the beginning of the nineteenth century: issues and prospects

Perspective

This volume looks at the history of Africa in the nineteenth century before the European Scramble and establishment of colonial rule. The century merits particular attention not just because it immediately preceded the colonial period but also because of the significant events and revolutionary changes which took place within it. It is necessary to begin by considering the general features of the nineteenth century and its overall importance in the history of Africa which have been subject to much debate.

Compared with earlier periods, the sources of African history became relatively abundant in the nineteenth century. There were new sources in the accounts of European travellers, missionaries, traders, consular and other government agents penetrating into the interior, often for the first time. Some previously unknown African scripts were discovered. Many African languages began to be written in European scripts. Some Europeans and their African agents took an interest in the historical traditions of various communities and began recording them. In spite of this, the myth was built up that African societies were static and that no significant change took place before the establishment of colonial rule. Once that myth was broken, it was then assumed that all important changes in African history took place in the nineteenth century. When that myth also was exploded – as evidenced by the significant movements and changes recorded in earlier volumes of the *Unesco General History of Africa* – it began to be argued that changes that took place in the nineteenth century were of a different kind from changes in the preceding centuries because they were due to external factors.

Because of the tendency to explain change in nineteenth-century Africa largely in terms of the increasing activities of Europeans on the continent, the nineteenth century has often been treated as only the prelude to the colonial period. All the significant developments that took place throughout the continent in the period have been explained as resulting from European interaction with African peoples and as foreshadowing the colonial period. In an attempt to provide an overall explanation, various scholars have turned to developments in Europe rather than to the internal workings and historical

1

tendencies in African societies. That is why, for instance, changes in Egypt are explained as the result of Napoleon Bonaparte's activities and not the pre-existing aspirations and the active participation of the local peoples. Similarly, the Mfecane in Southern Africa is explained not as the result of changes going on in Nguni society, but, vaguely, as caused by the European presence.

The aim of this chapter, therefore, is to focus on the nature of Africa in the nineteenth century, the general features of the period, the continuities with the past, the changes and new developments that occurred during the century, as well as the emerging trends for the future. It is important to determine the extent to which nineteenth-century changes were a continuation of eighteenth-century developments, how far they originated from internal factors and how far they were due to factors associated with the expansion of European activities and the increasing incorporation of African economies into the world system in the nineteenth century. By doing so, we will be able to understand better the course of African development in the century and the relevance of the European factor to either the development or underdevelopment of Africa.

Demography and population movements

By the beginning of the nineteenth century, African peoples were to be found in distinct cultural and linguistic groups each occupying a defined territory. The process of cultural identification was completed in most parts of Africa by the sixteenth century, but certain parts of East Africa (outside the central highlands of the Great Lakes region) and Madagascar still experienced large-scale migrations of peoples into relatively underpopulated areas in the seventeenth and eighteenth centuries. But by 1800, stability had been achieved in the region.

While migration, in the sense of large-scale movements of a lot of people over wide areas of land in Africa, could be said to have ended by the beginning of the nineteenth century, people still continued to move around as demanded by their occupations. Examples of such people were pastoralists seeking pasture, professional traders and specialist craftsmen travelling in distant places and establishing colonies as they pursued their trades, and hunters roaming over certain areas for game. Such movements did not involve the permanent abandonment of previous homes or a displacement of people. They were the regular flow of people usually within defined areas. However, certain occurrences such as prolonged drought and pestilence, war and the collapse of existing states, and excessive pressure on land due to overpopulation, could lead to movements of people permanently away from their original homes. Examples of this type of movement abounded in the nineteenth century, like those of the Fang in the forest belt of Equatorial Africa, the Chokwe of Angola, the Yoruba of Old Ọyọ and the Mfecane movement among the northern Nguni of Natal in Southern Africa.

It is said that in pre-1800 Africa, the overall population could not have been expanding much and the rate of fifty more births than deaths per ten thousand annually has been suggested. At that rate, a population would double itself in one thousand years. This estimation appears to be justified in the case of North Africa where intense agriculture and irrigation which could have shot the population up were balanced by periods of plague and drought. But in the case of the grassland and forest zones of West, Central and Southern Africa, the development of systems of agriculture (often mixed with pastoralism in the grasslands) led to population growth and high densities in some areas like the Igbo country in south-eastern Nigeria, the Cameroon grasslands and the Great Lakes region of East Africa. In these areas, however, especially in West and West-central Africa in the seventeenth and eighteenth centuries, population growth was seriously affected by the slave trade. It is true that the effects were not evenly spread. Some states seemed to have taken advantage of the trade to strengthen themselves at the expense of their neighbours. It was the weaker states, unable to defend themselves, who suffered such devastation and depopulation, the effects of which are still visible today. Many abandoned their homes in the fertile plains and the remnant populations tried to eke out some existence in difficult hilly areas.

The overall effects of depopulation arising from the slave trade was disastrous for all of Africa. From 1650 to 1850, the overall population of Africa was declining and the low performance of African economies at the beginning of the nineteenth century was largely the result of this depopulation. Even powerful states which seemed to have risen to prominence and experienced further internal developments suffered retardation because of the impoverishment of their neighbours. The slave trade would thus explain the fragility of the state systems in Africa at the beginning of the nineteenth century, and the instability and vulnerability of the political and economic structures. Population growth in the nineteenth century was not dramatic because the campaign to abolish the slave trade took a long time to take effect. It was only after 1850 that there was a significant reduction in the number of slaves exported overseas, across the Atlantic. Meanwhile the export to Zanzibar and the Indian Ocean increased. Moreover, the rise of alternative export items such as palm oil, rubber and ivory increased the demand for domestic slaves used in the process of obtaining the new trade items and transporting them to the coast. Internal slavery therefore increased tremendously in the nineteenth century, with significant loss from the wars and raids from which the slaves were procured. With the eventual abolition of the overseas slave trade, the overall population of Africa began to rise for the first time since the seventeenth century. It declined again with the initial impact of colonial rule and the wars of resistance before it began to rise again, slowly at first, and considerably from the 1930s.

Increased European interest

This first manifested itself in expeditions undertaken to obtain more accurate information about the major geographical features of Africa and its main agricultural and industrial products. The excuse to intervene in African affairs was provided by Britain's initiative first to curb the expansion of France during the French Revolutionary and Napoleonic wars, which spilled over to the continent, and then to abolish the slave trade. The French were already in Alexandria and Cairo in Egypt. The British had in 1789 converted the freed slave settlement in Freetown to a Crown Colony. They then seized the Dutch colony at the Cape of Good Hope in 1795. The French were expelled from Egypt and made to join the abolitionist movement. This spurred them to establish coastal bases and trading stations in West Africa.

Lingering Anglo-French rivalry and the campaign to enforce the ban on the export of slaves from Africa was the basis for expanding European and American interests in Africa, but it is necessary not to exaggerate the extent of their success in the first half of the nineteenth century. Abolition required the regular visits of rival British, French and American naval vessels, patrolling the seas and attempting to mount a blockade. The navies required bases on the coast. That encouraged traders who sought to profit from the transition from the trade in slaves to the one in palm oil, groundnuts, rubber, cloves, ivory or other products. That also provided opportunities for missionaries seeking to convert not only the coastal peoples but even more the larger populations inland.

The Portuguese made extensive claims to territory in Angola and Mozambique which they were encouraged by the British from time to time to keep alive if only to shut out the French. But they had great difficulties sustaining their forts on the coast or guaranteeing safe passage to the estates (*prazos*) they once established in the interior. In the first half of the nineteenth century, they depended mostly on African mulatto merchants (the *pombeiro*) and the goodwill of local rulers to trade with peoples in the interior.

The French after 1815 revived their trading posts in Senegambia, notably Saint-Louis and Gorée off the coast of what later became Dakar. Their attempt to establish an agricultural settlement in the interior failed. They seized Algiers in 1830 and had to contend with the resistance of the Algerians, led by Emir 'Abd al-Ḳādir, for over 20 years. The programme for the resettlement of freed slaves in agricultural villages around Freetown proved a spectacular success. This was due largely to the role of German and British missionaries who served as teachers, linguists, farm managers and overseers. There were attempts to repeat the Freetown experiment elsewhere on small scales – in Liberia by the Americans, Libreville by the French, and Freretown near Rabai in East Africa by the British. The spread of the Creoles from Freetown to other coastal towns like Banjul (formerly Bathurst), Cape Coast, Badagry, Lagos and beyond also helped to spread British missionary and trading interests.

Missionary influence also spread in South Africa but the effort to develop the economy was not so successful. The Boer farmers remained resentful of British control, particularly the abolition of slavery and the attempt to regulate their relationship with the Africans. The rebellious Boers trekked into the interior to take advantage of the Mfecane, but all they did was to drag British authority after them. Thus, up to 1850, South Africa remained a colony of poor British and Boer farmers spread thinly among African states, with the British colonial officials playing the role of partisan arbiters. The discovery of gold and diamonds and the prospects for an industrial economy lay in the future. Similarly, the missionary movement did not become a major factor of change in Africa until the second half of the nineteenth century. The Holy Ghost Mission was founded in 1847 and the White Fathers came into being in 1863. In 1850, David Livingstone was still on the first missionary journey.

European trading influence spread more widely and quickly than missionary influence in the first half of the nineteenth century. This was because the nineteenth-century European trade in agricultural and other products, usually referred to as legitimate trade, grew out of the pre-nineteenth-century slave trade. The Danes and the Dutch carried on trading from the slave trade era and did not pull out until the Dutch sold their fort at Accra in 1850 and ceded Elmina Castle in 1871. The structure of the new trade was very similar to that of the old. The same people who patronized the slave trade were more or less the pioneers of the new trade, while the same trust system of advancing goods on credit to African traders adopted in the slave trade was also the basis of the new trade. Europeans remained on the coast while dealing with African middlemen who took goods to the interior and brought back produce to the coast. The organization and demands of the new trade affected the social structure of some of the coastal states. The new trade, missionary influence and western education particularly among returned freed slaves, were producing a new elite. Some of those who amassed considerable wealth wanted to share in political power. However, this did not lead to a drastic change in the structure of society or to a total departure from the past because such people generally had to use their wealth to acquire traditional chieftaincy titles through which they could gain access to political power.

In other words, the expansion of European trade depended on the existing patterns of internal trade. The patterns of internal trade depended not so much on external stimulation as on factors within the African societies like the agricultural system of production, crafts and manufacture. External trade was important to some rulers who saw it as the main source of obtaining firearms. For the first half of the nineteenth century, external trade remained secondary in the life of the majority of Africans. As such, despite the growth of external trade, African peoples devoted their energies more to agriculture than to trade.

Agricultural systems

The basis of the economy of all African communities at the beginning of the nineteenth century was agriculture. All other activities including trade, politics, religion, crafts, building, mining or manufacturing could not have been carried on without agriculture. In fact, the agricultural system affected the structure of social relations, the pattern of authority, relations with neighbours, and even the response of African communities to external factors like trade. It is necessary to consider the main characteristics of the agricultural systems of a few African societies at the beginning of the nineteenth century to emphasize how much continuity there was with the past.

Few places could have been more remote than Bunafu in northern Busoga, East Africa. People migrated into the region at the end of the eighteenth and early nineteenth centuries. They lived in scattered homesteads and not in centralized village communities. There were no formal markets for regular exchange but through increased social dealings the people gradually developed a communal spirit. The individual household was the unit of production and land holding. But despite the remoteness of those homesteads, a system of exchange gradually emerged, demonstrating that the household even in Bunafu was not self-sufficient. Social changes took place in Bunafu in the nineteenth century in terms of the expansion of trade and the attendant social and political transformations. But these should be seen not merely as a result of external factors, but as a continuation and realization of tendencies and patterns carried over from the eighteenth century, including concepts of order and the hierarchical government that the migrants brought with them from the states from which they had migrated.

Agriculture in the villages and rural areas of Tunisia was obviously different from that in Bunafu, not just in the nature of the soils and the type of crops cultivated, but even more in the system of land tenure. In the fertile plains of Tunisia, the desert is never far away and only an intensive 'oasis' agriculture was possible. Land tenure was governed by Islamic law which the rulers in the urban areas and the local *kā'ids* (chiefs) in the rural areas interpreted differently. The basic principle was that land was owned jointly by the whole community and that the rulers allocated its use, with the judges arbitrating over disputes. In the urban areas, population pressure encouraged commercialization of land. This pressure was to be felt increasingly in the villages and rural areas, but throughout the first half of the nineteenth century, the traditional system in which land could not be bought and sold prevailed. Also, as in Bunafu, the households were units of productions and of landholding. Markets were predominant but households still exchanged products on the basis of trade by barter.

In the farming areas around Kano, the authority of the central ruler or *amīr* was more evident than in the Tunisian villages. Kano was a centre of both local and international trade based on the manufacture of textiles and the tanning of leather. The merchants and ruling elite of Kano played a great role in the management of the economy, affecting even the rural areas. But the bulk of agricultural production was in the hands of the villagers. The household was the unit of production. All its members took part in agricultural production and occasional communal labour. Land was in the custody of the ruler who regulated its acquisition, use and disposal. Industrious rulers took advantage of this by allocating land and encouraging foreign artisans and craftsmen to settle in and around Kano. In addition, the ruling elite and some merchants developed estates for agricultural and industrial production. The *djihād* of the early nineteenth century which resulted in the establishment of an Islamic government, brought the application of Islamic Laws (*sharīʿa*) to land tenure. But there was no sudden departure from eighteenth-century agricultural and land tenure systems. On the contrary, the new Fulani *amīrs* gradually re-incorporated more Hausa customs and practices as the century wore on.

Patterns of authority

Basically, there were two patterns of authority in Africa in the early nineteenth century. One was the centralized 'hierarchical, well-defined order based on the payment of tribute', which could be found in the kingdoms and centralized states. The other was the less authoritarian, and informal type of government by councils of elders and notables found in the non-centralized societies. These two types must not be seen as in opposition, but as two extremes of a spectrum, with most states falling somewhere in between and having elements of both. There were no 'stateless' societies because even in remote non-centralized societies, as we have noted in the case of Bunafu, there was a sense of community and orderly government. Many non-centralized communities developed associations, age-grade societies, secret clubs, initiation groups and other institutions which cut across lineages and were used to forge unity and maintain order. One of the best known examples is that of the Aro who maintained order over a wide area among the Igbo and other peoples of south-eastern Nigeria through a regional network of oracles and trading colonies.

However, developments in the early nineteenth century showed a tendency towards centralized power structures with executive rather than ritual rulerships. Vast, sprawling, decentralized empires tended to break up into smaller, more authoritarian kingdoms. The new Sokoto caliphate was large with the Caliph maintaining a theocratic supremacy, but real power was exercised by the *amīrs*. In Southern Africa, it was the Sotho-Tswana who lived in nucleated villages and chiefdoms, where the rulers centralized initiation rites. The northern Nguni lived in dispersed homesteads with chiefs exercising little power. However, increasing prosperity towards the end of the eighteenth century and the introduction of the maize crop, led to increasing pressure on the land. The agricultural system by which the cattle had access to both sour pastures in the spring and sweet grasses in the late summer could not contain the pressure on the land. This led to intensive competition for power over land and cattle, and the adaptation of Sotho-Tswana centralized initiation ceremonies for the recruitment of military regiments. This was the Shaka revolution that triggered off the Mfecane.

Internal initiatives

During the first half of the nineteenth century, European activities were confined largely to the coastal areas. However, the major revolutionary movements originated in the interior – the djihād movements in West Africa,

1.1   *Ceremonial dance at Mbelebele, a military camp of the Zulu in 1836*

the Mfecane of Southern Africa, the unification of Ethiopia, the expansion of the Imerina in Madagascar, the collapse of the Old Ọyọ empire in south-western Nigeria. It seems clear that internal factors such as changes in society, agricultural systems of production, and internal trade were more important than external factors of abolition, increasing European presence and trading interests in triggering off these movements. Even the reforms of Muḥammad ʿAlī in Egypt, though originating on the coast in Cairo, were based on a nationalist movement which had its roots in the eighteenth century before the coming of Napoleon to Egypt. The leading Egyptian shaykhs were determined to shake off Ottoman rule and they would rather rally round an Albanian Pasha sufficiently sensitive to those nationalist aspirations than risk the restoration of Ottoman misrule.

It seems clear that in many parts of Africa and in diverse historical, cultural, religious and economic circumstances, there was a deep-seated yearning for change. It was because of this that, in spite of many reservations, several African rulers gave Europeans a cautious welcome and sought to profit from their presence to consolidate their power and military effectiveness. For the same reason, many welcomed missionaries and their agents while trying to minimize their social and cultural impact. The nineteenth century may well be called an African Age of Improvement. Europeans exploited this yearning for change to consolidate their own positions and, in the end, used that to impose colonial rule and frustrate the internal initiatives for reforms and development.

Conclusion

New factors of change were introduced into African history in the early nineteenth century. Important among those factors were the campaign against the slave trade, the search for new items of trade and new missionary initiatives, all of which increased the European presence. The Europeans came to trade and subsequently intervened in the social, economic and religious life of the people. The new trade expanded commercial activity by giving an additional fillip to the existing pattern of trade. Thus the new trade was based on the pre-nineteenth-century African trading and agricultural systems. The continuities with the eighteenth century and the internal factors of change in the nineteenth century were therefore more important than the external factor represented by the European presence and the new trade.

2

Africa
and the world-economy

From 'luxury' to 'essential' trading patterns

The partition of Africa at the end of the nineteenth century should be seen as the result, not the cause, of the incorporation of Africa into the world-economy. This incorporation can be said to have begun in the middle of the eighteenth century and it marked a major transformation in the economy of Africa.

Before 1750, Africa had well-known trading links with the outside world. There were trading networks stretching beyond the continent, across the Mediterranean, the Indian Ocean and the Atlantic. Such long-distance trade however was generally for the exchange of luxury goods such as gold, beads, leather and salt which were small in bulk but high in profit. They formed only a minute fraction of the overall products of the area from which they came and a very small section of the population was engaged in producing them. Such trade can be described as non-essential in the sense that, for both sides of the exchange, interruption or cessation of the trade could take place without affecting in any fundamental way the productive processes.

The pattern of trade across the Indian Ocean did not change much between 1500 and 1800. The scope and nature of the trade was not altered even by the presence of Portuguese and other Europeans in the area, some of whom attempted estate agriculture in the Zambezi Valley. The traditional clear division between long-distance trade in luxury goods and non-commercialized agricultural production remained the same.

In West and Central Africa, there developed a long-distance trade in slaves. This slave trade was the product of the European-centred capitalist world-economy. The Caribbean zone of the Americas in which several plantations were established was part of the outlying areas of this capitalist world-economy, and slaves from West and Central Africa were used to man the plantations. The number of Africans exported to the Caribbean through the slave trade rose gradually between 1450 and 1650, and more significantly between 1650 and 1750 when the volume tripled. The mode of production and political systems in West and Central Africa began to be adjusted to meet the demands of the trade in slaves. In particular, the procurement of Africans as slaves became systematized and this affected social relations and political organization. At what point the adjustment can be said to have reached the stage when the trade ceased to be a luxury and became 'essential' cannot be precisely determined. But this was probably not before 1750 when the volume was increasing at an unprecedented rate. The period between 1600 and 1750 was, for the capitalist world, one of counting their gains and trying to build upon what they had achieved in the areas that had already been incorporated in the sixteenth century. Expansion and incorporation of other areas came after 1750.

Capitalist expansion

Africa was incorporated into the capitalist world-economy alongside with Russia, the Ottoman empire, India, and the rest of the Americas between 1750 and 1850. At the time it was drawn into the world-economy, Africa did not constitute a single economy although she had patterns of regional economy which cut across individual communities. The process of incorporation involved changes not only in some important sectors of production, but also in the political structure of the incorporated areas. It involved the weakening of some of the existing political structures and the establishment of new colonial political systems over them, though the latter process took a longer time to materialize. Integration was not achieved overnight. It was a slow process that did not immediately erase the persistence of previous patterns of agricultural production and the older ideas and values associated with it. What took place was that production of essential items was directed to a world market and this entailed the restructuring of the labour force which produced profitable returns. All these represented the economic basic of incorporation into the capitalist economy and its political consequences.

It is important to note that Africa did not choose to be incorporated into the world-economy. But it was overtaken by events despite its resistance and by 1850 it had been drawn into the world system. This integration did not begin with the shift from slave trade to legitimate trade. Integration antedated the shift in trade, and it took place even in areas where the slave trade did not exist, e.g. Southern Africa. The shift in trade came essentially because, with the incorporation of Africa into the world system, it soon became clear that the slave trade was no longer beneficial to the system as a whole. The calculation of profitability now had to include not only the cost of production or procurement of slaves but also 'opportunity costs' involved in moving them away from Africa where they could produce raw material for the world-economy.

Incorporation of Egypt and the Maghrib

The Egyptian economy before 1730 was linked to that of the Ottoman empire. Egypt supplied the Ottoman empire with grain and was the transit point for much of the empire's long-distance trade with the Middle and Far East. But in the second half of the eighteenth century, the economic weakness of the Ottoman empire led to heavy taxation and much discontent among the farmers in Egypt. This crisis coincided with the expansion of the capitalist economy of Europe and the search for new areas to incorporate. This was evident in the competition of France and England to control the region.

This was the background to the nationalist movement that Muḥammad ʿAlī tried to mobilize against the Ottoman regime. His reforms centred on the production of cotton for the European market under state control. This led to changes in the irrigational system, land tenure and social relations. The new system of agriculture and the ambitions of the new dynasty – notably the Suez Canal and the attempts to control the Sudan – put a lot of burdens on the farmers, and this culminated in the 'Urabist Revolt' of 1881–2.

Attempts to incorporate the Maghrib into the capitalist world-economy could be dated to the late fifteenth century. But these were not effective until the mid-nineteenth century when Morocco and Tunisia began to export considerable quantities of industrial and food crops, animal products and even mineral ore to Europe. Algeria resisted this economic incorporation most vehemently and that was probably why she was conquered earlier than the other Maghrib states, and forcibly incorporated.

The West African pattern

In West Africa, the new trade brought about changes, not only in the items exchanged, but also in the way people organized themselves for production which in turn affected their political structures. The change in the production patterns was accelerated by the abolition of the slave trade though the process had been initiated a long time before abolition. Of the new items of trade, palm oil was the most successful and it thrived in the Niger delta area. The palm oil trade at first coexisted with the slave trade before it finally displaced it, and by the end of the nineteenth century, the oil trade had begun to slump. The Gold Coast and Dahomey were also areas in which the palm oil trade was established but it could be said of Dahomey especially that the degree of active participation in the slave trade had already led to incorporation into the world economic system before the legitimate trade was established.

Other new products in the West African trade with the outside world were groundnuts produced on the Upper Guinea coast and Senegambia, and rubber. However, not all attempts to produce new cash crops succeeded especially in cases were Europeans were directly involved. More importantly, the Europeans were displacing the African merchants in their role as middlemen of getting produce from the interior and bringing it to the coast. New imports were introduced into the African economy during this period. The leading imports were cotton goods, the massive importation of which displaced some of the local manufacturers. Some of those local producers of cotton goods responded to this treatment by evolving special designs and directing their products to more limited markets.

Southern Africa

The pattern of incorporation of South Africa into the capitalist world-economy was different from that of the other parts of Africa due to the absence of slave trade and the presence of a white settler community in the region. The integration of the region into the world-economy began with the restructuring of its processes of production. Commercial sheep rearing was established in the Cape Colony while several sugar plantations were set up in Natal.

The pressures of the changing economy led to the migration of the Boers into the interior, called the Great Trek. The result of the movement was a serious struggle for the control of resources – land and labour – in production that was aimed at the world market. In the Cape Colony, African peasant agriculture continued to coexist with the plantations owned by the white settlers.

The Angolan case was different from the above. There, trade in slaves and ivory continued and it had the effect of causing the political structures of the interior to wear away. With the abolition of the slave trade, attempts were made by the white settlers to establish plantations, but the project eventually failed after which no important cash crop was produced in the area. With the decay of indigenous political systems, there was no alternative to conquest and incorporation.

Delayed incorporation of eastern Africa

Eastern Africa was incorporated late into the capitalist world-economy. Its early link with the outside world was via the slave trade that went across the Indian Ocean. The growth of Zanzibar as an important supplier of cloves to the outside world brought it into the mainstream of the world-economy by the middle of the nineteenth century. Madagascar produced rice and beef which were exported to Mauritius. The latter was also known for her sugar plantations. But the effective incorporation of the region into the world-economy was delayed till the time of the Scramble for Africa. The changes which then took place in the relations of production naturally triggered off other changes in the political structures of the African groups concerned.

Implications of incorporation

The effect of the external factor, viz, the European presence and trade, on state formation in Africa should not be overstated. Some states like that of the Rozvi developed without any contact with Europeans while some Niger delta communities that traded actively with the Europeans did not develop strong centralized states.

One major consequence of incorporation was that it led to the emergence of political structures that facilitated and ensured the performance of the economy, according to the necessities of the export trade. This meant that there was internal restructuring in some of the African states in the nineteenth century. The response of the other foreign powers to this was the eventual creation of colonial states in Africa. On the other hand, the immediate effects of the capitalist world-economy were the slave trade, plantation slavery and their abolition.

The incorporation of Africa into the world-economy further entrenched Britain's supremacy as the major power in the capitalist world. The policy of free trade gave Britain a lot of economic advantages on the African continent. British traders were miles ahead of others in Africa in terms of their economic gains and achievements. But this economic supremacy was later challenged by other powers in Europe and the USA. Eventually, by 1900 most of Africa was colonized by Britain, France, Portugal, and Germany.

Conclusion

Africa was incorporated into the capitalist world-economy as from 1750, with the exception of East Africa which was integrated later. Some African states were broken and forcibly integrated. With most of the others, the process of incorporation was more gradual, involving the adaptation of existing structures to suit the demands of the new trade, and the world-economy. This process resulted in the eventual colonization of Africa.

3

New trends and processes in Africa in the nineteenth century

In this chapter, we shall identify and analyse the new trends and processes that characterized the first eight decades of the nineteenth century. The impact of those trends will be assessed while attempts will also be made at the end of the chapter to consider what would have happened if Africa had not been colonized at the close of the nineteenth century.

New demographic trends

The first of these new trends had to do with population changes. The suppression of the slave trade led to a gradual increase in the population of Africa. This was so especially in the last three decades of the nineteenth century unlike the previous century when the African population was on the decline.

Apart from population growth there was also a redistribution of population in the nineteenth century. This redistribution took the form of internal migrations and movements. Such migrations included the movement of the Nguni from the Natal region of Southern Africa to different parts of South, Central and East Africa and the migrations of the Yoruba after the fall of Old Ọyọ, from the semi-savannah of northern Yorubaland to the forest areas to the south. In both cases, the activities of the migrants resulted in the formation of new political entities. In the case of the Nguni, there were new kingdoms like Gaza, Swazi, Ndebele, Sotho, and Pedi, and in Yorubaland new towns like Ibadan, Abẹokuta, Modakẹkẹ and Ṣagamu became centres of political power.

Islamic revolutions

The diffusion of Islam from Arabia into Africa which began around the seventh century remained, with few exceptions, a peaceful process facilitated largely by trade, until the end of the eighteenth century. But it took a militant turn in North-western and West Africa in the nineteenth century. In the Western Sudan, that is the savannah belt of West Africa alone, there were four major djihāds and several minor ones in the course of the century. The major ones were: the djihāds of ʿUthmān dan Fodio in Hausaland in 1804; that of Shaykh Aḥmad in Massina in 1818; that of al-Hadjdj ʿUmar in the Bambara areas from 1852; and that of Samori Ture in the 1870s.

15

Apart from that of Samori Ture, all the other *djihāds* were led and organized by the Fulbe or Fulani people who were scattered all over the Western Sudan. They saw the *djihāds* as an opportunity to reform Islam as it was then practised, as a way of redressing political and social abuses, and for alleviating the economic burdens of society. Their goal was the creation of theocracies – kingdoms administered according to Islamic law and injunctions. Samori Ture, though not a Fulani, belonged to the Islamized and learned section of the Soninke people, called the Dyula. His *djihād* was also successful and his aim was to convert the people and use the Islamic religion to forge unity among them, especially in the struggle against European invaders.

The success of the *djihāds* brought with it political and social changes. Politically, they led to the creation of large empires like the Sokoto caliphate, the Massina empire, which was later swallowed up by al-Hadjdj 'Umar's empire, and the huge empire of Samori Ture. They also led to major shifts in political authority in the Western Sudan. The Fulani *djihāds* replaced the old Hausa kings by new Fulani *amīr* while the Soninke ruling elite were replaced by Dyula scholars. The Sokoto *djihād* also left its imprint on the Borno empire. Through the activities of Shaykh Muhammad al-Kanēmi, the old ruling dynasty of Borno, the Saifawa, was replaced by a new and reforming dynasty which revived the fortunes of the empire.

Socially the *djihāds* led, through the teachings and preachings of the leaders, to the purification of Islam. They promoted a better knowledge of the teachings of the Ku'rān and the works of leading Islamic jurists, and discouraged the survival of the traditional religions that continued to be mixed with the practice of Islam. They also transformed Islam in the Western Sudan from a religion of the court and capital of rulers into that of the whole community. The establishments of different orders also polarized the faith. There were two rival orders: the Tijāniyya and the Kādirīyya brotherhoods. The Tijāniyya order, to which al-Hadjdj 'Umar belonged attracted a lot of ordinary folks and this explains the numerical preponderance of the order over its more aristocratically based counterpart, the Kādirīyya order. The *djihād* also resulted in an improvement of the standard of Islamic scholarship and mass literacy in the nineteenth century. Lastly, the *djihāds* forged a feeling of oneness and Islamic cultural unity which survives till today among the different peoples of the Sudanic belt.

However, the *djihād* leaders were not always able to adhere to their determination to administer their empires purely by Islamic laws. In a number of cases they had to allow some of the already existing socio-political institutions to continue functioning. This resulted in new cultural amalgams, Hausa/Fulani culture in Hausaland, and Juula (Dyula)/Soninke culture in the Niger bend. Islam also gained ground in other parts of Africa. It was extended in Senegambia through the activities of various reformers and *shaykhs*. It became entrenched in Cyrenaica, Eastern Sahara and Libya by the Sanūsī Brotherhood, in eastern Sudan through the activities of the Mahdī; and in Buganda through the efforts of Arab and Swahili traders, and Muslim mercenaries in the service of various adventurers.

Christian missionary activities

Another important trend in the nineteenth century was the revival and expansion of Christianity in Africa. The Early Church which flourished in North Africa and extended up the Nile River and into the Fezzan was overrun in the seventh century by the rising tide of Islam, and almost completely wiped out leaving pockets of Eastern Orthodox and Monophysite Coptic Church in Egypt and Ethiopia. Attempts by the Portuguese to propagate the Christian faith in the fifteenth and sixteenth centuries initially took root in places like the Congo, Benin and Warri, but its association with the slave trade ensured ultimate failure. By the last decade of the eighteenth and the beginning of the nineteenth centuries, the missionary fervour was up again in Europe. This could be attributed partly to the evangelical revival led by John Wesley, and partly to the spread of anti-slave trade ideas and the humanitarian spirit. The wave of Christian missionary activities in Africa in the nineteenth century was so strong that its impact was as revolutionary as that of the Islamic *djihāds*. There were notable differences, however. In our period, Islamic reformers rose from within the society and manifested the militancy of the sword, while the spread of Christianity was led by foreign missionaries preaching the virtues of the Bible and the plough, but drawing the military might of imperialist Europe after them. By 1840, there were more than fifteen missionary societies at work in Africa. These included the Church Missionary Society (CMS), the Basel Evangelical Missionary Society of Switzerland, the North German or Bremen Missionary Society, the United Presbyterian Church of Scotland, and the Society of African Missions from France. As the century dragged on, the number of the missionary societies functioning in Africa increased.

In East and Central Africa, there was only a single missionary society, namely the Church Missionary Society, by the middle of the nineteenth century. By 1873, when David Livingstone died, there were two others: the Universities Mission to Central Africa (UMCA) formed in 1857 and the Catholic Society of the Holy Ghost formed in 1868. But within four years of Livingstone's death, four more missions came into the region due to the publicity given to his travels and the circumstances of his death. The new missions were the Livingstone Mission formed in 1875, the Blantyre Mission formed in 1876, the London Missionary Society, and the Catholic White Fathers. Those missions were active in Malawi, Buganda, Tanzania and in other parts of East and Central Africa.

In the whole of Southern Africa, there were only two missionary societies at the end of the first decade of the nineteenth century. They were the Moravian Mission, and the London Missionary Society. But as from 1816, many missionary societies, Protestant and Catholic, from Europe and the USA flooded the region. Among them were the Church Missionary Society (CMS), the Norwegian Missionary Society, the Wesleyan Missionary Society, the Glasgow Missionary Society, the United Presbyterian Mission, the Berlin Society, the Rhenish Society, the Paris Evangelicals and the USA Mission to Zululand and Mosega.

Unlike most missionaries in other parts of Africa, those in Southern Africa were directly and actively involved in the internal political affairs of the region. Some of them even developed close friendship with some of the African kings. For example, Rev. Robert Moffat and King Lobengula were good friends. But the colonial authorities in Southern Africa disliked this friendship which they saw as being detrimental to colonial interests. The African leaders also became suspicious of the missionaries because they were used on a number of occasions as colonial agents negotiating with African rulers.

Activities of the missionaries in Africa were varied. In the first place, they built churches, preached the gospel and won converts. And as part of their religious commitment, they translated the Bible into African languages. Secondly, they sought to promote agriculture among the local peoples. To this end, they established experimental farms and plantations. In addition, they raised the standard of living of the people by teaching them valuable skills like masonry, carpentry, printing and tailoring. They also promoted trade. But most importantly, they promoted literacy and Western education. They established elementary schools, training colleges and secondary schools. It is necessary to elaborate briefly on these educational activities in different parts of Africa.

West Africa

The Church Missionary Society established Fourah Bay College in Sierra Leone in 1827 and by 1841 they already had twenty-one elementary schools. In 1842, they established two secondary schools, one for boys and the other for girls in Sierra Leone; and another for boys in Lagos in 1859. The Wesleyans (Methodists) also had twenty-four elementary schools in the Gold Coast by 1846 and they established their first secondary school, the famous Mfantsipim School, in 1876. Three years later, they established the Methodist Boys' High School in Lagos. The establishment of schools by the missions were not limited to the coast, but extended into the hinterland as the missionaries penetrated the interior.

East and Central Africa

In East Africa and Central Africa, the educational attempts of the missionaries began later, but were very productive. By 1830, there was a school in Livingstone which had an enrolment of four hundred students and with workshops and a printing press that was producing first-year textbooks for the elementary schools, and local translations of the Bible. The London Missionary Society reported in 1835 that it had 4 000 children in its schools in Madagascar and by 1894 the rate of enrolment in the local schools was comparable to that in Western Europe.

Southern Africa

Assistance from the governments of the Cape and Natal in the nineteenth century helped the missions to cover a lot of ground in the field of education. They established many elementary schools and began to found teacher-training colleges and secondary schools as from 1840. For example, the Glasgow

Missionary Society established a seminary in Natal in 1841 with an industrial department which taught several skills like masonry, carpentry, wagon-making, smithing and later printing and book-binding. The Roman Catholics were also involved in the same process. They established a boarding school attached to the convent of the Sisters of the Holy Family, besides a primary school, and a home of refuge, all in Natal. The French missionaries in 1868 established a teacher-training institute at Amanzimtote and a seminary for girls in Natal in the mid-1860s. The Anglicans established St Albans College among the Zulu in 1880.

The impact of the spread of Christianity and Western education in the nineteenth century amounted to a revolution in African societies. Africans gained technical skills and some European ideas. In many places, they improved the traditional patterns of house construction by the newly acquired skills, while some, mostly the converts, adopted Western clothes. The missionary enterprise dealt a nasty blow not only to the religious basis of African societies, but also to family relationships by condemning belief in ancestors, traditional gods, witchcraft, and the institution of polygamy. The introduction of Christianity increased the number of religions practised in Africa, and this in turn led to the division of African societies into rival groups. On the one hand, there was the division between converts and non-converts, while on the other hand there was division within the converts' ranks, as between Protestants and Catholics. The latter division was to be responsible for serious social tensions especially in Uganda and Madagascar.

Emergence of the Western-educated elite

The emergence of a class of Africans educated mainly in English and French represented perhaps the greatest social impact of the missionary enterprise. This Western-educated elite began to appear first on the coast, and later in the interior.

In South Africa, post-primary institutions like the Lovedale Missionary Institution in Natal became centres for the production of professionals who later constituted the elite. Such institutions turned out teachers, missionaries, clerks, journalists, interpreters, artisans, and agriculturists. Some of this elite like Tiyo Soga, Nehemiah Tile, Reverend Kenyane and James M. Divane, all clergymen, were to play leading roles in the spread of Christianity among the Bantu in the 1880s and 1890s. Others like John Tengo Javabu were to be very influential in the politics of the Cape later in the century. However, the number of educated elite in South Africa by 1880 was very small when considered against the entire black population in the area.

In East and Central Africa, the elite was also very small. For instance, it was not until the 1890s that Africans were ordained as priests of the Universities Mission to Central Africa in Tanganyika. And a politically conscious elite did not emerge in Kenya until the opening decades of the twentieth century due to the fact that post-elementary educational activities of the missionaries did not start there until the end of the nineteenth century.

3.1 *The Church of Scotland Mission's church at Blantyre (Malawi)*

3.2 *Tiyo Soga*

3.3 *Charlotte Village School, Sierra Leone, c. 1885*

In West Africa, a considerable number of educated elites had been produced by 1880, and the leading country in this respect was Sierra Leone. The educated elite in Sierra Leone, called Creoles, were the pioneers of most of the missionary enterprise in other parts of West Africa. They included James Africanus Horton, a medical doctor, Samuel Ajayi Crowther, the freed Yoruba slave who became educated and was consecrated as the first African bishop of the Anglican church; and James Johnson, another clergyman who was also to become a bishop. Others included Edward Wilmot Blyden of Liberia, originally from the West Indies; Otunba Payne, H. E. Macaulay, and Essien Ukpabio of Nigeria. From the Gold Coast were people like John Mensah Sarbah, J. P. Brown, A. W. Parker and J. H. Brew.

However, not all the educated elite in West Africa and even in Mozambique and Angola were in the professions, or worked as civil servants and church agents; a large number went into the commercial field as merchants and traders. This commercial elite, though concentrated on the coast, was also sprinkled throughout the interior. They cultivated foreign tastes, consumed imported goods from Europe, and played a major role in the penetration of the interior by European ideas and the taste for European goods. Thus, we can say that by the end of the 1880s, there had emerged a new social class in Africa made up of the educated elite in the civil service, church service and in private business.

Ethiopianism

Ethiopianism was one of the two important consequences of the emergence of the educated elite in Africa. The other, an intellectual revolution, was borne out of the former. Both were very significant in the history of Africa in the nineteenth century. Ethiopianism was a term believed to have been coined from the Biblical quotation (Psalm 68 v. 31) that Ethiopia will stretch out her hands unto God. The movement to which it was applied had both religious and political undertones. It grew from the humiliation and anger suffered by Africans as a result of European discrimination against them, in both the church and civil hierarchies, especially in the last quarter of the nineteenth century. This led to some Church elders breaking away from the existing churches, at first retaining much of the liturgy, while later on others established churches with their own new liturgies or adaptations of the inherited ones to conform more with traditional African modes of worship. From resentment against discrimination in the church, some began to lead their followers also in protesting against political and administrative injustices. It was therefore a movement for both religious and political independence.

The aim of the movement was to establish independent Christian churches under the control of Africans, free of foreign missionary control, and organized according to African culture and tradition. It began in South Africa around the 1860s and in the 1880s the first African independent church was formed in the region by an African Wesleyan minister, Nehemiah Tile. From South Africa, Ethiopianism spread throughout West, East and Central Africa. In West Africa, a group of Nigerian church leaders, prominent among whom was T. B. Vincent, later known as Mojola Agbebi, initiated the movement. Part of their contention was to retain local names, and dresses, and the use of the indigenous languages in worship.

The educated elite in West Africa went a step further than their counterparts in other parts of the continent. They set out to disprove ideas of the supposed inferiority of the black race. They did this through their articles, books, pamphlets and speeches. This gave rise to an intellectual revolution which in turn propagated ideas about the dignity of the African race, the unity and solidarity of black peoples (Pan-Africanism), and the unique African identity called the 'African Personality'. The leaders of this intellectual revolution in West Africa were James Africanus Horton, Edward Wilmot Blyden and James Johnson.

James Africanus Horton (1835–83)

A medical graduate of Edinburgh University, Horton was born of Igbo parents in Sierra Leone. He condemned racism and argued that the black man was not inferior to the white man. According to him, Africans were capable of development and what was needed were able men to prove the continent's worth to the outside world. In addition, he believed in Pan-Africanism and in preserving the political independence of African peoples. His works included *An African View of the Negro's Place in Nature* (1865), *West African Countries and*

Peoples: A Vindication of the African Race (1868) and *Letters on the Political Condition of the Gold Coast* (1870).

Edward Wilmot Blyden (1832–1912)

He was born in the West Indies and later migrated to Liberia where he studied and lived. He preached racial pride – that Africans should take pride in their race and not intermarry with non-Africans so as to preserve the purity and integrity of the black race. According to him Islam and polygamy were more in keeping with the African personality. He thus enunciated his belief in the 'African personality' to describe the corporate African identity. His works included *African Colonization* (1862), *Vindication of the Negro Race* (1857) and *From West Africa to Palestine* (1873).

James Johnson (1836–1917)

He was born of Yoruba parents and educated in Sierra Leone at the Freetown Grammar School and Fourah Bay College. He joined the Church Missionary Society (CMS) and was transferred to Nigeria in 1874. He advocated nationalism and Ethiopianism in Nigeria. The latter took the form of praising and glorifying past achievements of the black race and highlighting the struggle for power and position in church government and the civil administration. He spread the concept of Ethiopianism through his sermons and writings. He condemned the idea of black racial inferiority and believed that Africa should be evangelized by Africans. According to him, there should be an independent African church controlled and staffed by Africans alone. He saw the European presence as an obstruction to the full realization of the African potential. In 1880, he was relieved of his post as Superintendent of all CMS stations in the interior of Yorubaland by the Mission's authorities, even though he was later appointed an Assistant Bishop.

It is clear from the spate of writings produced by these educated elites, from the scholarly standard of their arguments, and the nature of the ideas presented, that there was indeed an intellectual revolution in Africa and particularly in West Africa in the nineteenth century. The main themes of this revolution included the idea of the corporate identity of African peoples (African personality); the unity and solidarity of African peoples (Pan-Africanism); and movement for political and religious independence, and the growth of a new dignity and confidence in black peoples.

New political trends

Important political developments and trends can also be discerned in Africa in the nineteenth century. These include features such as increasing centralization, modernization and the confrontation between the Africans and the Europeans.

There was a tendency towards centralization in the political structures being established in Africa in the nineteenth century. Examples of this tendency can be seen in the *djihād* states mentioned above – the Sokoto caliphate, the Massina empire, the empire of al-Hadjdj 'Umar, and the empire of Samori Ture – as well as in the Nguni states that followed the rise of Shaka the Zulu king, and the Mfecane. Further examples of this trend can also be found in Ethiopia, Madagascar, and Buganda. The rival states in Ethiopia were eventually united through military conquest under the leadership of Menelik II. In Madagascar, King Andrianaimpoinimerina and his successors also united the feuding states of Central Madagascar into one kingdom. In West Africa, Sierra Leone and Liberia, which were established as freed-slaves settlements, also developed centralizing tendencies. They absorbed other independent states in the interior and sought to become nation states. Such centralizing tendencies were also parallelled in Egypt and the Great Lakes region where Buganda, Bunyoro and Burundi expanded their power and influence over wide areas.

Another political trend in the nineteenth century, apart from that of centralization, was modernization or reawakening. This modernization manifested itself in the social field, the military sphere and the constitutional setting. In the social field, contact with Europeans brought new developments like railways, telegraphs, agricultural and mining machinery, the printing press, technical education and finance capital. The attitudes of Africans to these opportunities and situations were sometimes wary and cautious, and resulted not in blind imitation but in adaptation and compromise. For example, the printing press got to Egypt in 1822 and to Portuguese Luanda in 1841. The first modern mines were opened in Algeria in 1845 and in the Gold Coast in the 1870s.

Modernization was also evident in the constitutional field. The existence of a large educated Westernized elite and Muslum 'ulamā' called for a revision of the existing power structure in most African states. In the case of the 'ulamā', the answer to their demand for political participation was found in the *djihāds* of the first half of the nineteenth century. But the response was not always as militant as the Fulbe and Juula (Dyula) Muslim clerics made it in the Western Sudan. In other parts of West Africa, especially on the West Coast, the demand for power by the new elite was pursued by constitutional procedures. An example was the constitution of the Fante Confederacy of the Gold Coast in 1874. The spirit of the Fante Constitution was to promote cooperation among the several Fante groups that made up the Confederacy. This was indeed a remarkable development and it could have had a great impact on the history of the area if the British had allowed the constitution to be fully implemented. Another example of constitutional reform was that of the Egba United Board of Management at Abẹokuta which was set up to introduce European constitutional procedures into the traditional political system, promote 'civilization' and the spread of Christianity, as well as develop trade by protecting the property of European merchants and of the Sierra Leone immigrants as British subjects.

The nineteenth-century political trends discussed above were of such significance that they had their impact on the ensuing colonial state. A number of them cast their shadows forward and can explain some of the problems and patterns of colonial rule.

New economic trends

There were also new economic trends in Africa in the nineteenth century. The most dramatic change was that associated with the abolition and suppression of the slave trade and the switch to agricultural exports. The real significance of this change was that it led to a redistribution of income. With the suppression of the slave trade, the kings and rulers no longer had the monopoly of trade and the income accruing from it. Ordinary folks who now participated in the produce trade got their own share of the commercial income. This redistribution of income led to the rise of a new set of rich people in the rural as well as in the urban areas. The development of this export agriculture also led to the incorporation of the African economy into the capitalist world economy of profit maximization and capital accumulation. But because the change to export agriculture was not accompanied by a technological change in the means of production, nor in the industrial processing of the products before exportation, Africa remained a feeder to the capitalist and industrialized economy of Europe.

Another economic change in the nineteenth century was the completion of the commercial unification of Africa. This meant that different parts of Africa that were hitherto unconnected became linked via commercial transactions in the course of the century. Commercial routes developed linking East, Central and North Africa together through the instrumentality of Arab, Swahili, Yao, Kamba, and Nyamwezi traders in East Africa; Tio, Ovimbundu, and Chokwe traders in Central Africa; Arab traders in Egypt, and Arab and Sudanese traders across the Sahara. The outcome of this was the commercial unification of Africa, an increase in internal contacts in Africa, and also an increase in the number of African entrepreneurs, middlemen and traders. Most importantly, it led to the gradual opening up of the interior of Africa to European and Arab/Swahili influence with the unfortunate effects that constitute a major theme of vol. VII of the UNESCO *General History*.

Conclusion

From the above discussion, it is clear that, if there had been no colonial rule in Africa, most of the new trends mentioned would have continued unabated. Politically, the tendency towards centralization would have continued and resulted in the establishment of strong nation states; constitutional experiments like the Fante Confederacy would have established the basis of cooperation between the educated elite and the traditional rulers. Christianity and Islam would have continued as they did in the colonial period while the pace of the spread of Western education would have been quickened. Moreover, given the commercial unification of the continent, Africa would have become more inward-looking and self-reliant. Pan-Africanism and the feeling of racial identity would have led to the ideological unity of the continent. Unfortunately, colonial rule put an end to all such developments.

However, one important fact remains, namely, that the nineteenth century before the establishment of colonial rule was indeed a revolutionary century which witnessed the development of new trends and processes whose impact marks the end of the old and the beginning of modern Africa.

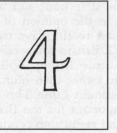

The abolition
of the slave trade

In this chapter, we shall examine the abolition of the trans–Atlantic slave trade: problems encountered in the process, the course of the abolition and its consequences. It should be pointed out here that not all African communities participated in the slave trade across the Atlantic. Some communities in the interior were not even aware of it while some coastal peoples, on the other hand, participated so actively in the trade that it affected their political and social structures. While a number of Africans made personal fortunes out of this trade in human beings, the overall effect on the continent was disastrous. The trade statistics show that during the eighteenth century alone almost seven million Africans were exchanged for European goods and firearms. This figure was much more than that of the slave trade across the Sahara and that of the Indian ocean put together. The campaign for the abolition of the slave trade did not come from Africa. It started from Europe partly on humanitarian grounds, and partly because of the relative decline in the importance of the Atlantic trade with the assertion of independence in the Americas and the gradual shift of European interest to the Far East and Africa.

The Western impetus for abolition

European ideas about the African began to change in the eighteenth century as they saw him in more humanitarian terms. This led to the demand for the abolition of the slave trade. The slave trade began to be seen as an evil transaction which led to the death of a large number of people, prevented the diversification of trade on the African coast, and allowed barbarism to thrive on the continent. Advocates of abolition sought to employ Christianity, Western technological civilization and normal trade largely in agricultural produce in suppressing the slave trade. But first, public opinion in Europe and America had to be won to favour abolition, while the attitudes of governments to the slave trade also had to be made to change.

In France, in the eighteenth century, secular thought and ideas publicized through the works of philosophers like Diderot encouraged the abolition of the slave trade. In Britain, the public was taught about philanthropy through religious means which were fuelled by a powerful evangelical revival. In the

27

USA the Quakers were already campaigning against the slave trade and were persuading others to do so. Apart from these changes in the opinion of the public, governments were also modifying their attitudes to the slave trade. The first official abolition was that of Denmark in 1802. Britain followed suit in 1807 after several parliamentary debates on the issue led by William Wilberforce. Some scholars have argued that economic rather than humanitarian considerations led Britain to champion the abolitionist cause. This was because the Atlantic slave trade was relatively more important for the British economy of the mercantilist period of the seventeenth and eighteenth centuries than it was for the industrial economy of the nineteenth century. In the latter period, Britain required the raw material and the markets of the Far East and Africa more than the sugar plantations of the West Indies. The humanitarian factor was important for moving people to take steps to stop the slave trade and abolish slavery. But it was the economic factors that made it possible for them to succeed.

The campaign for the abolition of the slave trade in the West was spearheaded by Britain. After the failure of its proposals for collective abolition made in 1787 and 1807, Britain devised a three-point plan of action for a forceful abolition of the slave trade. The first step was to get other nations to make laws that would make slave dealings illegal to their citizenry. The second was to make bi-lateral treaties to the effect that the navies of each had the right to search and seize the merchant ships of the other nation if they were caught in the slave trade. The third was cooperation through mixed commissions with the right of trying captured slave ships and setting slaves found in them free. It is rather strange that this plan did not begin with Africa which actually supplied the slaves but was concentrated on the European and American importers of slaves.

This initial plan produced a two-pronged result. On the one hand it appealed to people with kind hearts and it received their support. It was also supported by some governments as a way of courting British economic support. On the other hand, the plan was opposed by states which saw abolition as part of the British bid to achieve naval supremacy and control world trade. Such states saw the British plan as likely to do damage to their navies, colonies, and trading interests. For instance, Portugal, Spain, the USA and France consumed and distributed coffee, cotton, sugar and tobacco produced on their plantations tended by African slaves. There were also shipping agents and corporations which thrived on the slave trade, and such groups did not take the attempts to abolish the trade kindly.

Politically weak states yielded to British pressure for abolition, but in certain cases, only after threats from Britain. Denmark, the Netherlands, and Sweden signed treaties of reciprocal suppression with Britain. Spain and Portugal agreed to abolish the trade for some compensation from Britain in 1817, but the latter did not completely stop its slave dealings until 1842 after receiving threats from Britain. Brazil continued the trade till 1850 while Cuba did not stop until 1866. Politically stronger states on the other hand, reacted differently to resist

British pressure which they regarded as an invasion of their sovereignty. France and the USA continued the trade for several years before they eventually abolished it. France agreed to stop the trade in the 1830s while the USA did not stop until the second half of the nineteenth century.

The planters in America and the West Indies resisted abolition for a variety of reasons. They saw no sense in the humanitarian argument for the suppression of the trade. They were so racist that they did not believe that abolition could improve the lot of the blacks. They held on for as long as possible to the social prestige and economic advantages they had acquired from the ownership of slaves and slave labour on their plantations. Moreover, their opposition was strengthened by the increasing demand in the West for the products of slave labour. Meanwhile, this same West led by Britain was pressing for the prohibition of the importation of slaves which the planters saw as essential for increasing the supply of these products.

The process of suppression

The suppression of the slave trade was entrusted to commanders of warships which operated not only on the West African coast, but also in the Mediterranean. France spearheaded the operations in the latter as part of her attempt to gain naval supremacy in the landlocked Mediterranean Sea. For a while, in the 1830s, Britain seemed to have lost the lead in the abolition process. Activities of warships were more successful in some parts than others. British ships captured French slave ships between Mauritius and Madagascar on the Indian Ocean. But there were no fixed regulations to deal with those caught. Sometimes the slaves on board were freed and, at other times, they were dispersed on the local plantations. French ships captured by the French themselves in American waters were tried and the slaves recovered were taken to Cayenne. However, there were several inconsistencies in the suppression exercise. In cases where slave ships were caught and tried by the Mixed Commissions, sentence was pronounced on the ships and not on the traders. In the Americas, there were also a number of contradictions in the suppression exercise. In fact, the effectiveness of the Commissions that tried to apprehend slave ships depended on the dispositions of the planters at that point in time. Because of this, very few ships were caught despite the fact that nearly seventy warships from different nations operated in the area.

There were fewer warships on the West African coast; and the Dutch, Portuguese, and American naval squadrons in the area operated intermittently making their impact minimal. Only the naval squadrons of Britain and France were in continuous operation. France's squadron was established in 1818 and it remained independent until 1831 when it began to collaborate with the British squadron. But national pride and rivalries did not allow the 1831–3 agreement between Britain and France to succeed in suppressing the trade. In 1845, the number of warships on each side rose to twenty-six, and it was from that year that a real naval task force seemed to have emerged against the slave trade.

Added to this were the five American and six Portuguese ships off the Congo. However, in 1849 France defaulted on its obligations and, later, the Second Empire promoted covert slave trading. The French naval squadron, on the whole, did not achieve any suppression and its stance in the entire process was ambiguous.

The task of ensuring the success of the scheme fell on Britain. But Britain had many disabilities in this regard. One of its principal problems was that its twenty-six warships were not suited to the task of policing the Atlantic. They were not smart enough to outmanoeuvre the slave traders. Effective suppression therefore depended on the role played by British naval officers, many of whom had thoroughly assimilated the idea of abolition in London and were genuine converts to the cause. They consequently disobeyed their headquarters at home in certain cases and even ignored international law in their concern for human welfare. Imbued with humanitarian zeal, British naval officers illegally searched and seized French and American vessels even before the latter has made any commitment to the abolition exercise. This led to diplomatic protests and scuffles on the international scene. Added to these was a high death rate among the slaves in the process of their being freed by the navy. There were also deaths among the seamen, either from sickness or from artillery exchanges with opposing slave ships.

The slave traders also compounded the task of the naval squadrons. They evaded them successfully because they had adequate information about their movements. They used false flags and other devious means to escape detection and capture. This led to an increase in violence. Squadron captains and local governors of Western settlements like Liberia embarked on overland expeditions to punish the slave traders. Trading stations were subsequently attacked and destroyed. Examples of such stations were those at Cape Mount which were bombarded by the Liberian Governor, the Reverend Jehudi Ashmum. Slaves recovered from those expeditions were freed and sent to Sierra Leone, the Gambia and Mauritius.

These operations were regarded as successful in France and Britain. From these, it was recognized that it was necessary to involve African rulers in the process of abolition. Consequently, two new techniques were introduced. The first was that treaties began to be signed with local rulers who pledged either peacefully or forcefully to suppress the slave trade in territories under them. The second technique was that Britain and France blockaded the main export centres to stop the flow of slaves. This signified the beginning of diplomacy by armed intervention. And it was particularly the case between 1841 and 1850 on the West African coast which was the base of the slave trade across the Atlantic.

The period 1841–50 was also important for the trans-Saharan slave trade. The Western powers had no means of abolishing the trade because it was entirely in the hands of Africans and did not extend beyond the boundaries of Africa. But within the above decade certain states in North Africa were prevailed upon to abolish the trade. Between 1840 and 1842, the Regency of Tunis abolished the slave trade, while the Ottoman Sultan prohibited it in 1857.

All these attempts to erase the slave trade however did not significantly reduce the number of slaves still being exported and subsequent efforts were also fruitless.

In their bid to apportion blame for the stubborn persistence of the slave trade, the advocates of abolition argued in Europe that if there were no buyers the slave trade would not exist. On the other hand, slavers insisted that it was the regular supply of slaves from Africa that sustained the external demand for them. According to them, if there were no slaves made available, demand would at once dwindle. The blame for the persistence of the trade was, therefore, placed on Africans themselves.

African reactions

In the last two decades of the eighteenth century, before the official abolition of the slave trade by the West, over a million Africans were sold into the Americas. In fact, the act of legislating abolition of the slave trade in Europe was not decisive enough to put an immediate end to it. Nations like Portugal and Brazil still carried on with the trade which even in the nineteenth century sometimes thrived at the level which it had attained in the previous century. The effectiveness of the abolition order on the West African coast was even more limited. Traditional slave-trading centres in areas of European influence like Sierra Leone, Liberia and the Gold Coast were closed down but because the political authorities of these communities were weak, the abolition exercise did not extend beyond their boundaries. In a place like Dahomey, where the slave trade was a major pillar supporting the ruling house, and had influenced the fabric of the political structure, normal slave transactions continued. A regular supply of slaves from the Central Sudan was assured while the wars among the Yoruba overflooded the Whydah market with slaves. Local rulers and slave dealers on the coast supplied the Portuguese and Brazilian traders who fed fat on the trade before turning later to trade in other commodities.

In the Niger delta and Old Calabar, the slave trade was promoted by groups who carried on trade in other commodities simultaneously. There were local institutions and organized groups who were responsible for most of the slave trade in the area. They included priests and dignitaries, the Arochukwu Oracle, the 'Canoe Houses' and the Ekpe society. The trade was regulated by long-established principles and slaves were procured from such distant places as Sokoto, Benue, Nupe and north-western Cameroon. There were also traditional judicial and social customs by which slaves were recruited from nearer home, from the inner delta areas.

No accurate figures can be given for the actual number of Africans sold across the Atlantic during the first sixty years of the abolitionist period. Only rough estimates can be provided in terms of changes in the magnitude of the trade. Between 1807 and 1867, it is estimated that as many as 4 000 European and American vessels of about one-million tonnage were still engaged in the slave trade; that they made about 5 000 journeys and exported about

1.9 million Africans across the Atlantic from the region between Senegal and Mozambique, with more than 80 per cent being loaded south of the Equator. This was just a little less than the number of Africans involved in the trade across the Sahara, and the Arab trade on the Indian Ocean put together from about 1800 to the 1880s.

Although it is true that the slave trade had very destructive effects on Africa, it is not difficult to understand the resistance of African rulers. Some adventurers like Tippu Tip and Rabeh used the slave trade to consolidate their political power. However, the resistance of the coastal rulers and middlemen can only be explained in economic terms. While the peoples and rulers in the plundered areas lamented the evils of the trade, the coastal rulers and the merchants who dealt with the slave traders viewed the trade as a lucrative occupation with an established network and structure which they refused to give up in the absence of an alternative to replace it. Their resistance to the suppression of the slave trade was thus informed by short-term economic considerations with little thought for the long-term overall impact on themselves or their neighbours.

The suppression of the slave trade saved a number of people from slavery in America. About a quarter of the total number of slave ships involved in the trade were probably captured by the anti-slavery squadrons and subsequently tried by the courts set up for that purpose. In all, about 160 000 Africans were freed. But the process of their settling down into normal life was long and arduous. Some led an unstable existence in Brazilian and Cuban slave plantations; others in French settlements for freed slaves in Guyana, Senegal and Gabon had an unclear status. It was only in Sierra Leone and Liberia that some of them acquired genuine freedom backed up by clear legal political status.

Sierra Leone

The experiment at Sierra Leone represented the first viable solution to the problem of rehabilitation faced by the freed slaves. Sierra Leone was founded in 1788 as a philanthropic settlement and as part of the anti-slavery movement. The rehabilitation of the freed slaves was to be assisted by conversion to Christianity and exposure to Western civilization. They were also to be given a commercial orientation. But in spite of these lofty aims the settlement was not initially a success due to a variety of adverse conditions. Recruitment of settlers was not easy, and the forced emigration of some British prostitutes did not help matters. The settlers found the climate harsh and unhealthy, and the death rate was very high. Then there was the hostility of the African neighbours and invasions by the French during the Napoleonic wars. There was also political instability caused by internal intrigues, and the inability of the Company in charge of the administration of the settlement to discharge its responsibilities. By 1802, the number of the settlers had been reduced from 2 089 to 1 406. It was at that stage that the British government came to the rescue of the settlement by taking it over as a Crown Colony and using it as a depot for slaves freed in the Anti-Slavery crusade. More freed slaves were brought in and, by 1811, the population had risen to 4000. By 1831, there were 21000 Africans living in Freetown and the surrounding villages. By 1850, the population had almost tripled.

Different generations of settlers encountered different sets of problems. The first generation battled with the problems of creating a new society. The steady increase in the population called for an improvement in the available amenities. Governor Charles MacCarthy whose tenure fell between 1816 and 1823 rose to the occasion by improving the standards of living in the earlier former villages and building new ones. Subsidies from the British government proved very helpful. Freetown was the seat not only of the colonial administration and that of the naval Vice-Admiralty but also the official liberation centre for the Mixed Commissions which tried apprehended slave ships. The colony was opened to foreign trade in 1831; with this, subsidy from the British government was withdrawn and the inhabitants were expected to take charge of their own affairs and be self-supporting.

During the period of the trials, the role of missionaries in the survival and development of the colony was crucial. The missionaries, sponsored by the British upper and ruling classes, set out to spread Christianity and Western civilization, and to fight for the effective abolition of the slave trade. Despite a few confrontations with the local slave traders, the missionaries cooperated with the civil administration of the colony, particularly in the rehabilitation of the freed slaves in the agricultural villages round Freetown where they acted as Managers. Several schools were established and English became the lingua franca. The missionaries used Sierra Leone as a laboratory for the study and comparative analysis of African languages. They recruited interpreters, clerks and missionary agents from Freetown for the penetration of other parts of West Africa.

The problems faced by the second generation of settlers had to do with the growth of the settlement. With as many as 2 000 people coming in annually in the 1840s when the campaign for suppression was at its height, there was the problem of accommodation. Partly to relieve pressure on available space, some of the freed slaves were recruited into the British army, others left for the Gambia compulsorily, while some were given the choice of emigrating to the West Indies. This West-Indian alternative did not appeal to the Africans because they feared that a journey to the Americas would end up in some form of slavery or the other. They preferred to settle in the villages. But the missionaries also helped some of them to return to their original homes which were mostly in the Yoruba country. Meanwhile, some of those in Freetown rose to occupy high positions in the society but they had to contend with the attitude of superiority of the early settlers from Britain and Nova-Scotia who maintained a class distinction.

The development of the economy was gradual. Firstly, there was the production of food, especially rice. Secondly, there was the cultivation of export crops like sugar, ginger and indigo; and the exploitation of local natural resources like coffee and timber. The trade in natural resources flourished more than that in export crops, and the timber business became very lucrative. However, this economic buoyancy should not be over-emphasized. The British lent minimum administrative support to it. Its success proved only that the exercise was a viable one. The profit that accrued from it was not enough to provide the colony with a real capital base, though it generated some wealth for a few individuals. By the second half of the nineteenth century, the different cultures in Sierra Leone had been welded together into a Creole society, 'civilized' by its own internal developments. In 1853, Sierra Leoneans became subjects of the British Crown.

Liberia

The story of Liberia differed a little from the above. It was a product of philanthropic and civilizing aspirations. It was established by the American Colonization Society and the Federal Government of the USA helped to populate it by sending Africans freed by the naval patrol. Liberia was also the result of a desire to reduce the influence of emancipated blacks in the USA.

The first problem faced by the settlers in Liberia was posed by the hostile neighbouring African rulers who detested the foreign encroachment on their land and the threat to the slave trade which was their main commercial activity across the seas. Their opposition was largely checked by the settlers under the leadership of the Reverend Jehudi Ashmun, thus giving the settlement a chance to survive. It was given the name of Liberia in 1824 and Monrovia became its capital. It was administered by the American Colonization Society through an official who, because of the distance from the USA, had to be left relatively free to govern according to his interpretation of the charter authorizing the settlement. Trade was encouraged and the population of the settlement began to swell with the years. In terms of composition, Liberia was made up not only of liberated Africans – the majority of the earliest settlers were slaves manumitted in the Southern USA on condition that they would emigrate.

Three factors contributed to the survival and growth of the settlement. The first had to do with the courage of the inhabitants in the face of hostilities from neighbours and the harsh environment. Three more settlements were founded at Bassa Cover, Sinoe and Cape Palmas (Maryland); and the last was incorporated into Liberia only in 1856. The inhabitants of these settlements demonstrated a remarkable resilience in the face of all odds. The land was not fertile, there was no business, no capital, and labour was very expensive. But the presence of the settlers on the coast did not only drive the slave traders out, it also stopped the slave trade in the area.

The second factor was the personal qualities of the people who took charge of the administration of the settlement. Many turned out to be very capable administrators, down to earth and very practical. Examples of such men were Thomas Buchanan who moulded the constitution to suit local conditions; J. B. Russwurm, the Governor of Maryland from 1836 to 1851; and J. J. Roberts, Governor of Liberia from 1841 to 1847, and President from 1847 to 1856.

The third factor was the status of Liberia. It was officially declared independent on 26 July 1847 following the attempt of the British to challenge the attributes of an autonomous nation exercised by the settlers. With independence, the nationality of Liberia was open only to black people. It thus became the first African Republic, made up of freed slaves and some free-born African Americans.

In the nineteenth century, Liberia was not as economically developed as Sierra Leone. The significance of the experiment in the two countries was not that they anticipated the independence movements in the twentieth century, but that they represented the wonderful idea that new African nations could actually be created on the same soil that had been ravaged by the slave trade. Despite this significant achievement, the success of Liberia and Sierra Leone did not satisfy the abolitionists who could not agree on the particular methods to adopt in the effective suppression of the slave trade. The failure of another settlement attempted at Lokoja on the Niger–Benue confluence led to widespread criticism of the whole abolitionist strategy.

Protecting new trade

In the suppression era, Western countries were generally concerned more with the protection of the new trade in agricultural produce than with effective suppression of the slave trade. There was an increasing demand for the natural products of Africa. This trade in other commodities did not really compete with the slave trade; it developed alongside it. If there was any competition at all, it was among the Western nations who divided Africa into areas of economic influence. Moreover, the industrial and technological revolutions in Britain and France created a high demand for such African products as palm oil, which was needed as lubricant for machinery, and raw material for making soap and lamp fuel.

The amount of palm oil exported from Africa to Britain and France rose significantly between 1814 and 1870. France also imported groundnut and some other nuts from Senegal and the Gambia for the manufacture of household soap. The growth of this trade represented the establishment of an alternative to the slave trade. The main producing areas of palm oil were Dahomey, the Niger delta and Cameroon. However, the expansion of the new trade meant that internal slavery began to flourish as slaves were needed to aid the production and marketing of palm oil. These economic changes were in turn speeded up by the spread of Christianity, Western education and other cultural influences from Europe and America.

Protestant and Catholic missionaries became important agents of Western influence. In places like Senegal where Islamic culture had already been firmly established, the educational and evangelization efforts of the missionaries had very little success. The Saint-Coeur de Marie mission in Gabon also experienced limited success under Mgr Bessieux. The missions, having realized their relative helplessness in the face of Islam, decided to train an elite and they established many schools to this effect. They settled first on the coast. They got to Badagry in 1842, Whydah in 1843, Calabar in 1846; and their link with the interior was Abẹokuta.

4.1   *A group of Oromo women on board HMS* Daphne *in 1867 after being liberated from an East African slave-trading dhow*

4.2   *Released slaves on the Universities' Mission estate at Mbweni near Zanzibar – paying wages*

The Protestant missions, unlike their Catholic counterparts, involved themselves in local affairs and sought worldly influence. Christianity to them did not only embrace conversions, but also education, culture, class affiliation and political choice. They taught some skills like architecture, carpentry, printing, and European medical practices. This had a significant impact on the people. Some of them became Westernized in dress, food and in their homes. This was a new middle class whom the missionaries expected to expand the flow of trade to and from the coast. The Protestant missions thus took on the role of reformers. In Abẹokuta, they interfered in the political and military affairs of the people. They got the help of British troops against Dahomey which was encroaching on Abẹokuta soil. By 1890, the missions were really entwined in local development which gradually led to the imposition of colonial rule.

Conclusion

To conclude, we should note that in the first eight decades of the nineteenth century, the decline of the slave trade did not anywhere lead to a complete eradication. The slave trade ended in Senegal and Gorée in 1824 though irregular operations still continued in some of the adjoining areas till 1866 to 1867. In 1848 to 1850, Liberia got the assistance of French ships against international slave ships. The slave trade in the Côte d'Ivoire was not to supply the external demand, but for internal purposes in the region. The Gold Coast was also relatively unaffected by the slave trade in the abolition period.

In the region between Lagos and Whydah, however, slave dealings continued until they were curbed by diplomacy and force from Britain and France around 1860. A policy of concluding treaties and encouraging land occupation was used to subdue the trade in the region between Benin and Gabon. Between the Congo and Angola, slave dealings were discouraged by the coercive activities of British and Portuguese naval patrols. It could thus be seen that the slave trade was not brought to an end at the same time in different parts of the continent.

The east coast of Africa was an exception. Between 1860 and 1870 when the slave trade was dying out in the west and south, it was experiencing a revival on the East African coast. The British attempt to suppress the trade by signing an abolition treaty with the Sultan of Zanzibar was of no effect. It was only the imposition of colonial rule later on that saw the end of the trade. This delay was due to the fact that Western abolitionists were not immediately aware of the magnitude and impact of the Arab trade in slaves until the discoveries of Livingstone.

The doctrine of abolition led to a more humane treatment of African slaves, and the idea of opening Africa to the world. The Western interest in Africa was, however, due more to their desire to exploit Africans than to a respect for African values. By 1870, the slave trade had largely been suppressed not only by the activities of the West, but also through the cooperation of Africans. The African reaction to abolition demonstrated a high degree of adaptability at the risk of economic chaos. After a century of the struggle for abolition, the West felt satisfied and used the success of their abolitionist efforts as a moral justification for the conquest of Africa.

Thus, the slave trade was, in a sense, replaced by colonialism. Under colonial rule, the vestiges of the slave trade and slavery as a social institution, were abolished. However, some of the worst forms of colonialism, such as the apartheid system in South Africa, approximated to conditions of slavery. The struggle against abuses of human dignity has therefore had to be carried on, and appreciation of the inhumanity of the slave trade is increasing. It is noteworthy that during a visit to the island of Gorée in February 1992, Pope John Paul II, on behalf of European Christendom, apologized to African peoples for the centuries of slavery. A movement is also gaining ground for Africa and Africans in the diaspora to demand some restitution for the damage caused by the slave trade.

5

The Mfecane
and the rise of
new African states

This chapter is concerned with the nature of the Mfecane, a revolution that started among the northern Nguni and was popularized by the military and socio-political activities of Shaka, the Zulu king, and some of his lieutenants. Although the revolution started in Southern Africa, it spread into modern Mozambique and Zimbabwe, and as far north as southern Tanzania in East Africa. As it progressed, it first disrupted and then rebuilt the existing state systems in Bantu-speaking Southern and Central Africa.

The Mfecane means 'crushing' and 'hammering' in Bantu languages. As this name implies, it certainly had some crushing effects on political structures in Bantu-speaking Southern Africa. It started in the first decades of the nineteenth century and triggered off a chain of events in which established dynasties were overpowered and replaced; old states were conquered and incorporated into new ones; groups of people were forced to leave their traditional homes and resettle elsewhere; economies were impoverished and, in certain cases, whole village populations dispersed or captured as slaves. The Mfecane led to the depopulation of a large portion of Southern Africa thus facilitating the taking over of African land by white migrant settler communities called Boers. These Boers did not only appropriate the best part of African land for themselves, they also enslaved Africans and plundered what remained of their lands.

However, the Mfecane did not produce only negative results. It also had some positive aspects. In several parts of Southern Africa, it gave rise to large centralized kingdoms and empires, some of which survive to the present. Within the African states, it brought out the ingenuity of African political leaders and forced them to improve their military tactics and political skills.

In order to understand the forces behind this revolution, its fundamental character and the quality of the changes it engendered, it is important to first examine the physical environment of the northern Nguni region and understand how, on the one hand, it moulded the people and how the people in turn had shaped it. Of particular importance was the policy of some Nguni rulers to control the processes both of production and reproduction among their people so as to ensure the surplus labour on which the strength of the king and autonomy of the state depended.

The country and farming practices of the northern Nguni

The communities of the northern Nguni area have been able to adapt considerably to their physical environment due to centuries of settlement and farming in the area. The land of the northern Nguni lies between the rivers Pongolo and Tugela, and is bounded to the west by the valley of the Mzinyathi. It is a region of high relief into which several rivers have cut deep valleys. This high relief has meant climatic variations which in turn produced a wide range of vegetation variation. The farmers who reared animals and produced crops in the area had to adapt to the environment, but they also of necessity interfered with the natural vegetation.

The vegetation of the northern Nguni area was broadly twofold, on one was forest – real wooded forest and scrub-forest (stunted growth forest with trees and bushes of poor quality); on the other side, in the low-lying valleys was savannah (grassland). The original Nguni settlers had changed the vegetation of the area over the centuries. They drove the forest back and increased the area of grassland vegetation to their own benefit. This deliberate manipulation of the vegetation over several centuries eventually produced a complex pattern of vegetation in which there was a mixture of different kinds of pasture, determined largely by the amount of rainfall and the nature of the soil. For example, there was *sourveld* in the areas of higher rainfall which the farmers preferred for their cattle in the summer months, the *sweetveld* in the drier upland areas which they preferred in the winter months. It was access to a combination of the different varieties that farmers regarded as providing adequate pasture for their herds throughout the year.

Other areas in Southern Africa were not like the one described above. Even in areas occupied by Sotho-Tswana communities in the Transvaal grassland which had sweetpastures for their herds, there were no river systems like those of the northern Nguni area to keep it well moistured. Also, some of these other communities had pasturage which often occurred together with tse-tse fly which causes sleeping sickness in men and beasts. In addition, the pre-colonial farmers of the Transvaal grassland lacked the advantage of a mixture of different kinds of grazing land which the northern Nguni had. However, the settlement pattern of Sotho-Tswana societies showed that they had access to much more extensive and open land in comparison with that of the northern Nguni. The problem of crowded settlements that was eventually faced by the northern Nguni was not encountered by the Sotho-Tswana groups. The close settlements of the latter, on the other hand, were due, not to the pressure of population density as such, but to their convergence around the few and sparse water resources in the area.

The stability of the region was not threatened as long as there was a careful balance between the growth of human and animal populations on the one hand and free access to different types of pasture. But towards the end of the eighteenth century, population increase affected access to land and related resources. This population increase was caused partly by the adoption at that time of maize as a staple food in the region, thus increasing the pressure on the land. Added to this was the restlessness and violence generated by the fierce competition for the dwindling resources among the different states in the region. As if this situation was not bad enough, there was a severe famine in the area of the northern Nguni between the end of the eighteenth century and the beginning of the nineteenth century. This famine was characterized, among other things, by wandering groups of hungry people who plundered food stores and made matters worse.

The structure of northern Nguni society

It is clear from the foregoing that population increase among the northern Nguni was not due to any large-scale migration into the area but to natural growth which originated from within. As land and other related resources began to dwindle, some of the communities began forcefully to seize land and pasture belonging to others. This crisis also led some rulers to adopt methods of controlling production and reproduction. In order to understand this process clearly, let us examine the structure of Nguni society in the pre-colonial period.

The society was split into numerous homesteads or compounds each under a head chosen from the male line. The number of wives this family head had depended on his social status. Each wife and her children lived together in a house and they produced food for their own needs. There was a division of labour according to sex; the male took care of cattle production and hunting while the female was in charge of crop production. The royal families were however organized differently. Apart from the normal production activities of the members and their relations, the royal compounds also developed into military barracks as from the late eighteenth century onwards. Males were recruited from all over the country into the barracks and the tasks which they performed for the king included crop production among other things.

There were also female recruits but they did not stay in the barracks with their male counterparts. They lived in their fathers' compounds. However, neither male nor female recruits could marry without the king's permission. They sometimes stayed for as long as ten years before being released to marry. The kings of the northern Nguni states were able, through this practice, among other things, to control not only the rate of crop production but also that of human reproduction. The extact time when this practice began among the northern Nguni is not clear, but it is possible that in their expansion they incorporated some Sotho groups into their political orbit and consequently adopted the Sotho-Tswana method of centralizing initiation rites for purposes of political control.

Several explanations have been offered for the Mfecane. These range from population pressure to the factor of European influence. Among the examples of European influence cited are the crisis generated by the eastward movement of the Boer immigrant farmers in the eighteenth century, and the factor of European trade in Delagoa Bay. Of all these theories only that of population pressure seems to be borne out by the facts, and can be regarded as viable and able to stand the test of criticism. Towards the end of the eighteenth century and the beginning of the nineteenth century, a combination of factors revolving round the issue of shortage of land caused by increasing population led to unrest and violence in most of the northern Nguni states. It also saw crucial and fundamental changes in the structure of those societies in response to the changing situation. There were innovations in military tactics and organization, and examples of the great innovators of the period were Zwide of the Ndwandwe, Dingiswayo of the Mthethwa and Shaka of the Zulu.

Three powerful kingdoms emerged in the series of wars that engulfed the Nguni states. The first was the Ndwandwe confederacy under Zwide, the second was the Swazi state ruled by Sobhuza, while the third was the Mthethwa confederacy ruled by Dingiswayo. The three large states were ruled by paramount kings who exacted tributes from a host of other smaller states, communities and clans. The subordinate states recognized the control of the overall central ruler in issues pertaining to state rituals and initiation rites, payment of tributes and waging of war. But they enjoyed considerable autonomy in their day-to-day affairs.

The Ndwandwe

The Ndwandwe state came into prominence in the middle of the eighteenth century. The people that made up the state originally migrated from the Thembe kingdom in the interior of Delagoa Bay towards the end of the seventeenth century. They finally settled in the valley of the Pongolo together with some other Nguni groups. The Ndwandwe rulers then embarked on an expansionist policy by subjugating and incorporating other smaller communities in their neighbourhood. It was at this time that they took the name of Ndwandwe to distinguish them from their neighbours. The political authority of the Ndwandwe increased tremendously as they annexed several other communities to their own state, and their borders became quite extensive. This made the Ndwandwe rulers the first Nguni rulers that created a large state from the various small communities in the region. In achieving this, they did not only make use of military force, they also exploited old institutions and adapted them to serve new purposes.

The greater task of building the Ndwandwe confederacy fell on Zwide who came to the throne in 1790. He proceeded to build on foundations laid by his grandfather and father by making use of old customs and practices. He got to the peak of his rule about the same time as Dingiswayo of the neighbouring and rival Mthethwa confederacy.

The Ndwandwe kingdom like other Nguni states in the region made use of military regiments recruited through traditional initiation of males and females of the same age group. It is likely that Zwide and his predecessors were among the fist Nguni rulers to see some political significance in the practice of co-ordinating circumcision and initiation rites on a state-wide basis. These ceremonies were henceforth organized from the centre and youths (both male and female) from all the territories under the Ndwandwe were made members of national age groups. In periods of war, these age groups were converted into military regiments. Apart from the military utility of the national age-group, they also served to weld different parts of the Ndwandwe confederacy together.

In order to enhance their own authority and create an aura of invincibility round themselves, the Ndwandwe rulers relied on a widespread use of magical and religious influence. For example, Zwide made use of a large number of magicians and medicinemen to build up and spread news of his power throughout the neighbouring communities. He also made use of diplomatic marriages to cement relationships with some of the other states in the region. His sister married Dingiswayo, the Mthethwa ruler while his daughter married Sobhuza, the Swazi king.

However, Zwide was astute enough not to allow such dynastic alliances to stand in the way of his expansionist policy. Despite the fact that Sobhuza was his in-law, Zwide attacked his capital because Sobhuza laid claims to the fertile arable land of the Ndwandwe in the Pongolo valley. The Ndwandwe army emerged victorious and expelled Sobhuza from the Pongolo, driving him and his followers in a northerly direction where Sobhuza later laid the foundation of the Swazi nation.

The Swazi

The groups that later became known as the Swazi were different Ngwane and Tsonga clans under the leadership of Dlamini royal lineages. These groups became welded together and formed the core of the Swazi nation. The Swazi leader, Sobhuza, brought a lot of other clans and communities in the area under his political control, notable among whom were various Sotho groups.

The Sotho communities integrated by Sobhuza into his kingdom had an age-regiment system which he adopted and this enhanced the integration of other conquered communities. The Swazi age-sets functioned only in times of war. The chiefs of the conquered communities were not destroyed, but given a degree of independence in local affairs while their youth were incorporated to the age-regiment of the Swazi. With time, and as they demonstrated their loyalty, the Sotho clans were given the same treatment as the Nguni members of the Swazi state.

Sobhuza also sought to strengthen his own position and ensure the safety of his new kingdom by maintaining peaceful relations with his neighbours. It was for this reason that he married one of the daughters of Zwide, the Ndwandwe ruler, and also sent a number of young Swazi as tribute to Shaka, the Zulu leader. Sobhuza continued his peaceful overtures even when they were not reciprocated and this enabled his domain to enjoy relative peace from the destructive activities of Shaka's troops.

Sobhuza was succeeded in 1840 by his son, Mswazi. On his accession, Mswazi faced both internal and external problems. Internally, he had to contend with several palace rebellions aimed at unseating him and, despite his numerous reforms, those rebellions became a regular feature of his reign. He also embarked on a policy of diplomatic marriages in order to weld his state together. He married from many of the ruling families of the conquered groups while he also gave Swazi royal brides to the rulers of such groups. This principle of intermarriage was also widely practised by the populace. The effect of this was that ethnic divisions were practically wiped out from the Swazi society. Externally, he battled with several foes like the Zulu forces of Mpande in 1846, but his kingdom survived.

The Mthethwa

The Mthethwa kingdom was founded by Kayi, and it became famous under Dingiswayo, his grandson. Like the other Nguni states, the power of the Mthethwa was built on tribute collection from subject communities, cattle raiding, an army based on age regiments, and trade with Delagoa Bay. Dingiswayo reached the peak of his power at about the same time as Zwide of the neighbouring and rival Ndwandwe kingdom. He brought about certain changes in the age-regiment in his domain. He cancelled the circumcision rites that usually accompanied the formation of the age-grades in order to remove the period of seclusion which such rites demanded. He also adopted the chest-and-horns formation for his army.

The Zulu

Dingiswayo, the ruler of the Mthethwa, was killed in a war against Zwide and his Ndwandwe troops in 1818. Shaka, who was the head of the small Zulu chiefdom and a general in Dingiswayo's army became the ruler of the Mthethwa confederacy. He consequently made the Mthethwa part of the Zulu nation. He allowed the traditional system of government of the Mthethwa to continue under a young son of Dingiswayo and the supervision of a regent subordinate to himself. In dealing with other groups, Shaka insisted on total incorporation. The rulers of the conquered peoples were often wiped out and replaced by members of the Zulu royal family, though at other times, the chiefs of the larger groups were retained and allowed some measure of freedom in managing their local affairs.

Shaka's main achievement was in the reorganization of his army. He intensified the adaptation of social institutions like age grades for military purposes. He changed and perfected some of his military techniques and tactics during the wars that he fought for the expansion of the Zulu kingdom. He replaced the long throwing spear by a shorter one for close combat. He introduced long shields and prohibited the wearing of sandals by his troops so they could achieve greater mobility. He maintained a standing army of well-drilled and disciplined men who were kept in barracks and had to remain celibate sometimes for as long as ten years before they were discharged. Of his military tactics, the 'cow-horns' formation was the most impressive.

Shaka's army was tough and merciless with the enemy. His drive to conquer all the groups in the northern Nguni region brought him into a direct clash with Zwide, the ruler of the Ndwandwe whom he eventually defeated in 1820. The defeat of Zwide meant the collapse of the Ndwandwe state. While some of the component groups of the Ndwandwe fled the country, the bulk of them remained as vassals of Shaka.

The Gaza

The Gaza state was formed by a small group of people led by Soshangane which broke away from the Ndwandwe immediately after the defeat of Zwide. Soshangane established himself in Tsonga country from where he conquered and annexed several other smaller states.

The economic power of the Gaza kingdom was based on the control of trade between the interior and the Portuguese trading settlements on Delagoa Bay. However, rather than expand and exploit this commercial opportunity, the Gaza state relied too heartily on wars. Soshangane's troops fought all the neighbouring peoples. His authority was backed by an army based on the age regiment system, and which copied other military techniques of the Zulu army.

The Gaza society, however, remained divided along ethnic lines. The original Nguni group from the south formed a socially superior class while the newly incorporated Tsonga communities belonged to an inferior class. Soshangane did not use his age regiments to weld the subject communities into the central group. Instead, the age regiments of the Tsonga were kept in their own districts under Nguni officers. They were discriminated against and often made to suffer heavier casualties in war.

The Ndebele

The Ndebele state was founded by Mzilikazi, the son of a ruler of a small Khumalo chiefdom which was under Zwide, the Ndwandwe king. In 1818, Mzilikazi became the ruler of the Khumalo following the death of his father. With the defeat of Zwide by Shaka, the Zulu leader, Mzilikazi transferred his loyalty to Shaka. However, he eventually quarrelled with Shaka, and he fled the region with his people. He settled in an area inhabited by the Sotho people and there he established his Ndebele state which was a very powerful and rich one. Through wars, he incorporated many Sotho communities into the Ndebele state. Mzilikazi was seriously threatened by powerful enemies and marauders and this made him move his capital several times until he eventually settled at Bulawayo. Here again, he incorporated several other groups into his kingdom and had to fight several defensive and offensive wars until about 1850. He had cordial relations with Europeans. He opened up his state to missionaries, traders and hunters. His association with Europeans prepared the way for the eventual colonization of the region. Mzilikazi died in 1868.

The Ndebele kingdom was given to war and, in building it, Mzilikazi had copied some of the features of the Zulu empire. He used the age-regiment system to absorb conquered peoples and to cut across the social divisions in the kingdom. The position of the king was crucial in forging the unity of the kingdom. An annual event called the 'first fruit' ceremony was established to bring the different peoples that made up the kingdom together at the capital. As the ruler, Mzilikazi had control of the national herd. He also took care of all captured maidens and, through the age regiments, regulated when his subjects could marry. He thus controlled not only the economic productive ability of his people, but also their biological reproductive potential.

Because the Ndebele kingdom was a military state, the organization of the army was interwoven with, and sometimes overshadowed by, the political administration of the state. The army was divided into units each under a commander. The commanders in turn were under the control of four divisional commanders who took their orders from Mzilikazi. The age-set system was highly developed in the Ndebele state. Almost all adult men formed part of the army and belonged to regiments which lived in towns specially designated for them.

In the Ndebele kingdom, all powers revolved round Mzilikazi. The headmen or commanders of villages were personally appointed and supervised by him. His state was well-founded and thoroughly administered. The conquered peoples – mostly the Shona – were assimilated into the Ndebele polity, but they also contributed some aspects of their religious life to Ndebele culture.

The Sotho

The Sotho kingdom founded by Moshoeshoe was another state that sprang up during the upheaval of the Mfecane. It was made up of small independent Sotho-speaking communities located to the north and west of the Drakensberg mountains. Moshoeshoe came into prominence by defending his people against the attacks of some of their neighbours. He moved his people from their original abode to the mountain fortress of Thaba Bosiu. It was on this mountain that Moshoeshoe set out to build the capital of a Sotho state. He subdued the neighbouring peoples and placed mostly his relatives as governors over them. In a few cases, he allowed the traditional rulers of the conquered territories to remain as long as they acknowledged his supremacy and overlordship. He welcomed many small communities of people who had been dislodged from their original homesteads in the turmoil of the Mfecane, and incorporated them into the structure of the Sotho state.

Moshoeshoe was faced with the problem of hostile and powerful neighbours. His approach was to be ready to fight while seeking to placate such powerful enemies, and doing everything he could to avert any aggression aimed at the new Sotho state. He also played one powerful neighbour against another. He did not depend only on the military might of his army. He had the reputation of an accomplished diplomat and shrewd politician in his dealings with neighbours. If, in spite of these measures, he was attacked, he exploited the advantages of his mountain fortress and often got the better of his enemies. The victories of his army further boosted the morale of the state and spread Moshoeshoe's fame.

The Sotho state was very wealthy in terms of the herds of cattle it possessed. But it was incessantly harrassed by armed bandits who plundered the herds. The Sotho were eventually able to overpower some of the very difficult bandits like the Griqua and the Korana. The Sotho seized their horses which they subsequently used to breed their own national stock called the 'Basotho pony'. The use of these horses gradually turned the Sotho people, alone among the Bantu of Southern Africa, into a nation of mounted gunmen.

In 1833, Moshoeshoe invited Christian missionaries into the kingdom. He hoped that the presence of European missionaries would help to deter Boer aggression and that the missionaries would assist him to make foreign contacts and procure firearms. It was the Paris Evangelical Missionary Society that responded to his invitation. Their headquarters was at Morija where they established a school and training centre, a printing press and an agricultural station. They had a number of out-stations where they promoted agriculture, various trades and educational institutions. They were loyal advisers to the king and helped to mediate between him and the Boers and British officials in Natal and the Cape. By establishing the basis of a new Sotho Christian culture, they became a unifying force and a vital element in the king's nation-building efforts.

The 1830s was a decade of serious confrontations between the Sotho state and the Boers (white settler farmers). The intervention of the British in the issue was to the detriment of the Sotho because, while claiming to be impartial, the British gave their recognition to a Boer republic right on Sotho territories. This gave the Boers the opportunity to continue to threaten the survival of the Sotho state. Eventually, in a bid to save his kingdom from being swallowed up by the Boer state, Moshoeshoe implored the British to annex it. By so doing, he saved his kingdom from falling apart and also laid the foundation of the modern nation called Lesotho.

The Kololo

The Kololo were a Sotho-speaking group uprooted from their original home during the upheaval of the Mfecane. The invaders captured all their cattle and, impoverished, they had to flee for safety with Sebetwane as their leader. In their wanderings and search for a new home and cattle, they were joined by other roving bands. Following the disastrous defeat at the battle of Dithakong in 1823, they moved northwards through the territories of various Sotho and Tswana groups to Lake Ngami. Desert conditions and resistance from desert communities dissuaded them from moving towards the Atlantic coast. The Kololo then crossed the Zambezi, and settled down on the plateau at the confluence of the Zambezi and the Kafue. Although they were able to repel attacks from the Tswana, the Ndebele and other Nguni groups, they took the opportunity of a disputed succession in the Lozi kingdom to invade and occupy the kingdom on the western part of the plateau.

The Kololo state flourished very well under the rule of Sebetwane. He incorporated the Lozi into the Kololo state and tried to integrate them thoroughly by taking wives from them. He also brought the Lozi into the decision-making body of the state. He retained their political system and in certain cases it existed alongside the new Kololo system until the two became fused. Sebetwane grouped the conquered villages into provinces administered by Kololo officials who also collected tributes from the subject peoples.

Socially, the Kololo language was spoken throughout the kingdom. However, Sebetwane did not impose the Sotho age-grade initiation on any of his conquered subjects. Also, he did not seclude himself like the old Lozi kings but made himself accessible to all his people. Through this, he endeared himself to his people and by the time he died, they had developed a strong sense of belonging to the Kololo state.

After the death of Sebetwane, his successors imposed an iron rule over the Kololo kingdom. This made their Lozi subjects revolt and the Kololo were subsequently overthrown and the Lozi monarchy restored. However, this did not mark the end of Kololo influence. Some of them organized the inhabitants of the Shire Valley called the Manganja peoples, into several small communities which were later grouped into two kingdoms under Kololo chiefs. The Kololo thus ruled over the local Manganja. Their influence in the Shire Valley remained till the 1890s despite frequent harassment from the Nguni.

Trans-Zambezi Nguni states

After the defeat of the Ndwandwe by Shaka in 1820, the kingdom was broken and some of the inhabitants fled in different directions. The group led by Zwangendaba created serious upheavals as they migrated, with their successive military campaigns against settled communities that they encountered. They destroyed the Chamgamire empire, defeated the Rozwi and fought many wars against the Chewa and Tumbuka communities. After Zwangendaba's death around 1848, his group split into several factions which continued to terrorize the other states in the region.

One of the groups, the Msene Nguni, was led by Nqaba. This group engaged in several military campaigns against their neighbours. They were later defeated in a battle against the Kololo led by Sebetwane. The Maseko Nguni was another group from the broken Ndwandwe kingdom, which later established a state in south-eastern Tanzania under Mputa.

Conclusion

The Mfecane can thus be seen as the result of a combination of certain sociopolitical changes. It was sparked off by population pressure and land shortage aggravated by a severe famine. A struggle thus ensued for the declining resources of the northern Nguni area. The struggle for supremacy and survival no doubt included competition for the new trade in imported goods at the port of Delagoa Bay. However, as could be seen from the structure and character of the new states, it needs to be stressed that the revolution represented by the Mfecane was the result primarily of internal initiatives and not of external influences. Some of them developed powerful military systems based on the age-sets. Others utilized various aspects of traditional social structures to keep their nation-states together.

The Mfecane led to the rise of new states like Lesotho and Swaziland which have survived till the present and are part of the international community of nations. Some other states that emerged during the Mfecane did not survive the death of their founders while others were crushed by European imperialism. The Mfecane also led to the eclipse of existing states like the Mthethwa, Ndwandwe, Ngwane and the Hlubi.

The Mfecane states were in two categories. There were the conquest states with very aggressive military policies like the Zulu, Ndebele and the Gaza kingdoms. In the second group were the defensive kingdoms like Lesotho, Swazi and Kololo. In all of the Mfecane states, the institutions of kingship and kinship were very important. The Mfecane saw the rise of new men like Shaka, Mzilikazi, Sobhuza, Zwangendaba and Sebetwane who were to play crucial roles in the fortunes of their peoples in the nineteenth century.

The wars of the Mfecane period reduced the populations of the areas affected. Many Southern African states were thereby weakened and made vulnerable to Boer incursions. The Mfecane also redistributed African populations in Southern Africa by making the populations of certain areas concentrated and others sparse. The Boers took advantage of this and in what is generally referred to as the Great Trek moved in the 1830s into areas that were for the moment temporarily sparsely populated. From such established positions, they fought several wars to capture more settlements, cattle and cheap labour. Thus they established themselves in the Transvaal area and the basin of the Orange river at the expense of the Sotho nation. The British favoured them and while allowing them free access to arms and ammunition tried to prevent their African neighbours from having similar access to weapons. Thus the Mfecane facilitated the expansion of European settlements into the interior of Southern Africa.

6

The impact
of the Mfecane
on the Cape Colony

In terms of its intensity and impact, the Mfecane could be likened to the Fulani *djihāds* in West Africa. However, it should be noted that as sudden as the outbreak of the Mfecane appears to have been, the factors which sparked it off had been building up over several years. The last quarter of the eighteenth and beginning of the nineteenth century saw the gradual rise of such large states as the Ndwandwe and the Mthethwa, with strong military leaders. It was the competition of the large states for the territories and resources of the smaller communities that produced the explosion called the Mfecane.

The Cape Colony included the area occupied by the whites and that inhabited by Africans to the west of the Great Fish river. To the West around Cape Town was the area where the original Dutch farmers settled since the mid-seventeenth century. By the 1820s, they had become Afrikaans-speaking *Boers* (farmers). They preferred to live on large farms in lone homesteads, surrounded by large numbers of African servants, mostly Khoisan. The British had seized the colony in 1795, largely because of its strategic position on the route to the Far East. The Boers disliked British rule, and they regarded the activities of British officials, missionaries or traders as unwelcome interference with their way of life. The British on the other hand were determined to impose their authority. In particular, they wished to control the eastern border of the colony where the settlers began to confront various southern Nguni peoples, especially the Xhosa who were more powerful than the Khoisan of the Western Cape. Partly to strengthen the British presence and help to stabilize the situation, they allocated farms to some British settlers in Albany, near Port Elizabeth, in 1820.

Relationships between the various African groups in this region were relatively peaceful. There were occasional clashes between the southern Nguni in the Eastern Cape and their Khoisan neighbours to the west on the one hand, and among the various Nguni-speaking peoples on the other hand. But these quarrels were usually restricted to the locality and effectively controlled. However, the same cannot be said of relations between the Africans in the region and their white neighbours.

The eastern borders of the Cape around the Great Fish river was, in fact, a region of intense hostilities and open conflict between the blacks and the whites. The factors responsible for the conflicts ranged from boundary disputes, cattle raids and competition for the better areas of agricultural land. It is thus clear that on the eve of the Mfecane relationships particularly between the blacks and whites in the Cape region were not peaceful.

Economic situation and prospects

Before the outbreak of the Mfecane, the economic situation and prospects of the Cape Colony were also very dull. The new set of white settlers brought into the Cape in 1820 bore the brunt of this economic hardship. Agriculture, which was meant to be the mainstay of the economy and source of livelihood at Albany did not thrive. There were several causes for this. Many of the settlers were not qualified and had no experience of farming and, compared to the average Boer farm, the land given to each of them was small because the British authorities wanted the settlers to live close together to facilitate control and protection. On top of that the floods in 1823 destroyed much of their crops.

These problems led most of the farmers to abandon their land and besiege the urban centres where they sought new forms of employment. In addition, there was another chronic problem which faced not only the new settlers but also the old Dutch colonists in their old settlements in the Cape. This was the shortage of cheap labour to help on the farms. While the old settlers had been allowed to use slave labour and to employ Africans on their farms and in their homes, the pressure of the abolitionists meant that the new settlers were not allowed any of this. The result was that the new settlers felt this problem more than the old settlers despite the attempts made in 1824 by the Society for the Relief of the Distressed Settlers to raise funds to assist them.

These economic problems were also worsened by the dangerous security situation on the eastern borders of the Cape. This was because, in addition to their economic woes, the farmers were required to regularly defend the eastern borders against African aggression. Thus on the eve of the Mfecane, the issue of the shortage of labour remained a sore point among the whites in the Cape Colony, and there was no sign of lasting peace on the eastern borders.

The Cape's initial response 1823–8

The devastation occasioned by the activities of the Zulu led a lot of people – displaced groups and individuals – to flee from their homes westwards across the Drakensberg mountains. As these peoples fled they also attacked other settled groups whom they came across, raided their cattle, and devastated their homes and crops. This sparked off other series of migrations as more people were displaced by the wandering bands. Some of the refugees that managed to get to the Cape Colony had lost their group identity and leaders. They were homeless, hungry and insecure. They did not constitute a military threat as they were unarmed and without leaders. They were just seeking help, and a chance to settle and make a new beginning.

6.1 *Dolls representing a San man and woman on sale in Cape Town, early nineteenth century*

The response of the whites to the influx of these black refugees was conditioned by the two most pressing needs of the Cape before the outbreak of the Mfecane. As mentioned above, these were the scarcity of cheap labour and the insecurity of the eastern borders. Coincidentally, Sotho and Tswana refugees began to trickle into the Cape just as some of the new settlers in Albany were abandoning their farms because of the lack of cheap labour. So with the help of the Cape government, the white farmers were able to make maximum use of the refugees as cheap labour on their farms.

As time went on, the opinion of the white settlers began to differ as to the worth of the Sotho and Tswana refugees. While some saw the refugees as lazy and dishonest, others saw them as being of great use and advantage. Indeed, it should be noted that whatever opinions the white settlers held about the usefulness of the refugees, the Sotho and Tswana peoples were very useful in undertaking menial jobs for the settlers which their Khoisan neighbours were no longer willing to provide.

While one cannot give precise figures of the number of Sotho and Tswana peoples that sought refuge in the Cape, a rough estimate would be between several hundred and a thousand. The influx of refugees into the Colony increased annually during the first five years of the Mfecane. But by the late 1820s, they had started to return to their countries; the number of such refugees returning home increased considerably with the establishment of the Sotho state by Moshoeshoe.

However, the significance of the presence of those refugees while in the Cape Colony should not be overlooked. Their timely arrival helped the settlers to solve the problem of labour scarcity that had been plaguing them. Their presence also strengthened the sense of dependence on cheap black labour in the Colony's economic development which undermined the principle of self-reliance that was intended to operate in the new areas of white settlement. In addition, as cheap labour was made readily more available in the Cape, there was the tendency to acquire more land, forget about intensive agriculture, and consolidate the old Boer pattern of large-scale agriculture on massive plots of land.

The Tswana and Sotho refugees also benefited from their sojourn in the Cape Colony. Not only were they provided with shelter when they were desperate, they were also paid for their services. Through this, many of them acquired some property which they were allowed to take back to their countries.

While the presence of the Sotho and Tswana refugees adequately solved the problem of labour shortage facing the white settlers in the Cape, it did not solve their other problem, namely the tension on their eastern border. This is not to suggest that relations between the white settlers in the Cape Colony and their southern Nguni neighbours like the Xhosa on the eastern frontiers was always hostile and bloody. In fact, there was a pattern of commercial relationships between them.

The realization of both groups that they were dependent on each other for the acquisition of certain items forced them into commercial transactions. The

Xhosa had ivory, horns, hides, beef and gum which they exchanged for imported items like copper, beads, buttons, guns, gunpowder and liquor from the whites. Thus a system of exchange by barter developed between the white settlers and their Xhosa neighbours. This commercial interdependence became so strong as to defy efforts by the colonial government in the Cape to stop it. Stricter government control of the border only encouraged smuggling to flourish.

A regular trade fair was eventually allowed to be established on the eastern border in 1821. This began as an annual event and by 1824 it had gradually become a weekly market. Increasingly, the fair became not only a commercial depot but also a forum for interaction and meaningful communication between blacks and whites. However, beneath the rapport created by the market were deep-seated hostilities between the blacks and the whites. In Xhosaland the people also engaged in a secret arms trade with some white smugglers. The Xhosa were acquiring firearms in preparation for a major clash with the whites in which they would avenge the seizure of their ancestral lands by the settlers. The clash came in 1834 and 1835, followed by several other wars which the Xhosa fought with the whites, besides the routine capturing and kidnapping of the children of the whites, some of whom they eventually killed.

External threat and black–white concerted response

The stability of the relationship between blacks and whites in the Cape was not seriously threatened by the events of the Mfecane before 1828. The Tswana and Sotho refugees who trickled into the Cape after 1823 did not constitute a threat to the settler community; rather they were peacefully absorbed into its economic life or they later returned home. Occasionally, there could be active cooperation between blacks and whites as when the Mpondo, a southern Nguni group, prevented Shaka's army from penetrating their land, and thus acted as a shelf for the white settlers.

However, in 1828, a different group of refugees, the Ngwane, under Matiwane came to threaten the inhabitants of the Cape. They were unlike the Sotho and Tswana refugees because they had a group identity and a military leader. To make matters worse, the advent of the Ngwane in the Cape region coincided with the bid of the Zulu army under Shaka to penetrate the Cape. This event created a lot of anxiety among the white settler community. Therefore, immediately the Ngwane entered the African portion of the Cape region, they were attacked by the colonial forces of the Cape who mistook them for the Zulu. This confrontation, however, did not produce any definite result. Preparations were therefore made for a major battle against the Ngwane. To this end, the whites enlisted the support of their Xhosa and Thembu neighbours. Thus it was a combination of black and white troops that attacked and defeated the Ngwane.

This battle was very important for two reasons. One was that the defeat of the Ngwane effectively removed one of the strongest and most destructive agents of the Mfecane. Thereafter, the Cape Colony and its African neighbours were free from any serious external threat. Secondly, while the reason for the white involvement in the battle is not clear, especially as their territory was not in any immediate danger of being invaded by the Ngwane, the 1828 campaign was an occasion when black and white (British and Xhosa) suspended their hostilities and cooperated in a joint venture. This presupposes that despite the previous incessant clashes between the British settlers and the Xhosa, there was a balance in their relationship which was felt to be threatened by the outside invaders and which necessitated the subsequent cooperation of the two groups.

The emergence of the Mfengu

As we have noted above, the Mfecane rendered many people homeless, without group identity or leaders, and they wandered from place to place. Some of these displaced peoples, mainly from northern Nguni, began to drift into the Cape Nguni (that is, southern Nguni) territory. They came in trickles of individuals and small groups, and because they were homeless and poor they took to begging. It was from this act of begging that they got the name 'Mfengu'. The term, 'Mfengu' was therefore collectively applied to the refugees from the northern Nguni territory who were accommodated in the southern Nguni area after they had been displaced and scattered by the Mfecane.

The number of those refugees began to increase considerably between 1822 and 1828 and it was further swollen by the Ngwane survivors after their defeat by the joint forces of the blacks and whites in the Cape region. The Mfengu were received with warmth by the southern Nguni groups – the Xhosa, Thembu, and Mpondo – who provided them with food, land and cattle. Most of the Mfengu were able to acquire some property of their own through hard work. Consequently, those in Mpondoland and Thembuland were integrated into their host societies. But those in Xhosaland felt discriminated against and were not integrated into the Xhosa community.

It is not clear what caused the originally warm relationships between the Mfengu and the Xhosa hosts to become bitter. But immediately this bitterness developed, Xhosa–British relations which were already tense became worse. Moreover the hostile relation between the Xhosa and the Mfengu were exploited by certain external forces to perpetuate the division between the Africans and to promote their own interests. The external forces were the Wesleyan Methodist Missionary Society, the white settlers and the government of the Cape Colony.

The presence of the Wesleyan missionaries in Xhosaland in 1827 interfered with the process of the integration of the Mfengu which was already problematic. The missionaries interpreted the ruler–subject relationship between the Xhosa and the Mfengu as a master–slave relationship. Consequently, the missionaries became more sympathetic with the plight of the Mfengu and, together with the Cape government, they felt they ought to do something to solve the problems of the Mfengu. The latter, on their own part, began to look up to the missionaries, the Cape government and the white settlers as their liberators.

These external groups, however, had their own ulterior reasons for taking sides with the Mfengu. The missionaries wanted the Mfengu to be more receptive to Christian teaching. The Cape government and the white settlers hoped that by fuelling the disenchantment of the Mfengu with their Xhosa rulers, they would be more readily available for recruitment as cheap farm labour. Moreover, as the Mfengu recoiled from the Xhosa emotionally, they also looked for opportunities to withdraw from them physically, and seek out new homes and fresh opportunities.

This was the background to the Sixth Frontier War of 1834 to 1835 between the British and the Xhosa. In defining their own role in the conflict, the Mfengu decided not to join with the Xhosa in the invasion of the Colony; but rather to defend and protect missionaries and traders, and to act as spies on the Xhosa, revealing their plans and movements to the British. Finally, on 9 May 1835, about 16000 Mfengu left Xhosaland with many cattle and goats belonging to Xhosa chiefs, under military escort provided by British troops, for the new place provided for them in the Cape by the colonial government.

Immediately they got to their new site, the Mfengu assisted the British to attack and dislodge the Xhosa. They also provided cheap labour for the white settlers. In cooperating with the missionaries, not only did the Mfengu allow their children to be taught by the missionaries, many adults also attended church services. Moreover, the Mfengu were used to weaken the Xhosa in subsequent conflicts with the whites because the area in which the Mfengu were settled became a buffer zone located between the Xhosa and the Cape Colony.

The trekboers

The defeat of the Xhosa in 1835 did not end the border crisis. More frontier wars were to come in 1846, 1850–53, and 1877–78, as the British tried to shift the border from one river to the next, further and further to the east. The truth was that many of the Boers were nomads at heart, practising mixed farming, and searching restlessly for more and better land. As we have seen, this was also true of the southern Nguni who thus constituted a barrier to the eastward expansion of the Boers. At the time of the Mfecane, several Boers had already settled beyond the Great Fish river which was the official boundary with the Xhosa. Taking advantage of the Xhosa defeat, Cape authorities annexed a large part of Xhosa land as an extension of the Cape colony. When the colonial office, partly under missionary pressure, rejected the annexation, several Boers in the proposed province decided to emigrate beyond the areas under British influence. They hated British missionaries, British labour laws, British legal system and land policies. This mass emigration is often called the Great Trek, and the Boers who took part in it the trek boers.

Between 1835 and 1841, no fewer than 6 000 Boers – men, women and children – with all their movable possessions loaded into their ox wagons, and with their African servants, cattle, and sheep, moved out of the new province and other parts of the Eastern Cape. They went in organized groups of caravans into lands which scouts had indicated were not heavily populated. These, in fact, were choice fertile lands, well populated, but temporarily depopulated by the Mfecane as various groups who coveted the lands fought over them. The two most powerful groups in the area were the Zulu now under the rule of Dingane, and the Ndebele under the rule of Mzilikazi, one of Shaka's former generals.

A group of the Boers went towards Natal, negotiated with Dingane for land where they could have access to the sea. Dingane seemed to have agreed, but since he did not trust the Boers, he ambushed them, killing some 350 Boers and about 250 of their servants. The Boers regrouped and came back to inflict a heavy defeat on the Zulu. This marked the beginning of the decline of the Zulu as the royal family became split, some of them using Boer allies against the others.

Most of the Boer groups, however, went northwards to the very fertile land on the high plateau, on both sides of the Vaal River. They soon confronted Mzilikazi who had earmarked the same land for his troops and Ndebele followers. The Boers were able to secure enough African allies who felt threatened by Mzilikazi. Thus supported, and armed with guns, they succeeded eventually in displacing Mzilikazi who decided to move further north, across the Limpopo towards present day Zimbabwe. The Boer settlers to the south of the Vaal later grouped together to form the Orange Free State, while the land settled by those on the other side of the Vaal became known as Transvaal.

Conclusion

The Mfecane produced changes that affected the economic, political, social and military aspects of the life of the peoples in Southern Africa. The intensity of such changes however varied with locality and with the calibre of people involved. From the discussion above, it is clear that three kinds of victims of the Mfecane entered the Cape Colony. The first were the homeless and hungry refugees, that is, the Tswana, Sotho and the Mfengu and other northern Nguni, who came in search of shelter, food and protection. The second was the army of Shaka the Zulu which got to Mpondoland, but could not penetrate because of the resistance of the Mpondo. The third were the other aggressive groups like the Ngwane who created some anxiety in the Cape region by their presence in Thembuland. These Ngwane were mistaken for Shaka's Zulu, and a combined force of British, Xhosa and Thembu attacked and defeated them. This military unity of black and white did not last because it dissolved with the disappearance of the Ngwane threat.

However, the economic, social and cultural effects of the Mfecane were more permanent in the Cape Colony than its military or political effects. The timely arrival of the Sotho and Tswana refugees saved new settler districts like Albany in the Cape from total collapse from lack of labour. The abundance of cheap labour thus created undermined the twin principles of settler self-reliance and intensive agriculture on which the new agricultural settlements had been founded.

In addition, the migration of the Mfengu to the Cape in 1835 also ensured a steady supply of cheap labour to the white settlers. The political impact of the Mfengu on their Xhosa hosts was erased by their withdrawal to British territories in the Cape where, as British subjects, they fought against the Xhosa. The cultural impact of the Mfengu on the white settlers and their black neighbours is not easy to assess especially as the Mfengu shared the same culture with the Cape Nguni. The Mfengu impact was more important in the sense that since they were the first Nguni group to accept Christianity and Western education, they were to play crucial roles as agents of modernization among other African groups in the Cape as teachers, clergymen, secretaries and agricultural demonstrators.

Finally, the Mfecane was significant for Southern African history not only because of the groups of people it brought into the Cape Colony. Perhaps, even more important was its role in attracting the trekboers into lands where they were surrounded by powerful African states. Hitherto, European settlers were in one corner of South Africa, pushing against the southern Nguni barrier. The Mfecane and the Great Trek came like a great explosion that scattered Boer settlers among both the southern and northern Nguni states, already reshaped and consolidated by the Mfecane. The racial tension that characterized the eastern border of the Cape Colony was thus, within a few years, spread across the whole of South Africa.

7

The British, Boers and Africans in South Africa 1850–80

Before 1880, South Africa had no specific political significance; it was a mere geographical expression which comprised British colonies, Boer republics and African states. Up to 1870, the British, who claimed some supremacy in the area, were reluctant to take over political control of the whole region because of financial considerations. But as from 1870 onwards, they began to conquer many of the African states in the region. This imperial drive brought the British into several wars with the Boers. As a result of these wars, the British got hold of a substantial part of South Africa. Thus in the period between 1850 and 1880, the Africans gradually lost their land and freedom, the Boers became more united, while the British colonies acquired some self-rule.

British withdrawal from the interior

The British began to withdraw from the interior of South Africa in the 1850s. They had earlier occupied the area at the instance of Sir Harry Smith, the Governor and High Commissioner of the Cape. He annexed Xhosa country and a vast territory between the Orange and Vaal rivers containing African and Boer communities. This expansionist policy naturally produced violent wars because the subjugated peoples cherished their independence and the Africans were particularly unhappy about the loss of their land.

The first armed resistance came from the Boers who in 1848 chased the British out of their territory. But they could not consolidate their victory because the British retaliated by inflicting a crushing defeat on them and reoccupied the area. However, the issue of boundary delimitation became a problem for the British. Every attempt they made to define Boer/African borders always satisfied one group and left the other disgruntled. This led the disenchanted group to violate the boundaries and raid the other group's livestock. The Sotho kingdom under Moshoeshoe particularly suffered from these unfavourable boundaries while the British sought to consolidate their own position in the area by playing one group against the other through their unsolicited mediation. An instance of this which backfired on the British was the outbreak of a war between two African groups, the Taung and the Tlokwa. The British came to the aid of the Tlokwa and defeated the Taung army making away with over 3 000 head of cattle. This led the Sotho under

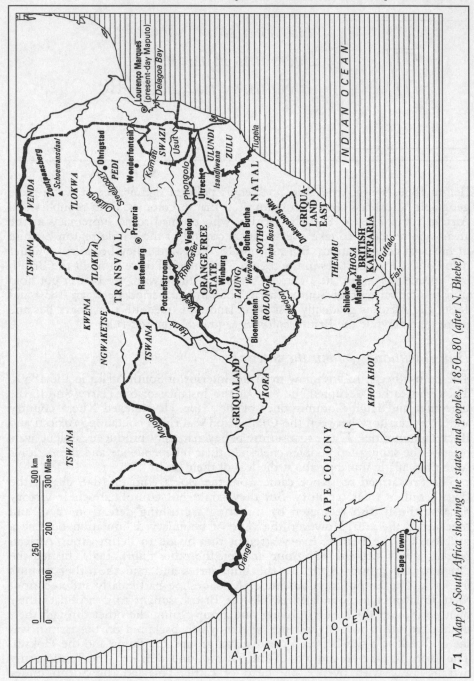

7.1 *Map of South Africa showing the states and peoples, 1850–80 (after N. Bhebe)*

Moshoeshoe to ally with the demoralized Taung army, and together inflict a crushing defeat on the British and their African allies, leading to the collapse of British administration in the area in 1851.

This was the period when the British were also having serious troubles with the Xhosa in the Cape Colony. The Anglo-Xhosa war of 1850–3 was caused by British interference in Xhosa affairs. By declaring a colony on Xhosa terri-tories, the British deprived them of their land and even gave parts of it away to the Mfengu and other African groups who were loyal to them. In addition, the British imposed white magistrates with no idea of African laws on the Xhosa. They also outlawed some Xhosa institutions like bridewealth for example. All these infuriated the Xhosa and they sought opportunities to throw off the British yoke. The chance came when the British deposed a Xhosa chief and attempted to install a white one in his place. The people rejected this and began to attack British forces and military installations on their land in December 1850. A lot of other Africans identified with the Xhosa cause and fought on their side against the British. The war dragged on till October 1852 when the British eventually defeated the Xhosa and seized most of their cattle.

The expensive war with the Xhosa and the disruption of British administration in the South African interior led the British to begin to withdraw from the area. To facilitate easy movement in the interior without any interference, the British granted the interior Boers independence and made an agreement with them to the effect that they were not to sell arms and ammunition to the Africans, thus guaranteeing the military superiority of the whites over the Africans.

Before withdrawing completely from the interior, the new British High Commissioner wanted to refurbish the military image of the British by attack-ing Moshoeshoe's kingdom. However, the stiff resistance which he met from the Sotho made him withdraw quickly. This experience further reinforced the belief that it would be too expensive for the British to maintain their hold on the South African interior. As the British were alienated by Moshoeshoe's kingdom, they sought an alliance with other Boer groups in the region.

To the east of the Cape Colony, the British dispossessed the intimidated Xhosa of their land which they sold to the white farmers and gave to the Mfengu. The British also sought to develop the area as a buffer zone to check black aggression from the east. By 1854, the British had left the Africans and Boers in the interior alone. But they maintained their authority in the Cape Colony and Natal in order to deny the Boers direct access to the sea and the British naval base. Natal and the Cape Colony were granted self-rule so that they would be responsible for their own defence and administrative costs. In 1853, the Cape Colony was granted a parliamentary constitution while Natal got a legislative council in 1856.

The Cape Colony and Natal before 1870

The British granted the Cape Colony some self-rule in 1853 because of a combination of factors which ranged from colonial pressure to economic considerations. The self-rule was enshrined in a parliamentary constitution. This constitution, while it protected the interests of the wealthy English merchants, offered only limited political participation to the Boers, the coloureds and the Africans. The right to vote was restricted by property qualifications, while a person must be an enfranchized British subject and own immense property in the Cape before he could contest for a seat in the legislature. The legislature which was bicameral restricted the upper house only to the very wealthy. The lower house comprised British subjects with property worth 25 pounds sterling or a salary of 50 pounds sterling per annum. The use of English to transact parliamentary business also kept a large number of Boers from standing for election even to the lower house.

The Cape parliament was dominated by two burning issues. One was the demand for the partition of the colony by the English-speaking eastern districts of the Cape who had a fear of being dominated by the Dutch-speaking western districts. The other issue had to do with repeated conflicts between the executive and legislative authorities. Due to the lack of ministers in the political structure, the constitution gave a lot of discretionary powers to the governor. The smooth working of the constitution therefore depended on the personality of the governor and the economic situation in the colony. In cases where the economy was bad and the governor inept, there was a lot of friction between parliament and the executive authorities. However, even the concession of responsible government to the Cape in 1872 did not put an end to the frequent clashes between the governor and parliament. The constitutional powers of the governor continued to fuel conflicts between him and the Cape Cabinet which comprised bureaucrats.

During the tenure of George Grey and Philip Wodehouse as successive governors of the Cape, the Xhosa on the east completely lost their independence. White settlers were planted in Xhosaland to 'civilize' the local population while the political power of the chiefs was drastically reduced. To confirm their subordination, Xhosa chiefs were paid salaries by the British. The Xhosa were also taxed and made to work on public projects for meagre wages. All these problems led the Xhosa and their Thembu neighbours to seek religious solutions in 1856–7. In response to a religious prophecy, they killed all their cattle and destroyed their grain stores in the belief that, through some supernatural occurrence, the British would leave and they would recover their cattle and grains, and yet obtain European manufactured goods. This envisaged relief did not come and many people died of starvation while some went to the Cape to seek employment from the whites as a means of survival.

The Cape governor took advantage of the helplessness of the Xhosa and Thembu by taking away large pieces of their land on which he later encouraged white immigrants to settle. He eventually annexed the area to the Cape Colony in 1865 because financial problems made it difficult for him to maintain it as a separate colony.

Natal also witnessed some constitutional developments in the period before 1870. Many of the Boers in the Natal region began to emigrate because of certain grievances associated with British policy. Some of the initial difficulties faced by the colonial government of Natal had to do with the administration of the Africans. To solve this problem, Africans were put in reserves under local chiefs and headmen where African customary laws were allowed to operate. To administer the colony, the British imposed a hut tax on the Africans whose natural resources were also exploited with perfect immunity. With the exit of the Boers who had emigrated into the interior during the Mfecane, more British subjects came to settle in Natal. In 1856, Natal was made a separate colony and granted a legislative council. But only the whites had the right to vote. The vote was denied the blacks through very high property, residential and other qualifications.

The economy of Natal depended on the sugar industry. The blacks, however, refused to work on the plantations because of the very low wages. Eventually, Natal planters resorted to the importation of indentured labourers from India to work on the sugar plantations.

Thus both in Natal and the Cape Colony the whites entrenched their political supremacy while the blacks were exploited and deprived of their right to land. Various measures were also adopted to ensure that the social cohesion of the blacks was severely battered.

The Boer republics before 1870

At the time of the British withdrawal from the interior of South Africa, the Boers were divided into numerous groups. Some were to the north of the Vaal river while others were to the south. Two Boer republics eventually emerged in these areas: the Orange Free State in the south and the Transvaal (South African Republic) in the north.

The Orange Free State had some problems at its inception. Apart from poverty and lack of administrative infrastructure, it was also very weak militarily. This made it a victim of its powerful neighbour, the Sotho kingdom of Moshoeshoe with which it had no settled border. Violent border disputes always erupted between the two and they exposed the Boer republic to undue interference from the British in the Cape Colony and the other Boer Republic – the Transvaal – in the north.

Another problem faced by the Orange Free State was internal disunity. This was caused by the creation of three opposing factions in the republic. The first group called the 'loyalists' comprised Boers who wanted the republic to be re-annexed to the Cape Colony. The second group consisted of 'unionists' who wanted unification between the Orange Free State and the Transvaal Republic in the north. The third faction comprised those who stood for the complete independence of the Orange Republic. As each of these three groups strove to make its position accepted by the others several crises were brewing in the republic. By 1863, all attempts to unite the Orange Free State with either the Cape Colony or the Transvaal had failed and the Orange people began to look inwards in shaping their national destiny.

The relationship between the Orange Free State and the Transvaal before 1850 was very fluid. There were frantic attempts to unite the two but all proved abortive. In June 1857, the two republics signed an agreement by which they recognized each other's independence. However, this did not end efforts to bring the two republics together. In 1860, the Orange Republic voted the Transvaal president, M. W. Pretorius, to be their own president also (1860–63). This would have been the golden opportunity to unite the two republics, but the Transvaal legislature refused and forced Pretorius to resign his presidency in the Transvaal. The British did everything they could to forestall a union of Boer states. They feared that with unification the Boers could enter into relations with foreign powers who would certainly become a threat to British colonies and naval bases. They therefore took steps to dissuade the Boers and discourage the unification of the two republics.

Apart from the disunity between the two republics, internally, the Transvaal was also disunited, and it took a longer time before it emerged as a stable state. The Transvaal Boers were widely dispersed and they had deep-rooted religious differences, all of which stood in the way of its unity until 1860 when they were able to draft a workable constitution which provided for an executive and a legislature. Pretorius was re-elected President of the Transvaal in 1864 and he ruled the republic till 1870.

Boer relations with the Africans before 1870

The depredations occasioned by the Mfecane led to the destruction of many African communities in the Transvaal and the Orange Free State. Some of them were absorbed into the Ndebele kingdom while others were able to regroup under powerful leaders like Moshoeshoe. The Ndebele were however expelled by the Boers while some of their subject peoples were subdued and incorporated into the Boer states. These Africans suffered not only direct exploitation but also racial discrimination from the Boers. In the Transvaal constitution, for instance, blacks were not equal to whites and the former were forced to carry passes supplied by government officials and their employers at all times. Africans provided free labour on white farms; their children were also recruited as 'apprentices' to work for white farmers until the males were twenty-five and the females twenty-one. In addition, Africans were to assist the Boers in times of war.

The Boers in the Transvaal sought to consolidate their position by expanding at the expense of their African neighbours. They were however met with stiff resistance by the Africans. To the west, the Tswana resisted them while the Pedi fought them relentlessly with firearms in the east, until a satisfactory border was drawn in 1857. In the north, the Venda and the Sotho held out against the Boers. After defeating some Sotho groups in a twenty-five-day siege, the Boers thought they had put an end to African resistance in the north. But the uprisings of the Venda in 1859 and 1867 drove the Boers out of their territory.

The toughest opposition to the Boers came from the Sotho state of

Moshoeshoe who valiantly resisted Boer encroachments on their land. However, with the ageing of Moshoshoe, fratricidal strife tore the people apart. Moshoeshoe was losing his hold on some of the subordinate groups. This made them vulnerable to the Boers. Eventually, in the face of increasing Boer aggression, Moshoeshoe invited the British to annex Lesotho which they eventually did on 12 March 1868.

British expansion in South Africa 1870–80

British interest and expansion in South Africa coincided with the discovery of minerals – diamond and gold – in the region. Meanwhile, Boer republics and African states clashed over diamond fields. The British offered to arbitrate and would not allow arbitration by any outside power. They allocated the disputed fields to the Africans and then annexed the area as Griqualand West which was later incorporated into the Cape Colony. The British action in taking over the diamond fields and the way they disallowed the territorial expansion of the Boer republics into the area made the Boers bitter and soured their subsequent relationship with the British.

The explanation for British expansion in South Africa in the 1870s after the initial withdrawal of the 1850s lies in economic considerations and especially the discovery of diamonds in the area. To further secure their interests in South Africa, the British tried to sponsor a subordinate confederation of white states in the region. This was to comprise the two Boer republics – the Orange Free State and the Transvaal – the Cape Colony, Natal and Griqualand. All peaceful attempts made by the British to bring these states together failed woefully as they were not willing to federate. Moreover, quarrels over diamond minefields stood in the way of a South African confederation.

The British then resorted to forceful means to bring about the federation. Taking advantage of a border clash between the Transvaal Boers and the Pedi – an African state – the British annexed the Transvaal in 1877 with the hope of using it to champion the confederation scheme. For the scheme to succeed, the British also thought it necessary that African states in the area should be annexed. Their first target was Zululand. In spite of the heroic resistance of their king, Cetshwayo, and his brilliant generalship manifested in the famous battle at Isandhlwana of January 1879, the Zulu were eventually defeated by the firepower of the British guns. Cetshwayo was captured in August 1879 and taken to imprisonment in Cape Town. The British did not annex Zululand but rendered it impotent by dividing it into thirteen independent chiefdoms.

The Zulu war did not achieve the purpose for which it was fought, namely, to serve as a prelude to the incorporation of African states into a federation in South Africa. This was because the British officials both in London and South Africa had different approaches to the federation issue, and more importantly, the Zulu war was followed by the Anglo–Boer war and the Cape–Lesotho war, both of which shattered the idea of federation.

7.2   *Boer commandos, c. 1880*

The failure of federation

The Boers in Transvaal were not pleased with the annexation of their republic by the British in 1877 and for three years they tried to persuade the British to grant them independence and pull out of their territory. The agitation of the Boers increased as the British turned down all their pleas and insisted that all Transvaal could get was self-government within a confederation. By December 1880, the Boers' patience had run out and they declared their independence by reinstituting their republican government. This led to war with the British and in February 1881 the Boers led by Paul Kruger, Piet Jourbert and M. W. Pretorius won a decisive victory at the famous battle at Amajuba hills. The war ended officially with the signing of a peace settlement called the Pretoria Convention in August 1881 which marked the beginning of increased Boer freedom. This was followed by the London Convention of 1884 in which the British confirmed full independence of action to the Boers in all matters except foreign relations, and particularly a free hand in dealing with the African states who continued to be denied access to arms and ammunition.

The Lesotho war was related to the efforts of the colonial government at the Cape to disarm the African states as a first step in implementing the plan to impose confederation on the people of South Africa. It was the refusal of the Sotho to surrender their guns that led to the Cape–Sotho war which broke out in September 1880. After seven months of fighting, the war came to an end with neither of the sides scoring a decisive military victory. However, it was a political victory for the Sotho because they still retained their guns after the war.

Conclusion

British activities in South Africa in the period under review (1850–80) produced several results. While their attempt to forcefully federate the region failed, they succeeded in weakening and reducing the several African peoples like the Xhosa, Sotho, Mfengu and Khoi Khoi who were all subordinated to the Cape Colony. The political system of others like the Zulu and the Pedi who were not yet incorporated was disrupted and chaos erupted among the people. Some Boers like those in Griqualand West lost their sovereignty, but the major Boer Republics in Orange Free State and Transvaal won their right to independent action except in relations with other European powers besides the British. Meanwhile, the British maintained a loose control over the various parts of South Africa by monitoring the situation through their resident officials.

The countries
of the Zambezi basin

In this chapter, we turn our attention to Central Africa to consider the main changes that took place there between 1800 and 1875. The area under consideration includes that occupied by present-day nations like Malawi, Mozambique and Zambia. Internal factors of change in the local communities will be examined briefly as these affected not only local developments but also the people's reaction to external factors of change. The notable external factors were the overseas slave trade which brought Central Africa into the world economy, and the Nguni/Sotho incursions. The relative importance of these sets of factors will also be discussed. As background to this discussion, we should first look at pre-nineteenth century tendencies in the area and later conclude with a brief examination of the region on the eve of the European 'Scramble'.

On the eve of the nineteenth century

The political and economic changes of the nineteenth century were part of a continuous process of change which antedated the century. Economic and political changes had been taking place in the region in the previous centuries with concrete effects. The significance of nineteenth-century changes was that they were more rapid and their impact more far-reaching.

Major political changes had taken place in the Zambezi valley before the nineteenth century. Several waves of Shona and Lunda groups had conquered many of the indigenous peoples in the region, and had settled there. The result was that many of the indigenous groups were absorbed into either the Shona or Lunda state system. This process of state formation probably started in the region south of the Zambezi river with the imposition of Shona authority on the local peoples. This saw the emergence of a number of independent Shona states which maintained effective control of the Zambezi region till the nineteenth century. The Lunda also made significant inroads into the region before 1800. The first Lunda migrations took place in the seventeenth century and throughout the eighteenth century they consolidated their hold and expanded their authority in the region. By the beginning of the nineteenth century, quite a number of Lunda states had reached their peak while others were rapidly expanding.

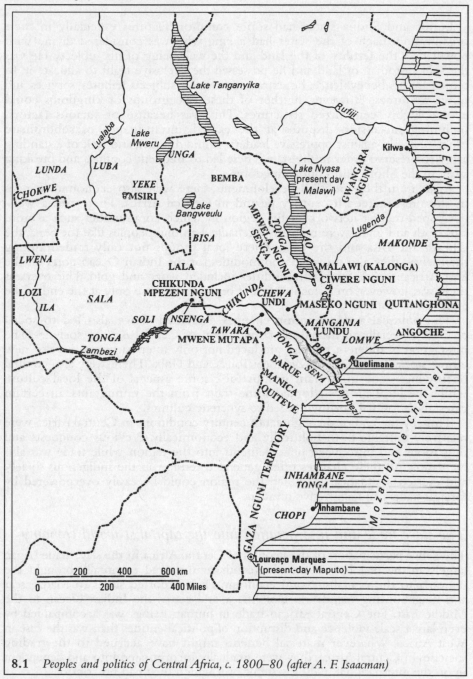

8.1 *Peoples and politics of Central Africa, c. 1800–80 (after A. F. Isaacman)*

Lunda and Shona states had some common features especially in their organization. Each of the states had a king who was considered divine with power over the fertility of the land and the well-being of his subjects. He was the sole custodian of land and he possessed the exclusive right to allocate it. In return for his benevolence, he extracted from his subjects tributes, services and other resources. However, neither of these two groups of kingdoms could evolve highly centralized structures. This was because of various factors, including succession disputes at the capital, intransigence of subordinate officials, revolts against oppressive leaders, ethnic disunity, and lack of a standing army to preserve order in the state. These led to frequent conflicts and breaking away in the Shona and Lunda kingdoms.

Apart from these political developments, there were also economic changes in the pre-nineteenth-century period in Central Africa. There was a well-developed trading network in the region in which commodities such as iron, salt, cloth and grain were regularly exchanged among peoples like the Sena, the Chewa, the Bisa and the Lozi. These local groups not only traded among themselves, they also provided commodities for the Indian Ocean ports on the East African coast. Such commodities included ivory and gold. This overseas trade was, however, on a small scale and began to increase only at the end of the eighteenth century.

The political and economic changes described above also led to social changes especially in the ethnic composition of Central African societies. The interaction of different peoples produced not only intermarriages but also new ethnic stocks like the Sena, Zambezi Tonga, and Goba. There were also cultural borrowings – the immigrant groups took some aspects of the local culture while the local groups adopted some traits from the immigrants. In certain cases, these mutual borrowings led to syncretic cultures.

Thus, by the end of the eighteenth century conditions in Central Africa were relatively unstable both politically and economically. Previous conquests and migrations had introduced new elements into the region while trade was also increasing. All these changes often generated tension in the indigenous society and created a situation in which the region could be easily overpowered by foreign traders and aggressive invaders.

The slave trade and incorporation into the capitalist world economy

The active participation of the peoples of Central Africa in the slave trade began largely in the first half of the nineteenth century and eventually brought the region into the capitalist world economy. They exported slaves to Madagascar and neighbouring islands via East Africa, and across the Indian Ocean to the Middle East. The Central African trade in human beings was accompanied by even larger scale violence and disruption of political entities than was the case in West Africa. Whatever material benefits might have accrued to the trading societies in Central Africa, they were gradually incorporated into and dependent upon the international trading systems over which they had no control.

Certain factors led to the expansion of the slave trade in Central Africa at the time when the struggle against the trade in West Africa was just beginning to gain momentum. First, there was the demand for labour on the expanding sugar plantations of Cuba and Brazil which could no longer be satisfied by the supply from West Africa and the Congo region. Slavers began to explore the markets of Mozambique. Then there was demand from French planters in Bourbon (now called Réunion), Seychelles and the Mascarene islands in the Indian Ocean, as well as from rulers who were consolidating their rule in Madagascar. The largest demand, however, came from the Omani rulers of Zanzibar and surrounding areas. Local trade networks already linked the interior with the coastal markets of Kilwa, Mozambique island and Quelimane where, apart from slaves, ivory was also offered for sale. A contributory factor was the relative inactivity of the British naval force in the areas.

Local slave dealers – the Yao, Bisa and Chikunda – responded to the increased demand for slaves by expanding their own activities. They extended their commercial contacts to new areas both north and south of the Zambezi in their search for slaves, and the Indian Ocean ports became major exporting centres. Meanwhile, ivory also became an important component of the trade. The two items of trade were closely linked as the slaves carried the ivory on their heads down to the coast. By the middle of the nineteenth century, Central Africa had become a major supplier of both slaves and ivory. The East African coast from where the slaves were shipped overseas experienced an economic revival. A substantial number of the slaves were exported to Brazil, but the island of Zanzibar was the principal recipient.

The growth of the slave and ivory trade brought a number of groups into competition with the Yao, Bisa and Chikunda for the control of the trade. Groups outside Central Africa such as the Makua, Swahili and Arab traders also became prominent in the regional commerce. By the mid-nineteenth century, others like the Mambari, Lozi and Kololo also sought to partake of the expanding regional economy. Increasing external demands for slaves thus created a situation in which much of the area to the north of the Zambezi was actively involved in the supply of slaves and ivory.

The character of the trade underwent a noticeable transformation after about 1840. The mode of acquiring slaves changed radically in that raiding and conquest replaced the hitherto peaceful commercial means of obtaining slaves. All the trading groups now resorted to violence as a means of maintaining their economic overlordship and of satisfying the ever increasing coastal demand for slaves. This in turn affected the political configuration of the region. New states were carved out by a number of trading groups to ensure a steady supply of captives and ivory. Using European weapons, they conquered many local groups and exchanged their captives for more weapons thereby facilitating further expansion. Although these states were politically independent, they constituted an indirect extension of European economic and military power into a substantial part of Central Africa. The long-distance trade therefore brought to power in the region new dominant classes whose authority lay in the exploitation and oppression of the local population in order to meet the demands of the world capitalist economy.

In places where the slave dealers did not impose themselves outright as political rulers, they were instrumental in the erosion of the political authority of the local rulers by fuelling internal divisions and sponsoring intra-group uprisings. They also intervened directly in local politics thus leading to the eventual collapse of already weak states. However, it was not in all cases that the impact of the slavers on the political fortunes of local peoples were negative. In the case of the Bemba kingdom, for example, an alliance between the local rulers and the Arab/Swahili traders strengthened the state and released substantial wealth to its rulers. This situation also applied to some other local chiefs in the region. The foreign slave traders were always ready to befriend any local group in their bid to prevent the establishment or expansion of the commercial influence of a rival.

Yet, even the strengthening of the state that resulted from such cooperation with the external long-distance traders could eventually prove a source of weakness. The demand for slaves and ivory could become insatiable with the pressure to produce more and more slaves as the only way to sustain the wealth of the state and to acquire the weapons to sustain its regional supremacy. A few states, after they had over-exploited the weakness of their neighbours, seizing their cattle or destroying their farms, and enslaving the people or causing them to flee to more defensible sites, turned on themselves and began to enslave their own subject peoples. This was a self-destructive strategy as it could lead to mass revolts, and destruction of the cohesion and stability of the state. A good example was the Makua who were recognized in the 1850s as a major state and the principal exporter of slaves to Mozambique. By the 1870s they had become fragmented and unable to stand up to the invasion of the Portuguese. The same short-sighted policy was in part responsible for the destruction of the *prazo* system on the Zambezi when the Afro-Portuguese *prazeros* over-reached themselves, began to enslave the Africans on their land, causing widespread revolt and the explusion of most *prazeros*.

However, the Shona-dominated region to the south of the Zambezi was not so susceptible to attacks from the foreign slave traders. The Shona states were relatively powerful and could thus repel most raids. Moreover, with the coming of the Gaza Nguni into the area in the period after 1830 and the British blockade of the slave-exporting ports, the slave trade in the area soon became very problematic and later unprofitable. The result was that slaves were no longer exported but utilized internally. In Central Africa, the slaves were recruited into forced labour for local production. In a few cases, the reliance on slaves enabled freemen to collect other commodities like ivory, wax and rubber for overseas export thus maintaining their commercial prosperity.

The slave trade had a few positive effects like the introduction of some crops such as tobacco, maize, rice and cassava; elementary technological innovations like the Chikunda traps, granaries and weapons; and the expansion of some local industries. But these were rather insignificant developments when compared with the overall economic retardation of the region caused by the slave trade. The trade in human beings no doubt led to depopulation and the disruption of the rural economy with the exportation of able-bodied men and women out of the local communities. This situation also engendered famine. In addition, infectious diseases like cholera and smallpox common to the Indian Ocean communities were inadvertently introduced into the Central African interior. These epidemics took a very high death toll. This further reduced rural productivity which in turn produced malnourishment and disease. The social effect of this was a significant increase in accusations of witchcraft among the local peoples. Some rulers reacted to these problems by seeking additional slaves to populate their depleted communities which only further intensified the slave trade.

On the whole, the participation of Central Africa in the slave trade created a growing dependence of the region's economy on the world trading system and this intensified the process of underdevelopment in the region. The great commercial states lost their economic independence. Competition for slaves also generated intense hostility among the trading groups. Meanwhile, the dependence on European weapons and foreign allies made the local trading communities very vulnerable to external intervention. Some, like the Sena, even lost their sovereignty.

With the abolition of the slave trade, some African merchants and rulers sought to maintain their economic ascendancy by searching for other commodities like wax, coffee, groundnut and vegetable oils which they could exchange for European weapons and consumer goods. The success of this move only emphasized the growing dependency of the local communities on a world economy whose control eluded them. The subordinate role of Central Africa in the world trading system could also be seen in the unequal exchange that characterized the slave trade in which able-bodied human beings were exchanged for various glittering but valueless and perishable goods.

There were also wide disparities in the society. While the region as a whole was gradually becoming poorer, the rulers together with the merchant class became wealthier. However, in some cases, the local merchant class allied with foreign traders to weaken the economic position of the local rulers and established their own economic hegemony thus leading to the rapid disintegration of such states.

One important result of the increased commercial interaction was the considerable amount of cultural borrowing that took place among the different groups. Three broad patterns of acculturation occurred. In the first example, the alien group were absorbed into the culture of their host (Chikunda hunters incorporated into Nsenga, Ambo and Valley Tonga communities). In another case, the local peoples adopted the culture of the alien groups (e.g. Yao traders became Muslims because of their contact with Arabs). The third pattern was a case of compromise whereby the interaction of different cultures led to new ethnic and cultural groups.

8.2   *A 'Ruga-Ruga' (slave-raider)*

8.3 *Soshangane's Shangana arrive at Shapanga to collect the annual tribute from the Portuguese*

The impact of the Nguni and Kololo invasions

The Nguni and Kololo invasion of Central Africa which began in the 1820s represented a continuation of previous developments in new forms and on a larger scale. The influx of these Southern African peoples into Central Africa was part of a larger pattern of migrations and state formation which had started several centuries before. Three principal groups of Southern Africans came into Central Africa during the nineteenth century. The first were the Nguni followers of Soshangane, the second were also Nguni peoples led by Zwangendaba while the third were Kololo migrants of Sotho descent under the leadership of Sebetwane.

These three groups had some common characteristics. Their military strategies and weapons were derived from the Zulu pattern and they all fled their original homes in Southern Africa in search of security. They all saw the need to absorb a great number of aliens in order to become a viable military-cum-political force. Each of them established military states in Central Africa by conquering the local peoples, and they placed a lot of importance on gaining access to new weapons for expansion of territories and acquisition of wealth.

The Gaza Nguni under Soshangane
This group left their original habitation for fear of a Zulu attack. As they moved northwards they absorbed other Nguni groups to swell their ranks. In

1831, they had a military confrontation with the Nguni of Zwagendaba whom they defeated. This victory enabled them to expand their frontiers. They further moved into Central Africa where they defeated several Shona kingdoms. The areas conquered by the Gaza Nguni in present-day Zimbabwe were not incorporated into their empire but were occasionally plundered and subjected to annual tribute payment.

The core of Soshangane's empire was southern Mozambique and the areas to the west. The subject peoples there were treated harshly. They were made to pay heavy taxes and their young men recruited into the Soshangane age-regiments where they were discriminated against by the Gaza Nguni. This generated serious animosity between the oppressed majority and the Nguni rulers. Some of the local peoples attempted to regain their independence by moving out of the jurisdiction of Soshangane's authority; others even allied with the Portuguese as a step towards the expulsion of the Nguni. The eventual death of Soshangane was believed by the Nguni to have been engineered by their disgruntled subjects.

The Nguni of Zwangendaba

Zwangendaba and his Nguni followers left their historic home in Southern Africa and embarked on a twenty-year trek in search of a suitable homeland. During this period they came across many groups and acquired new followers. They struggled with the Gaza Nguni for control of the Delagoa Bay area, crossed the Zambezi, dealt the final blow to the fragmented Rozwi empire of Changamire, and swept through the western parts of Lake Malawi before finally settling down at Mapupo. Zwangendaba then embarked on an assimilationist policy to properly integrate the foreign elements which formed the greater percentage of his followership into Nguni culture. The Nguni age-regiments and lineage system were used as important socializing institutions.

Zwangendaba also evolved a centralized administration. As the king, he became the personification of the state and its ultimate authority. The age-regiments were transformed into the military arm of the state with its leaders appointed by, and made responsible to the king. Thus by the time Zwangendaba died, the Nguni state had become a major power in Central Africa. However, his death brought about many succession disputes which eventually broke the state into several units. The hostility of powerful indigenous states in the region did not help matters. By 1870, two of the units – the Mpezeni Nguni and the Mbwela – were able to carve out substantial domains. Others like the group led by Ciwere Ndhlou and the Gwangara also established themselves as separate units with the latter eventually moving into Tanzania in East Africa.

The Kololo

The Kololo were Sotho people escaping like the others from the Mfecane. They fled from Dithakong under Sebetwane their chief in search of a new home. In the course of their flight northwards, they suffered defeats from other groups like the Tswana and the Ndebele. Eventually, around 1835, they arrived on the borders of the large and powerful Lozi kingdom on the flood plains of the Zambezi. It was an opportune moment when the Lozi king had just died after 50 years on the throne, which precipitated internal rivalries among the ruling aristocracy and challenges from subordinate groups. Even then it took several years before the Kololo finally claimed victory over the Lozi.

Sebetwane then embarked on the political and social integration of the vast Lozi people into Sotho culture. To this end he contracted many diplomatic marriages and adopted a conciliatory policy towards the Lozi. Within a short time, Kololo became the lingua franca of the state while the Lozi demonstrated their allegiance to the Kololo by defending the new state against external aggression. However, several factors frustrated this assimilationist policy. The death of Sebetwane in 1863 unleashed a spate of succession disputes which shook the new state to its roots. The new king reversed his father's policy of conciliation to the Lozi and instituted an authoritarian rule that was anti-Lozi in all its ramifications. In 1864, the Lozi rose up against him, liberated themselves and killed virtually all Kololo men.

This however did not end Kololo influence in the Zambezi region. Kololo refugees regrouped and followed the missionary, David Livingstone, into the Shire Valley where the fragmented Manganja people were at the mercy of Yao and Arab slave-traders. By 1870, the Kololo had succeeded in taking over the politics of the Shire Valley and organized the Manganja into a state over which they established their authority.

The Nguni–Sotho incursions into Central Africa had lasting effects on the political structure of the region. The newcomers established new kingdoms which incorporated a number of the local groups. In the process, they were instrumental to the fall of some of the older states such as the Rozwi, Undi and Lundu. The new states were densely populated and centralized. In addition, the age-regiments constituted the most distinctive feature of such states.

Despite the initial success of the Nguni and Kololo invaders and their substantial territorial gains, they were challenged periodically by the local peoples who wanted to regain their independence. Also their efforts to expand the frontiers of the new states were violently repelled by their powerful neighbours. All these constituted military setbacks to the new states and the Lozi example shows how effective local resistance could be.

As the Nguni and Kololo established states in Central Africa there were also some socio-cultural changes in the period. Because the new states comprised different cultural strands, the rate of assimilation was more rapid at the beginning of the state formation process than when the states had fully developed. The actual pattern of acculturation also differed from place to place. In certain places the dominated population adopted the culture of the invaders. In other cases the situation was reversed. Between these two extremes were cases of cross-fertilization of ideas and values which led to the formation of syncretic cultures.

A major effect of the Nguni diaspora which has not been adequately tackled is the growth of new classes within Nguni kingdoms. The insecurity occasioned by the Mfecane led to the rise of a military leadership whose power was based on the tribute and plunder which they acquired. Economically, they enjoyed a status comparable to that of the Lunda and Shona rulers of Central Africa. As the Nguni groups moved north of the Zambezi they gradually lost access to such plunder. They subsequently depended more on tributes and began to exploit their slaves to ensure a continued source of wealth. This reduction of much of the local population to such servile status could well explain the subsequent local resistance to the Nguni.

The Nguni and Sotho immigrants were not directly involved in the slave trade. Rather than exporting slaves, they chose to utilize them internally. However, their military activities did much to weaken many societies making them more vulnerable to the attacks of the slave-trading warrior/merchants. Thus the Nguni incursions can be said to have retarded the socio-political advance of many of the communities and heightened the process of underdevelopment.

On the eve of the 'Scramble'

On the eve of the 'Scramble', conditions within Central Africa were very unstable. The first seventy-five years of the nineteenth century saw such developments as the emergence of new ethnic groups, increased cultural exchange and growing class divisions. The incorporation of the region into the world economy via its participation in the slave and ivory trade also retarded rural growth and increased its economic dependency. The military activities of the slave traders and the Nguni–Kololo migrants did not augur well for the tranquillity of the region. Added to these were internal divisions and strife which left African societies in no position to resist European imperialism.

However, there were a few exceptions to this. Some states like the Bemba kingdom, the liberated Lozi kingdom under Lewanika and the Mwenemutapa kingdom all became very strong and regained pre-eminence. On the whole, however, the tendency of nineteenth-century developments was to weaken the kingdoms in Central Africa and subsequently make them more vulnerable to European invasion.

9

The East African coast and hinterland 1800–45

Coastal communities, c. 1800

In order to understand the changes that took place in the lives of the peoples of the East African coast and its hinterland in the period covered by this chapter, it is necessary to examine the political and economic conditions on the coast around 1800. Politically, the coastal communities were disunited, each one virtually independent of the other and each with its rulers. The overall influence of the Omani Arabs was limited to only Mombasa, Zanzibar and Kilwa and even in those places they were content to share power with the local Swahili and Shirazi.

In Mombasa, the leaders of the local Swahili peoples participated in the political administration of the town. The Mazrui family from Oman remained independent of the Omani rulers of Zanzibar because of their close cooperation with local Swahili _shaykhs_ with whom they shared rule. Even for some time after the rule of the Mazrui had been overthrown, Swahili leaders remained influential in the administration of the town. In Zanzibar, the local ruler at first had some say in the government of his people, being largely in charge of collecting taxes levied on the local population. However, with increasing Omani interest in the region, he gradually lost his political authority. At the same time, the local population in Zanzibar lost more land to Omani settlers who began to encroach particularly on the fertile areas to the north and east of the island.

Despite the presence of an Omani garrison on the island of Kilwa, the local Sultan retained his title and one-fifth of customs dues, and he enjoyed some overlordship over the coast beyond Kilwa Kisiwani. His loss of authority was owed not so much to the Omani presence as to the economic decline of Kilwa Kisiwani itself, which was the result of the rise of a rival Kilwa Kivinje on the mainland which successfully diverted the slave and ivory trade from the island to the mainland depot.

The rest of the coast was still under the authority of local rulers and free from any Omani overrule. The people of Vumba Kuu who were a blend of Shirazi, African and Arab Sharifian elements had an autonomous political authority. By 1800, Malindi, another of the coastal towns had declined

79

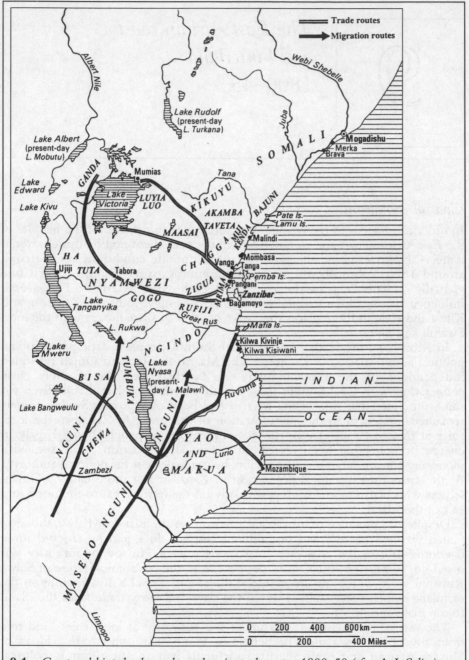

9.1 *Coast and hinterland: peoples and major trade routes, 1800–50 (after A. I. Salim)*

considerably owing to the movement of its ruling family to Mombasa in the sixteenth century. To the north of Malindi were the Lamu and Pate islands. By 1800, Pate had fallen from the position of commercial prominence which it had enjoyed in the seventeenth and eighteenth centuries due to internal succession disputes and conflicts with neighbouring Lamu. The rivalry between these two islands was to later facilitate their subordination to Zanzibar. On the mainland opposite the Lamu and Pate Islands lived the Bajuni people who inhabited also the chain of small islands along the Somali coast. Theirs was a maritime economy and throughout the period under review they were able to maintain their political autonomy.

At this same time, the Benadir coast further north with Mogadishu, Merka and Brava as the major towns was largely self-governing. From the beginning of the century, some Arabs and Indians participated in the trade of these three towns, but the area remained autonomous until 1842 when Omani influence reached Mogadishu. Even then, the relationship remained more economic than political.

The Omani Sultanate

The emergence and growth of Omani influence in East Africa was the result of various factors, some springing from within the Sultanate of Oman, some from without. However, the most important factor was undoubtedly the economic ambitions and acumen of Sultan Seyyid Sa'id (1806–56) who considered himself first and foremost a merchant prince. By maintaining a policy of neutrality towards both France and Britain during the Napoleonic Wars, Sa'id was able to expand the shipping and foreign contacts of Oman to the point where he became a potential threat especially to British shipping, and both powers tried to cultivate his friendship. The British in particular, so as to safeguard their route to India, helped Sa'id to achieve stability in Oman, and eventually occupied Aden in 1839.

Domestic stability enabled Sa'id to expand his economy without distraction. With the disunity and instability on the East African coast, he saw the opportunity for both economic and political expansion, and the need to counter European ambitions by his own activities. He began to make contacts with local peoples and rulers by negotiating treaties, and involving himself in their internecine rivalries.

By 1823, he had succeeded in establishing a firm footing in Pate and Lamu Islands, and a few other neighbouring communities. His major rivals were the Mazrui – the ruling dynasty in Mombasa, also of Omani origin – who got the British to declare a protectorate over Mombasa in 1824. This action strained relations between Sa'id and the British. However, the protectorate was short-lived because the British developed a preference for Sa'id and the Mazrui were no longer enthusiastic about the protectorate as it obliged them to share their revenue with the British who had failed to help them regain their lost possessions.

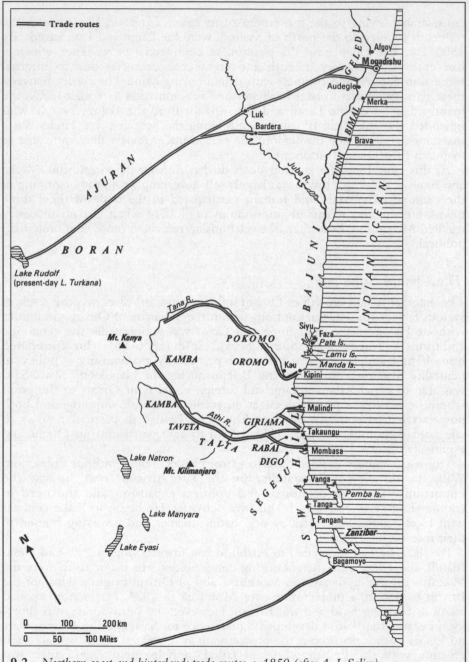

9.2   *Northern coast and hinterland: trade routes, c. 1850 (after A. I. Salim)*

9.3 *Saʿid bin Sultan, Sultan of Zanzibar (1804–56)*

Coast/hinterland trade relations

It was soon after gaining control over Mombasa that Saʿid decided to shift the capital of his sultanate to Zanzibar which was fast becoming a very busy commercial centre. Saʿid was attracted not only by the maritime facilities of Zanzibar, but also by the fertility of the island and its potential for agricultural production. He declared a monopoly over the trade of the island and proceeded to make it the most important economic centre on the East African coast.

Among the items of trade to be found there were ivory, slaves, cloves, gum copal, cowries and imported goods such as cotton cloth, beads, wires, chains, muskets, gun-powder, china, glass, knives and axes. Its position was also enhanced by the recognition it received in terms of commercial agreements from foreign powers such as America, Britain and France.

Ivory and slaves were the most profitable items to the Omani Sultanate because of the high demand for them both locally and overseas. The Yao, a hinterland group, had a long-distance trading network through which they brought ivory and slaves to the coast. Their activities covered the Lake Nyasa region and their goods got to the coast of Zanzibar via Kilwa Kivinje. In fact, the rise of Kilwa Kivinje to prominence and prosperity could be traced to the increased commercial intercourse between the coastal and hinterland peoples in the nineteenth century.

The Bisa, another hinterland people, also participated in the trade with the coast. Together with the Yao, they brought ivory and slaves to Kilwa Kivinje. But competition between them made the Yao concentrate more on the slave trade while the Bisa carried more of the ivory trade. By 1850, Kilwa Kivinje had become the most important commercial centre on the coast between Mozambique and Zanzibar where slaves, ivory and other products like rice, copal and tobacco were exported.

Slaves were acquired through raids or warfare though not all conflicts and raids were necessarily motivated by the desire to capture slaves. Moreover, the people enslaved were often from hinterland groups who were themselves slave traders like the Yao, Bisa, Makua and Ngindu. The slaves were collected inland and assembled at caravan centres from where they were taken to the coast.

There were other long-distance traders to the north of the Lake Nyasa area, the most notable being the Nyamwezi, the Kamba and the Miji Kenda. They made their first contact with the coast around 1800 and soon developed commercial networks between that part of the hinterland and the coast.

Later, as prices for slaves and ivory began to rise, some non-African traders started to move into the interior. The first caravan led by non-Africans to reach the hinterland got to Unyamwezi in 1824 and by 1845, many coastal traders, mainly Arabs, had penetrated into the interior, reaching as far as Buganda where the king welcomed them with the hope not only of increasing trade but also obtaining strategic goods and military assistance.

Further north, other traders in the hinterland were establishing links with coastal peoples, and large commercial networks like those of the Miji Kenda brought the hinterland and coast together into a common economic system where ivory, tobacco, cloth, fish, beads, coconuts, sesame, sorghum and wire were exchanged.

Socio-economic effects of expanding trade

The expansion of trade on the East African coast and hinterland had some significant results. For example, the expansion of the Kamba beyond their original home into less fertile areas led them to undertake hunting, pastoralism and barter trade as their means of subsistence. They traded with neighbours like the Kikuyu, Embu and Maasai, and later extended their trading network to the coast. They set up their own caravans to travel to the coast and they dominated the long-distance trade in the northern sector of the East African interior until the 1850s when they were displaced commercially by the Arabs and the Swahili.

As a result of the trade relations between the coast and hinterland, the system of living in fortified settlements by the Miji Kenda called *kaya* began to decline. The people started to abandon their *kaya* in order to pursue commercial opportunities. This dispersal undermined the togetherness enjoyed in the *kaya*, eroded the authority of elders and brought an end to the age-set system. The society became ordered on a smaller scale – the lineage or subclan – and there was the rise of wealthy individuals who built a following and influence for themselves. Among such men were Ngonyo of Giriama, Mwakikonge of Digo and Kivui of Kamba.

To the north, there was also a well-established commercial link between the dwellers of Lamu and Pate islands on the one hand, and the Pokomo and Oromo peoples on the other hand. Further north, the Benadir towns of Brara, Merka and Mogadishu on the Somali coast were also linked commercially with the interior. All these commercial links between the coast and hinterland gradually produced obvious socio-cultural effects.

One of such effects was the custom of acquiring foreign wives. These intermarriages among different groups led to the development of brotherhoods among the peoples concerned. There was also the adoption of new ritual practices among the groups in eastern Kenya. In addition, new elements were introduced into the coastal towns, making them bigger and ethnically differentiated. Arabs and African traders and slaves from different parts of the interior were to be found in all those towns. Cultural interaction and integration between Bantu and Arabs, and between Bantu and Swahili resulted from the growing use of domestic slaves on plantations and the spread of concubinage. In the Omani Sultanate the idea of taking foreign wives was very widespread especially among the ruling class. The cultural intercourse between the Arabs on the coast and their hosts was pronounced to the extent that there were clear cultural differences between the Omani Arabs based at home and their Africanized counterparts in the Swahili towns. Meanwhile, relationships between African groups on the coast deepened with economic and social ties.

There were also several changes in the interior arising out of the people's participation in the coastal trade. There was the expansion of certain states according to the level of their participation in long-distance trade. Also, the Swahili mode of dressing for men was copied in the interior. Some hinterland rulers rebuilt their capitals in coastal style, adorning their courts with coastal goods and even cultivating a taste for coastal food. The Swahili language – Kiswahili – as the lingua franca of the commercial classes also spread widely into the interior.

However, not all hinterland groups were affected by coastal culture. The Kikuyu, for instance, did not show any interest in the coastal trade, even when Arab and Swahili caravans came into their land. The Maasai prevented Arab and Swahili traders from penetrating their land.

Apart from the commercial developments discussed above, important socio-political developments also took place among the peoples of the Great Lakes region. There was the development of political entities with distinct identities like that of the Baganda. Buganda developed as a centralized state with elaborate political institutions. But the groups to the east of Lake Victoria, with the exception of the Wanga kingdom, did not evolve any centralized states.

Omani international trade

Seyyid Saʿid adopted an economic policy of encouraging Indian enterprise and settlement in Zanzibar. These Asians had remarkable business acumen and played dominant roles as customs agents, middlemen, financiers, or money-lenders and whole traders in Zanzibar. Although their presence and activities in Zanzibar did not win them any political influence or any say in running the affairs of the government, their economic position was greatly enhanced. Some of them became very rich to the extent that even some Sultans of Zanzibar were indebted to them. Also goods imported from Asia became indispensable to Arab and Swahili caravans. This was an important source of wealth for the Asian middlemen and financiers who reaped the greater benefits of the Asian sector of the Zanzibar trade.

Saʿid also introduced clove growing into Zanzibar. He used slave labour to develop the clove industry and became a major exporter of the produce which got as far as Bombay in India. In fact, by 1843, India had become a major importer of Zanzibar cloves.

Due to the growing importance of cloves, a number of Omani Arabs in Zanzibar and Pemba began to cultivate cloves on large plantations. This had many results: it broke the monopoly of Saʿid in the clove business; it saw the development of cloves as a national industry among the Omani Arabs; it increased the demand for slave labour, and also increased the East African slave trade; it led to the neglect of other crops like coconut and rice; and it created land problems in Zanzibar. These land problems particularly soured relations between the Omani Arabs and the original inhabitants of Zanzibar whose land the Arabs had seized by force.

Furthermore, Saʿid signed commercial treaties with the USA, Britain, France and German states. This contributed in no small way to the economic development of Zanzibar in East Africa. American goods such as sugar, beads, brassware, gums, gunpowder and cotton cloth were imported by Zanzibar while the Americans shipped ivory, gum copal, and cloves to their land. The British soon realized that the Sultan of Zanzibar held the key to the abolition of the slave trade in East Africa and therefore sought some measure of political influence in Zanzibar in addition to the small share they had in the East African trade.

However, the commercial and economic policies of Sa'id not only turned Zanzibar into the most important commercial centre on the East African coast, they also gradually integrated the East African economy into the Western capitalist system. The negative impact of this was that European, American and Asian merchants were enriched at the expense of East African peoples thus causing their low level of development. The human and material resources of East Africa were exploited via the unequal exchange that transpired between the foreign merchants and the local peoples. The importation of some manufactured goods like cotton cloth undermined and even destroyed some local textile industries. Equally important was the export of slaves and the depletion of human and material resources that attended it which contributed largely to the under-development of the region.

Conclusion

In the period under review – 1800–45 – the East African coast and hinterland consisted of independent states which were involved in trade either at the local, regional, or overseas levels. Gradually, the Omani rulers began to extend their economic and political influence and to demand nominal allegiance to Zanzibar. There was also the development of long-distance trade which was initiated by African groups in the interior. Later, Arab and Swahili traders moved inland in search of more products. The expanding long-distance trade had its social, economic and cultural impact on many of the hinterland groups. Such impact included the spread of Islam and the Swahili language. But some important developments like the Nguni invasion took place in the interior independent of the long-distance trade.

Lastly, the development and growth of the economic influence of Zanzibar led to unequal exchange between East Africa and the West. It also brought the East African economy into the capitalist system thus contributing to their under-development of the region.

10 The East African coast and hinterland 1845–80

In the last chapter we saw how, by the first quarter of the nineteenth century, the societies in the East African interior were developing independently. Various changes like population movements and political adaptations were taking place in many of these societies, but only the coastal regions and the islands of Zanzibar and Pemba had by then been drawn into the world economic system. This chapter will therefore examine the drawing of the interior into the international economic system, the Nguni invasion from Southern Africa, the struggle between the Maasai groups, and the increasing European interests and incursions into East Africa from about 1845 to 1884.

Omani penetration and the expansion of trade

The foundations of the trade that was to bring the coastal regions and the interior of East Africa together into one commercial empire had already been laid in the early part of the nineteenth century. By 1840, the ivory and slave trades were rapidly expanding and drawing the interior into the coastal trading network. These two commodities facilitated the incorporation of East Africa into the world economic system which in turn affected the development of trade in the region before the establishment of colonial rule.

The establishment of a plantation economy in Zanzibar and Pemba facilitated the expansion of the slave trade into the interior. By 1840 when Zanzibar became the capital of the Omani sultanate, clove plantations had become the primary economic activity of the sultanate and were operated mainly by slave labour. This produced a class of land owners which initially comprised Arabs and later indigenous Shirazi and Indians. The high demand for slave labour in the clove plantations and overseas meant that the slave trade increased tremendously around the middle of the nineteenth century.

The ivory trade also expanded rapidly in this period. There was an increasing demand for ivory from Europe and America. But the ivory trade was firmly under the control of Indian merchants who had established themselves on the East African coast. From there, the ivory was exported to India and later re-exported to Europe. A few Americans were also to be found on the East African coast participating, albeit on a small scale, in the ivory trade and heavily dependent on the Indian merchants.

These commercial developments also saw the growth of long-distance trade which gradually linked the interior with the coast. From different coastal towns, long-distance trade routes spread to various points in the interior. These commercial networks gradually integrated the hinterland and coast into the international trading system.

However, one should not see the role played by Africans in the long-distance trade as minimal or insignificant, reducing them to mere victims of European commercial interests. It is true that the slave trade had an obviously disastrous moral and social impact on East African communities. But the Africans participated actively in the trade. In certain cases, the extent of their participation was such that it affected the development of the societies involved in that the social structure was gradually adapted to cater for the needs of the trade. In addition, the trade made some positive contributions to the economic life of African societies in that it led to the introduction of rice and maize. It also made cultural contributions through the spread of Islam and the Swahili language.

Nonetheless, the overall impact of the long-distance trade and the consequent integration of East Africa into the world commercial system was disastrous for the region. Coastal traders such as the Indians and their African allies served as middlemen for European traders who got the largest profits. East Africans were thus drawn into the world economy on terms unfavourable to them. The energies they could have used to develop their own economies and internal trading networks to benefit the region were diverted to the supply of raw materials and slaves in exchange for ephemeral luxury goods which benefited only a few people in the society. In some cases, African local industries such as the handwoven cloth in south-western Tanzania and the bark-cloth industry in the Lake Region were stifled as a result of the importation of European-manufactured cotton cloth.

The integration of the East African interior with the coast was achieved through the expansion and assimilation of existing trade routes. The network of long-distance trade routes in the region may be classified into four, namely, the Kilwa-hinterland routes, the Central Tanzanian routes, the Pangani Valley route and the Mombasa-hinterland routes.

The four major routes

The Kilwa-hinterland routes were the oldest set of long-distance trading routes leading into the interior of East Africa. They were stimulated by the eighteenth-century demand for slaves on the French dominated islands of Réunion and Mauritius. The routes cut across the Lake Nyasa region linking it with Kilwa. This area was controlled by the Yao who brought ivory, wax and slaves to Kilwa. The crucial role they played in this trade during the first half of the nineteenth century led to their prominence in the second half of the century. This regional trade therefore had a lasting effect on Yao society. The Yao who had been previously organized into small chiefdoms became grouped together

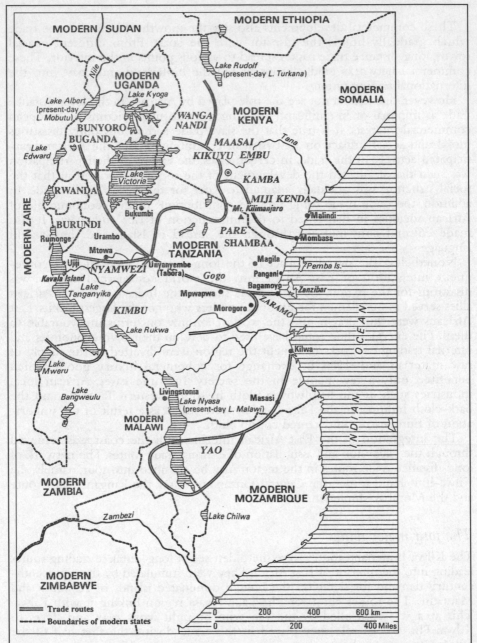

10.1 *Trade in nineteenth-century East Africa (adapted from P. Curtin, S. Feierman, L. Thompson and J. Vansina,* African History, *1978, p. 399)*

into larger communities by the middle of the nineteenth century, even before the Nguni invasions. Yao chiefs consequently became stronger and could not be easily challenged or intimidated by the Arabs who later began to penetrate into the hinterland. The Yao continued to control the regional trade but welcomed the partnership of the Arabs who supplied them with guns and other trade goods. The only areas outside their control were Khota-Khota and Karonga in present-day Malawi.

In the opening decades of the nineteenth century, most of the trade along the central Tanzanian routes was carried by the Nyamwezi. But later, Arab traders financed by Seyyid Sa'īd and Indians on the coast began to penetrate the interior. Thus, while in the Kilwa hinterland the Arabs worked as customers to Yao chiefs, they played a more prominent role in the central region. The central routes linked coastal towns like Bagamoyo with the Nyamwezi country, and with Ujiji which was further on the western shore of Lake Tanganyika. Some of the routes even reached Zaire in Central Africa and areas like Karagwe and Buganda to the north of the East African interior. A southward route joined the Kilwa routes in the Lake Nyasa region. On these central routes, the Arabs established their own trading centres which served as collecting points for ivory and slaves.

Two principal Arab settlements developed in these trading centres. The first was an Arab colony at Unyanyembe in the Nyamwezi country, while the other was at Ujiji on the shores of Lake Tanganyika. The Arabs in Ujiji did not constitute on autonomous colony since they were more or less incorporated into the indigenous state system. But because those in Unyanyembe remained a distinct group they competed for trade with the Nyamwezi rulers and traders and this often produced conflicts between them.

The Pangani Valley route was not controlled by any one group. It was the Shambaa who pioneered trading activities in the Pangani Valley between 1836 and 1862. They had acquired knowledge of long-distance trade from the sojourn in Zanzibar from where famine had dispersed a large number of them. Later, Semboja, ruler of the Zigula kingdom, participated actively in the trade and sought to control it. But neither Semboja nor the Zigula traders fully explored the Pangani Valley route to the interior. It was the Arab and Swahili traders from the coast who went beyond the Zigula trading stations in the Shambaa and Pare plains and got as far as modern-day Kenya. The absence of a dominant power necessitated the establishment of trading centres where coastal traders could maintain direct contact with the different local rulers. This caused rivalry and led to frequent clashes among the various local rulers and their subordinates.

Trade in the Mombasa hinterland was controlled by the Kamba before 1880. The north route which passed through Ukambani country was directly under their surveillance, while the other route which went towards Mount Kilimanjaro was controlled by Arab and Swahili traders from the coast.

Long-distance trade among the Kamba was quite old because they had dominated the regional commerce for about a century before 1836. In the

10.2 *Nyamwezi hairstyles and head-dresses*

10.3 *Nyamwezi traders on the road*

nineteenth century they were gradually drawn into the international trading network where they exchanged their local items for imported goods. By the mid-nineteenth century Kamba caravans were visiting not only their Kikuyu neighbours and the coast, but also places far beyond the Mount Kenya region.

By the 1880s however, the Arab and Swahili traders were in control of the Kamba trade route. They achieved this by having gained control of the local sources of ivory. The slave trade also became important at this period. Famine and intergroup conflicts disrupted Kamba society and forced them to sell their own people to the Arabs and Swahili who played the prominent role in human traffic.

The effects of long-distance trade on East African societies

In examining the effects of long-distance trade on East African societies, it should be understood that not all East African communities were directly involved in this trading system. While capitals of strong kingdoms and states became trading centres, non-centralized states did not enjoy this advantage and were, in fact, often subjected to slave raids from the stronger states. Non-centralized pastoral societies like the Maasai, however, were an exception during this period.

Long-distance trade essentially affected the economic base of the society. Some of the effects were seemingly constructive but had destructive undertones. Large states emerged in areas where smaller states had existed. For example, the previously small Wanga state in Kenya became enlarged and centralized. It grew to cover two neighbouring areas, namely, Kisa and Buholo. Wanga military power was due to the use of Maasai mercenaries as well as the acquisition of guns from coastal traders who had penetrated the interior. The rise of a centralized Wanga state was thus at the expense of its weaker neighbours who bore the brunt of many Wanga raids and were later incorporated into it.

Long-distance trade also had the effect of destroying the existing solidarity of the states. It encouraged independent action by subordinate rulers who sought to make themselves more powerful by allying with intruding coastal traders and this led to the weakening of some of the kingdoms. In the Pangani Valley, there were two fairly large states, the Shambaa and the Gweno kingdoms. They could not participate actively in the regional trade because of their location in mountainous areas. They were thus unable to control the caravan routes which passed through the plains. Subordinate rulers who were nearer these routes thus attracted Arab and Swahili traders to their districts independent of the capital. From their control of the trade, they built up well-armed groups which enabled them to defy the capital. This engendered instability and caused the break-up of the kingdoms into smaller units. Apart from the Shambaa and the Gweno, this kind of fate also befell the Pare states in the Pangani Valley.

There were other generally destructive effects of the long-distance trade. The slave traffic was not only dehumanizing but also socially and economically destructive. Local industries were unable to withstand competition from imported European manufactured goods. The most notable victim was probably the handwoven cloth industry in south-western Tanzania which was stifled by the importation of European manufactured textiles. Moreover, there was the neglect of subsistence agriculture caused by an emphasis on trade in luxury goods and the general violence and instability which accompanied the slave raids. The Zigula in the Pangani Valley appeared to have been strengthened by the trade. From their control of the trade, they were able to build larger states. However, with only a few exceptions such as the kingdom founded by Kisabengo near Morogoro which survived till the German invasion, such states were generally subjected to the pressures of internal conflicts and fragmentation.

In western Tanzania, long-distance trade produced commercial rivalries. There were hostilities among African chiefs, among Arab settlers, and between African chiefs and Arab settlers. This rivalry for control of trade led to social disruption which was in turn intensified by population movements caused by the Nguni invasions. In this atmosphere of insecurity, enterprising leaders like Msiri and Musumbwa, Simba and Nyungu ya Mawe of Unyamwezi built up personal followings and established new kingdoms. Other rulers in western Tanzania like Mirambo used the opportunity of the general insecurity and their increasing power to expand their states. But the survival of such states depended not on the initial military exploits of their leaders but on the establishment of a solid foundation based on an effective administration and the integration of conquered peoples. That was why the kingdom of Nyungu ya Mawe, for instance, was able to survive his death while Mirambo's state broke up immediately on his death.

Some of the large kingdoms in the Great Lakes region were greatly strengthened by their association with coastal traders. They accumulated firearms and raided their neighbours and other non-centralized states in the region. Other groups to the north-central interior of East Africa were less affected by this long-distance trade. They had limited dealings with the coastal traders and were actually unwilling to welcome the foreigners into their communities. Rwanda and Burundi, for instance, held out against foreign trade and successfully withstood the aggression of their neighbours in the Great Lakes region who had acquired firearms from long-distance trade. The Maasai also, as noted above, remained largely unaffected by long-distance trade.

The Nguni invasion

The Nguni came from Southern Africa where they had fled their homeland around 1820 in the face of the increasing aggression of Shaka. They moved northward under Zwangendaba, their leader, and continued to wander until they reached the Fipa plateau in western Tanzania in the early 1840s by which time they had become organized into an armed nation.

The transformation of these Nguni refugees into an armed nation was due to their adoption of Zulu institutions by which foreigners could easily be

10.4   *Mirambo in 1882 or 1883*

absorbed into the society through both the lineages and the centralized age-regiments. The Nguni were thus able to absorb and integrate the peoples they encountered and conquered on their northward march. They also used their superior military organization to survive by raiding other peoples for able-bodied young men, women and cattle. They were thus able to swell their number with war captives who were assimilated into the Nguni social system. By the time they reached the Fipa plateau, these assimilated elements already made up the majority of the Nguni nation.

The death of Zwangendaba in 1848 triggered off a series of succession disputes which finally split the nation into five factions. Three out of these factions moved south and established kingdoms in Zambia and Malawi. The fourth settled to the north and continued to raid the neighbouring peoples. The last group called the Gwangara were in turn split into two kingdoms – the Mshope kingdom and the Njelu kingdom.

The importance of the Nguni invasion lay in the creation of Nguni states on Tanzanian soil. The two Nguni kingdoms mentioned above remained strong centres even in the colonial period. The adoption and adaptation of Nguni military techniques by certain Tanzanian societies was another significant result of the Nguni invasion. Nguni military techniques strengthened the societies that adopted them and enabled them to be better able to cope with the insecurity and instability caused by the long-distance trade, the incursion of coastal traders and the increased demand for slaves. Beyond the need for self-defence, some of the indigenous societies like the Sangu and the Hehe in modern Tanzania used Nguni military techniques to build up large states which remained powerful enough to offer fierce resistance to the Germans in the colonial period.

Southern Tanzania thus witnessed a lot of social and political changes in the second half of the nineteenth century. Some of these changes were initiated by long-distance trade and were then accelerated by the Nguni invasion. By the period of the colonial invasion in the 1880s, southern Tanzania had come to possess some of the most powerful states in the region, such as the Nguni kingdoms, the Hehe and the Sangu.

The Maasai wars

The Maasai wars of the mid-nineteenth century affected the history of a wide area of the north-eastern interior of East Africa throughout the second half of the century. This was because the long series of civil wars ultimately weakened the Maasai whose control of the Uasin Gishu plateau had been a major factor in the distribution of power in the region.

The wars were caused basically by conflicts arising from the competition to control cattle and pasture land, both of which were considered important to the Maasai cattle culture or pastoral way of life.

The first series of wars may have been caused by pressure on grazing land on the Uasin Gishu plateau. The second series of wars began after the famous

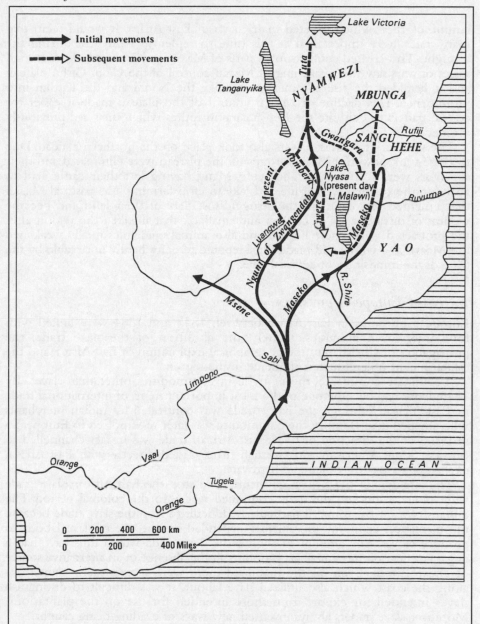

10.5 *Northward migration routes of Zwangendaba's Nguni, the Maseko Nguni and the Msene (from J. D. Omer-Cooper,* The Zulu Aftermath, *1966, p. 66)*

famine of 1836 which affected many parts of East Africa. It would seem that many raids were undertaken at this time to replenish herds lost during the drought. This created conflicts in all parts of Maasailand. The end of the second series of wars saw the weakening of Maasai control of the Uasin Gishu plateau and it heralded the rise of other groups like the Nandi and the Kipsigi into prominence. This decline of Maasai control of the plateau made it easier for coastal traders to cultivate the Kenya caravan routes which they had previously avoided.

The final series of Maasai wars also took place on the northern plateau. Due to these wars, powerful Maasai groups on the plateau were eliminated and their survivors were scattered far and wide. Many, having lost their cattle, had to abandon the pastoral way of life and take to crop farming. The pastoral Maasai that emerged victorious in the struggle lost part of their land and became victims of diseases such as cholera and smallpox that infected the region after the protracted wars. These human and also animal epidemics finally weakened the Maasai as a whole and made their reputed ferocity hardly noticeable by the time of the imposition of colonial rule.

Increased European pressures

European pressures in East Africa between 1845 and 1884 were linked with four interwoven activities, namely, the abolition of the slave trade, the propagation of Christianity, the geographical exploration of East Africa, and the establishment of legitimate commerce in the region.

'Legitimate commerce' meant trade in commodities other than slaves. By 1845, ivory had become one of the most important items of international trade in East Africa. Although the ivory trade was controlled by Indian merchants who shipped it to Bombay, the commodity was later re-exported to Europe. So in terms of the direction of trade, East African trade was in fact channelled to Europe. Some American and German firms traded directly with East Africa, exchanging ivory for calico and hardware.

The attempts of the British government to stop the East African slave trade were unsuccessful and the trade continued well into the colonial period. The Sultans of Zanzibar found it particularly difficult to stop the slave trade because the plantation economy in Zanzibar depended on the use of slave labour to produce cloves. Any attempt to abolish the slave trade would thus have had a negative effect on the Zanzibari economy in the absence of an alternative source of cheap labour. Even on the mainland there were several grain plantations along the coast which also utilized slave labour. It was difficult to distinguish slaves intended for export from those intended for use on the plantations. Moreover, slave traders always invented new ways of evading being caught.

Until 1856, European anti-slavery activities were concentrated on the coast and in Zanzibar. The European world thus had little knowledge of the hinterland. The accounts of the travels of several explorers were later to draw their attention to the East African interior.

The travels of David Livingstone in East and Central Africa were a major factor in drawing the attention of the European world to the interior of East Africa. Before these travels, three German missionaries sent by the Church Missionary Society (CMS) with their base near Mombasa had ventured into the interior. These men gathered considerable information about the East African interior which became valuable to later explorers and missionaries. As a result of the insight he acquired into the condition in the East African interior through his travels, Livingstone advocated intensive trade with East Africa to link the interior with Christian Europe and purge it of all the evils of the slave trade.

Intense missionary activities thus began in East Africa with the question of freed slaves. The CMS, the Universities Mission to Central Africa, and the Holy Ghost Fathers were all involved in this problem between 1858 and 1873. Meanwhile, as the missions were taking root on the coast, European explorers were also active in the interior, having been inspired by the pioneering efforts of the missionaries. These explorers exposed the inhuman character of the Arab slave trade and this in turn gave a vigorous fillip to missionary zeal.

European pressure in the East African interior before 1884 was exerted mainly by missionary societies. Protestant missions such as the CMS, UMCA (Universities Mission to Central Africa), London Missionary Society, the Scottish Free Church, and the Roman Catholic White Fathers all launched into the interior after the death of Livingstone in 1873, establishing many stations and spreading the Christian faith. The commercial activities that existed were very few and were carried out mainly under the auspices of the missions, such as the Livingstonia Central African Trading Company and the British India Steam Navigation Company both of which were associated with the Scottish Free Church.

It should be clear from the foregoing discussion that missionary work in East Africa between 1845 and 1884 was in its pioneering phase. Even then it had a considerable impact on the local peoples. The fact that the missionaries had a free hand to operate, unlike later during the colonial period, led them to establish colonies which attracted not only freed slaves but also political exiles, runaway slaves, and other groups of discontented people. This helped the mission stations to thrive and swell at the expense of the existing African states. The indigenous societies which were already drained economically by the international trade thus became more fragile and were very vulnerable by the time of the colonial conquest. In this sense, the missionaries could be said to have prepared the way for the colonial rule which was established during the closing decades of the nineteenth century.

People and states of the Great Lakes region

Introduction

The Great Lakes region is a densely populated and well watered area of Eastern and Central Africa covering parts of modern Uganda, Kenya, Zaire and Tanzania. Its geography is dominated by the great Rift Valley in which the huge lakes are located and into which several rivers drain. Before the imposition of colonial rule the states in this area shared some common features in terms of their history, migration of peoples and social and political structures.

The nineteenth century witnessed in the Great Lakes region a continuation of previous developments in the area. At the beginning of the century, the states in the region were still developing and trying to establish themselves firmly by evolving new institutions and incorporating new areas into their jurisdiction. The region retained from the eighteenth century the character of a troubled zone because of the constant opposition and frequent acts of rebellion against the rulers – for example, rebellious members of the royal lineage or other unsuccessful aspirants to high office retreating to remote areas to gather an invading force or allying with ambitious rulers of other states. This instability, however, did not preclude interaction between the states. The states were not isolated entities but, rather, constituted a communicating network of diplomatic relationships, alliances, dynastic marriages, commercial exchange and military activities all of which the rulers found necessary for coping with the instability of the area. Internally, each state had an important impact on the lives of the people that constituted it, especially by determining their attitudes towards their domestic existence, production, trade, religious thought and practice.

The political order

The Great Lakes region in the nineteenth century comprised many states of varying sizes and strength. Each state had a king who came from a royal lineage. In the service of the state were also a court of advisers, councillors, other state officials hierarchically placed, and artisans. As stated earlier, conflict, both from within and without, remained an important element of local politics.

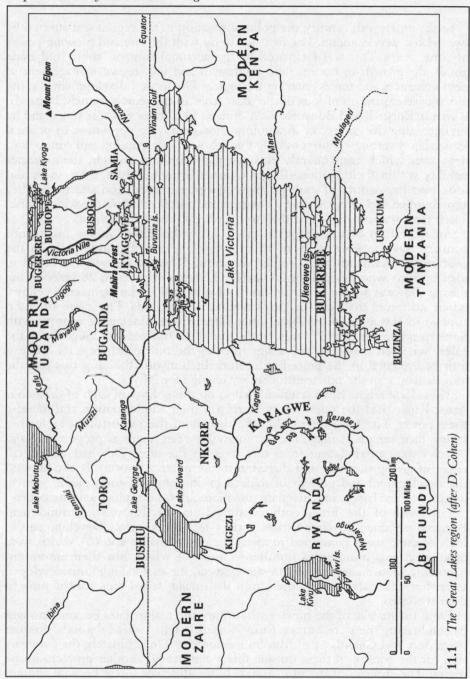

11.1 *The Great Lakes region (after D. Cohen)*

In the nineteenth century, the political situation in the region was affected by two related developments. The first had to do with the rise and growing power of some states. This was facilitated by the accumulation of labour and trade goods, the growth of bureaucratic institutions and the shrewd management of new influences and forces entering the region. The second development was the remarkable expansion of four of the older states in the region, namely, Buganda, Rwanda, Burundi and Bunyoro. Each of these four states was able to expand by strengthening the control of its administration, removing opposition to political leadership, diverting conflicts outside through wars of expansion and conquest of new areas which consequently enlarged the states and brought them greater stability within their borders. To get a firmer economic base, these states also took over the control of strategic areas of regional production and trade. They also absorbed and integrated new elements and forces entering the wide region. Their fame was enhanced and they were brought into the limelight.

An indication of the change in these major kingdoms in the nineteenth century was the long reign of their rulers. The first Baganda ruler in the century was Kamanya who reigned for about 35 years. He was succeeded in turn by Suna who reigned for 20 years and Mutesa who spent 28 years on the throne. This was a great departure from what existed in the eighteenth century when no fewer than eleven kings reigned in Buganda. The same situation applied to Rwanda where three kings ruled in the nineteenth century with none spending less than 30 years on the throne. In Burundi the longevity of the rulers was such that only two kings ruled in the nineteenth century whereas four had reigned in the preceding century. In Bunyoro, the king that had the longest tenure in the nineteenth century reigned for 29 years.

These long reigns had a stabilising effect on the politics of each of these four states. Rulers had the opportunity to reform their administration and increase their power. The long reigns also afforded them the opportunity to further secure their tenure. It made for continuity between reigns as programmes and policies were carried over from one reign to the next. This had the overall effect of giving meaning and direction to the political process. It also allowed the development and growth of societal institutions of family, public service, production, exchange and adequate provisioning of the capitals and the courts.

For most of the nineteenth century, Buganda, Rwanda, Burundi and Bunyoro remained the largest states in the Great Lakes region. Developments in each of these states continued to affect the other smaller states – which were more than two hundred in number – many of which lost their autonomy, becoming subordinate entities. In other words, the major kingdoms developed as centres of attraction to people from the smaller states thus contributing to their weakness.

From the middle of the nineteenth century, the major states became stronger by embracing new resources from outside such as trade goods, foreign merchants, and Christian and Muslim missionaries. Unfortunately, the competition for the control of these outside forces constituted another problem in the region. The rivalries of the protagonists of the different forces became another

11.2 *Buganda in 1875: The Kabaka's Capital*

11.3 *Kabaka Mutesa with chiefs and officials*

factor of division. While, on the whole, these new forces brought increasing strength to the four major states, they allowed them to heighten the sense of insecurity in the area.

Production and extraction

As the states in the Great Lakes region expanded politically, they sought to establish a firm economic base and sustain their courts and capitals by controlling the production of food and trade in the region. In fact, this had been their major preoccupation since the eighteenth century as exemplified by the expansion of Buganda into Kyaggwe during that century. Buganda's target then was the productive regions of Kyaggwe. Thus, the major states of the Lakes region had their eyes on the centres of production surrounding them which they exploited for their own benefit.

There were several patterns of extracting revenue from these rich areas. In the first place, the component units of a major state and its dependent entities regularly brought tribute into the capitals and courts of the reigning monarch. However, this tribute payment was by no means voluntary. It was forcefully extracted by the agents of the rulers of the dominant state. This generated a lot of conflicts and soured relations between the dominant and the dependent areas. These conflicts negatively affected trade in the region and were most apparent in the centres of food production. Foodstuffs from the subordinate areas of the region thus fed the courts and capitals of the major kingdoms. While contributions of food from those areas to the centre were regular and seasonal, there were occasional emergencies such as times of war necessitating the sending of military expeditions to make extra demands on the producers.

Another pattern of extraction was that represented by the establishment of governmental farms under the supervision of appointed officials whose sole task was to provide for the needs of the capital and courts of the ruler. For example, in Buganda, Rwanda, Nkore, Karagwe and Burundi, there were such royal farms which provided food not only for the rulers' households but also for their senior chiefs. These governmental farms functioned so effectively that they could step up production at very short notice.

Apart from this centrally organized production, powerful kingdoms had programmes of extraction and of tribute-taking from areas beyond their political jurisdiction. This fell into two categories. The first comprised irregular but expected extraction. These extractions were irregular because they were carried out at different intervals. However, the victims never lacked the resources with which to pay up. The fact that they always obliged, after some initial resistance but without being actually coerced, makes it clear that they anticipated the demands. An example was the exploitation of central Busoga by Buganda for dried bananas and some other commodities. This routine collection forced the Basoga to increase production beyond what they could consume, keeping the surplus for the purpose of tribute payment. Another example was the extraction of salt by Bunyoro from the Lake George area.

The second category comprised the irregular and unexpected collection of tributes from more remote areas. Extractions in these remote zones were more military in character. Armed groups attacked an area and took over whatever captives, cattle, ironware, back-cloth and other valuable and movable resources they could get. The expeditions of Buganda into Busoga clearly illustrates this. The presence of the Ganda army in central Busoga disrupted the system of food production in the area. In the nineteenth century, Rwanda also sent such military expeditions into areas to its north and west to extract valuable commodities and cattle. These expeditions had the overall effect of disrupting production and trade in the affected areas. Some of the areas attacked for food got their supplies in turn from neighbouring areas which increased their own production to meet the external demand. In addition, these expeditions also had the result of establishing fairly stable transit routes into the target regions.

The programmes of extraction of some of the major kingdoms in the region were actively resisted in the areas of production in the nineteenth century. For example, Buganda military expeditions were resisted in eastern and northern Busoga. But in order to increase its collection, Buganda embraced ways of acquiring firearms, intervened in the local politics of other groups and increased the scale of its military expeditions to exploit new areas as old productive zones collapsed. All these were fiercely resisted by the centre of production. The situation, however, was not peculiar to Buganda. Rwanda extractions were also resisted by the people to its west and north-west throughout much of the nineteenth century.

Coercion, violence and the market

Resistance to the extractions of the major states produced several results one of which was the eventual decline of productivity in the tribute-paying areas. This in turn affected the courts and capitals as more elaborate and expensive means had to be adopted to maintain the high levels of tribute from areas beyond the regular producing centres. Resistance also increased the level of violence in the region. In addition, trade suffered severely as a result of all these disruptions.

In the nineteenth century intense conflict was generated when certain productive areas in the Lakes region became targets of two or three tribute-collecting states at the same time. For example, the Budiope area of northern Busoga and the Bugerere area to the west of the Nile became simultaneous targets of Bunyoro and Buganda, both of which sought to extract the produce of those areas. This led to intense conflict between the two states for much of the century. This scramble for tribute among regional powers might have had several results. In some places it probably led to the formation of various defensive alliances among the tribute-paying groups. In others, it might have reduced the population and output of the contested areas. In still others, it probably increased production far beyond local needs.

11.4   *Treasure house, and regalia of King Rumanyika of Karagwe*

11.5   *Naval battle on Lake Victoria between the Baganda and the people of the Buvuma Islands, 1875*

But while some areas in the Lakes region were producing beyond local needs, others experienced acute food shortages. These shortages, experienced at the beginning of the wet season and during long seasons and years of poor harvests, were relieved by the operation of occasional markets in the region. These markets were organized during periods of crises for the exchange of livestock, grain, fish, vegetables and manufactured goods; and they were regulated by members of the dominant lineage in the areas.

In some areas, for example in western Kenya, staple foods were scarce because of irregular rainfall and an extended dry season. This led to population movements away from the area to more hospitable zones and higher lands in the region. This process of upland migration, which continues today, has produced very high rural population densities which in turn has contributed to the exhaustion of the soil and the depletion of forest reserves.

Some people remained in the lowlands and continued to suffer food shortages, with the occasional market providing some relief for them. They kept cattle which served as a means of accumulation of convertible wealth.

Trading circuits

There were extensive trading networks in the Lakes region in the nineteenth century. On the one hand there were regional networks or circuits which were controlled by certain groups within the area, while on the other hand there were international exchange routes which linked the Lakes region with the East African coast. Regional commerce indicated, and was necessitated by, the lack of self-sufficiency of different groups in terms of production. Commercial exchange thus led to the establishment of a wider communication network.

One such regional trade network was centred on Lake Kivu. Rwanda participated actively in this trade system. The major items exchanged were woven bracelets, cattle and foodstuffs. The woven bracelets called *butega* were used widely in exchange in the Kivu zone and this, in a way, stimulated production in the area.

Another regional network connected areas on the eastern side of Lake Victoria. The Bukerebe state dominated the trade of the southern sector of this eastern Lakes network. This state had witnessed an agricultural revolution earlier in the century and so was able to organize the production of several new crops such as maize and cassava, and also introduced new kinds of sorghum and millet to the region. The ability to produce surplus foodstuffs enabled Bukerebe marketeers to profit from famines in Buzinza and Usukama to exchange food at exploitative rates for metalware and cattle, and thus to play a central role in the trading circuit.

The northern reaches of the eastern Lakes trade network was controlled by Basuba traders. They transported salt, slaves, dried bananas, grains, beans, livestock, fish and iron across Lake Victoria, thus linking the Bukerebe markets in the south with south Busoga and Buvuma markets in the north.

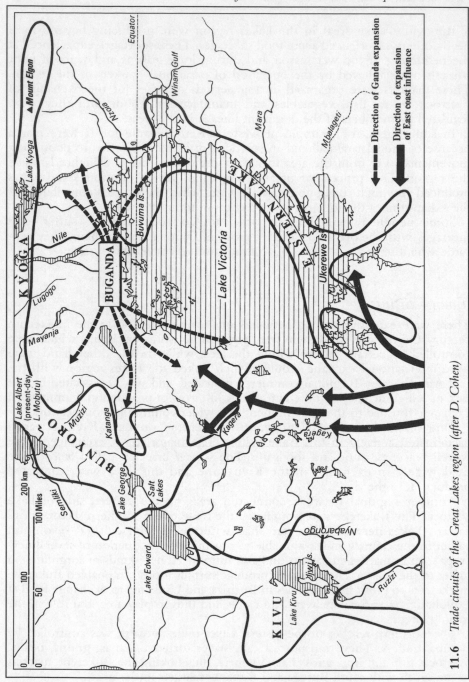

11.6 Trade circuits of the Great Lakes region (after D. Cohen)

Bagabo and Bashingo traders developed another regional network in the area of the salt lakes in western Uganda. These groups maintained a firm monopoly over the production and marketing of salt. In both the salt lakes area and the eastern Lakes network described above, the traders developed their monopolies and markets independent of the states in the Great Lakes region and only supplied the needs of those states when they were militarily forced to do so.

Another extensive commercial network in the nineteenth century was centred on the general Bunyoro area and extended into neighbouring regions. Ironware and salt were the principal items in the exchange though other goods such as foodstuffs and livestock were also traded. This exchange had the result of stimulating further production in some of the areas involved in it. An example of this was the increase of sesame production by the Lango.

Bunyoro played an important role in this trade network. Production from the Lake Kyoga basin was directed to the Nyoro market. Agents of the Bunyoro kingdom and of its dependencies levied taxes on the production, carriage and marketing of goods, foodstuffs and livestock coming both from Lake Kyoga and western Uganda. The importance of Bunyoro in this regional market cannot be overemphasized. Its rulers and those of Toro played crucial roles in the exchange system of the western part of the Lakes region without destroying the routines of commodity traffic and exchange.

International exchange involved the penetration of the region by Arabs and Swahili traders operating in the Unyamwezi area. They first came in through the Bukerebe network which they eventually displaced. They moved further into the region via the routes used by the salt lakes traders. They introduced firearms into the region in exchange for slaves and ivory. European explorers, Muslim and Christian missionaries later followed the tracks of these external traders, thus opening the way for new forces of change in the Great Lakes region.

While these Arabs and Swahili were penetrating the region around Lake Victoria, Buganda was seeking to establish direct commercial links with them at the southern side of the lake. This had the effect of further displacing Bukerebe influence in the east and north. However, Buganda's influence in the region did not create a new marketing network as the Bukerebe had done.

If Bunyoro's authorities as earlier discussed stimulated the expansion of commercial exchange in the western flank of the Lakes region, Buganda's activities tended to destroy and stifle market activities in the same area. In the nineteenth century, Buganda was a warfare or tribute state with no plans for the expansion of sub-regional exchange. But at the same time Buganda was participating actively in external exchanges from the shores of Lake Victoria to the East African coast. The difference between the roles played by Bunyoro and Buganda in the economic life of the Lakes region lay essentially in the levels at which they participated in the trade. While Bunyoro participated actively in the regional trade and even contributed to its expansion, Buganda raided other states in the region as a solution to whatever shortages of local commodities it encountered, thus exploiting rather than contributing to the regional trade. At the same time, Buganda joined the broader international trading system which was steadily getting into the lakes region from the East African coast and managed, to some extent, to exclude Bunyoro from participating in this external commerce. This had the result of reducing Bunyoro's influence in the region.

The external commerce from the East African coast to the Lakes region involved the exchange of firearms for ivory and slaves collected in the region. Other luxury goods were also imported into the Buganda court. The Buganda court consequently developed a taste for foreign goods and this later facilitated its colonization.

Growth of inequalities and tension

By the last quarter of the nineteenth century, a lot of inequalities and tension had developed in the Lakes region which made the people, both the weak and the powerful, seek the help of Europeans when they began to penetrate the region. The acquisition of firearms by the most powerful states had further increased their military might and strengthened their hands in relations with their weaker neighbours. This increased the spread of inequalities as represented by the exploitation of the weak, and slave-gathering expeditions by the more powerful peoples.

At the close of the nineteenth century, there was a new wave of resistance and conflict as certain groups tried to overthrow the rulers of the major kingdoms in the Lakes region. The growing power concentrated in the region's capitals began to generate tension during the last three decades of the century. In Bunyoro, Rwanda and Busoga, common people resisted the excessive demands of the powerful kings by moving away from their homes, or by building up their settlements as defensive villages.

In Busoga, by the second quarter of the nineteenth century, the people had developed a new outlook to the state. The readiness of the people to emigrate and abandon their lands undermined the authority of the state. Thus, while the capital was accumulating more arms, the people were releasing themselves from whatever legal hold the state had on them by emigrating to seek more attractive opportunities elsewhere.

Resistance to organized political authority in the nineteenth century also involved the enhancing of the authority of religious institutions if only for a short while. Thus, religious institutions began to thrive and attract more patronage at the expense of the political institutions. For example, in the Bunafu area of Busoga, there was the rise of a religious sect organized around the possessed child called Womunafu. Also in Rwanda, Bunyoro and south-western Uganda, there were religious movements called *kubandwa* based on the female deity Nyabingi. These movements often developed in opposition to political authority as happened in Rwanda. Later, they were used as foci of resistance to European colonial authority in the region.

Conclusion

The Great Lakes region in the nineteenth century was a large area of conflict and struggle among different groups and forces. These conflicts were on two levels. At one level, states competed for the control of agricultural zones and special resources, such as salt, cattle and iron. They also struggled for access to the control of trade systems.

At another level, individuals sought to preserve their areas of economic, political and social operation. But in the nineteenth century, the state in the region was more interested in ruthlessly exploiting the people than in protecting their interests. This produced different reactions from the people according to their limitations and opportunities. Some diverted production and marketing away from the demands of the state, others left their areas as a form of protest against increasing state pressure, while some sought refuge by joining religious communities through which they subsequently worked to overthrow the existing political authority. The peoples in the Great Lakes region thus tried several times in the nineteenth century to change their orientations to state authority, public service, production and the market. Consequently, these states underwent significant changes in production, exchange, relations among states, as well as in relations between the state and the people.

12

The Congo Basin and Angola

The area covered by this chapter is bounded on the west by the Atlantic Ocean, on the east by the Nile–Zaire ridge, on the north by the Ubangui savannas, and on the south by the plateau separating the Zaire and Zambesi basins. A number of themes will be treated in the history of this area between 1800 and 1880. They include production, trade and politics. In addition, we shall look at the way of life of the communities in this area in order to see what continuities and links they were able to maintain with the remote past. The changes brought by the nineteenth century especially in the economic sphere and the extended impact this had on the social and political history of the people will also be examined. In this connection, the chapter will thus discuss the impact of fluctuations in the world economy on this part of Central Africa and the peoples' response to these external and internal challenges.

Production: models of sparse and dense populations

Central African communities in the period under consideration showed the persistence of some patterns carried over from the previous century in the distribution of their population, systems of production and basic socio-economic aspirations. Of particular importance was the uneven distribution of population caused by various geographical, economic, social and historical factors.

Sparse populations existed in the south of the rain forest where agriculture was practised on a small scale because of the poor soils. The major crops were old African cereals, namely, 'finger millet', and sorghum. Because this small amount of agriculture could not support the people, it was supplemented with food-gathering, hunting and fishing. In fact, these other sources provided most of the food consumed.

Areas of sparse population were in contact with densely populated areas which tended to shed their excess population on the thinly populated areas. Areas of sparse and dense population merged; improvement in the availability of water and therefore arable land, or in the techniques of agriculture or cultivation of new crops led to more intensive agriculture and population increase. In other words, the existence of the thickly populated areas in Central Africa was facilitated by the improvement or expansion of agriculture. There were some ancient areas of intensive agriculture in the Lualaba valley and in the

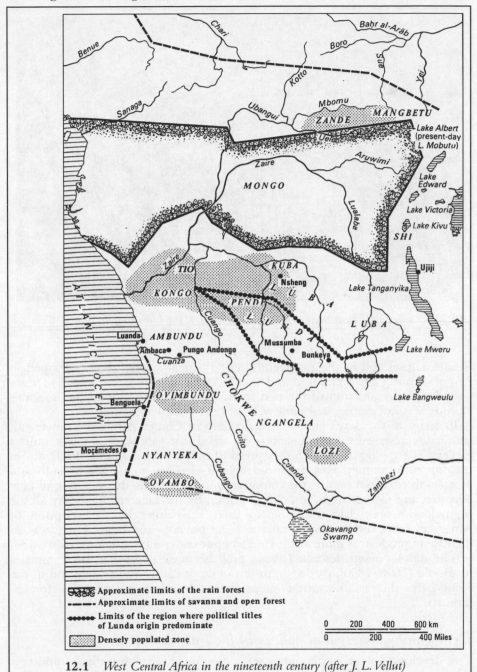

12.1 *West Central Africa in the nineteenth century (after J. L. Vellut)*

12.2   *A village in Manyema, a north-eastern province of the Luba Empire, in the 1870s*

Kongo region and in the nineteenth century high-density areas developed in Angola among the Ambundu and the Ovimbundu. In Zaire, a high-density corridor at the junction of the rain forests and savannah around the 5° south latitude was not demarcated until well into the twentieth century.

In terms of the development of agriculture in Central Africa, the nineteenth century represented the culmination of a trend that had begun a few centuries earlier. The trend started with the spread of iron-working among the Bantu in the fifteenth century. This produced several changes in the seventeenth and eighteenth centuries such as the colonization of new lands, the founding of new dynasties and the extension of political power. By the nineteenth century, all the high-density areas had strengthened their agriculture by the adoption of American crops such as maize, cassava, sweet potatoes and beans. There was an increase in produce as more arable land was put under more intensive cultivation.

The developments described above probably took more than two centuries to unfold (1600–1850). By 1850, American crops had spread widely and in the Kongo area they had become domesticated and no longer regarded as foreign imports.

Demography, society and politics in high-density areas

The development of communities with diversified agriculture had important consequences for the demography of Central Africa. This was because unlike communities which gradually took to agriculture and animal domestication, and those that hunted and gathered food, communities with a more diversified agriculture had a higher growth rate. Nevertheless, the growth rate of even these complex agricultural societies was low when compared with twentieth-century figures because of the high rate of death in such societies in the nineteenth century.

Many factors were responsible for this high death rate. There was the slave trade and its attendant violence. There were also endemic diseases and epidemic outbreaks which defied the medication offered by local healers or by traders from Angola and the Swahili Coast who had acquired some knowledge of European medicine. Although population growth in the nineteenth century was still low by modern standards, it was no doubt an improvement on previous centuries. Excess population migrated into areas practising a more diversified mode of agriculture. This saw the development of more settled communities which finally tamed the hostile environment.

The material development and the socio-political history of the area had a mutual effect on one another. In some cases, high-density areas developed as bases for centralized political structures. Examples of this were Mangbetu and Zande in north-eastern Zaire. In other places, political factors sped up population growth which in turn intensified production as exemplified in Burundi, Rwanda and, in the experience of the Shi, in the nineteenth century. This relationship between material and human forces was not a one-sided affair; production of increasing surpluses led to population growth, and this in turn further boosted production. But this could sometimes lead to the decline of political power as in the case of western Zaire where population growth led to radical changes in the structure of the society.

Increased migration led to the development of a strong community to the west of the Luba heartland in the nineteenth century. The individual identities of each of the migrants were shed for a corporate one, consequently forging an ethnic consciousness among them. Their common historical experience greatly fuelled this group identification while individual enterprise, increase in population and agricultural productivity remained vital aspects of the society's existence. Many Chokwe also left their homes in the upper Tshikapa and upper Kasai to hunt and gather food in the open forest, with several Lunda women who had been captured as slaves. The Lunda women who were assimilated into Chokwe society knew how to cultivate cassava even on poor soils and the Chokwe thus became introduced to agriculture.

The conquest of poor soils

Another important aspect of the history of the area under discussion is the conquest of poor soils in the nineteenth century. Together with animal domestication, this facilitated the setting up of human communities in arid areas, and increased the population of some areas with sparse densities. An example of this was southern Angola.

12.3   *Nineteenth-century royal drums from the Kuba kingdom*

Southern Angola was a sandy, dry area with irregular rainfall. The peoples of this region shared a common historical experience and this forged an ethnic solidarity among them. They were distinguished by their soil and by the importance they attached to agriculture and animal production. They are known generally as the Ovambo, of whom the most numerous subgroups were the Kwanyama, the Ndongo and the Kwambi. The rise of the Cuvelai river and the flooding of the grassland in parts of southern Angola enabled the Ovambo to overcome the drought and cultivate the area. They made use of irrigation and also used animal manure as fertilizers on their farms.

The assimilation of newcomers, especially of captives taken during raids, into neighbouring lands facilitated the change to a more intensive type of farming among the Ovambo. The staple crops were millet and sorghum. American plants such as groundnuts, beans and maize were also cultivated but to a much lesser extent. Production was controlled by the king who shared out land and organized irrigation works.

Thus, the increase in productivity facilitated by the conquest of poor soils accentuated the hitherto existing disparities in population distribution. There was a rapid increase in the population of areas that enjoyed a surplus from an increase in agricultural production. Examples of such areas were Ovambo, Ovimbundu and Luba. This meant that people from other areas were attracted to these agricultural zones, thus depopulating their own home base. This depopulation was also facilitated by certain economic factors. For instance, the practice of food gathering promoted the dispersion of people in the forest as they went out to collect ivory, wax and other items. Moreover, the creation of centres of trade in the river valleys brought different peoples together thus producing a concentration of population.

Central Africa in the fluctuating world economy

The economy of Central Africa was not only given to productive activities such as agriculture, animal production, fishing and gathering; trade also existed, and its importance depended on historical circumstances. In general, the problems of transportation limited trade items to a few major products that were in high demand such as salt, iron and luxury goods. On the other hand, agricultural produce was seldom carried over long distances.

The rise of an international trading economy which began in the sixteenth century gradually affected the economy of certain areas of Central Africa. By the nineteenth century, there was an expansion of trade and Central Africa became more active in world-wide trade. Its principal export to the outside world during the first half of the century was slaves. However, from the 1850s, other products such as ivory, wax, copal, oil and coffee began also to be exported. There was indeed a remarkable growth in the market economy of Central Africa in the second half of the nineteenth century.

The manner in which trade and communication networks functioned within the African continent determined the volume of African products that got to the world markets. These networks delineated the major economic zones in Central Africa in the nineteenth century irrespective of the previous political and economic arrangements in the region.

Each of these new economic zones had its own history as well as political and social features. They came to be dominated by the demands of the external trade. A common feature among the different zones was that each succeeded in changing important aspects of the old African economic system, linking it however loosely with the world economy.

Economic zones and trading networks

There were four main economic zones in Central Africa during the period 1800–80. Two of these zones were characterized by the important role played in them by Muslim traders, while the other two zones were centred around the outposts of European traders on the Atlantic coast.

The first was the Arab/Sudanese trading network located in the north-eastern part of Central Africa which comprised the outposts of traders from Cairo, the Red Sea and Khartoum. It developed as a result of the commercial and military activities of Egyptians in the Sudan and Darfur. The Egyptian, Coptic and European traders involved in this network built forts which they used as bases during barter exchange. This Sudanese network had some important characteristics. One was the distinction maintained between state monopolies and private trade. Another was the use of force to capture slaves and raid for ivory, and a policy of developing plantations, especially those of cotton, to meet trade requirements.

The second economic zone was the Swahili network with its bases in the ports on the Swahali coast and in other places on the Indian ocean such as Zanzibar and Bagamoyo. The Swahili routes were in two main groups. One passed through Unyanyembe in the centre of present-day Tanzania, crossing Lake Tanganyika. The other linked the Luapula-Moero region either through Lake Malawi or through south-western Tanzania. This trading network was operated by small caravans which stopped at the courts of influential chiefs. It also led to the development of settlements of trading communities as from the 1870s, for example that of Tippu Tip which was established at Kasongo in 1875. More importantly, it was through this network that the Swahili country became the first base for colonial penetration into the eastern part of Central Africa.

The third was the Zaire river trade zone centred around the Dutch, French and English trading stations on the lower Zaire river and along the northern coast of Angola. It received supplies from both the Kongo trade and the river trade. The river trade developed in the second half of the nineteenth century and soon overshadowed the old land routes. Groups living along the river monopolized this river trade. They collected ivory and slaves from the interior and took them down the river as far as the Tio markets on the Pool. They set up trading centres and introduced new commodities like guns, copper rings and

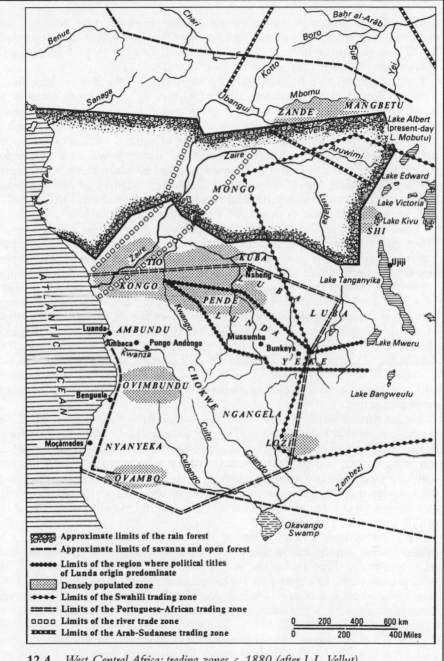

12.4   *West Central Africa: trading zones, c. 1880 (after J. L. Vellut)*

new varieties of crops into the rain-forest regions. The trading centres comprised slaves, refugees and other groups which swelled their populations. Small population centres, on the other hand, also developed around private individuals who had made their fortune in trade.

Last of all was the Portuguese/African network which was the oldest and most extensive in Central Africa. Throughout the nineteenth century there were many changes in its routes. In the first half of the century, the principal routes led to Luanda and Benguela. Another route linked the Ovimbundu highlands to the coast. The Lozi and Lunda kingdoms were also incorporated into this network in the 1840s. However, the network was vastly extended in the second half of the century. A new route linked Malanje with the capital of Mwant Yav. Other sets of routes took the African traders of Ambaca into the Lulua valley in the Luba region, and also to the markets around Kuba. At Kuba, they encountered some competition from Ovimbundu traders.

These commercial centres on the different routes performed important functions. Such functions included giving credit to traders, providing storage facilities and packing and equipping trading expeditions. The most important centres in the first half of the nineteenth century were Luanda and Benguela, while Moçamedes rose to prominence in the second half of the century. In Luanda, Creole and African culture took pre-eminence over the Portuguese section of the population. There was also room for social mobility and plenty of opportunity to amass wealth. In fact, by about 1850, Luanda was bigger than all the other Angolan posts in the interior. Such other posts as Dondo, Pungo, Andongo, Caconda and even Bie were important secondary centres of the network. Capitals of small chiefdoms or the markets of non-centralized communities constituted the termini of the network where active transactions were negotiated.

Under this network system, there was an increasing distinction between the major centres that handled a lot of the revenue-yielding market operations and those with few opportunities to acquire wealth. In the more fortunate areas, items like arms, textiles and domestic slaves were plentiful while they were scarce in other places. During periods of economic growth, most of the trade in the interior was carried on by Africans, but in times of economic recession, the Portuguese tried to monopolize all the profits by elbowing the African middlemen out of business.

This Portuguese/African network also had to adapt to certain major trade cycles in the nineteenth century. By the 1840s, the most important trading activity was the slave trade. The major importer of Angolan slaves was Brazil which used them to expand its coffee-plantation economy. By the end of the 1860s, the exportation of slaves had completely died down and for the rest of the century, coffee, sugar, wax, ivory, copal, palm oil and natural rubber were exported in their place.

Finally, the development of Central Africa's major economic zones increased social oppression. All the trading zones favoured the growth of an aspect of production based on slave labour. It was not that slaves were not used for

12.5   *King Munza of Mangbetu in 1870*   **12.6**   *Kazembe in 1831*

12.7   *Kimbundu woman of the chiefly class with her slave-girl, in the 1850s*   **12.8**   *Kimbundu warrior with woman of the chiefly class, in the 1850s*

12.9   *Mid-nineteenth-century carved tusk from the Loango coast of Congo/Angola showing scenes from trade and Europeans*

production before the nineteenth century, but in the course of the century slave labour was on a much grander scale as goods produced by it were in high demand. Moreover, the use of domestic slaves led to agricultural expansion which in turn produced population growth in some of the communities of the region such as the Kongo, Ovimbundu and Ovambo. The use of slave labour was carried even into the Angolan colonial society. Although slavery was formally abolished in Angola in 1878, slave labour continued to boost its plantation economy. In fact, by 1880, brandy distilled from Angolan sugarcane was a very important item of trade with the Portuguese. As whites began to settle in the region, slave labour also rose higher in demand.

Portuguese imperialism in Angola

Having examined the major trading zones in Central Africa, and the nature of their relations with the world economy, we are in a better position to understand the history of foreign interests and activities in the region in the nineteenth century. In fact, it is possible to identify a number of stages in the expansion and contraction of Portuguese possessions in Angola in the course of the century. These contractions and expansions reflected the indecision of the Portuguese governors of the colony as to which particular policy to adopt in order to dominate the African trading economy. On the one hand was the idea of commercial domination with the aim of promoting free trade with the Africans; while, on the other hand, was the policy of total incorporation of the African colonies into the Portuguese economic system, in which case the colonies would be politically administered as 'provinces' of Portugal with a white settler community. This second alternative also involved the promotion of colonial traders at the expense of African middlemen. Due to the fact that the Portuguese could not decide on which of these two policies to adopt for the domination of African trade in Angola in the nineteenth century, there was an alternation of both policies. Other factors such as the economic situation of Portugal, the military resistance of the Africans, the personalities of Portuguese governors, and world economic developments also affected these fluctuations in the Portuguese imperial policy in Angola.

Portuguese imperialism in Angola started with the policy of total incorporation of African colonies. This was pursued until about 1860 when the Portuguese started to withdraw especially after suffering some military defeats from the Africans. By the early 1870s the withdrawal was complete. The colonial powers were on the coast only and African traders were rapidly gaining control of the trade. During the years between 1867 and 1873 Angola experienced a rapid growth in trade.

Soon after this, the Portuguese began to revive their policy of territorial expansion as other foreign powers began to show interest in Angola. The Portuguese began the construction of a railway from Luanda to the interior; they made several diplomatic agreements and also began to venture into the interior in their bid to remove the threat posed by new arrivals in Central Africa.

Society and power in Central Africa (1800–80)

There were two types of political system in Central Africa in the period under study. One was the hierarchical, well-defined structure based on the payment of tribute, the other was an informal type of government by a council of elders and notables. In practice, to varying extents, aspects of these two systems were to be found together in most communities. Whichever of the two predominated in individual societies depended on factors such as the nature of the environment, population density, type of economic activities, historical circumstances, and the personal considerations of the leaders.

There were several examples of societies with permanent hierarchical structures and with large populations at their capitals. But these were very few because certain – largely economic – factors had to be present before such a state could emerge. Among such factors were a strong agricultural sector, levying of taxes on the production of important commodities like salt, copper and iron, collection of tribute from conquered territories and from trade. The power of the chiefs depended on the economic sectors of the society; growth or decline in any of these sectors was bound to affect the power of the state. An important nineteenth-century development in these communities was the increase in the opportunities for social mobility whereby enterprising individuals could rise to positions hitherto held only by chiefs. The power of the chiefs increased, but the expansion of trade was often at the expense of the relative wealth of the rulers.

There were also ritual aspects of power as seen in the insignia of office and charms made against enemies expected from within and outside individual communities. However, the correlation between the extent of this ritual power and the decline of the economic and military fortunes of the societies is a matter requiring further research.

State-organized societies

One of the ancient kingdoms which continued into the nineteenth century was the Lunda state of Kalagne and it will serve as an example of a centrally organized state. It reached its peak in the first half of the nineteenth century and began to decline in the 1870s. The highest political title among the Lunda was Mwant Yav. One of the great rulers of Kalagne in the century was Mwant Yav Nawej (1820–52). He was ambitious, widely feared by the people, and he greatly increased the powers of his office. It was during his reign that firearms were introduced to the Lunda. He attempted to forge good relations with the Chokwe whom he allowed into his capital. Another important feature of Nawej's reign was the rapid increase in long-distance trade with the Imbangala, the Ovimbundu and the Mambari.

Despite the fact that long-distance trade thrived under his rule, Nawej had a bad reputation with the traders. After his death in 1852, he was succeeded by his brother Mulaj as the new Mwant Yav, but his rule was torn by internal

12.10 *A Chokwe carving of Chibinda Ilunga, the legendary founder of the Lunda empire. The carving is probably nineteenth-century.*

disputes. Things were brought to normalcy by the long reign of Muteba (1857–73). The peaceful atmosphere in this reign gave a real boost to trade.

As trade flourished in the reign of Mwant Yav Muteba, groups of Mbundu travellers were allowed to stay in his capital. One of such groups was that led by Lourenço Bezerra, known to the Lunda by the nickname Lufuma, who later became very influential in the Lunda court. This group introduced Mbundu agriculture and animal production into the region, and imported plants such as rice, maize and tobacco began to be cultivated on the farms. The Mbundu also served the Lunda state as craftsmen in various capacities. Thus, during the period 1800–80 trading activities in this area were controlled by Lunda rulers and Angolan businessmen who were bound to the region by marriage and other economic ties. In 1882, Lufuma and his group left Lundaland for the Malange region for good.

Meanwhile, the dispersion of the Chokwe from their villages into this region between the Tshikapa and Kasai rivers continued through the 1870s and gradually they were strong enough to overshadow the power of the Lunda chiefs. This decline of Lunda power was further aggravated by internal disputes. The Chokwe assisted a chief to seize power as Mwant Yav Mbumba. He continued to rely on the Chokwe to keep other Lunda out of power. Following a violent reign, he died in 1883 and the Chokwe seized the throne for one of Mbumba's sons who had been adopted and raised by a Chokwe family.

The chiefdoms and fragmentation of power

Apart from strong states like the Lunda state of Kalagne, there were other smaller units in the region under discussion. These small communities were, in some cases, the products of broken states and they were not subject to any common centre despite their cultural affinity. In other cases, where the states did not outrightly break up, there was always a tendency towards decentralization and fragmentation which resulted in the eclipse of the power of the chiefs.

An example of this process of fragmentation of power could be found in the region to the south of the Ovimbundu highlands in Angola where there previously existed important kingdoms which later disintegrated into large chiefdoms. One such was the Nyaneka kingdom of Mwila which dominated the region in the eighteenth century but broke up in the middle of the nineteenth century. Its successor chiefdoms became trading centres for wax, ivory and livestock, supplying the whole of southern Angola in the second half of the nineteenth century. Raids and plundering expeditions by adventurers contributed to the political break-up of the region.

Another example of this disintegration was the Luba 'empire' which covered a very vast area. At its peak in the first half of the nineteenth century powerful Luba states held sway over smaller chiefdoms. The penetration of the area by trading caravans from the Swahili area and Angola accelerated internal disputes in the land. By 1880, the Luba states and chiefdoms had become independent of one another and power was virtually decentralized.

12.11 *Mwant Yav Mbumba*

Adventurers, traders, condottieri: the new masters

A significant aspect of the nineteenth-century history of the region being examined was the appearance of new forms of power. In some areas, the role of chiefs became irrelevant while in others the expansion of trade had brought certain enterprising individuals or groups into the limelight as chiefs. Examples of this could be found throughout Central Africa. For example, in the rain forest of the central basin, several canoe-traders on the banks of the Zaire river became rich by the slave trade, accumulated arms and built up a commercial centre. The best known example of this was, of course, the rise of the kingdom of Msiri. The process started with trading expeditions from Tanzania to the Luapula valley and surrounding country. The traders were mainly attracted by ivory and copper which were plentiful in the region. In 1855, Ngelengwa Mwenda, a son of one of the traders, settled in the territory of Chief Katanga, a major centre of copper production.

Mwenda was able to command a large and well equipped army which facilitated his settlement in a chosen area. He attracted a lot of people to his base and intervened in the political disputes of the other chiefs in the region, playing one group against the other. By 1880, he had set up a state of his own with his capital at Bunkeya. He attracted many neighbouring groups into his kingdom and dispensed patronage to them at the capital. He also adopted the title of 'Msiri', meaning the owner of the land.

His kingdom was very active in the trading networks of the region. It disposed of goods from Zanzibar to Benguela and from the Luba country to Portuguese outposts in Mozambique or the Arabs on Lake Malawi. It was more or less a clearing depot. As a ruler, Msiri was not only benevolent, he was also ruthless – a typical product of his age.

Conclusion

From the foregoing discussion it is clear that conditions for the accumulation of wealth were altered in the nineteenth century as a result of the rise of more densely-populated areas, improvements in agricultural productivity and in the various crafts, and the rapid expansion of certain sectors of economic activity. Trade was developing according to prevailing circumstances and it contributed to the beginnings of social stratification in many of the societies.

Also in the course of the century, traditional political office came increasingly to adventurers who had either captured the trade and the economic base of the state, or created a new centre of power to replace the old. The position of the chief became very unstable in the century. Moreover, there were several chiefdoms without any territorial centralization of authority. However, fragmentation was not the predominant theme in Central African history between 1800 and 1880. Boundaries were no longer being defined by political or ethnic forces as before, but by economic forces as we have seen in the several economic zones in the region.

13

The renaissance of Egypt 1805–81

The Egyptian national movement

Contrary to views propagated by colonial historiography, the rise of Egyptian nationalism did not originate with the French Expedition led by Napoleon, or the British effort to dislodge the French. The Expedition was directed at British interests, but the Egyptians saw it as an invasion, and neither French revolutionary ideology nor the academic merits of French research later published in the monumental *Description of Egypt* had any appeal to the Egyptians of the time. While the lower classes – the 'retailers, street porters, craftsmen, donkey drivers, stable boys, pimps and prostitutes' – felt liberated, the notables and middle classes were subjected to all kinds of economic constraints due to the suspension of imports and exports.

The roots of Egyptian nationalism lie further back and the eighteenth century should be seen as the laboratory from which the new Egypt emerged. Three tendencies in the eighteenth century pointed in this direction. First were the reforms of people like 'Alī Bey al-Kabīr to reduce the number of feudal structures controlled by the Mamlūks in the delta of Lower Egypt. Then there was the revivalist movement in Islam led by Shaykh Ḥassan al-Attar; and thirdly, the rise in the cities of Cairo, Alexandria and others of a group of local notables, scholars and traders, deriving wealth mostly from the land, and willing to place their resources at the disposal of what came to be known as the 'national effort'.

All these converged with some other factors to produce the Egyptian national movement which had widespread influence. It led to the two Cairo revolts of 1798 and 1800 led by Egyptian notables. The evacuation of the French invasion force in 1801 provided the Egyptian national movement with the opportunity to strengthen itself and demand autonomy within the Ottoman empire. In other words, the Cairo revolts which weakened French positions strengthened the local leadership. However, the status of Egypt in 1805 was still that of a province of the Ottoman empire. The essential elements for the emergence of a strong state were present however, namely a central authority with an effective military force and a genuine mandate representing all the social classes in Egyptian society. What was lacking was strong and clear-sighted leadership that could manipulate circumstance and turn the tables in

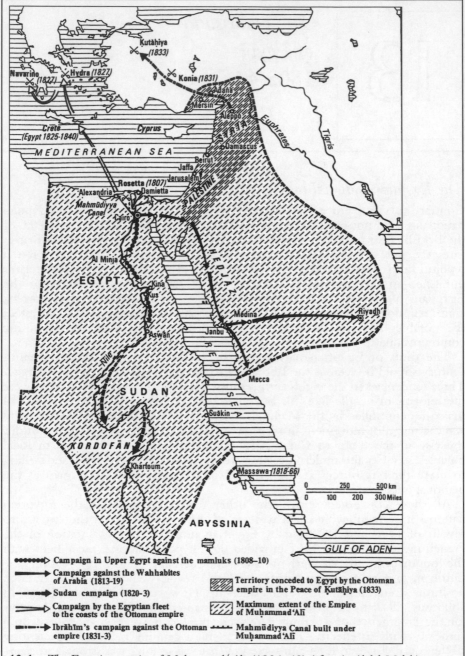

13.1   *The Egyptian empire of Muḥammad ʿAlī (1804–49) (after A. Abdel-Malek)*

Egypt's favour. All was thus set for a reawakening in Egypt when the leadership emerged.

Muḥammad ʿAlī and Ismāʿīl

The idea of an independent Egypt did not originate with Muḥammad ʿAlī either. Before he came to the scene, the 'Coptic Legion' of General YaʿḲūb's 'Independent Brothers' had already proclaimed it but their movement crumbled with the departure of the French Expedition and the removal of their leader. No doubt the French encouraged the idea of an independent Egypt in opposition to British supremacy. However, Muḥammad ʿAlī's idea of Egyptian independence was different from that of the Egyptians or the French. His aim was to build Egypt up militarily, economically, politically and culturally, and use it to supplant dying Turkey as a new Islamic empire. Thus the campaigns of ʿAlī and his son Ibrāhīm were geared to project Egypt not only as an African country, but also as an Islamic and Arab state.

After seizing power in Egypt, ʿAlī settled down to consolidate his own position and build up his power. In this respect, in 1807 he defeated the British who were involved in subversive acts against his authority. He then put an end to the Mamlūk influence in Upper Egypt especially as they were British allies. In 1811, he eliminated the leaders of the Mamlūk opposition who had constituted themselves into an obstacle to his political advance in Lower Egypt. Having removed the Mamlūks, ʿAlī embarked upon the building of the empire and the task of national revival.

It may be of interest at this point to examine Muḥammad ʿAlī's concept of Egyptian autonomy and how it fitted into his role in the Ottoman empire. He wanted Egypt to become an independent state while still remaining part of the Ottoman empire. In 1810, he secretly sought the help of France at the court of the Sultan to support his bid for autonomy, after which he approached the Sultan to grant Egypt an independent status within the empire. His military incursions into Arabia (1813–19) and the Sudan (1820–23), however, brought him into conflict with the British who felt threatened because he was penetrating their areas of influence. Indeed the growing power of Egypt was creating real concern in Britain. A rejuvenated Egypt within the Ottoman empire would soon take over and reinvigorate the Ottoman empire. This was not what Britain wanted.

This eventually led to military confrontation in 1827 between Britain and the Ottoman empire assisted by Egypt. The Egyptian fleet was destroyed in the encounter. Meanwhile, France had withdrawn its support of Egypt and Muḥammad ʿAlī had to seek the goodwill of the Ottoman Sultan for his plan of revival of the empire. This was refused by the Porte, resulting in a series of other events which eventually led to war between Turkey and Egypt. The early victories of the Egyptian army led by Ibrāhīm, Muḥammad's son, alarmed the European powers, who decided to save the Ottoman Sultan. This was because they knew that if Muḥammad ʿAlī was left alone to destroy the Ottoman empire and establish his own authority, their own colonial expansion would be

13.2 *Muḥammad ʿAlī (painting by Sir David Wilkie)*

13.3 *Ibrāhīm, Muḥammad ʿAlī's son and leading general*

opposed and the other provinces of the Ottoman empire would be revived and made more formidable under his leadership.

Moreover, Ibrāhīm had a different idea of Egyptian independence from that of his father. While Muḥammad ʿAlī conceived of Egyptian autonomy and influence initially within the Turkish empire, Ibrāhīm believed that Egypt's independence could only be meaningful if it supplanted the Turk and became the heart and head of an Arab empire. In fact, Ibrāhīm emphasized the importance of the Pan-Arab factor in the process of building up the power of Egypt, namely, that Egypt was to become the centre of an Arab revival. This idea, however, disappeared with Ibrāhīm after 1840.

Ismāʿīl (1863–79), who succeeded after the short reigns of al-Abbās and Saʿīd, saw the national problem in terms of independence and sovereignty. He devised a scheme of reducing Egypt's dependence on Turkey by negotiation, after which he would make it an autonomous state and then develop the institutions of self-government later. In other words, Ismāʿil felt a gradual approach to the issue of Egyptian independence would be more fruitful than forceful and sudden action. To secure his own position, he established a system of hereditary succession to the throne of Egypt, and also created the title of *Khedive* for himself. In addition, he assumed the right of promulgating administrative ordinances and of negotiating economic arrangements with foreign countries without the necessity of prior ratification by the Sultan. And in 1873, he defined Egypt as a 'state'.

In his governmental policies, Ismāʿil showed that he saw the importance of building a powerful independent state out of Egypt, as well as the necessity to seek international recognition for the nation through expansion in Africa like one of the rising European colonial powers. In fact, such expansion into the heart of Africa was opposed neither by Turkey nor Britain at the initial stage. The liberal press in Europe was actually full of praise for the infrastructural achievements of Egypt, namely, a war fleet of average strength, 18 forts, a good telephone and telegraph service and the beginnings of a railway that was planned to reach Khartoum and Suākin.

Moreover, the penetration of the Egyptian economy by foreign capital after 1840 was to curb Egypt's drive towards an independent economy. Indeed, the construction of the Suez Canal completed the integration of the Egyptian economy into the world system and led directly to the military occupation of 1882. Egypt was thus subjected to the fluctuations of the international economy from which it had earlier been isolated.

Another distortion in the Egyptian economy was created by uneven development. Lower Egypt (i.e. the north) was more developed than Upper Egypt (the south). This was because most of the arable land was found there due to the Nile Delta and this led to the growth of large towns. Alexandria and Cairo thus became important commercial centres with an indigenous ruling class made up of leading landowners, while Upper Egypt, having been marginalized, remained the hinterland.

Agriculture and land use

Since agriculture was tied to land use, the management of land became a crucial issue. Before the nineteenth century, land was managed by the *multazim* whose main task was to collect and transmit the revenues owed by their respective villages to the central treasury. However, the powers acquired by the *multazim* over land were such that stood in the way of Egypt's development as a modern, centralized state. To rectify the problem, Muḥammad ʿAli devised a policy of land allocation in which all the arable land in Egypt was divided into six categories which were given respectively to Muḥammad ʿAli's family and military officers; the Mamlūks; the *ʿulamāʾ*; foreign experts in Egypt; the *fallāḥin* (peasants); and the Beduins.

This policy of land allocation did not go down well with the people especially those whose land was seized by the state. However, Muḥammad ʿAli's land policy should rather be seen as a transition between feudalism and capitalism. In other words, it was a necessary step if Egypt was to move from a state of high dependence on land to that of capital and market forces. It was also during Muḥammad 'Alī's period that the development of large private estates began. These were introduced to facilitate administration and tax collection.

Muḥammad 'Alī also transformed the Egyptian agricultural economy from a subsistence level into a cash crop economy by intensifying the growing of cotton alongside the cultivation of cereals. Over thirty canals were dug to irrigate the state farms. However, the real significance of 'Alī's achievements in irrigation was not that he had the most impressive irrigation system in Egyptian history, but that he set about to modernize Egypt with a view to ensuring its independence from other countries.

The period 1840–79 marked the transition of Egypt from feudalism to a rudimentary capitalist economy which was predominantly agrarian. In fact, the policy of state ownership of land was to prepare the way for private ownership of land. In 1858 a law was passed which instituted the right to private ownership of land and by 1880 several individuals possessed large tracts of land.

The policy of using foreign loans to fund capital works began with 'Abbās who in 1851 raised a loan for the construction of the first railway in Egypt, to link Alexandria with Cairo. Under Ismā'īl, a number of capital projects were carried out in Cairo and Alexandria, such as the construction of canals, bridges, railways, coastal lighthouses, sugar refineries, telegraph lines and other municipal works.

The big landowners were the first social group to emerge as a class in the rural areas. These were people to whom Muḥammad 'Alī and later Ismāīl gave large tracts of land. They included high government dignitaries, military officers, some village notables, some Beduin chiefs, 'ulamā', and Copts. This group held 14.5 per cent of the cultivated land in 1863 which rose to 28.8 per cent by 1891. The remaining land outside the framework of the large farmholdings was 85.5 per cent in 1863 and 71.2 per cent in 1891.

The 'ulamās and shaykhs also enjoyed some prominence under Ismā'īl. Although the emergence of private ownership of land under Sa'īd had reduced their influence, Ismā'īl reinforced their authority. In fact, while 'Abbās and Sa'īd sought to reduce the power of these village dignitaries, Ismā'īl relied heavily on them for political support and gave them the opportunity to manoeuvre within the national political scene. This group was later to stand him in good stead during the 'Urābī revolution in 1882. But meanwhile some of the fallāḥīn were getting poorer while others in the society got wealthier.

Cultural development

In the quest for national renaissance, the issue of cultural development deserves attention. Some people thought that modernization of the economy, industrial and political processes must be accompanied by imitation of Western values,

13.4   _Shaykh Rifā-ʿa al-Ṭahṭāwī_

while others believed in promoting the emergence of an authentic philosophy of national culture. It should be noted here that while the state provided the driving force in this cultural development, the writings and ideas of Shaykh Rifāʿa al-Ṭahṭāwī (1801–73) were crucial to this process. He advocated the reconquest of Egyptian identity which he felt was necessary for the nationalist phase of development. This could only be possible if pursued within the framework of the nation. According to him, radical thought and a critical approach to foreign ideas and the national heritage would transform the fatherland and bring about the prosperity of the collectivity through freedom, work and positive ideas.

The duality of tradition and modernity was most glaring in the field of education, since two distinct systems of education existed in Egypt. The first was traditional and classical, based on Egypt's heritage. The second was modern and it was tailored to meet the requirement of the military state and the ongoing cultural revival. The advanced educational institutions of Muḥammad ʿAlī's time were extended and enforced by the national educational policy of Ismāʿīl. The Egyptian educational system was thus both modern and traditional in character; it had a traditional university of high academic standards and numerous scientific institutions with a curriculum based on modern scientific and humanist ideas.

Consequently, there developed an intellectual community in Egypt which in turn nourished a powerful press and publishing movement. In addition, Egypt served as a refuge for thinkers and writers from different parts of the Ottoman empire fleeing from persecution by the Porte. This provided new stimulus to the intellectual culture in Egypt and produced myriads of ideas and dynamic social and political movements. Egypt thus made an immense contribution to education and general enlightenment in the entire Arab and Islamic world. However, for the driving force of its political life, Egypt eventually replaced the concept of 'community of believers' with that of 'fatherland', thus representing the political effort made by Egypt to become independent of Turkey.

Placed in the wider context of the struggle of European states for colonial acquisition, Egypt now sought a way of legitimizing its own bid for independence and imperial designs. The solution was not to be found in a large scale imitation of the West under the guise of 'reform'. This was, in fact, denounced by the people for more viable solutions.

Geopolitics and compradors

The penetration into Egypt of European big business supported by the 'compradors' (local collaborators) of the time which was strongly resisted by ʿAbbās took root during the reign of his successors. Saʿīd (1854–63) granted the concession for the construction of the Suez Canal to Ferdinand de Lesseps, a foreigner, in 1854 and this marked the beginning of the penetration into Egypt of European big business capital. De Lesseps contracted a number of foreign loans to carry out the project and this further drew Egypt into the mainstream of the capitalist world economy. The situation was so bad that Saʿīd had to sell some of his estates for a paltry sum in order to ease his indebtedness.

Ismāʿīl, who succeeded Saʿīd, tried to reduce the financial burden imposed by the construction of the Suez Canal on Egypt. But other national undertakings such as the major drive to develop the national economy, the diplomatic missions and military operations outside Egypt, added enormously to Egypt's debt. As Egypt got deeper into debt, the terms of loans became harsher. Moreover, the reduction of land tax by 50 per cent in 1871 did nothing to help matters. Eventually, in 1875, in an attempt to get Egypt out of its economic mess, Ismāʿīl sold all Egypt's holdings (shares) in the canal to Britain for a ridiculously low price.

The foreign residents in Egypt were a mixed multitude which kept on increasing in number throughout the nineteenth century. By 1897, they were as many as 112 568. They were made up of Mediterraneans, Levantines, and Europeans. Some were gainfully and meaningfully employed while others not. They were to play an important role in the occupation of Egypt in 1882.

Towards the end of the nineteenth century, the control of the Egyptian economy gradually slipped from the hands of its nationals. The wholesale trade, imports and exports, moneylending and banks in Egypt, as well as retail trade, were all in the hands of foreigners. The craftsmen and artisans were also foreigners – Mediterraneans and Levantines. Thus by 1897, only 17 per cent of Egyptians as against 50 per cent of the foreign working population were engaged in industrial and business activities, whereas the majority of the indigenous working population (64 per cent) were working in the agricultural sector where there were 0.7 per cent of foreigners.

Land also slipped from the hands of Egyptian nationals. By 1918, each foreign landowner held as much as 400 *feddans* of land while leading Egyptian landowners could only boast an average of 150 *feddans* each. In terms of income the foreigners also earned much more than the Egyptians.

The Egyptian Revolution: 1881–2

While the Egyptian bourgeoisie rose to prominence after 1840 and the likes of Ṭahṭāwī and A. Mubārak engineered the establishment of a truly national culture, the Egyptian army became the most powerful in Africa. This army was to play a crucial role in supporting the forces that launched the revolution in Egypt. The rise of a powerful group called the 'Ḥilwān Group' led by 'Urābī provided the prelude to the revolution. The group imposed its demands on the nation and had its way in certain cases. It eventually metamorphosed into a national party in 1879 which allied with the country's most influential groups and leaned heavily on the army.

Following the forced abdication of Ismāʿīl in 1879, the party denounced the growing influence of European powers in Egypt. The national party, supported by the army, manipulated the new ruler Khedive Tawfik, and turned him into a puppet. Given this situation, the European powers decided to deal with the Egyptian question by military intervention. Thus in 1882 the British fleet bombarded Alexandria. This invasion led to the destruction of the Egyptian army. Seeing the manner in which some of the leaders of the revolution who were top military officers were either killed or exiled, a large number of local leaders crossed to the side of the occupation forces, denying the cause of the revolution.

Despite the fact that the Egyptian revolution failed in its immediate objectives, there were some achievements that could be attributed to that period. The first was the revival of Islamic thought. This was used to mobilize popular support for the revolutionary cause. The root of the national decadence that fuelled the revolutionary fervour was identified as being in the distortion of Islam. Any meaningful reform in the state was thus to be within the religious framework. This Islamic fundamentalism therefore played an important role not only in the political revival that led to the abortive revolution, but also in the social dimensions of the national revival.

Another important product of this period of Egyptian history was the rise of 'Abdallāh al-Nadīm (1843–96) who inculcated nationalist principles and ideas into the masses. He was able to rouse public opinion through his newspapers. Through his writings, he fuelled the national ideology which was then becoming radicalized and was a stimulus for patriotic revival. He thus became the spokesman for the *fallāhin* masses whom he later proclaimed as the controllers of the revolution.

The impact of Egypt

In conclusion, we must attempt to account for the Egyptian renaissance and its fading out.

The first thing to note when considering the turn of events in Egypt during the nineteenth century is the position of Egypt and the effects of this on its politics. In fact, a large number of the forces at play in the Egyptian situation had external roots which fuelled the renaissance. However, the inspiration for the awakening and the causes of its temporary collapse can be traced to internal factors. Egypt lacked a coherent system of social thought that could have guided its policies. There was a dichotomy between liberal modernism and Islamic fundamentalism which was not bridged until the middle of the twentieth century. This ideological disarray could not sustain the Egyptian renaissance.

Notwithstanding, the Egyptian revival had a far-flung impact. Some areas in Africa like Sudan, Ethiopia, the Horn of Africa and the Great Lakes region in Central Africa had a first-hand encounter with Egyptian imperialism which was hatched during the renaissance. The awakening of Egypt also threatened the 'world order' as it then existed, and the colonial powers found the solution to this threat in the dismemberment of Africa. The Egyptian experience also provided an object lesson for Japan in 1868 during its restoration in the Far East – that a prior condition for development is the preservation of national autonomy. In Turkey, the constitutional reforms effected by the *Tanẓimāts* was directly based on reforms earlier carried out in Egypt. Thus the Egyptian national renaissance which provoked some crises at home was to be a contributory factor in the resurgence of Africa, Asia and the Middle East in the nineteenth and twentieth centuries.

The Sudan in the nineteenth century

14

Introduction

The beginnings of Arab influence among the peoples of the eastern Sudan could be dated to the ninth century. By the early sixteenth century the area was controlled by two Muslim Sultanates: the Fundj and the Fūr. The Fūr Sultans ruled Dārfūr to the west till 1874 while the Fundj Sultanate based in Sennār was conquered in 1820–1 by Muḥammad 'Alī, the Pasha of Egypt. In fact, before Muḥammad 'Alī struck in 1820–1, the Fundj Sultanate had been torn apart by dynastic rivalries into weak and warring shaykhdoms. It was this instability and chaos that led the Fundj to fall easy prey to Muḥammad 'Alī and it remained a colony for the next sixty years.

It should be pointed out that when Muḥammad 'Alī conquered this portion of the Sudan, Egypt was still a province of the Ottoman empire and not a sovereign state. The conquest of the Sudan should thus be seen as a 'Turkish' rather than an 'Egyptian' affair. This was more so given the fact that the senior political and military officers in the conquered Sudan were not all true Egyptians but Turkish-speaking peoples. Muḥammad 'Alī was himself an Albanian officer of the Turkish army, but he identified himself with Egyptian aspirations. Egyptian elements in his army increased gradually, but a wide range of people were used in the administration of the Sudan, including Europeans. The Sudan was therefore a Turkish, rather than an Egyptian or even a Turco-Egyptian colony.

Three issues need to be considered here: the strategy of the conquest and the response of the northern Sudanese people; resistance to the imperial drive in the South 1840–80, and the role of the new regime in modernizing the Sudan.

Conquest and reaction in northern Sudan

In explaining the strategy of the Turkish invasion of the Sudan, one needs to exercise caution. Muḥammad 'Alī's primary objective in establishing his authority over the Sudan was not the welfare of the country and its people, neither was it borne out of a desire to safeguard the unity of the Nile Valley by keeping Egypt and the Sudan under one political umbrella as some writers have argued. Rather, his primary objective was the exploitation of the Sudanese

140

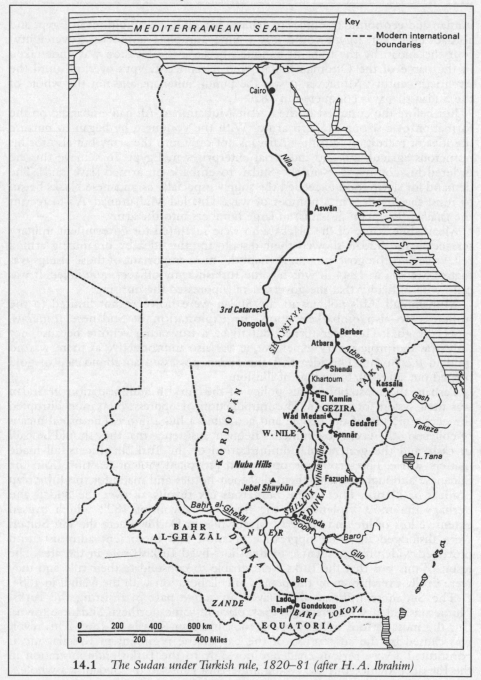

14.1 *The Sudan under Turkish rule, 1820–81 (after H. A. Ibrahim)*

human and economic resources to achieve his extensive ambitions in Egypt and abroad. However, Egypt could not assume complete authority (sovereignty) over the Sudan by the right of conquest because the invasion was undertaken in the name of the Ottoman Sultan who remained Egypt's overlord until the twentieth century. Moreover, it was the Fundj Sultanate, and not the whole of the Sudan that was conquered in 1820–1.

Just before the conquest of the Sudan, Muḥammad ʿAlī had embarked on the formation of a strong modern army. With the conquest, he began to nurture the idea of recruiting Sudanese Africans not only into the army but also for his numerous agricultural and industrial enterprises in Egypt. To achieve this, he ordered his commanders in the Sudan to embark on armed slave raids. The demand for slaves soon exceeded the supply, especially as Sudanese blacks began to resist the invaders in a number of ways. This led Muḥammad ʿAlī to recruit the *fallāḥin* (Egyptian peasants) in large numbers into the army.

Meanwhile, some of the blacks who were recruited for government military service in the Sudan showed their distaste for this idea by organizing armed revolts against the government. Perhaps the most important of those risings was that of Medani in 1844 in which some Turkish army officers were killed. It was only with difficulty that the government suppressed the uprising.

Muḥammad ʿAlī's policies in the Sudan were however not limited to the military. He also embarked upon the exploitation of Sudanese minerals, especially gold. This later turned out to be a frustrating venture because, not only was the project very expensive, it was also unproductive as there was no gold in the Sudan. The idea that the Sudan possessed an abundance of gold turned out, after all, to be a great illusion.

Perhaps the most obnoxious policy of the Turkish administration in Sudan was their system of taxation. The introduction of oppressive taxation disrupted the economic life of the people and generated a huge furore. The brutal means of collecting the taxes, government's frequent insistence that they should be paid in cash, and the general maladministration of the Turkish officers, all made matters worse. This economic oppression provoked violent reaction from the Sudanese although some of them fled their homes and made for the Ethiopian borders or Dārfūr. There were numerous tax revolts all over the Sudan and perhaps the most violent was the Sudanese revolt of 1822 which caused extensive loss of life and property. Meanwhile in Dārfūr where the Fūr Sultans were dislodged in 1874, oppressive taxation and inefficient administration provoked widespread resistance to the short-lived Turkish rule in the area. The result of this was that the Turks were unable to consolidate their rule and they were finally overthrown by the people in collaboration with the Mahdī in 1884.

The Sudanese military also played an active part in resisting the Turks. Numerous military insurrections took place in some northern Sudanese towns. But the most serious military revolt took place in Kassala in 1865. This revolt was caused by the suspension of the pay of the regiment in Kassala, and it constituted a very serious challenge not only to the Turkish administration in the Kassala province but also to the imperialist cause in the Sudan as a whole.

14.2   *Sennār in 1821: the capital of the Old Fundj Sultanate at the time of the Turco-Egyptian invasion*

14.3   *An encampment of Turco-Egyptian slave-raiders in the Kordofān*

The only success of Turkish imperialism was in the expansion of agriculture in the Sudan. They improved the irrigation systems, developed existing crops, introduced new ones and effectively fought plagues and pests. They also took great care of the livestock and taught the Sudanese the preservation of hides and skins. But the wealth derived from the expansion of agriculture was not meant to cater for the welfare of the Sudanese people. Instead, it was exported to Egypt as Muḥammad ʿAlī imposed a government monopoly on almost all Sudanese products and exports.

Resistance in the south, 1821–80

The nineteenth century, especially its second half, was a period of great material loss and chaos for the peoples of southern Sudan. They experienced a lot of miseries as a result of Turkish imperialism in the Sudan and they were victims of numerous wars, slavery and conquest. Wars of conquest and armed slave raids were waged against the people by Turkish and Egyptian colonial officers in the Sudan whose major objective, as noted above, was to collect tributes and slaves to swell the Egyptian army. These slave raids were not restricted to the north but also extended into the south. This led to a phenomenal rise in the volume of the slave trade which became big business after 1840.

European traders were also involved in this slave traffic. They initially participated in the Sudanese ivory trade but as profits on this fell, they decided to pay their Arab aides and guides in slaves rather than in cash, and this intensified the slave trade. During the mid-nineteenth century, Kaka in northern Shillukland developed as a major slave market and it received a lot of slaves from the south.

However, the southerners refused to cooperate with the slave traders and entirely resisted their presence in their land. There were many military confrontations between the two sides. The Bari people were the first to attack the invaders. In 1854, they attacked two European trading missions in their land and they killed a lot of people in the process. The Bari also attacked any of their own chiefs who showed signs of collaboration with the slave traders. Chief Nyagilo, for example, was hunted down and killed by a band of armed Bari youths in 1859 for collaborating with the traders. The Lokoya, another southern group, also killed some slave traders in 1860.

Perhaps the most notable case of resistance against the traffic in human lives was that of the Shilluk who repeatedly fought the traders in the White Nile. At first, the relations between the Shilluk and the immigrants who moved into Kaka from the Turkish-ruled north was cordial. But as trade in Kaka continued to be dominated by these foreigners, the Kaka king reacted by expelling many Arab traders from his kingdom in 1860. Some of the traders fought back destroying Fashoda, the royal capital of the Shilluk. The latter's reaction to this was equally devastating and brutal, and it led to protracted conflict between them and the Turkish government.

The Turkish government then decided to teach the Shilluk a lesson especially after its inability to defeat them in the 1868 military confrontation. The administration levied oppressive taxes and tributes on the Shilluk, and forcefully recruited them for the cultivation of cotton in the Fashoda area. The Shilluk answer to this was rebellion. In 1874–5 they took up arms against the government troops in their land and killed most of them. The Turkish government retaliated in 1876 by attacking the Shilluk and killing many of them. A large number of those remaining were conscripted into the army and sent to Cairo. Fashoda became a slave market where government troops sold captured Shilluks to a group from the north called the Jallāba. Thus the Shilluk population dwindled and the land became a shadow of its former self.

But not all southern groups had experiences as bitter as those of the Shilluk. The Jieṅ and Noath, for instance were able to protect themselves against slave raids by retreating into the inaccessible swamps from where they inflicted severe defeats on the invaders. The strong political system of the Zande also helped them to withstand the slavers' assaults. There were, however, some weak groups that could not put up a fierce resistance against the invaders. The people in such groups were either killed or enslaved in battle. This led to the decimation of a number of communities in the south.

Meanwhile, the accession of Ismāʿīl to the leadership of Egypt marked an intensification of Turkish incursion into the vast hinterland of the southern Sudan. Ismāʿīl's desire was to advance up the Nile and build for himself an African empire. He hoped by the imposition of his rule to establish orderly administration and end indiscriminate slave raiding. This attempt to annex Equatoria was under the command of two British officers: Samuel Baker, 1869–73 and Charles George Gordon 1874–6, as governors of Equatoria. Gordon was also governor-general of the Sudan 1877–9.

Their activities produced minimal results because of the recalcitrance of local groups. Baker could not secure the co-operation of Africans in the southern Sudan. He faced the hostility of the Bari and Lokoya peoples. He later moved to the Acholi area of northern Uganda where he established some government stations and recruited mercenaries into his government forces. In the west, he also met the opposition of the Kabarega, ruler of Bunyoro and he had to turn back in 1872.

The experience of Gordon was no better. He also encountered tough local opposition. Gordon faced the hostility of the Moogie Bari who killed many of his troops. His advance toward Buganda was also blocked as the Kabaka of Buganda, Mutesa, outmanoeuvred him and frustrated all his plans. All these brought the Turkish advance in Equatoria to a disastrous end.

During this same period, the Turkish advance in the south was threatened by the vast trading empire of al-Zubayr Raḥama Manṣūr in Baḥr al-Ghazāl. His influence and power led Ismāʿīl to acknowledge him as the governor of Baḥr al-Ghazāl and he was instrumental in the annexation of Dārfūr to the Turkish regime in 1874. But the Turks were not able to establish an effective rule in Baḥr al-Ghazāl after the fall of Zubayr. Eventually, in 1883 the local people cooperated with the Mahdist forces to throw off Turkish rule.

14.4   *A Zande minstrel*

While the advent of Turkish administration in the south brought an end to widespread indiscriminate slave raiding, it also resulted in a greater disruption of southern Sudanese society. The Turks employed force to suppress the numerous risings against their domination because the people refused to accept their rule. This eventually led to the crystallization of the resistance movement which ultimately succeeded in bringing Turkish rule in the region to an end.

Modernization and reaction

Despite the fact that the Turkish adventure in the Sudan was largely unsuccessful, there is general agreement that modern Sudanese history starts with the Turkish conquest of the country in 1820–1. In other words, Turkish rule made some significant contributions to the modernization of the Sudan.

In the first place, the Turkish regime united the Sudan in its present frontiers. Thus by the 1880s the Sudan comprised an immense block of territory which extended from the second cataract to the equatorial lakes, and from the Red Sea to Dārfūr. Turkish rule started the process of modernization in the Sudan by the introduction of European methods of political and economic organization, and techniques of production, communication and transportation. All these produced notable innovations and changes in Sudanese society.

The three most outstanding technical innovations introduced by the Turkish regime were firearms, steamships and the electric telegraph. Handguns had been introduced into the Sudan by the second half of the seventeenth century, but it was only during the period of Turkish rule that they were used on a large scale. By the 1860s and 1870s not only had the steamship been introduced into Sudanese waters, but a substantial fleet had also been established there. The electric telegraph was extended to the Sudan during the reign of Khedive Ismāʿīl.

Moreover, the expansion of Turkish influence to the south was greatly facilitated by firearms and steamers. These two inventions enabled the colonizers and their Sudanese collaborators to overcome the two principal obstacles to their push up the white Nile, namely, the stubborn resistance of the Sudanese and the immense barrier of the Sudd, which blocked the approach to both the Equatorial Nile and the Baḥr-al-Ghazāl.

The imperial expansion to the south led to the rise of a local group known as al-Jallāba. They were northerners who took the opportunity offered by the opening up of the south by imperial forces to rush there and make some economic gains. They originally went to the south as servants and armed guards of foreign merchants but they later became traders in their own right, thus acquiring increasing responsibility and power for themselves. Their activities in the south had a dual significance. On the one hand, they accelerated the process of Arabization and Islamization in the south while, on the other hand, they provoked a lot of hostility from the southerners through their frequent resort to violence and their overbearing attitude. This second aspect of their activities also succeeded in fuelling the distrust and fear that still dominate relations between the northern and southern parts of the Sudan.

14.5 *Turco-Egyptian administrative consolidation and modernization: the Ḥukumdār's palace at Khartoum with a paddle steamer on the river*

The Turkish regime also succeeded in establishing a centralized administration in the Sudan. No doubt the administrative machinery was oppressive, corrupt and incompetent, especially as the Turkish officials were of low quality, but it was highly centralized in contrast with the previous types of government that had obtained in the country. The administration was headed by a governor-general with the title *ḥukumdār*. Even some Sudanese who collaborated with the imperial regime were made responsible to the central government. During the brief periods when the governor-generalship was abolished, as in 1843 and 1882, Sudanese provinces were placed directly under a department in Cairo, in keeping with the policy of centralization. Moreover, improvements in communication such as the steamers and telegraph networks made an important contribution to centralization. The army was also an important instrument in the hands of government for the control of the Sudan. In other words, the Turkish administrators made use of the army and effective communications to maintain public security, repress the restive Sudanese and force the payment of taxes.

The changes produced by imperial rule also affected the religious life of the northern Sudanese. Though the Sudanese and the Turks were both Muslim, there were some denominational differences between them. While the Sunnite Islam of the Turkish administration tended towards the orthodox, the Ṣūfī Islam of the Sudanese was a bit more sectarian. The Turkish administration undermined the prestige of the leadership of the local Ṣūfī orders by promoting orthodox Islam and by establishing a rival group of religious leaders which was more orthodox and alien in outlook, and more directly dependent on government. This undermining of the prestige of the traditional religious leaders later made them oppose the imperial government and support the Mahdī's efforts to overthrow it.

Another aspect of Turkish imperial rule that produced a negative reaction from the people was the infiltration of the Sudan by foreigners. The employment of Europeans in governmental services and the army caused much offence where they stood in the way of the promotion of the Sudanese, and even of the Egyptians, to senior posts. There were also Europeans and Americans who came into the Sudan as travellers, missionaries, experts and consultants. Because of the alien language, customs and religion of these foreigners, their presence created tension among the Sudanese people to the extent that the people not only distrusted the foreigners but also feared them. There was, on the eve of the Mahdiyya a general feeling of being ruled by infidels and that Egypt had ceased to be an Islamic country. Thus the proclamation of the Mahdī, freeing the country from alien and Christian control, received enthusiastic support from the people.

Conclusion

The Turkish drive to exploit Sudanese resources, as well as the socio-economic and technological innovations which they introduced, created widespread discontent among the people. The uprisings and revolts that this provoked were, however, not powerful enough to overthrow the government because they lacked a revolutionary ideology. It was only in 1885 when the Mahdī provided this and massively mobilized the people that Turkish rule was brought down and the Sudan became independent. In the north, this period was marked also by confrontations with advancing British imperial rule.

However, in the south, slave raiding, plundering and pillage continued without any check. Plundering was even encouraged by the Mahdist government which raided the south for people to conscript into its army. All these activities presented the Arabs and Islam in a bad light before the southerners. What eventually emerged was the crystallization of a culture of resistance among the peoples of southern Sudan.

15

Ethiopia and Somalia

Ethiopia in the first decades of the century

The first few decades of the nineteenth century saw large-scale disorganization of political, economic and social life in Ethiopia. There was a loss of royal authority and the emperors held only nominal sovereignty. They were overshadowed by feudal lords who had become independent of them. Moreover, relations between the feudal lords were so tense that they were always fighting among themselves. The depredations caused by these wars were to lead to the impoverishment of several provinces. Even the province of Bagemder, in which the capital was situated, was not left out of this dislocation: agriculture was neglected as many peasants left their farms in the face of the general insecurity to seek their fortunes elsewhere. Gondar, the capital and prominent urban centre, was deserted and there was a drastic fall in the patronage of works of art.

On the whole, there was a major shift in the location of authority in the state. There was an uprising of regional warlords at the expense of imperial authority and this unleashed forces which caused some other dislocations in the economic and social structure of the society. This period in Ethiopian history has been described as the period of the *Masafent,* meaning 'judges', a spiritual reference to the time in the Book of Judges when 'there was no king in Israel: every man did that which was right in his own eyes'.

On account of this political disintegration, the Christian highlands which had hitherto constituted the core of the empire were divided into three independent states, viz., Tigré, Amhara and Shoa, with other smaller political units. Tigré was the northernmost and most powerful of the three states. It had a predominantly Christian population with some Muslim elements in the east and south. Because of its location near the coast, it was easy for its rulers to acquire wealth from trade and to procure more firearms than any of their neighbours.

During the first half of the nineteenth century, Tigré was ruled by powerful chiefs whose reigns were characterized by wars against their neighbours. Perhaps the most notable of them was Ras Walda Sellasé (1795–1816) who was known for his military prowess. Apart from demonstrating a high administrative

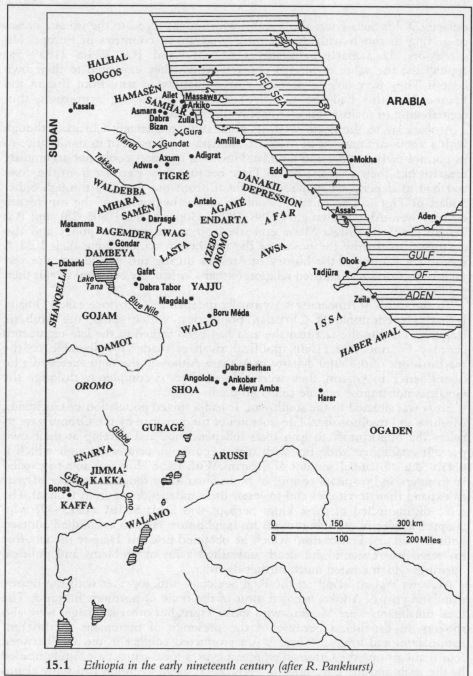

15.1 *Ethiopia in the early nineteenth century (after R. Pankhurst)*

capacity, Walda Sellasé was also a realist who sought access to the sea as a means of getting in touch with the technically advanced countries of Europe. His successors, Dajazmach Sabagadis (1822–31) and Ras Webé (1839–55) appreciated the value of foreign contacts which they exploited to their own benefit. They were able to procure a large quantity of arms from Britain and France. But this had the negative effect of promoting aggression, thus contributing to socio-political instability in the area.

Amhara lay to the north-west. Its population was largely Christian, though with a significant number of Muslims. Amhara owed much of its significance to its control of Bagemder and Gondar. However, its rulers could not accumulate firearms like their counterparts in Tigré because they were far from the coast and had to depend on supplies brought in from the Red Sea through either Sudan or Tigré. The rulers of Amhara at the beginning of the nineteenth century were Aligaz Gwangui (1788–1803), Gugsa Mersa (1803–25), and Ras Yeman (1825–8). Gugsa Mersa embarked on an expansionist policy and also attempted to destroy the power of the nobility by nationalizing their land. A prominent feature of the history of Amhara during this period was the way each of its rulers manipulated religion (either Christianity or Islam) to suit their political ends.

To the south of Amhara was a virtually independent province called Gojam. It had a predominantly Christian population which spoke the Amharic language. Despite the fact that the area had been united in the late-eighteenth century by one Ras Haylu, political rivalries made it vulnerable to the machinations of the Yajju dynasty in Amhara. Although the Yajju exercised a lot of influence in Gojam, they were able neither to completely dislodge the Gojames nor impose outside rulers on them.

Shoa was situated to the south-east. It had a mixed population of Christians, Muslims and traditionalists. The isolation of the province by the Oromo gave its rulers the opportunity to gain their independence and develop at their own pace. It established wide ties with major economic centres through which it obtained a substantial amount of firearms. With these Shoa was able to expand its frontiers and maintain control of trade. Shoa kings fought a number of wars to expand their territories and to wrest their independence from Gondar. The most distinguished of these kings perhaps was Sahla Sellasé (1813–47) who adopted a tolerant attitude towards his neighbours. He also established contacts with Britain and France from which he obtained firearms. Despite the fact that his reign was peaceful, his death unleashed a lot of problems and political uprisings which created much further disorder.

Massawa was an island off the Red Sea coast and, together with the nearby mainland port of Arkiko, handled most of the trade of northern Ethiopia. The local inhabitants were Muslims who spoke Tigré, but other languages were also spoken on the island because of the presence of merchants of different nationalities and tongues. There was a protracted conflict in the area between four main groups: the Ottoman empire, Egypt, a local aristocratic family headed by the na'ib, and the governors of Tigré. Each of these groups had some claims

15.2   *Dajazmach Webé of Tigré*

to the port, and the history of the port during the first half of the nineteenth century was full of conflicts and tensions between these four rival parties. While the na'ib's authority on the port was strongly threatened by the rulers of Tigré and Egypt, Tigré actually went a step further by soliciting for foreign help in order to acquire the land from both the na'ib and the Egyptians because it considered the port indispensable for access to the sea. The Egyptians established their authority over Massawa in 1846 after the ruler of Tigré had made several unsuccessful attempts to capture it. However, the mainland port of Arkiko suffered great devastation from the successive attacks of Egypt and Tigré.

The Afar Lowlands, located to the south-east of Massawa, were occupied by a Kushitic-speaking nomadic people. At the beginning of the nineteenth century these people were ruled by the Sultanate of Awsa. The death of the Sultan around 1810 however brought confusion to the area as the southern Adoimara, who had been enemies of the sultanate, sacked Awsa and forced the Sultan's successor to share power with them. Moreover, their growing strength was reinforced by the emergence of the port of Tadjūra and the increasing importance of trade with Shoa. With the British occupation of Aden in 1839, the Danakil coast began to acquire international interest. British and French officials subsequently began to make commercial deals with the different local chiefs.

The Somali and the Horn of Africa

To the east were the Muslim Somali who inhabited the desert lowlands on the Gulf of Aden. They spoke a Kushitic language and had long been under Arab influence. Zeila was controlled by the Arabs while the rest of the coastal strip, including Berbera, was claimed by the nomadic Somali. During the first half of the nineteenth century, the Egyptians began to encroach on Berbera. Their withdrawal from the area in 1841 led to the rise of an ambitious Somali merchant, Hadjdjī 'Alī Shermerki, to political prominence. He bought the governorship of Zeila and also seized Berbera but he later came into conflict with the ruler of Harar which eventually led to his downfall.

The coast from Bender Ziada on the Gulf of Aden to Illig on the Indian Ocean was controlled by the Majerteyn sultanate. This sultanate comprised semi-nomadic people who derived their revenue from the export of incense and aromatic wood and from seafaring. By the nineteenth century the Sultan had nominal authority over the hinterland peoples. He signed a treaty in 1839 with the British at Aden in which he got an annual stipend from them in return for protecting the lives and property of British seamen shipwrecked off his coast.

Power in the Benadir was shared between the Sultan of Geledi, who controlled a vast section of the interior, and the Zanzibari authorities. In the 1830s a *djihād* was launched by some reformers at Bardera against the peoples of southern Somalia. The response of the Geledi Sultan to this in 1843 was a massive expedition against the reformers which led to the sack of Bardera. This made the Sultan of Geledi the most powerful leader in southern Somalia. Meanwhile, the last great wave of Somali migration which began at the turn of the century brought nomads towards the Juba river and beyond, where they came into conflict with the Oromo whom they ultimately pushed towards the Tana river.

Harar was a Muslim city located on the hinterland of the Somali coast. Its inhabitants spoke Adare, a Semitic language not known elsewhere. For several centuries, the town had been an independent state ruled by an *amīr*. It coined its own money and did a flourishing trade in coffee, saffron, hides and skins, ivory and slaves, *chat* (a narcotic leaf), textiles and other imported goods. It was a centre of trade for neighbouring groups such as the Shoa, Arussi, Guragé and the Ogaden. Harer was also a centre of Islamic scholarship with its many mosques and Muslim shrines and it exerted religious and cultural influence on its neighbours.

By the early nineteenth century, the city was torn by internal strife but its adroit *amīr*, Aḥmād ibn Muḥammad (1794–1821) was able to keep it together and hold its enemies, especially the Oromo, at bay. However, things fell apart after his death, and the Oromo took advantage of the internal strife within the town to seize Harari land and encroach upon their territories. The town itself would have been taken but for the strength of its walls, its handful of artillery and small band of gunmen.

The Guragé region was also located in the interior. Its inhabitants spoke a Semitic language and were divided into Muslims and Christians. By the early nineteenth century the area was no longer ruled by a local dynasty but by seven independent houses whose lack of unity made them an easy prey to slave raiders, and led to their annexation by the ruler of Shoa.

The kingdom of Kaffa lay to the south-west of the Ethiopian region. Its population spoke its own Katicho language. The area was a source of valuable exports which included civet, ivory, slaves and coffee. In the eighteenth century the Kaffa kingdom had been encroaching on the territories of its neighbours such that by 1820 its king Hotti Gaotscho, ruled northwards and eastwards as far as the Gibbe and Omo rivers.

The Oromo were to be found in the region south of the Blue Nile. Early in the nineteenth century they were experiencing political change. The old system of government by rotating age-groups was challenged by rich and powerful military leaders who began to claim the right to establish dynasties which they in fact did. Three Oromo dynasties thus emerged in the first decades of the century: Enarya, Goma and Guma. Enarya, the most powerful, was ruled by Bofu who embraced Islam in order to strengthen his power. His successor, Abba Bagibo (1825–61) built up his own power by forging dynastic alliances with neighbouring ruling houses and by obtaining guns from Gojam. Trade flourished during his time and the kingdom became rich and powerful. However, his death was followed by the rapid decline of the kingdom.

15.3   *King Sahla Sellasé of Shoa*

15.4   *Amīr Aḥmād ibn Muḥammad of Harar, 1794–1821*

A few years after the emergence of Enarya, some other kingdoms sprang up in the south. The most enduring of such states was Jimma–Kakka which was founded by Abba Magal. His military tradition was continued by his sons who also effected political and administrative innovations as well as spreading Islam in the provinces.

So far, we have examined a number of states and polities, each independent in its own right. There were, however, inter-relationships among them especially along commercial lines. While ethnic and linguistic differences were maintained, there was much cultural exchange which bred bilingualism in some trading communities.

The unifying efforts of Emperor Téwodros II

The second half of the nineteenth century saw two notable attempts at reunification in Ethiopia. The first was made by Dajazmach Kassa Heyku who later became Emperor Téwodros II, or Theodore of Ethiopia.

Kassa was born in 1820 to a chief of Qwara, a community located on the borders of the Sudan. He was brought up in a monastery and he later became a freelance soldier. He made himself master of Qwara and assumed the title of Dajazmach. As his power grew, he rebelled against the Yajju ruler of Bagemdar a couple of times before eventually defeating him in 1853 in a military encounter in which the ruler of Tigré had also been brought in to aid the Yajju. This defeat marked the end of the Yajju dynasty and closed the era of the *Masafent*. Kassa also subdued the rulers of Gojam and Tigré thus removing his main rivals in northern Ethiopia. He then had himself crowned as Emperor and chose Téwodros as his throne name.

Emperor Téwodros set himself the task of unifying the diverse provinces of Ethiopia. After his coronation, he marched into Wallo and seized the natural mountain fortress of Magdala which he later made his capital. He also conquered Shoa and took Menelik, the king's son, as hostage.

As part of his reforms he decided to reorganize his army – the only effective means through which he could control the country was to build a well-equipped army of professional soldiers. He made use of some Turks and a British adventurer, John Bell to discipline this army. He also introduced the idea of regular pay to his army. He divided his soldiers into regiments each of which comprised men from several provinces, thus striking a blow against the feudal system, under which men gathered round the chief of their native district. He established granaries for the army and ordered his soldiers to purchase their food instead of raiding the peasants. He also increased his firepower by compelling missionaries and other foreign craftsmen to manufacture guns, cannons, mortars, and bombshells for the use of his army. He embarked on a road construction project in order to facilitate the rapid movement of troops. The roads were to link Dabra Tabor with Gondar, Gojam and Magdala.

Téwodros also attempted some economic reforms. He put an end to oppressive commercial levies and ordered that duties be levied only at three

15.5 *Emperor Téwodros inspecting road-building*

15.6   *Emperor Téwodros's great cannon 'Sebastopol'*

places in his dominions. He also restored peace and safety on the trade routes.

In the field of politics, he suppressed the power of the feudal chiefs. He placed the army of the provincial lords under the command of his own followers and not that of the provincial chiefs. In order to pacify the war-torn land, he proclaimed that the people should return to their vocations. His social reforms included the abolition of the slave trade and the eradication of banditry and bribery. He attempted to eliminate religious differences by ordering the Muslims in his dominions to become Christians and by expelling Roman Catholics. The most problematic of his reforms were the church reforms. He attempted to reduce the number of clergy, to curtail church land and make the priests dependent on state salaries. All these provoked a lot of opposition from the clergy and, coupled with the hostility of the provincial nobles, a substantial portion of the population was turned against the emperor and this contributed to his downfall.

Téwodros had a tough time battling with provincial opposition. The first challenge came from Tigré, with Agaw Negusé leading the rebellion. He ceded the port of Zulla to the French and offered to accept a Roman Catholic bishop as *abuna* of the Ethiopian Church. But because of British opposition, Negusé did not receive the expected support from the French and he was routed in 1860. Next came a series of rebellions in the latter years of his reign from nobles in Wallo, Shoa, Gojam and Gondar. In 1865 Menelik, heir to the throne of Shoa, escaped from Magdala and proclaimed himself an independent sovereign. Faced with these problems, Téwodros became more and more violent and temperamental; he sacked Gondar and Dambeya and executed several people.

Conflict with Britain

Téwodros's reign as emperor of Ethiopia ended with a dispute with Britain. The need for technical assistance from Europe made him write to Queen Victoria of England in 1862, proposing to send her ambassadors. The British government ignored his letter because it was not anxious at the time to get involved in Ethiopian affairs. Téwodros became impatient as time passed and his letter remained unanswered. It irritated him that the British government showed no interest in Ethiopia. A number of other events served to confirm his fears that the British were not ready to help. The report from the head of the Ethiopian Convent in Jerusalem that the British had not been helpful when Egyptian Coptic priests attempted to seize the convent did not help matters. Téwodros felt slighted by the British attitude and, in a fit of rage, he imprisoned the British representative, Consul Cameron and his party.

News of Cameron's imprisonment alarmed the British government and Téwodros's long-forgotten letter was immediately replied to. This made him release Cameron but he soon detained another set of Europeans in Ethiopia. His insistent demand for technical assistance from Britain; the tactlessness of some of the Europeans in Ethiopia; some incidental occurrences, such as a report which came to the emperor's notice that a British company was to construct a railway in the Sudan to assist in the invasion of Ethiopia, brought relations between Téwodros and the British government to a head.

Meanwhile, things were not going well at home for Téwodros. His power had sharply declined and his empire was on the verge of collapse. The British knew this and they decided on a military confrontation with him in 1867 in order to release the people he had imprisoned. The British force, led by Sir Robert Napier, inflicted heavy casualties on Téwodros's men whose artillery was not effectively used. Appreciating his helplessness in the face of continued British assault, Téwodros killed himself, thus forestalling any humiliation to which the British could subject him.

Though the captives had been released and the objective of the expedition accomplished, the British destroyed Magdala fortress and most of its cannons and took away Téwodros's young son and some Ethiopian manuscripts. They rewarded the ruler of Tigré with a gift of some arms for his co-operation with them.

Meanwhile, the second half of the nineteenth century was witnessing increasing French interest in the port of Obok. In 1856 the French Consul in Aden purchased the port but this did not lead to any effective operation. A new treaty was signed in 1862 according to which four Afar chiefs ceded the territory to France for a substantial amount of money. In 1869, an Italian

15.7 *Emperor Téwodros committing suicide in front of Sir Robert Napier (a modern interpretation)*

missionary also purchased the port of Assab on behalf of the Italian ministry of Marine from some Afar chiefs.

Emperor Yohannes and the forging of Ethiopian unity

Ethiopia became divided again after the death of Téwodros. Of the three personalities that held power in this period, Kassa of Tigré was the most powerful and, after defeating the ruler of Amhara, he was crowned as Emperor Yohannes IV at Axum in January 1872.

In order to succeed in the task of national unification, Yohannes adopted a more conciliatory policy towards the nobles. As part of his religious reforms, he

15.8   *Emperor Yohannes IV*

befriended the clergy and obtained an *abuna* from Egypt. He also sent funds to the Ethiopian community in Jerusalem. He built many new churches, for example at Adwa and Magdala. He gave extensive land to the church at Axum and renewed a grant to the monastery of Dabra Bizan. In addition, he attempted the mass baptism of Muslims and persecuted Roman Catholic missionaries. He tried to purify religious practices by forbidding the practice of witchcraft and prohibiting smoking and the taking of snuff.

Yohannes's major military confrontations were with Egypt because of Egyptian incursions into his domains. After asking Britain for assistance against Egypt without any response, he gathered his forces together in 1875. During the encounter, the Egyptian invaders were almost wiped out. A counter-attack by Egypt in 1876 was also severely defeated. The Ethiopian victories not only destroyed Egyptian dreams of empire, they also caused much embarrassment for Khedive Ismā'īl at home. These problems were to eventually lead to his deposition in June 1879.

Ethiopia, though the victor, also suffered from the fighting. Some territories were deserted and vast areas were devastated. However, the victories over Egypt boosted the prestige of Ethiopia and Yohannes became the first well-armed ruler of his country, having obtained significant quantities of arms from the Egyptian campaigns. As part of his efforts at national unification, Yohannes entered into a peaceful settlement with Menelik of Shoa. They discussed religious controversies in the country and decided to work together to make Ethiopia a thoroughly Christianized country. Meanwhile, peace talks initiated by Egypt were inconclusive as Yohannes refused to reconcile with Egypt, a Muslim state that refused to give up Massawa, Ethiopia's only access to the sea.

Taken together, the achievements of Yohannes as emperor of Ethiopia were many and significant. He established peace in Ethiopia by dealing with the Egyptian menace and by creating unity at home. But this peace was shattered by future events such as the Mahdist Revolt of 1881, the Italian seizure of Massawa in 1885 and the outbreak of epidemic and famine toward the end of the nineteenth century.

Conclusion

The dominion of Yohannes, although the most powerful in the area and the only one significantly involved in international relations, embraced only a fraction of the territory covered by this chapter. The empire which was based in Tigré covered virtually the entire Christian highlands. Gojam, Shoa and Wallo recognized his imperial authority. The Sultanate of Awsa to the east was independent, while the lowlands to the north-east and north-west of Tigré were under the control of the Egyptians. The lands to the west, south and east such as the region of Guragé, the Oromo states and others also maintained a separate political existence.

Harar to the south-east was under the occupation of Egypt though Menelik later gained control of the town. The Somali coasts along the Gulf of Aden which were under Egyptian domination were later to pass into the hands of Britain, France and Italy. The remaining Somali ports under Oman later passed into the hands of Italy. However, foreign influence in the Somali region was limited to the coast.

16

Madagascar
1800–80

Introduction

Nineteenth-century Madagascar comprised some eighteen ethnic groups of which the largest and most important were the Merina who inhabited the central plateau of the island. This group constituted only a sixth of the entire population of Madagascar but they ruled the greater part of the island before it was colonized by the French. The fact that all Malagasy groups spoke the same language and shared similar customs and traditions forged a cultural and ethnic unity among them, making them basically one people.

The Merina established their seat of government in Antananarivo from where they extended their authority to other parts of the island. This discussion of the socio-economic history of Madagascar in the nineteenth century, therefore, focuses mainly on the history of the Merina of the central plateau because by 1880 they were in control of over two-thirds of the entire island.

In this context we shall examine two major trends which characterized the history of Madagascar between 1800 and 1880. One was the political evolution of the country and the diplomatic relations between the evolving state and foreign powers, especially France and Britain. This political evolution consisted mainly of the consolidation of the Merina authority and its expansion to the rest of the island while its diplomatic relations with other powers served as a cornerstone of the country's development. The other trend had to do with major changes in the administrative and social organization of the country which facilitated economic development. The process of social reorganization also had to do with modernization, a crucial feature of which was the embracing of foreign religion.

The era of Andrianampoinimerina 1792–1810

An examination of how Andrianampoinimerina, the founder of the Merina kingdom, came to power and consolidated his position on the central plateau is crucial to an understanding of the history of Madagascar in the nineteenth century. About 1785, Andrianampoinimerina proclaimed himself king of one of the warring kingdoms in central Imerina after overthrowing the previous ruler. Using diplomatic and military means, he went ahead to incorporate other

164

neighbouring polities into his own political orbit. In 1792 he moved his capital to Antananarivo where he began to build the political and social structures of the new kingdom. After 1800 he embarked on the policy of conquering the other states on the islands with a view to uniting all the eighteen ethnic groups. In this task, he faced serious opposition from some other groups on the island such as the Sakalava, the Bezanozano and the Ambongo. Nevertheless, by the time of his death in 1810, Andrianampoinimerina had made Imerina probably the most powerful kingdom on the island of Madagascar.

The great modernizer: King Radama I (1810–28)

King Radama succeeded to the throne in 1810 at the age of eighteen. His immediate task on accession was to subdue revolting groups in the kingdom. He thus succeeded in consolidating his position in Imerina. His most remarkable achievement, however, was in the area of territorial expansion. He sought a direct access to the sea in order to facilitate trade with Europeans and expand the Merina political influence.

Radama's desire to get to the coast, especially to the important port of Tamatave which was then controlled by a powerful chieftain dictated his diplomatic contacts with the governor of Mauritius, Sir R. T. Farquhar. Incidentally, Farquhar was also interested in extending British control to Madagascar or at least to influence events on the island. This gave rise to many treaties between Radama and the British authorities represented by the governor of Mauritius. As a result of these treaties, a British presence was established in Madagascar in 1820 with the appointment of James Hastie as the British resident on the island.

The diplomatic agreements between Radama and the British also encouraged missionary activities on the island. The London Missionary Society (LMS) arrived in Antananarivo in 1820 and they made significant contributions to Madagascar in the field of education and technical assistance. They opened the first school in 1820 with three pupils and, with the support of Radama, by 1829 there were 23 schools with 2 300 pupils. The missionaries translated the Bible into the Malagasy language which they had already reduced to writing. Thus the development of education not only helped the spread of Christianity and literacy but also facilitated the evolution of the Malagasy language and literature as an instrument of national integration on the island.

In addition, the missionaries sent young Malagasy to England or Mauritius for technical education. They also introduced many technical skills like carpentry, building, tannery, tin-plating and weaving to Madagascar. One of the missionaries, James Cameron, greatly assisted the Malagasy in technical education. The wives of the missionaries were not left out of this drive. They gave useful instructions on housekeeping to the local households and also served as dressmakers and designers to aristocratic ladies.

The most important technical assistance that Radama got was in the task of building a standing army. The British helped him to train his army based on

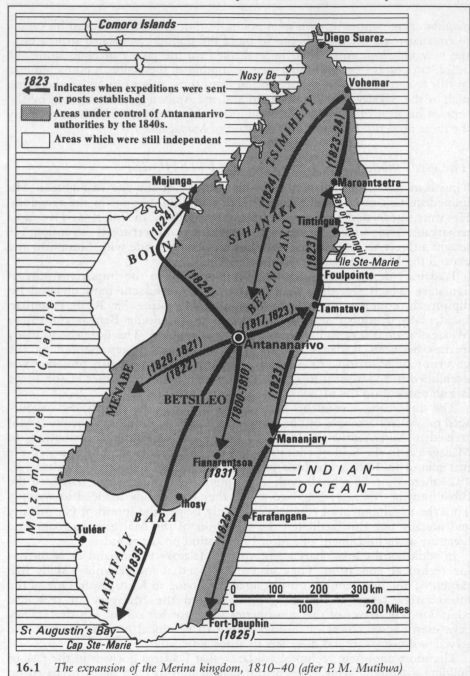

16.1   *The expansion of the Merina kingdom, 1810–40 (after P. M. Mutibwa)*

the English model. They also assisted him in procuring guns for the use of the army. The result of this was that Radama's army became the best on the island in terms of discipline and weapons, and this greatly facilitated his expansionist plans. The army was not only used to conquer other territories but also to maintain law and order in the conquered areas. By 1825 Radama had subdued the whole of the eastern coast of Madagascar from Vohemar to Fort Dauphin. He also made extensive conquests in the west, but there the Sakalava remained a difficult nut to crack. Despite this, Radama was able to extend Merina authority over most of the island by 1823. Even though his authority on the island was strictly-speaking not complete, there was no effective challenge to his title as king of Madagascar. He died in 1828 at the age of 36.

Ranavalona I (1828–61): reaction or stabilization?

Queen Ranavalona I was the cousin and first wife of Radama I. Because she was helped to the throne by the nobles and army chiefs whom Radama had removed from influential positions in his drive for modernization, her advisers were men who opposed the main policies of the late king. The thrust of Ranavalona's policies was to safeguard Madagascar's independence from foreign influence particularly as this affected national institutions, traditions and customs. In terms of foreign policy, she was bent on disengaging the country from British influence particularly in the political and religious fields

In the religious field, Malagasy leaders tried to ban Christianity which had been spreading since the period of Radama. They discovered that the religion was undermining their traditional institutions, especially the monarchy. It shook the foundations of royal power by discouraging the worship of the royal divinity believed to be responsible for the well-being of the state. Its principles of equality also contracted the traditional social divisions. All these led the Queen to take serious measures against the spread of Christianity and by 1835 the religion was officially banned. Christians were severely persecuted with some people dying as martyrs; but rather than being completely eradicated, the religion went underground. This was indeed a dark period for Christianity in Madagascar.

In pursuit of these policies, Ranavalona asked the British Resident to leave Madagascar in 1828. She also removed all British nationals holding significant positions in the country. In addition, she nullified all previous treaties with Britain. But when Malagasy leaders later realized that the country needed contact with the outside world to secure European manufactured goods such as guns, ammunition and other luxury goods, they sent a delegation in 1836 to conclude treaties of amity with Britain and France. It was the failure of this diplomatic mission, followed by the Anglo-French attack on Tamatave in 1845 which led Queen Ranavalona to expel all foreign traders and suspend overseas trade, especially the export of beef and rice to Mauritius and Réunion.

The severance of foreign commercial dealings, except with the USA, bred a culture of self-reliance among the Malagasy. They continued to promote

16.2 *Andrianampoinimerina, d. 1810*

16.3 *King Radama I, 1810–28*

16.4 *Queen Ranavalona I, 1828–61*

16.5 *King Radama II, 1861–3*

16.6 *Queen Rasoherina, 1863–8*

16.7 *Queen Ranavalona II, 1868–83*

Western education and used foreign nationals like the American William Marks and the French de Lastelle and Jean Laborde, especially Laborde, to establish industries to produce the essential goods which they could no longer import from outside. In this respect, several industrial ventures were embarked upon such as sugar plantations and a factory, and an industrial complex which produced various goods ranging from guns and cannon to glass, rum and soap.

Queen Ranavalona continued the expansion which Radama I had begun and consolidated her administration in the conquered territories. The Sakalava, however, continued to resist her authority. When government forces eventually defeated the Sakalava chiefs, they fled with their people to some neighbouring islands from where they placed themselves under French protection. This later formed the basis of France's claims to the western territories of Madagascar.

The last decade of Queen Ranavalona's reign witnessed a radical change in Malagasy policies. This was due to the death in 1852 of Rainiharo who had been at the head of the government since 1830, and the rise of some younger men in Malagasy politics who did not share the conservatism of the Queen's past advisers. The most prominent of these younger men were both sons of Rainiharo. The elder, Rainilahiarivony later became the virtual ruler from 1864–96, while his younger brother was the head of the army. They also included Rakoto Radama, the Crown Prince. They were very pro-European in their outlook and they ensured a re-orientation of Ranavalona's policies. The ban on trade between Madagascar and the islands of Réunion and Mauritius was lifted in 1853. Christian missionaries were readmitted into the country in 1856. Then in 1857 there was a coup attempt to overthrow the Queen in which the Crown Prince was an accomplice, but it was foiled.

Ranavalona died in 1861 after having proclaimed Rakoto Radama as her successor. Her reign can be described in two ways. On the one hand, it was a reign of terror for missionaries and many of the peoples brought under Merina authority. On the other hand, it was a period of considerable industrial development and one in which European education took root and the country was launched on the path of modernization. On the whole, Ranavalona was a symbol of Malagasy nationalism to many of her subjects.

The open-door policy: King Radama II, 1861–3

The activities of King Radama II were geared towards the reversal of all the anti-European policies of his predecessor. This attitude provoked a lot of opposition against his reign from the leading men in the country and this eventually led to his fall.

Radama's ambition was to modernize his country by attracting foreign traders, investors and missionaries. To this end, he recalled all exiled Malagasy Christians and as a result other European missionaries also began to troop into Madagascar. Both the Roman Catholic Mission and the London Missionary Society arrived in the capital and began their operations. The king also

16.8 *The Queen's palace in Antananarivo begun in 1839 by Jean Laborde at the request of Queen Ranavalona I*

re-established diplomatic links with Britain and France both of which appointed consuls to Madagascar.

Problems started, however, when Radama contracted many treaties of friendship and commerce with these European powers in which he gave them many concessions and privileges. Malagasy officials were dismayed and threatened by such actions. The king's policy of signing secret treaties without the knowledge of his officials increased the latter's suspicions. Moreover, the increasing influence of missionaries and other Europeans at the royal court did not help matters. The king was relying more and more on these foreigners in the running of government as could be seen in his appointment of an American and a Frenchman as secretaries of state for foreign affairs in 1862.

The last straw was his attempt to remove some of the principal officers of state who had been the backbone of the government and replace them with his friends of younger days. This brought into focus all the accumulated grievances against the king and on 12 May 1863 he was assassinated.

Madagascar's policies reviewed, 1863–8

After the death of Radama II, the effective government of Madagascar passed into the hands of the leading officials of the administration, who enthroned Queen Rasoherina as a puppet ruler. These men were not against the modernization of the country, neither were they anti-European. But their foreign policy was tailored to reflect the independence of their country, and they believed that modernization should not be pursued at the expense of Malagasy traditions. Thus the new government set out to make significant modifications in Radama's policies.

They cancelled all commercial concessions previously granted to European nationals by Radama. They also embarked on the revision of the treaties with France and Britain in order to remove the excessive privileges such as ownership of land and exemption from customs duties granted to European traders in Madagascar. This did not stop foreign nationals who wanted to come and assist in development projects in their country from doing so, neither did it drive missionaries away although their activities were restricted to certain towns. The Malagasy government however encountered problems mostly from foreign countries in the implementation of some of these policies.

Britain and France reacted differently to the overthrow of Radama and the proposed changes in Malagasy foreign policy. While Britain refused to be drawn into a quarrel with Madagascar because of the proposed revision of the treaties between the two countries, France was hostile and deeply hurt by the Malagasy line of action. France certainly knew that it would lose a lot if the existing treaties were revised, so it insisted on the payment of an indemnity by Madagascar before it could agree to any such revision. A new Anglo-Malagasy treaty was signed in 1865 while the Franco-Malagasy treaty was also signed in 1868. In both treaties, the Malagasy were able to achieve all their demands especially the cancellation of land-owning privileges previously granted the Europeans. However, Britain's conduct – its immediate acquiescence to Malagasy proposals – during the crisis, endeared it to the Malagasy while France's hostile and expensive demands evoked an opposite reaction. This was to affect future relations between the French and the Malagasy.

Internal developments 1861–80

We turn now to the administrative and socio-economic developments in Madagascar between 1861 and 1880. One of the most important events that affected later developments in the country was the conversion of its leaders to Christianity. The rapid expansion of the missionary enterprise in Madagascar after 1861 and its positive results made the Christian group a powerful force in the country. They could no longer be ignored nor relegated to the background especially as most of the country's influential citizens were numbered among them. Consequently, in order to consolidate their position and get Christian support, the key leaders of Malagasy, namely, Queen Ranavalona II and Rainilaiarivony, the prime minister – who was also her husband, as of the previous queen, Rasoherina – embraced Christianity in 1869.

The fact that it was the Protestant brand of Christianity that Malagasy leaders embraced is important because it came shortly after the conclusion of the Franco-Malagasy treaty of 1868 which had been preceded by a great show of

French hostility. Malagasy leaders saw Protestantism as the religion of Britain and Catholicism as belonging to the French. The acceptance of the former was thus to cement their friendship with the British and demonstrate their rejection of French culture and influence on the island.

This period also witnessed a wave of religious revival in the country. The Catholics intensified their efforts to reach the common folk in the rural areas and they were very successful in this regard in the Betsileo country. Further-more, there was a revival of traditional religions and the influence of traditional priests in a rearguard action to the very rapid spread of Christianity. With this medley of creeds, Madagascar was thus gripped with religious fever in the second half of the nineteenth century.

The missionary societies, especially the British, with the close alliance of the government, were able to achieve a lot in Malagasy society. Their most important achievements were in the field of education, architecture and medical services. In the field of education, more schools were opened and compulsory school attendance for all children over the age of seven was decreed in 1881. It has been said that the proportion of Malagasy children going to school in the 1880s compared well with that of most European countries. A number of students were also sent abroad for further studies. This educational expansion was greatly facilitated by the number of printing presses established by the missions which published books, magazines and newspapers. Another important social change which took place in this regard was the introduction of the Gregorian calendar by British missionaries in 1864 which replaced the traditional lunar calendar.

There was also missionary influence on architecture especially with the building of many churches and other monuments to the martyrs in the bid to make Antananarivo, the capital, a sacred city. Medical services began in Madagascar with the opening of a dispensary in 1862 and a hospital in 1965 at the capital by the London Missionary Society. In 1875, the Malagasy government set up its own medical services with paid personnel. And by 1880 the country had produced its first set of qualified doctors.

Apart from the spread of Christianity and the activities of Christian missions, the period under consideration also saw significant developments in the constitutional and administrative fields in Madagascar. There was a change from absolute monarchy to constitutional monarchy. This occurred as power gradually slipped from the hands of the Merina monarchy to the Hova oligarchy. The Merina monarchs still reigned within the period under consideration, but the act of rulership and actual exercise of government powers and authority were in the hands of the Hova oligarchy who occupied the topmost administrative positions in the state. With the passage of time, the monarch could no longer be said to rule according to her own discretion. In fact, in 1864 the Prime Minister overshadowed the Queen and became the most powerful person in the state when he also took over the command of the national army, and married the Queen.

With regard to administrative developments, a Code of 101 articles was

16.9 *The palanquin of Queen Rasoherina in front of a venerated building of Andrianampoinimerina's reign. In the background the Protestant church built during the reigns of Rasoherina and Ranavalona II*

promulgated in 1868 and by 1881 the number of articles had increased to 305. The essence of this was to improve the maintenance of law and order and the functioning of the administrative organs of the state. There were also reforms in the administration of justice. Three high courts were set up in the capital, each with thirteen judges, while magistrates and village heads administered justice in the provinces. However, final decisions in all cases rested with the prime minister. While this placed a lot of responsibility on one man, it enabled central government to know what was happening in the provinces. There was a reorganization of governmental machinery with the creation of a cabinet with eight ministries.

There were also military reforms. The prime minister in 1872 revived hitherto moribund policies of modernizing the army. Assisted by a British army instructor, the government recruited and trained an enlarged and professional army. A large quantity of arms was imported from England and the USA to equip the army and smaller arms were manufactured at home to conserve foreign exchange. Military reforms introduced in 1876 included the eradication of the abuse of the system of aides-de-camp. In 1876, compulsory military service was introduced for a period of five years. This led to the production of a very powerful army which was instrumental in the suppression of provincial revolts.

Other moves made in the bid to modernize Madagascar were: the banning of the liquor trade, the enforcement of the abolition of slavery and the slave trade, and the withdrawal of inhuman laws. Some British and French nationals, however, carried on with the slave trade in defiance of the Malagasy government. In 1877, all the slaves on the island, about 150 000, were set free by the government.

Economic development

Before Madagascar began to participate in international trade, especially before the mass arrival of Europeans on the island in 1860, the Malagasy had a virtually self-sufficient economy. The bulk of the population was engaged in agricultural production. Rice, the staple food on the island, was produced in large quantities to the extent that the Malagasy became specialists in its production. Livestock such as sheep and pigs were reared and fish were plentiful but cattle were the most important in this area. Rice and beef became important items of export. The Malagasy also developed some local industries such as spinning and weaving, mining and iron-working. In the 1830s, as mentioned above, an industrial complex was established in Mantasoa where a variety of goods were manufactured under the supervision of Jean Laborde.

The accession of King Radama I to the throne saw the beginning of Madagascar's active involvement in international trade. The chief imports into the island were slaves from the African mainland. This traffic in human beings was abolished officially in 1847 but it continued for some years after that before it finally died down. Other items imported into Madagascar included cloth, guns, rum and machinery while its chief exports were rice and beef. In the

16.10 *Ranavalona II's encampment upon her return from Fianarantsoa, 1873*

nineteenth century, the Malagasy traded with Britain, France, Réunion, Mauritius, Zanzibar, Seychelles and the USA.

This international trade was based on the conclusion of treaties of friendship and commerce. In 1862 such treaties were concluded with Britain and France and they were later revised in 1865 and 1868 respectively. In 1867, another treaty was concluded with the USA. Madagascar also established embassies in Mauritius, Britain and France to facilitate trade. The island encouraged private enterprise in international trade but the state had a clear lead. Concessions were granted to foreign capitalists to attract their investments in the country but they were not allowed to own land.

Conclusion

In this chapter we have been able to examine the modernization of Madagascar which started with King Radama I in the early nineteenth century. The process of modernization involved the encouragement of foreign trade and influences, the embracing of Christianity and the institution of certain reforms aimed at harnessing the human and natural resources of the country for greater development in the political, social and economic fields. The importance of this is that on the eve of the 'Scramble' Madagascar was not poor and undeveloped and was quite capable of ruling itself. Thus, the need for alien rule did not arise. But all the same, the island was colonized largely because, although the policy of modernization had in some ways strengthened the resistance that the Malagasy were able to put up, overall, it had weakened the kingdom by increasing its dependence on the outside world.

New trends in the Maghrib: Algeria, Tunisia and Libya

Introduction

The Maghrib experienced several major upheavals in the course of the nineteenth century. The most important of these developments was the loss of independence of the states to European powers. Algeria was conquered by the French in 1830; Libya fell under Ottoman rule again in 1835 only to be invaded by Italians in 1911; Tunisia became a French protectorate in 1881, and Morocco was invaded by the French and Spanish in 1912. These events represented either the culmination of, or, in certain cases, the prelude to, far-reaching new trends which affected the economic, social and cultural fabric of society. Thus the explanation of the problem of underdevelopment in North Africa at this period should be sought not only in local circumstances but also in the general situation prevailing in the outside world, especially Europe, since the phenomenon of 'underdevelopment' in Africa is intimately linked with that of 'development' in Europe.

In this chapter, we shall examine the basis of society in the Maghrib and also assess its strengths and weaknesses at the beginning of the nineteenth century. In addition, we shall look at the nature and impact of European influence in the Maghrib given the different local situations. The Maghrib in the period under consideration comprised an independent Morocco and three Regencies of the Ottoman empire, namely, Algeria, Tunisia and Libya. Attention will thus be focused on the common characteristics of these Ottoman regencies and on the nature of societies in the different countries.

The Makhzen at the beginning of the nineteenth century

A major feature of the Makhzen (state) in Algiers, Tunis and Tripoli was that it did not blend with the people over whom it ruled. The men who wielded power and authority saw themselves as being separate from their subjects. These men were Turks and *Mamlūks* who were assimilated in varying limited degrees in the regencies. The *Mamlūks* were former slaves of Christian origin who had been converted and suitably trained to serve at court or in the army. The main tools of government such as hard currencies, modern weapons, writing paper

17.1   *The interior of the Ketchawa mosque in Algiers in 1833 (built in 1794)*

and book-keeping techniques were drawn from outside the local society. The Makhzen thus represented a half-way stage between Turkish or European modernity and the traditions of local societies. The state was able to exploit the local societies with the collaboration of some notables in the cities and this was responsible, to a large extent, for the underdevelopment and even the decline of rural societies.

In pre-colonial times, the Makhzen received a lot of support from various local groups such as warriors, notables in the cities, prominent families in rural areas and religious leaders such as the *'ulamā'*, (scholars), the *murābits* (holy men) and heads of the *tariqa* (brotherhoods) both in the cities and in the countryside. Moreover, the amount of local support a regime was able to mobilize determined not only its nature but also its chances of survival. Thus in Algiers, the rise of Turkish janissaries and Levantine deys undermined all attempts to integrate the government into the larger society; whereas, by the opening decades of the eighteenth century, the rulers in Tunis and Tripoli respectively had been assimilated much more into the countries which they governed.

Urban society

Despite the existence of a common kinship system and the same Muslim culture in the Maghrib, by the nineteenth century the society was already a heterogenous one in which one could roughly distinguish townsmen, sedentary village ethnic groups, and highlanders, especially mountain Berbers. There were several cities because the city was an important feature of Islamic culture; but, of all the states in the Maghrib, it was in Tunisia that urban life was most established. Such cities included Rabat, Fez, Tripoli, Tlemcen, Algiers, Constantine, Tunis, Susa and Kayrawān. These cities were the centres of the most lucrative and important activities such as trade and handicrafts; religious teaching, culture and general education; and the performance of political, administrative and military functions because the power of the state was concentrated in the towns. Town life was therefore associated with a monetary economy, a literary culture and an individuality in human relationship as opposed to the solidarity and interdependence of rural society.

However, this urban society was incapable of transforming the whole of the country. This had to do with the role of the middle class. The middle class in the Maghrib had a lot of weaknesses. Its own development was hampered by the resistance of rural communities to its overtures, the fierce competition from European capitalists, and the paralyzing monopoly policies of the state to limit middle-class business interests. Thus members of the middle class in trade and handicrafts had difficulty in developing their activities on autonomous lines. With all these problems the middle class lacked the technology to lead the rest of the country along the path to the kind of radical changes that took place in contemporary Europe.

17.2   *A Ḳurʾānic school in Algiers in 1830*

Rural society

A clear distinction has often been made between city and country dwellers in the Maghrib. This distinction was based on a number of issues. On the one hand, there was a complex city culture based on the literary tradition while the oral culture persisted in the rural areas. In religious matters, the legal instruction given by the scholars in the city was different from the teaching of the holy men in the rural areas. In the economic field, a monetary system was evolved in the cities whereas a subsistence economy and a poorly developed technology characterized the countryside. And in the social realm, city dwellers were becoming more rank-conscious and individualistic while the country folk remained dependent on each other with strong kinship ties.

This distinction should however, not be overstretched. This is because not all rural communities shared all the features outlined above. Some rural areas exposed to the influence of towns or market centres shared some urban features. Even though the genealogical factor continued to be of fundamental importance in these areas, they undoubtedly displayed features that were unknown in the more remote rural areas.

The weakness of the North African communities in general and the *Makhzen* that ruled them in particular was their great diversity, their comparative isolation and their use of inefficient technology. But, on the whole, the *Makhzen* succeeded in maintaining a balance in the society which was disturbed after 1815 by the incursion of Europeans into the region.

The European offensive

The European onslaught on the Maghrib in the nineteenth century took two important forms both of which culminated in the colonization of the region. The first had to do with commercial relations between European nationals and the state in the different countries of the Maghrib which exceptionally favoured the Europeans. French traders derived the greatest benefit from this commercial exploitation. European aggression in the Maghrib was used partly to boost the national honour of European countries and partly to protect the very unjust privileges secured by treaty in the commercial transactions.

This onslaught also took the form of overflooding the Maghrib with European capital. This had to do with the expansion of moneylending or usury. In times of difficulty, the rulers of the Maghrib turned to European merchants for loans and the latter were quick to turn this to their own advantage by increasing the former's dependence on them through the granting of more loans and the extraction of many outrageous concessions from them. This lending process gained ground gradually in the course of the century and was accelerated after 1860 as the independent states of the Maghrib sought more loans to carry out 'reforms' in their drive towards modernization.

The trend was more pronounced in Tunisia where the country's financial resources were first exploited and then brought entirely under European control within the space of ten years, between 1859 and 1869. All the loans acquired within this period were unfortunately wasted on unnecessary projects. The profligacy of state officials did not help matters and in 1869 the country had to accept an International Financial Commission to control all its revenue and ensure the repayment of all its debts. Despite the relief which the state enjoyed between 1870 and 1881, capitalist penetration continued unabated through the operations of banking establishments. It is not surprising therefore that the spokesmen of capitalism called for direct colonization to protect their interests and this resulted in the establishment of the French protectorate in Tunisia in May 1881.

European penetration took a different turn in Algeria due to the early colonization of the country in 1830. Not only did capitalist commercial and banking interests arrive in the country, colonial settlers also gradually took over the people's land from them. And by 1890, a lot of the people had become landless.

Factors of change

The existing balance in the Maghribian society described earlier was disturbed by European penetration in its various forms. The effects of this were felt in the commercial and financial fields either directly or indirectly. We shall now examine the main factors of change, the nature of the change and the impact of European pressure on the various categories of the local population.

The first factor of change was the maritime trade conducted by European merchants which gradually weakened, and eventually superceded the traditional long-distance caravans and the seaborne trade with the Levant. The expansion of this trade introduced a lot of European manufactured goods into the Maghrib and raised the value of imports above the value of exports. This not only drained the financial resources of the states, it also stifled local industries. Small traders lost their well-to-do customers who developed a taste for imported goods.

The introduction of a monetary system into the economy, and the general impoverishment of the people led to an increase in money-lending and usury. Money lenders, most of whom were Jews, thrived in this situation while the local people sank deep into various debts. This development was, however, not limited to the urban areas; it also spread to the rural communities.

Oppressive taxation also fuelled a social crisis in the Maghrib. In Algeria, the increase in taxes by the colonial administration led to many revolts. The great uprising in Tunisia in 1864 was caused by the decision to double the rate of taxation. Similar developments also took place in Morocco. As if all these problems were not enough, there were several climatic crises in the course of the century which took a heavy toll on human lives. The crisis of 1866–89 in Tunisia and Algeria and that of 1878–81 in Morocco reduced the population significantly and led to the weakening of the economy and the indigenous social order.

Beneficiaries of the crisis

Some groups of people benefitted from the crisis in the Maghrib in the nineteenth century. The first were the European settlers who were more in Algeria and Tunisia than in Libya. Although most of them were men of humble origins, they enjoyed a very privileged status in comparison with the majority of the local people. There was also a Jewish minority who played an important role as intermediaries between the European capitalist network and the local population. Some Muslims also collaborated with the Europeans and stood between them and the indigenous people. Such Muslims included high-ranking officials of the state who misused their positions and corruptly enriched themselves at the expense of the state.

Other beneficiaries of the crises were some of the influential citizens who exercised authority over the communities within their jurisdiction and on whom the state in Tunisia and Algeria had to rely. A number of religious families also rose and monopolized the key positions either in the learned Islamic communities where they enjoyed a semi-official status or among various Islamic brotherhoods as in Algeria and Morocco.

The victims of the crisis

A large number of people suffered from the changed situation in nineteenth-century Maghrib. The immediate result was the large-scale impoverishment of the populace and the disruption of traditional social structures. Because of this, economic and demographic disaster was inevitable during the 1866–9 crisis.

The reactions of the victims took various forms. First they resigned themselves to their fate and embraced the Muslim brotherhoods more than before. This was the situation in Algeria, Tunisia and Morocco. This trend was most pronounced in Morocco. But it was in Libya where the Sanūsiyya, founded in 1843 in Cyrenaica, came to acquire a major social, economic and even political significance. Another form of reaction was evident in the high incidence of revolts in the Maghrib in the nineteenth century. Local rebellions were widespread not only in Algeria where there was already colonial rule but also in Tunisia and Morocco where they became common occurrences. Libya was not left out of this upheaval. However, the revolts failed because the authorities who were being attacked were better armed and because there was no cohesion among the revolting peoples.

It is significant to note that all attempts at reform carried out in various fields to restore the societal balance that had been disturbed proved futile. Let us now turn our attention to those attempts in each of the states of the Maghrib.

Algeria

By the beginning of the nineteenth century, the Regency of Algiers of all the regimes of the Maghrib was the most successful in preserving its non-indigenous features. Government remained exclusively in the hands of the Turks who stood apart from the rest of the society. This was due to Algeria's rural nature which did little to encourage the middle class that could have assimilated these rulers.

This is not to say that the Algerian political regime was totally opposed to change. Since the eighteenth century, many changes had taken place which led the rulers to modify their policies concerning cooperation with local leaders. But despite these changes, the leadership of Algeria continued to retain its non-indigenous character and this provoked a lot of conflicts in the society. Thus a kind of 'national' reaction was already taking shape before the French conquest.

The years following the French conquest of Algeria saw a number of contradictions and hesitations in French policy, particularly with regard to the issue of land tenure. Coastal areas were occupied by the French while plans were made to rule the hinterland through local administrators. Aḥmad, the Turkish Bey of Constantine and Amīr ʿAbd al-Ḳādir were two prominent personalities in the affairs of the hinterland. While the former continued with the Turkish system of government, the latter rallied the people round a religious cause, appealed to their patriotic sentiments and led a resistance movement against the French between 1832 and 1847. Despite the fact that he was able to mobilize two-thirds of the Algerian population, ʿAbd al-Ḳādir was eventually defeated by the French.

The French thereafter established a colonial society with all its institutions in Algeria. The country was placed under a governor-general and divided into a civilian territory where Europeans lived and French customs and institutions were developed, and military territories where the local communities were subject to the authority of the army. The defeat of France by the Germans in 1870 and the threat of an extension of the area under direct European rule – where Europeans owned all the land – led to a major revolt in Kabylia and the neighbouring regions in 1871. This was brutally suppressed by the French and the local people were brought under a more stringent rule by the French. The people were reduced to poverty as they were deprived of their land. In addition, they were deprived of many of their social and cultural traditions. The indigenous population thus lost all their rights and were openly exploited for the benefit of the European minority in their midst.

Tunisia

Tunisia was the first country in the Maghrib to introduce Western-style reforms because of its exposure to foreign influence. The results of their modernization drive were, however, disastrous.

Tunisia's exposure to foreign influence through commercial contacts coupled with the increasing power of the local notables began to influence the political system. Consequently, the leadership tried to identify with the populace, thus producing a quasi-national monarchy, while the Turkish janissaries and *mamlūks*

17.3 *Upper-class Algerian women with a black slave attendant*

17.4 *Members of the Tunisian nizāmī (army) in European-style uniforms*

continued to be the mainstay of the regime. A lot of support was also acquired from the local population. The regime reached the peak of its power under the rule of Ḥammūda Pashā, from 1782 to 1814 after which problems set in.

Faced with the problems generated by the infiltration of Tunisia by European enterprise and a military threat from its neighbours, France and the Ottoman empire, Aḥmad, the Bey of Tunis (1837–55), decided to borrow money from Europe. He also introduced some ill-fated reforms without taking into consideration the country's human and financial resources. Such reforms included the creation of a new army based on the Western model. To meet the needs of the new army, he set up modern factories to manufacture guns, gunpowder, cloth and footwear. He also abolished slavery in 1846 and, imbued with the spirit of nationalism, he reduced the privileges of the Turks thus placing them on an equal level with the indigenous population. Most of these reforms, however, did not produce the desired results and, to make matters worse, they ate deep into the financial resources of the state. A solution was sought in an increase in taxation but, rather than address the problem, it generated opposition and enmity against the regime.

The failure of these reforms could be attributed to the fact that they were not suitable for the human environment to which they were introduced. Moreover, the European states saw opportunities in the inauguration of the reforms for obtaining lucrative contracts. They were basically not interested in the success of the reforms. By 1885 when Aḥmad Bey died, the reforms had promoted the formation of a group which favoured modernization, and sown the seeds of a nation-state. At the same time, they had increased the danger of foreign intervention and accentuated internal weaknesses. This situation was exploited by the Europeans and their local allies.

By 1856–7, the European powers brought greater pressure to bear in favour of reforms which were to lead to the development of capitalist enterprise by allowing foreigners to own property, and pursue any occupation they chose, on the principle of free trade. This also led to the drawing up of a constitution in 1861 for Tunisia in which the three arms of government, namely, judicial, legislative and executive were separated and a municipal council set up in Tunis. In addition, ministries and administrative services were reorganized and a printing house established in Tunis.

Notwithstanding the failure of these reforms, the activities of European firms were expanding especially with regard to foreign trade. The level of expenditure of the Tunisian government rose without a corresponding rise in its income. The result was that the state sank deeper into debt. In order to alleviate this problem the Bey, Muḥammad al-Ṣādiḳ, decided to double taxes at the end of 1863. This sparked off a mass rebellion in 1864 which the government quelled with some difficulty. To make matters worse, the country experienced poor harvests in 1866–70, a terrible famine and a cholera epidemic in 1870 which aggravated all existing problems, leading to bankruptcy. In July 1869, an International Financial Commission was set up in Tunis to control all the state revenue and ensure the payment of its debts.

The calibre of ministers that the Bey supported also determined how Tunisia fared during those hard times. Whereas the corrupt government of Mustafā Khaznadār (1837–73) spelt doom for the country, the tenure of Khāyr al-dīn (1873–7) witnessed an improvement in the general conditions of the country due to his integrity, patriotism, insight and political sagacity. Yet, with the famine of 1876–7, and the rising prestige of France, even Khāyr al-dīn could not survive. He was replaced by Mustafā ibn Ismā'īl, the bey's former time-serving minister under whom Tunisia became a French protectorate in 1881.

Libya

Due to the fact that more of Libya is covered by the Sahara desert than any other country in the Maghrib it was less coveted by Europeans. The old caravan trade was thus able to continue to thrive in the country till the twentieth century.

From the last decade in the eighteenth century to 1835, Libya was embroiled in a power struggle between central authority represented by the Ķāramānlī dynasty and nomad groups. The urban middle class on the coast constituted the mainstay of the ruling Ķāramānlī dynasty. This middle class comprised large families who were prominent in the military, commerce and religious affairs. Their sources of revenue included long-distance trade, regional trade, handicrafts, and, up to 1815, privateering. The struggle for power was eventually resolved when the Ottoman Porte resumed direct control of Libya. The Ottomans made use of the military and diplomacy to weaken the opposition of the nomads, and after 1858 they extended their rule over the whole of Tripolitania and part of the Fezzān.

A small section of the population cultivated the little arable land in the desert while the remaining majority were nomads rearing sheep and camels. The most powerful communities were those that lived deep in the desert. It was among them that the Sanūsiyya flourished, in their *zāwiya* around the major oases. They concentrated their attention on raising the level of religious life among the nomadic groups. They promoted trade by organizing the caravan route from Barķa in Cyrenaica to Wadaī and offering accommodation and other facilities to the caravans. They also used their influence to settle disputes among the different nomadic communities. To ensure that the nomads no longer posed any threat to their administration, the Ottomans made use of the Sanūsiyya in Barķa as intermediary between themselves and the nomad population.

In order to further secure their authority, the Ottomans began to introduce some reforms into Libya. Judicial reforms, administrative reforms, a municipal government, schools, hospitals and a central market were all introduced between 1865 and 1880. Centres of distribution of food in times of famine were also established. While all the previous reforms benefitted only the middle class, this last one was particularly advantageous to the ordinary people. In addition, the economy remained healthy despite the increase in imported European goods after 1850.

17.5   *The tomb of Muḥammad ben ʿAlī al-Sanūsī*

Problems came with the continual shortage of food in 1881–9. This affected exports adversely and the volume of imported foodstuffs increased. The income from the Saharan trade also declined. This coincided with the time when the Sanūsiyya was facing both external pressure and internal difficulties. With the decline of its revenues from trade, it turned to landholding and agriculture at the expense of some of its followers. This encouraged the rise of rival brotherhoods and other religious organisations. By 1910 its influence in the region had been drastically reduced.

The picture presented above is that of a society undergoing a process of radical change in which old patterns were fast disappearing. Europeans were not slow in taking advantage of this situation by positioning themselves strategically in the local economy. From 1911 there was the attempted Italian conquest, resistance and war until 1932.

Conclusion

The countries of the Maghrib were subjected to colonial rule at different times. The reason for the loss of independence should, however, not be sought in local events only, but in the expansion of western capitalism. This experience was not peculiar to the Maghrib; it was shared by some other parts of the non-European world which became the target of European imperialism.

Nonetheless, certain local conditions would explain the differences in the rate at which the various countries of the Maghrib were reduced to a state of dependence, the methods used for the subjugation, and the reactions of the local population. Algeria was forcefully taken even before the middle of the century and there the European assault involved settlers and large-scale land alienation which was most ruthless and traumatic for the traditional society and culture. Tunisia was penetrated gradually through the influx of capital, while Libya was protected for some time from European ambitions by the re-establishment of Turkish rule in 1835 and also by its poverty and remoteness. All these experiences had an enduring impact on society in the Maghrib.

Morocco from the beginning of the nineteenth century to 1880

The foundations of modern Morocco were laid in the eighteenth century during the reign of Sultan Muḥammad III (1757–90) which came after a period of anarchy in the history of the country. This modern state was consolidated by Sulaymān (1792–1822) who governed more according to the _sharīᶜa_ (Islamic law) and gave government a more urban basis. He administered directly the agricultural communities of Haouz, Dir, and Gharb, whereas he ruled the mountain and desert regions indirectly through the great chiefs – _ḳāids_ and the leaders of different religious brotherhoods. This created a duality between the areas of sovereignty, the _bilād-al-makhzen_ under direct rule of the Sultan, and the areas of suzerainty, the _bilād-al-sibā_, that he ruled indirectly at the discretion of the chieftains, though in practice the distinction was not always so sharp.

Subsequent rulers of Morocco were faced with the task of reorganizing the country. Groups of people enjoying excessive privileges from the _Makhzen_ (government) were removed from power. It was at this time that Europeans began to make incursions into Morocco especially after the conquest of Algiers by the French in 1830. The Moroccan government was therefore preoccupied with broadening its political and territorial base as well as strengthening itself to withstand foreign danger. Despite the sterling qualities of Moroccan rulers in the nineteenth century, they encountered domestic opposition and mounting European pressure such that the country could not totally escape foreign control. But the major achievement of the period was the development of a traditional Moroccan identity which gave Morocco a special position in the Maghrib.

The politico-social structure

In the period under consideration, an important political institution in Morocco was the _bayᶜa_ (investiture contract) which bound the sultan and the various groups in the population together. It was a written contract which legitimized political authority. According to it, the sultan was expected to defend the land against foreign enemies and to maintain peace at home. The people in turn owed him complete obedience as long as he did not break the law and custom of Islam. Among other things, they were to comply with the orders of government, pay the legal taxes, provide armed contingents when necessary in time of peace and rally massively round the state in time of war.

To carry out his duties, the sultan had a *Makhzen* composed essentially of an army and a bureaucracy. The army consisted of three groups: the *bwakher* comprised slave troops numbering a few hundreds; the *gish* were composed of contingents from certain communities; and the *nuaib* were temporary troops provided by other communities at the sultan's demand. This army had the major task of policing the state and maintaining domestic order. The bureaucracy was made up of viziers and secretaries of the ministries which were broken down into several departments. A number of these officials were of Andalusian origin and the bureaucracy carried on the Andalusian tradition through courses of instruction proferred at Ḳarāwiyyīn University at Fez. A new type of government official, however, emerged in the second half of the nineteenth century to meet the needs arising from expanded relations with Europe. These were people less versed in history and rhetoric but more acquainted with European languages and financial problems.

Because the Moroccan state was based on Islamic ideas and precepts, its sources of income were those approved by the religion while other means were considered illegal. The legal sources of income were the receipts from state lands, a tax on commercial capital and farm produce, and taxes on foreign trade. With this limited means of income, the Sultan had to reduce his spending to a strict minimum. Various attempts made by Sultans Muḥammad III, Sulaymān ʿAbd al-Raḥmān and Muḥammad IV (1822–59) respectively to increase taxes or institute new ones, all met with failure. Thus throughout the nineteenth century the problem of taxes remained central to Morocco's history and it was never resolved satisfactorily. Even as the *Makhzen* sought the solution in reducing its expenditures, overall reforms became more imperative, especially with increasing European pressure.

Apart from the army and the bureaucracy there were some other intermediate bodies in the society. These stood between the government on the one hand and the people – urban and rural – on the other. In a sense, these bodies were also part of the *Makhzen*. They defended the traditional rights of the people against the Sultan, and also carried out government orders because they were responsible to the sultan. These bodies comprised the clerical class, the *shurafā*, the *zāwiyas*, and the *ḳabīla* chieftains.

The clerical class was made up of the *ʿulamā'*, (teachers), *ḳādīs* (judges) and other administrators of the religious foundations and officers in charge of the markets. This group strictly applied the commandments of the *sharīʿa*, and, although they were under the supervision of the sultan, they enjoyed unquestionable authority. In a number of ways, the Sultan could not over-ride the prerogatives of this class. Even the *sharīʿa*, the body of Islamic laws governing social life, was under the jurisdiction of the *ʿulamā'*, and the Sultan could not attempt to change it.

The *shurafā* were direct descendants of the Prophet Muḥammad and they constituted a sort of religious aristocracy found in all parts of Morocco. They

18.1   *Sultan ʿAbd al-Raḥmān (1822–59) in 1832*

were numerous and they enjoyed a privileged status and social prestige. They were exempted from several taxes and they received numerous obligatory gifts from the Sultan. Their connection with the Prophet Muḥammad gave them not only an elevated social standing but also supernatural endowments which they employed to generate considerable income for themselves. The Sultan was even on their list of clients.

The *zāwiyas* were social groups with a religious basis and they were in two major forms in nineteenth-century Morocco. One was the *zāwiya* brotherhood with an open membership without any discrimination as to social class, wealth, occupation or ethnic origin. Examples of such brotherhoods were the Tijāiyya and Darkāwiyya. The other was the *zāwiya* principality in which the chief of a religious foundation ruled over a specific area of jurisdiction with virtually complete authority such as the Wazzāniyya and the Nāsiriyya. These two *zāwiya* forms were not mutually exclusive: some tried to incorporate features of both. But their major role was that they served as forums of social discipline and as extensions of *Makhzen* authority despite their apparent independence.

The *kabīla* chieftains ruled over specific regions (*kabīlas*), either a mountain canton, a nomad confederation or a community of soldier shepherds. In each case authority was delegated to a *kā'id* appointed by a decree after the approval of the people of the district had been obtained. The *kā'id* performed a dual role: he was the sultan's representative as well as the people's spokesman. In some cases, he also performed the duties of a governor by collecting taxes and troops' levies. In each *kabīla* there grew two kaidal families (from which *kā'ids* could be chosen) which formed part of the country's administrative elite.

In the final analysis, these intermediate bodies, either urban or rural, were cogs in the wheel of the Sultan's government. The socio-political system of Morocco, as reorganized by Muḥammad IV, marked a return to traditional Islam. It not only recognized the autonomy of the intermediate bodies, it also limited the ambitions of the central government. By allowing all groups to voice their claims inside the governmental structure, the system reinforced the idea of the Moroccan state. The system can neither be categorically described as direct government by the *sharīʿa* nor as one in which the sultan was only a unifying symbol with delegated authority – it incorporated both elements. But before it could be stabilized, the system had to cope with stronger European pressures.

Limited reforms of the *mashzen*

The period between 1800 and 1880 was one in which Morocco enjoyed relative peace from European intervention, unlike the other states in the Maghrib. Neither France nor Spain embarked on any territorial expansion that could threaten the sovereignty of Morocco while British goods were not granted special commercial privileges in the country. There was no meeting point for the demands of the European powers and the Sultan's authority. This was due to the fact that the Sultan's hands were tied by the *'ulamā'*, who

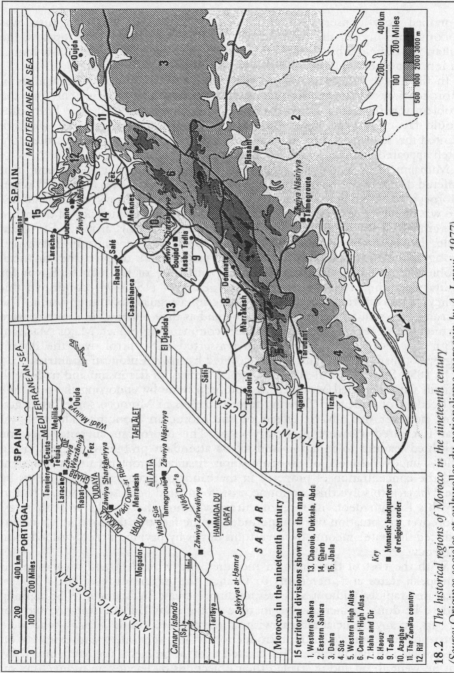

18.2 *The historical regions of Morocco in the nineteenth century*
(*Source*: Origines sociales et culturelles du nationalisme marocain by A. Laroui, 1977)

remained very conservative and upheld the *sharī'a*, which in turn was uncompromising on the demands of the Europeans. To the Europeans, the Sultan was therefore backward and unenlightened while the *'ulamā'*, saw him as an innovator seeking under European pressure to reform the state.

In the nineteenth century both the Sultan and European representatives in Morocco saw the need for reforms in the army and government. But the problem was the form which the reforms were to take. While the Europeans would favour reforms based on Western ideas and concepts, the *Makhzen* wanted the reforms to be based on the *sharī'a*. The resulting reforms therefore often appeared ambivalent and ambiguous.

Muḥammad IV as crown prince was commander-in-chief of the army that suffered defeat by European troops in 1844, and he was sultan (1859–73) when Morocco was again defeated in 1860–1 and made to pay heavy war reparations. He was therefore determined to reform and improve the efficiency of the army. He employed the services of some Tunisians to train his army in European style. He also set up an engineering school at Fez to train surveyors, topographers, cartographers and artillerymen. And despite the financial problems that faced him after 1860, he sent some of his men to Egypt for military training. His son and successor, Hasan I (1873–94) continued this policy of reorganizing the army by setting up a regular recruiting system. The recruits were sent to Europe for training and as they returned home they were formed into a regiment under a British commanding officer, Major Maclean. With this reorganized army, Hasan reasserted his control over the distant regions of his kingdom which were coveted by many European countries.

In 1856, Sultan 'Abd al-Raḥmān signed a treaty of friendship and trade with Britain which opened Morocco to European trade by endorsing the principle of freedom of trade, and allowing foreign traders in Morocco some privileges. This, however, had adverse effects on the Moroccan economy. The first was that it created a severe monetary crisis. The Moroccan currency became devalued leading to inflation and all its attendant problems, namely, rising prices, impoverishment of the population, financial problems for government and the concentration of property in the hands of a minority. All attempts by the *Makhzen* to solve this economic crisis foundered because the Sultan had to pay his foreign debts in foreign currency which he sought at high rates. Moreover the situation was compounded by the fact that the foreign merchants reduced the state's income from customs duties by paying in the devalued local currency.

With the cost of these reform measures, and with debt and reparations to European states and merchants to finance, the expenditure of the *Makhzen* increased rapidly without a corresponding increase in its income. Something had to be done to increase the income of the state. But the sultan could not embark on any financial reform without the approval of the *'ulamā'*, who were not ready to acquiesce to the introduction of any permanent and extra tax on the people for that purpose. This created a lot of problems for Muḥammad IV, but he went ahead and overruled their objections by levying an indirect tax on

18.3 *Sultan Ḥasan I*
(1873–94)

18.4 *Silver rial minted in*
Paris in 1881 for Ḥasan I

the people. This met with stiff opposition especially from urban dwellers. Ḥasan I faced similar problems and strong public opinion and opposition from some army leaders which prevented him from carrying through his fiscal reforms.

In the 1860s the *Makhzen* launched a programme of government reforms in response to the complaints of the European community in Morocco which had grown considerably by that period. A corps of customs inspectors called the *umanā* was set up in 1861 to oversee the collection of customs duties in the eight ports open to foreign trade in the country. Sixty per cent of these customs receipts were allocated to war reparation payments. The *umanā* and another group of officials called the *tulba* enjoyed increasing prestige in the bureaucracy. The latter had been sent to Europe for training and to learn foreign languages and on their return they were used in the ministry of foreign affairs and in the tax division of the department of the mint, part of the armaments factory managed by Italians in Fez.

The European traders also sought to restrict the authority of the local administrators by devising means of extricating themselves from the latter's jurisdiction. The Europeans would rather be judged by the governor or by a joint tribunal made up of the governor and European representatives. In 1863 Muḥammad IV concluded an agreement with France which granted judicial privileges to both foreign merchants and their Moroccan associates. They were thus to be judged by the governor in the presence of the European consul concerned. But this provision for their Moroccan associates was regularly abused until 1880 when the arrangement was reviewed.

On the whole, European pressure brought about a reform of Morocco's army, government, monetary and tax systems. The scope of the reforms was, however, limited both by foreign hindrances and domestic problems. While Europeans welcomed any measure that guaranteed their security and favoured their commercial operations, they did not want the Moroccan government to be strong enough to interfere with their privileges and profits. On the other hand, the Sultan was not given a free hand to operate at home: some areas like education, judiciary and religious institutions were not open to reform due to the uncooperative attitude of the '*ulamā*'. The sultan was also handicapped by meagre financial resources. Consequently, with each reform, the Sultan was gradually tied more closely to Europe because, as foreign traders increased in Morocco, there were more incidents which resulted in Morocco paying heavy fines or making territorial concessions or losing its prestige.

This chain of events provoked a lot of opposition from the Moroccan populace as the people traced their national poverty to the admission of foreigners into their land. Public opinion was thus incensed against the foreigners, for all the woes of the country.

Popular reactions

The nineteenth century which saw increasing European pressure on Morocco also witnessed some other socio-economic problems all of which were resented by the populace and attributed to the European presence. Due to increased pressure on the land because of the growing demand of European exporters, and the vagaries of the local climate, there was a series of famines in the latter half of the century which had severe effects on the urban and rural population. The rural population became impoverished. Many crop and livestock farmers left their land for the urban areas. This drift to the towns affected about one-third of the agricultural land in Morocco.

The urban population was also in a very bad state. By 1881, it was estimated that about fifteen per cent of the inhabitants in the towns survived on public charity, and about 64 000 Moroccans had been forced to emigrate. In addition, slums were springing up outside the town walls. There was a hike in the prices of basic necessities such as grains, wool and hides. Imported goods were relatively cheap but they posed tough competition for the local industries which constituted the strength of the urban economy. Government workers also suffered from the devaluation of the national currency as their purchasing power was greatly reduced.

The *Makhzen* too had its own share of this misery. There was a decline in the receipts of the tax on both commercial capital and farm produce due to the hardships suffered by the rural and urban population. The government was also asked by the Europeans to pay the debts of private individuals such as governors. To make matters worse, some European merchants and their local collaborators embarked on acts of economic sabotage which the sultan found very difficult to control. They were the only set of people who escaped the general impoverishment in the country. They enriched themselves at the expense of the state by paying ridiculously low prices for their local purchases and lending money out at very high rates.

Apart from these economic hardships, there were other social problems. There was a great decline in the authority of religious officials, the sultan, and Islam generally. This was at a time when Europeans were insisting on their national respect and individual rights. This situation put government officials in a very difficult position: to satisfy the Europeans would mean flouting their local custom, while refusing the Europeans could create problems for the sultan in his external relations. On whichever side they stood, these officials always suffered the consequences of their actions.

Religious officials in Morocco therefore fiercely opposed any attempt by the sultan to protect or allow any foreign interest in the country. They were also hostile to individual Moroccans who collaborated with the Europeans, and they mobilized public opinion against them especially when the Sultan failed to side with the *'ulamā'*, because he did not want to create problems with the European powers. The result of this was a general hatred for foreigners in Morocco. This was heightened by the fact that the populace attributed their poverty to the European presence.

Everybody strove to cut away from the foreigners or reduce contact with them to the barest minimum. The society thus turned away from external influences and began to look inward. This inward-looking took the form of the glorification of their past when things were better and life was more enjoyable. The religious officials called for a strict application of the *shari'a* in all areas of social life, and for personal, moral and religious renewal. Reform was no longer seen in the Western sense; it was taken to mean a return to the ancient ways of life in which Islam and the society was untarnished by foreign influence. This was the movement called *salafism* (Muslim fundamentalism). To restrict the Europeans' sphere of operations, the sultan also dragged out every negotiation and, whenever possible, tried to frustrate them with delay.

Thus a general xenophobia was planted in the society as a result of the collective experience of the people. Societal ills were attributed to the penetration of European capital and Moroccan leaders sought to undo this malaise. but they were only pre-occupied with bemoaning a past that had vanished. They glorified the past and failed to see the promise of a different future.

Conclusion

While Morocco was facing the domestic problems described above, it did not fare badly on the international scene. By 1880 it was getting over most of its economic problems which also meant that its external debts were almost repaid. The international convention signed in July 1880 guaranteed the independence of Morocco. Thus the country was protected jointly by the French, the English and the Spanish. The reign of Ḥasan I was thus a golden age for Morocco which made him appear as a great Sultan both at home and abroad.

Moreover, the internal problems of the country seemed controllable at the time. The reforms undertaken during the reign of Ḥasan I were considered adequate to give birth to a strong, modern and independent Morocco if not for the attack of France and Spain. However, the reformist tendencies of the *Makhzen*, the Islamic fundamentalism of the *'ulamā'*, and the xenophobia of the rural population all combined to give rise to the virile spirit of twentieth-century Moroccan nationalism.

In evaluating the results of this policy of reform, one must recognize the fact that it took place within the framework left by Muḥammad III who had had to handle the change in the power relationship between Morocco and Europe. Thus a thorough understanding of the situation in which Muḥammad III operated is needed before an objective assessment of the evolution of the Moroccan society in the nineteenth century could be made.

19

New patterns of European intervention in the Maghrib

Introduction

European colonialism in the eighteenth and nineteenth centuries was marked, among other things, by commercial expansion and the struggle for control over trade routes. This struggle was in the form of naval wars between European states and the Maghrib. By the beginning of the nineteenth century, North African pirates had become a terror to European merchants. Relations between Europe and the Maghrib also became strained because of quarrels over the commercial dues and duties payable by the Europeans to the Maghrib states.

The situation was worsened as pirates from Naples and Malta began to plunder Muslim merchant ships from the Maghrib. As if that was not enough, after the Napoleonic wars, Europeans began to organize massive naval expeditions against the Maghrib under the pretext of a struggle against piracy. The states of the Maghrib were bombarded in turns, and by the end of the third decade of the nineteenth century, Maghribian shipping and naval tradition had been destroyed. This was followed by an intensive expansion of European commerce into the Maghrib.

Attempts made by Morocco and Algeria to defend their positions led to a deterioration of relations between them and the European powers. The Algerian government not only refused to grant special rights and privileges to the French, it also refused any special concessions in commercial dealings involving the two countries. The French response was the naval blockade of Algiers in 1827. Morocco for its own part decided to shun foreigners and closely monitor its relationship with them.

European pressure on traditional society

Tunis and Tripoli encountered a number of financial problems as a result of the growth of European trade and its attendant difficulties. While the governments of Tunisia and Tripolitania (Libya) were signing debtors' bills, their ministers also sank into debt. This meant they succumbed easily to European pressures and gave up all political resistance. The treaties between Tunis and Tripoli on the one hand, and the European powers on the other, were lopsided. European countries, especially France, were given a lot of privileges in Tunis and Tripoli: they were not to pay any commercial dues, the principle of free trade was entrenched, and France was declared to be the most favoured nation. Consequently, the position of France in North Africa was considerably strengthened while Tunisia was almost turned into its vassal. The increasing influence of France in North Africa greatly alarmed Britain, its greatest rival, and in order to limit French power in the area, Britain did its best to ensure the success of the Turkish expedition to Tripolitania in 1835.

The Ottomans, however, encountered a lot of opposition from the local population after reestablishing their authority in Tripoli and they had to crush many rebellions. As the Ottomans were pacifying the land, they introduced reforms along European lines into the country. They reorganized the administration, the system of justice, taxation and laws. In 1851, a mixed court of justice was established in Tripoli which strengthened the position of the foreigners. All these reforms however undermined the foundations of traditional society and gave rise to protests among the indigenous population.

In Tunisia, reforms were begun in 1830 and continued by Aḥmad Bey (1837–55) who reorganized the army and established an armaments factory. He also nationalized the economy by establishing government monopolies. A national bank was founded in 1847 and a new currency put into circulation. In addition, he abolished slavery and banned the sale of slaves in 1841. There were also some educational reforms. In 1838 a military college and polytechnic were established and Tunisians began to travel abroad for foreign studies.

The governments of Tunis and Tripoli also allowed the activities of Christian missionaries. The Catholics established schools in Tripoli, beginning with a boys' school in 1816, followed by a girls' school in 1846. In Tunisia they founded the College Saint-Louis and a few primary schools. The rise of an Arab printing press could also be traced to this period. The first Tunisian newspaper appeared in Italian in 1838.

With all these modern developments, the anti-European fear in Tunisia and Tripoli gradually died down. Increased contacts with Europeans contributed to the intellectual awakening of these countries and to the Westernization of their rulers. However, the populace, on whose shoulders the burden of the reforms fell, were dissatisfied with the growth of foreign influence and Westernization on their land. They regarded their rulers as traitors and continued to follow the traditional way of life. Meanwhile Moroccan and Algerian rulers remained suspicious of Western influences, and they remained unaffected by them.

The conquest of Algeria

The conquest of Algeria was largely facilitated by the inactivity of its government. Having provoked France, Ḥuṣayn Dey, the ruler of Algeria, did nothing to fortify and arm his country in anticipation of a French attack. Thus it was that at the time of the French attack, Algeria was not in the least prepared for war. Despite the large number of its forces, 40 000 as against France's

37 500, Algeria was completely defeated. This was also due to the inadequacies of the army both in military strategy and technology. With this defeat, Algeria was occupied by France in 1830.

In July 1830, Ḥusayn Dey officially surrendered Algiers to the French. He was then allowed to leave the country with his family, members of the Dīwān (Council) and their families, and the janissaries. The control of Algeria thus passed into the hands of the occupying army who lacked administrative organization. The country was divided into two: the city of Algiers and some coastal centres were assigned to the French while the provinces of Oran and Constantine in the hinterland were brought under the rulers of Tunis. This division was however infringed continually by the French who extended their influence into the hinterland at will.

In 1834 a governor-general was established over French possessions in North Africa. The idea of a limited occupation according to which Algeria would not be directly ruled by the French was officially adopted till 1840. In most cases, this was taken to mean a system of indirect government in which indigenous chiefs were used to rule the people. 'Arab bureaux' were established to link French commanders with the local peoples. Meanwhile civil administration based on the pattern in France began to evolve in the coastal cities and towns. In 1845, the whole of Algeria was divided into 'Arab territory', where the *sharīʿa* was in operation and 'civil territory', where a French social order developed.

The resistance in Algeria

The French conquest and occupation of Algeria which led to the surrender of Ḥusayn Dey, the ruler, created a political vacuum in the land. Various local centres no longer recognized any authority and the bulk of the population regarded the French occupation with intense hostility. The people were determined to defend their culture and independence. However, this resistance was limited to the local level because of the lack of any centralized authority to mobilize the entire populace. The resistance was not well coordinated and it took many forms ranging from refusal to recognize the occupation to the assassination of certain Europeans and their local collaborators.

Two main centres of resistance were formed as the struggle gathered momentum: one was in the east and the other in the west. The eastern resistance led by Aḥmad Dey, the former governor of Constantine, constituted the main threat to the French in the early days of the struggle. Aḥmad attempted to restore the dey system and he strengthened himself with the remnants of the janissaries. He stopped the decay of the administration, consolidated the state machinery and reinforced the army.

The revolt in the west of the country was led by 'Abd al-Ḳādir who relied on the political support of Morocco. His objectives were: to put an end to the confusion in the land; to uphold the *sharīʿa*, and to lead a holy war against the French. He became the governor of western Algeria in 1832 and was recognized as such by the French. He was able to consolidate his authority through his energy, determination, and courage, and his victory over the French in 1835. In his bid to reform Algeria, he had to contend with some opposition from certain groups and individuals like the beys of Oran and Titeri. Eventually, he succeeded in creating a unified and centralized Arab state which encompassed two-thirds of contemporary Algerian territory. After putting an end to the confusion and disorder which prevailed in the land, he set up a coordinated legal and administrative system. He also established a standing army, introduced a state-controlled economy by establishing a system of monopolies, founded arms factories, and built fortresses for the defence of the country.

At the initial stage, the Algerian resistance against the French was very successful because of the latter's unstable policy and their inability to handle guerilla tactics. Up till 1837 the Algerians were able to effectively hold out on the French. But in 1837, the French attacked Constantine, the base of the eastern resistance and occupied it. Aḥmad Dey fled to the mountains from where he harrassed the French and the government which they set up in the east until 1848.

The fall of Constantine left the west as the main theatre of the struggle. 'Abd al-Ḳādir was routed by the French in 1843 after which he fled to Morocco with some of his followers. The administrative and military system which he had set up consequently crumbled. His defeat at this period was due to the total warfare which the French waged on him. He thereafter attempted to renew the struggle from his base in Morocco with the support of the Moroccan Sultan. This led to war between the French and Morocco in 1844. The result of this year was so disastrous for Morocco that the Sultan denounced 'Abd al-Ḳādir as an infidel and withdrew his support for him. This did not deter 'Abd al-Ḳādir who continued to fight the French without Moroccan support. His efforts were supplemented by that of the Taibiyya brotherhood who also proclaimed a *djihād* against the French. His resistance was eventually crushed in 1847 by the French and he was forced to surrender.

After this, other smaller groups carried on with the resistance in Algeria but all of them were eventually overpowered by the French. It was not until 1857 that the entire country came under the control of the French military command.

Colonization and financial servitude

The French did not colonize the inland regions of Algeria because of the threat of a general uprising by the people. In administering the colonized coastal areas around Algiers and other cities, the French first adopted the system of assimilation which made Algeria an integral part of France. But this policy was halted under the Second Empire. Napoleon III not only issued a wholesale condemnation of the policy, he also abrogated the representation of the Europeans in Algeria in the French parliament. He then went ahead to declare Algeria an 'Arab kingdom' in favour of the traditional chiefs, and much to the chagrin of the colonists. The area in which French colonists settled (civil territory) was also strictly limited. In the rest of Algeria, power was shared by

19.1 '*Abd al-Ḳādir*

19.2   *Infantry of ʿAbd al-Ḵādir*   **19.3**   *Cavalry of ʿAbd al-Ḵādir*

19.4   *Surrender of ʿAbd al-Ḵādir*

the French military and the traditional Muslim administrative authorities acting under the supervision of the 'Arab bureaux'.

Napoleon III also made some other administrative arrangements in Algeria. European settlers were asked to stay only in the towns, practise trade and technical occupations and not venture inland. After 1863, land was to be reserved for the Algerian communities and held according to traditional Islamic principles of land tenure. Only 'surplus' land was taken by the colonial state and granted to foreign companies and individuals. Private enterprise was not restricted in industry and trade, and all monopolies established by the previous rulers of Algeria were abolished. Furthermore, the Muslim system of justice was reorganized in 1854: mixed Franco-Muslim courts and the Muslim high council of justice were set up. Muslim religious observances such as the building of mosques, and the pilgrimage to Mecca were encouraged. Algerians were given the right to join the French army and the administration. Lastly, in 1869, a draft constitution was prepared for Algeria, providing for the country's autonomy and Muslim representatives in all elected assemblies.

In the mid-nineteenth century, Tunisia was virtually an independent country ruled by the bey, while Tripolitania had fallen under direct Ottoman rule since 1835. Yet, because of the rising tide of European influence and capital throughout the Maghrib, similar reforms were carried out in Tunisia and Tripolitania. In Tunisia, the liberal group, supported by the European powers, produced a reform programme in 1857 as a result of which state monopolies were abolished and private enterprise established. The municipality was reorganized and a constitution was promulgated in 1861 which made ministers responsible to a representative assembly called the Supreme Council. In Tripolitania the administration was reorganized, and courts to deal with commercial, civil and criminal matters were established in 1865.

These reforms led to the development of private enterprise and the advent of foreign capital in the Maghrib. The abolition of customs barriers between Algeria and France, for instance, opened the markets of these countries to foreign goods. Various firms with large capital were subsequently introduced to the Maghrib. The first foreign bank in Algeria was opened in 1851, while that of Tunisia was in 1873. In Tripolitania, the first banks made their appearance in 1880. Banks, concession-holders and companies were closely linked, and they enjoyed special privileges in Algeria and Tunisia. In Tunisia, those companies mined lead, exported esparto grass and experimented with the cultivation of cotton, potatoes and tobacco. The building of railways was started in Algeria in 1857 and in Tunisia in 1859. The foreign companies also modernized the ports, set up telegraph lines, built roads and started town-planning along the coast.

The 'development' of North Africa by foreign capital was reinforced by the training of Europeanized personnel. In Algeria the first Franco-Arab secondary school was established in 1875 followed by a teacher training school. Also in Tunisia and Tripoli there were schools where foreign languages were taught. An Arabic press consequently emerged in Algeria, Tunisia and Tripoli producing local newspapers.

The advent of foreign capital into the states of the Maghrib took place at different times. In Algeria, it began after the colonial occupation of the country and French capital was dominant. But in Tunisia and Tripolitania, it preceded the conquest and it was more multi-national. The reforms in these other countries were funded by foreign loans obtained under very harsh conditions. This led to an increase in their foreign debt. The case of Tunisia was so critical that by 1869 its foreign debt had risen to twelve times the amount of its national revenue. This led the government to declare itself bankrupt and accept an International Financial Commission (IFC) which took over the control of its finances, and turned Tunisia into a semi-colony of the European powers.

British and Italian interests on the IFC were substantial. But while Britain decided to focus its attention on Egypt, the Italian government was in no position to press Italian claims until the 1880s. France, on the other hand, once it had recovered from the 1870 defeat, began to dominate the IFC. The Italians shifted their attention to Tripolitania. But Ottoman rule and Tripolitania's relative poverty protected its autonomy till after 1911.

Morocco also experienced the same pressure from European capital, although it managed to resist longer than any other North African country. While the treaty of 1856 between Morocco and Britain opened the country to foreign capital, that of 1860 concluded with Spain imposed heavy financial conditions on it. Similar treaties with France and other European countries paved the way for the country's eventual colonial subjection.

The conquest of Algeria and the commercial penetration of Tunisia, Morocco and Tripolitania were followed by the settlement of foreigners in those countries in large numbers. These foreigners were commercial agents who represented foreign firms and traded extensively, thus acquiring great wealth. They also enjoyed a number of privileges which were not extended to the local inhabitants. Of all the foreign settlers, the Algerian colonists were in the most privileged position. They were not interested only in trade, but also in private ownership of land and agriculture. They had their own legal and administrative system and formed a compact society which was hostile to the indigenous population. As their numbers increased much more rapidly than in the other states, they hatched plans of extending their influence on the administration of the country and seizing more land from the local people than the metropolis allowed them.

The reaction of traditional society

The indigenous population became increasingly incensed by the foreigners who were penetrating every aspect of their national life in addition to dominating their economy. While some of the liberals in North Africa appreciated their countries' problems and understood the need for reforms, the majority of the population was hostile to the foreigners and to the states' reform programmes. The reforms aroused the particular hatred of the *marabouts* (holy men) and the rural population who saw them as another phase in colonial subjection. Moreover, the Europeanized Muslims were regarded by the peasants and nomads as traitors and collaborators and they refused to place any confidence in them.

Thus the struggle against the foreigners was widely supported among the people in nearly every Muslim country at the beginning f the 1860s. While the people embarked on an active propaganda for a pan-Muslim *djihād*, local insurrections sprang up almost everywhere. It was at this time that the Sanūsiyya brotherhood who fiercely protected the purity of Islam against European contamination came into prominence. The insurrections were not organized and they took the form of looting, assassinations, and the destruction of European structures. Later they were followed by major national uprisings.

The first national rebellion broke out in Tunisia in 1864 and it was led by the Tijāniyya brotherhood. However, it was the isolation of the rebels and their vacillation which made it possible for the bey's government to save the capital and destroy the rebellion. A similar rebellion led by the Dergawa brotherhood broke out in western Algeria in 1864 and it was with much difficulty that the French were able to put it down. In 1871, a national rebellion, tagged a *djihad*, broke out in eastern Algeria and spread widely, and it was not until 1872 that the French were able to take control of the situation.

The suppression of these revolts was accompanied by wholesale repression, fines, seizure of land and disarmament of the communities. However, while all this was going on, the European settlers did not take sides with the Muslims; rather they supported the armed struggle against them. Even in Algeria where the white settlers were also fighting for democratic and socialist ideals, they did not identify with the national aspirations of North African Muslims.

Towards an imperialist policy

With the suppression of the insurrections described above, the way was opened for the colonization of North Africa. This was at a time when developments in Europe and the spread of capitalism favoured colonial expansion. This expansion gradually took the form of a struggle among the European powers for dividing up the world and for the monopoly of sources of raw materials.

Colonialism had one of its greatest triumphs in Algeria. The country was directly administered and the colonists therein constituted themselves into a privileged social class that enjoyed all civil and political rights and referred to themselves as 'citizens'. The indigenous population, however, were denied any rights and were derogatorily referred to as 'subjects'. The white settlers also acquired a lot of land at the expense of the local inhabitants. In addition, French capital investment increased considerably and economic ties with France expanded.

Tunisia experienced a similar situation towards the end of the nineteenth century. In 1881, French troops moved into the country and the local ruler was made to sign some treaties which gave the French the right to establish a protectorate over the country. Morocco and Tripolitania succeeded in postponing the European occupation of their territories, though Morocco did not succeed in curtailing the privileges and high-handedness of the foreigners resident there.

To the Muslims in North Africa, the European occupation of their countries was seen as an attack on Islam. The struggles of the Muslims thus received the moral support of the other Islamic countries in the East. Relying on this support, Muslims in Algeria and Tunisia made fresh attempts to forcefully resist colonization. But despite the heroism and ferocity of such movements the uprisings failed to achieve their objectives. These moves could in fact be seen as belated actions by the people to defend their traditions, culture and identity which had already been undermined by foreign conquest and eroded by the development of colonial capitalism in their land.

20

The Sahara in the nineteenth century

This chapter looks at nineteenth-century Saharan history at two levels. The first deals with the internal history of the Sahara which had to do with changes and fluctuations in the lives of Saharan nomads and inhabitants of the oases. The second examines contacts between the Saharan peoples and the outside world, with emphasis on the effects of European economic penetration on their lives. Due to the dearth of material on the history of some of the Saharan societies, we shall attempt only a survey of developments in the desert with special emphasis on the camel nomads. This group was very prominent in the Sahara because their wealth in terms of camel acquisitions conferred a great military power on them which they used to plunder and loot the oases dwellers and other agricultural communities. It should be pointed out, however, that although these nomads raided the agriculturists for slaves and even demanded tributes from them in return for protection, their ultimate aim was not to destroy these agriculturist groups but to exercise some control over their produce. Therefore, as the key actors in political, military and religious changes in nineteenth-century Sahara, the camel nomads deserve to be given a special focus.

Society and environment

Due to the arid environment of the desert, the people developed as nomads rearing different kinds of animals. But this is not to say that the whole of the Sahara was arid or that all its inhabitants were nomads. There were variations not only in the climate but also in the terrain of the desert both of which affected the inhabitants and shaped their societies.

Rainfall in the desert varies from one side to the other. While the driest part of the desert is the eastern central segment, in present-day Egypt and eastern Libya, some other parts enjoy a higher than average rainfall which cuts across the desert from north to south, traversing the dry central portions. Population in the well-watered areas is dense and travellers avoided the driest regions. Agriculture is possible in the moist areas and in some cases, even irrigated agriculture is practicable.

These disparities in the desert environment have affected the people in it. Those who kept livestock had to move from place to place with their herds in search of pasture for them to survive. The people at the edge of the desert have taken maximum advantage of their environment and adapted to it accordingly. At the southern shore of the desert, called the Sahel, cattle nomads and settled agricultural communities lived in a dependent and harmonious relationship. Because of the demands of the environment, some nomads had to turn some members of their families into farmers while the rest tended the herds. Others sowed the crops, went away with their herds in search of pasture, and returned to harvest the sparse yields of the untended fields. In the central, dry parts of the desert, nomadic peoples kept different kinds of animals but they relied heavily on the camel which could adapt beautifully to the dry environment. In addition, they had to migrate either for short or long distances, and at regular intervals, depending on the availability of the required pasture.

The dry environment also affected the political structures of the nomads. They evolved similar non-centralized political systems which have been described as 'segmentary lineage systems'. While this structure met the need for dispersal in search of pasture, it also provided for unified action when necessary in the face of external aggression. Such societies were organized according to descent from a common ancestor. As long as the lineage authority was intact, internal conflict could be resolved without recourse to any external 'central authority'. At the same time, the different lineages could also unite to face an external threat with the core of such a union representing a central authority. However, sedentary or partly sedentary people could also be assimilated by the nomad group thus showing that kinship was not the only principle of association among the desert inhabitants.

Another similarity among Saharan people was a hierarchical social structure. At the top of the social ladder were lineages of aristocratic warriors. Under them were groups of free but politically subordinate people who were the descendants of conquered nomads. At the bottom of the social ladder were slaves, or descendants of slaves who worked as servants, herders, artisans, trade specialists and farmers.

Changing relations with the outside world

Life in the desert was not in complete isolation. Despite the fact that the nomads, for instance, lived in a world of their own, they had to rely on the settled agricultural communities for grains and other essential items that they needed as they could not subsist on livestock alone. To obtain these other items they depended not only on plunder and tribute, but also on peaceful trade with the sedentary states. Thus the nomads were not cut off from external influences. Cordial relations between nomads and sedentary groups was also encouraged by the fact that aggressive nomads did not always pose an effective military threat to dense sedentary populations who employed their large numbers to good advantage.

At the beginning of the nineteenth century, the pattern of interaction between nomads and sedentary states at the northern edge of the desert differed greatly from that at the southern edge. At the southern fringes of the desert the sedentary population sought to reduce the nomad menace by involving them in the economy of the fertile areas. This was done by giving them a stake in desert-edge commerce, agriculture and urban growth. They also tried to play the nomad groups one against another. Despite the fact that geographical barriers in North Africa, such as the Atlas and other mountain ranges, kept the desert nomads at a safe distance, the settled population at the northern edge of the desert still had to contend with them. In addition to the methods used by the southern population to tackle the nomads, the states of the Maghrib to the north of the desert demonstrated considerable skill in manipulating the nomads and playing one group against another thus sparing themselves direct confrontations with them. Also, the wealth of the Maghribian states afforded them the chance to support well-armed forces which intervened from time to time to bring recalcitrant nomads to order. But rather than rely solely on force, the North African rulers also used their position as rulers of Muslim states to enhance their chances in diplomatic dealings with the nomads most of whom had accepted Islam.

As the French began to advance in Algeria, and the Ottomans penetrated Libya, there was a change in relations between Saharan societies and the outside world. The southward push of the Ottomans and the French in the desert had a similar aim, namely, to control and tax the trans-Saharan trade, and to prevent other powers from gaining a foothold in the hinterland of the Mediterranean. But despite the similar timing and speed of the penetration, the style of the two powers differed greatly.

The Ottomans were very cautious in their dealings with the nomads in the interior of their domains in Libya. They exploited the divisions and friendships between nomad groups to their own advantage. Their knowledge of local politics and experience of governing segmentary societies stood them in good stead in their relations with the desert nomads. They established diplomatic links with the groups they could not govern and drew a lot of influence from the prestige which they enjoyed as rulers of the political centre of the Muslim world. They took direct control of Libya in 1835 from the Ḳāramānli dynasty in order to stop the spread of French influence from Algeria into Libya. Ottoman officials were then stationed in the desert to supervise efforts to collect taxes levied on the date palms of Djalo and Awḏjīla and to maintain order in the surrounding desert. As time went on, the Ottomans became involved in nomad conflicts as they protected the oasis dwellers of Awḏjīla from nomad attacks. The Ottoman officials also attempted to rule through some local rulers, but overall Ottoman influence in the desert was very limited. And by the end of the nineteenth century, the desert interior was effectively governed by the Sanūsiyya, a religious brotherhood established in the 1840s.

It is instructive to note that Ottoman interference in the Sahara, though limited, met with stiff resistance from the nomads. But despite their negligible military resources, the Ottomans were able to manipulate the politics of the nomads and produce considerable disruption among them. An instance of this was the disruption of the Awlād Sulaymān group and their allies which the Ottoman Pasha (governor) of Tripoli, ʿAlī Askar effected in 1840–1.

The French, on the other hand, lacked the skill with which to manipulate local politics and they relied instead on the force of arms. They started by defeating ʿAbd al-Ḳādir whom they saw as the first obstacle to French expansion in Algeria in 1847. In order to provide security for the trans-Saharan trade between Algeria and the Western Sudan which they wanted to promote, the French established many outposts in the desert. However, their activities in the desert were disrupted by revolts from nomad groups such as the Awlād Sīdī Shaykh and the Ahaggar Tuareg. It was only when the French began to recruit nomads into their army of occupation that they were able to put down all the serious resistance to their expansion. This was because they were able to combine the mobility and local knowledge of the recruited nomads with their own superior firepower.

The Moroccan government also had some stake in the Sahara, namely, to extend its territory beyond the Atlas mountains into the desert. But unlike the French, it did not have the means to finance an army capable of doing this. What Moroccan sultans did was to manipulate existing political and diplomatic ties with the desert societies. They entered into nomad politics by supporting one nomad group against another, by mediating disputes, and by capitalizing on their prestige as religious leaders just as the Ottomans did. This last avenue of influence was particularly potent as the religious influence of the Moroccan sultan in the nineteenth century extended as far as the Western Sudan.

Of all the external forces penetrating the desert in the nineteenth century, the French were the most significant. This was because the French occupation of the Algerian desert marked a turning point in relations between the desert societies and the outside world. The French occupation was far more permanent than either the occasional expeditions of the Moroccan sultan into the desert or the irregular visits of Ottoman officials to the oases of Cyrenaica. The nomads, for the first time, had to contend with an army armed with modern weapons and manned by local guides and recruits who knew the desert very well. Not only that, the French administered the nomads through the Arab Bureaux, an elite group of officers who studied the ways of the Muslims so as to be better able to administer them and ruled the local population through appointed chiefs. On the whole, the French occupation of the Sahara was far more complete than other settled communities on the fringes of the desert had ever attempted. It also led to a major drain on the meagre agricultural resources of the desert.

In reaction to the French occupation, the nomads tended to cooperate among themselves to protect their vital interests and to avoid their unconditional submission to the external invader. Religion served as the unifying factor in most of the larger scale resistance movements which transcended kinship ties. The religious orders and their respected leaders, who had hitherto performed valuable political and religious services, became the political and military champions during such crises. Resistance to the French thus crystallized around religious leaders and the brotherhoods.

Apart from provoking resistance, the French push into the desert also produced unusual economic circumstances. The Ahaggar Tuareg, for instance, having been cut off from their northern markets, transformed the basis of their economy. This economic adjustment took the form of a diversification of the articles of trade and the development of a new trade route in the 1880s. This was made possible through the unity of the Ahaggar which, in turn, had resulted from conflict with their neighbours in the 1870s.

Another aspect of the resistance against the French was the increased mobility of camel nomads with their herds. A classic example of this was the adventure of the Djeramna who had a clash with the French in 1881 near Géryville from where they began to roam the desert from one end of the Sahara to the other for almost fifty years before returning in 1925 to their initial location near Géryville.

Desert trade and the nomads

Technological change in Europe in the nineteenth century did not only facilitate the conquest of the Sahara, it also transformed the economic life of the desert. This was because the manufacture of cheap products promoted a new phase of European penetration. Trade with Europe increased tremendously in the nineteenth century with different effects on the regional economies of the Sahara. Various groups at the edge of the Sahara involved themselves in the export of goods such as gum, ostrich feathers and tanned goat skin. European economic penetration also affected the tastes of consumers; for instance, the custom of drinking heavily sugared tea spread during the century.

The trans–Saharan trade was also responsible for establishing closer contact with the world economy. Involved in the trade were Saharan merchants, guides, transporters, and suppliers of the Saharan exports. Inhabitants of the northern oases such as Tafilālet and the Fezzān played a crucial role in the organization and financing of the trade. Although nomadic groups such as the Ahaggar Tuareg and the Tubu traded in small quantities of slaves and other products on their own account, their main role was to provide transport animals, guides, and military escorts for caravans. Thus, most of the Saharan nomads participated actively in the trade that passed through their territory.

Trade, however, on the different Saharan routes was not stable. There were many fluctuations due to either a decline or a rise in trade, and these affected the development of desert societies. The control of trade routes was much sought after because of the large revenue it brought. Meanwhile the concentration of wealth in the hands of particular groups often upset the socio-political equilibrium, while the decline of a hitherto active trade route also led to readjustment by the affected groups. This readjustment could either be in the

20.1   *Desert-edge trade: 'Moors' trading gum at the* escale *of Bakel on the Senegal River*

form of an increased commitment to desert-edge regional trade, or raids on wealthy neighbours, or the practice of animal husbandry.

As the location and volume of the trans-Saharan trade shifted, the trade moved away from the French in Algeria much to the chagrin of French imperialists. The French tried to remedy the situation but trade failed to respond in their favour. The situation was such that while some trade routes were rising into prominence, others were declining. The Tripoli–Kano route, for instance, became particularly important after the middle of the nineteenth century as trade on the route increased. The trade along this route which was carried by Tuaregs began to decline due to a number of factors, prominent among which was the arrival of the railway in Kano in 1911. The Benghazi–Wadai route succeeded the Tripoli–Kano route in importance and lasted past the turn of the century because of the Sanūsiyya and because the areas served by the route were very extensive.

The Sanūsiyya was a Muslim brotherhood that spread among the Beduin of Cyrenaica after 1843 and later extended southward along the Benghazi–Wadai route. The brotherhood spanned the entire length of the route, providing merchants with a common legal, social and commercial framework plus a postal system. The leaders of the brotherhood strove to promote trade by maintaining peace along the route. However, they also benefited from the trade: from the revenue from tolls, payment for storage space, and gifts from merchants.

The trans-Saharan trade affected the lives of nomadic people in a number of ways. Some nomads near the West African Sahel raided Sudanese populations for slaves which they traded on their own account although they were largely

20.2 *Minaret of the Agades mosque*

transporters and not merchants. The most important impact of the slave trade on Saharan societies was, perhaps, the ready supply of slave labour which was used to expand the societies, especially those on the desert edge where labour was needed for herding, agriculture and artisan occupations. This was especially the case among the Tuareg populations. The volume of slaves carried across the desert increased in the course of the century with North Africa and the Middle East receiving more than they did in the previous centuries.

Trade in firearms across the desert also continued despite attempts by Europeans to stop it. European arms became very popular in the Sahara to the extent that European rifles had become commonplace by the 1890s. This spread of firearms to raiders must have been responsible for increased insecurity on the Tripoli–Kano route after 1898. Another effect of the trans-Saharan trade was the strengthening of the Tuareg whose economic strength in the desert depended not only on their mobility and possession of camels but also on their possession of firearms procured from the trans-Saharan trade. This made them very strong and formidable: they were powerful allies because of their economic potential and devastating enemies because of their military prowess.

Desert people also had an economic, political and religious influence on the Sudan. Politically, the nineteenth century *djihād* led to the formation of the Sokoto Caliphate, a large state which promoted economic growth in its centre near Kano, Katsina and Zaria. The surplus products of these areas, especially cloth, were exported to the central Sudan and the Tuareg country to the north. Economic growth in the desert thus complemented the developments in the savannah.

The southern Sahara also served as a reservoir of Islamic learning from which the savannah continued to tap, especially in the nineteenth century. An important aspect of Saharan societies was a division into warrior and saintly lineages. While the first aspired to warfare and politics, the second had an ideology of moderation and peace, experience in commerce and a shared intellectual tradition. The clerical lineages mastered the two politically useful sciences of jurisprudence and mysticism. They thus performed the task of mediation and their activities had economic, political and scholarly aspects. They maintained and developed Islamic scholarship and their influence extended south of the desert.

Conclusion

The nineteenth century was a period of dramatic changes in the desert. The economic unity of North Africa was shattered by the French occupation of Algeria which diverted trans-Saharan trade routes east and west of Algeria. By the end of the nineteenth century, the trans-Saharan trade had almost completely collapsed. However, more research still needs to be done on the impact of this trade on the lives of the nomads. The arid environment limited the reaction of the nomads to external incursion like that of the French. But more research is also needed on the effects of the European penetration on regional economies at the fringe of the desert. Nonetheless, an important theme which runs through Saharan history is the strong influence of climate on the people and their historical development although there is presently a lack of detailed data to substantiate this.

21 The nineteenth-century Islamic revolutions in West Africa

The area we are going to examine in this chapter was known to Arab travellers and historians as *bilād al-Sūdān* (land of the black people). This region had some unique characteristics which affected its historical importance. One was the delicate balance maintained between the environment, man, and animals. This equilibrium could also be found between settled agriculturalists and pastoral nomads; between freemen and slaves; and between Muslims and adherents of traditional religions. The region was also an important commercial centre where foreign imports and local goods were exchanged. Furthermore, the area permitted immense mobility and population mixing as illustrated by the spread of the Fulbe from their original homeland in Futa-Toro over a wide area of the *bilād al-Sūdān* stretching from the Atlantic Ocean to Lake Chad and the Cameroon. Again, the region saw the beginnings of *dār al-Islām* in West Africa, and after a long period of the spread of Islam through teaching and preaching, the region witnessed in the nineteenth century the movements which gave birth to three major caliphates: the Sokoto Caliphate of Northern Nigeria, the Ḥamdallahi Caliphate in Massina and the Tijāniyya Caliphate in Senegambia and Massina.

The religious background

The primary objective of the nineteenth century West African *djihād* movements was religious, namely, to restore Islam to its original purity. But because Islam is a comprehensive religion that incorporates all aspects of human life, the *djihād* also had social, political and economic undertones which were all products of the circumstances prevailing in the Western Sudan at the time.

The *djihād* movements were led by devout and pious men such as Shaykh 'Uthmān dan Fodio, Shaykh Aḥmad Lobbo (Seku Ahmadu) and al-Hadjdj 'Umar. These men were not only learned but also very committed Muslims who obeyed the *sharī'a* to the letter. They saw themselves as having been ordained by Allah and their *djihād* as the fulfilment of prophecies by the Prophet Muḥammad. As far as they were concerned, they were executing the divine will.

218

To support their cause, the leaders of the *djihād* relied on several kuranic verses, the *ḥadīth* (prophetic traditions) and other Islamic literature. The idea of *djihād*, at this time, had acquired mystical undertones which obliged the leaders to observe a strict code of moral conduct and self-denial. The advocates of the *djihād* were thus expected to live exemplary puritanical lives and to practise what they preached. In proving the propriety of the *djihād*, its leaders also turned to Muḥammad's prophecy that Allah would send a reformer to all true Muslim communities after every hundred years to purify and renew the religion. Twelve of such reformers were said to have been foretold by the Prophet: the first ten were believed to have appeared in the Muslim East and the eleventh had come in the person of Askia al-Muḥammad, the king of Songhay in the *bilād al-Sūdān*. The twelfth was expected in the nineteenth century. The *djihād* leaders were quick to exploit this belief: both Shaykh 'Uthman dan Fodio and Seku Ahmadu claimed to be the last reformer promised by Allah while al-Hadjdj 'Umar also saw himself as fulfilling a pre-ordained divine mission.

To further prove their legitimacy, the three reformers claimed that the divine assignment of carrying out a *djihād* was committed to them both by the Prophet and the heads of the respective brotherhood to which each of them belonged. According to 'Uthman dan Fodio, he was ordered in a vision to carry out the *djihād* by the Prophet Muḥammad and 'Abd-al Ḳadir al-Djilani, the head of the Ḳādirīyya brotherhood. In the same vein, al-Hadjdj 'Umar also claimed to have been commissioned by the Prophet and Shaykh al-Tidjāni, the mentor of the Tijāniyya, in a vision to carry out the *djihād*.

The Torodbe heritage

However, despite the mystical overtones of the nineteenth-century West African *djihāds* they were not isolated developments. Rather, they represented fresh waves in the long tradition of religious reforms already existing in the Western Sudan directed at establishing the rule of justice and equity which had been neglected by the local rulers. The leaders of the *djihāds* drew immediate inspiration from contemporary sources closer to their home base such as: the achievements of the Torodbe in Bundu, Futa Jallon and Futa Toro; the peaceful reform attempts of Shaykh al-Kunti and Muḥammad ibn 'Abd al-Karīm al-Maghīlī; the reaction of the brotherhoods to the outbreak of Wahhābī fundamentalism in Arabia; and the outbreak of the *djihād* of 'Uthman dan Fodio in Sokoto which served as precedent for Seku Ahmadu and al-Hadjdj 'Umar.

The Torodbe 'society' comprised Muslim scholars drawn from diverse ethnic groups throughout Western and Central Sudan, such as the Fulbe, Wolof, Mande, Hausa, and Berber of either free, slave or caste origin. Fulbe culture was however predominant as the Torodbe who originated from other ethnic groups, spoke the Fulfude language and embraced their customs and beliefs. They also intermarried with the Fulbe and accompanied them on their endless migrations. Consequently, the Torodbe became identified with the Fulbe and they were in fact the scholarly branch of the Fulbe. The Torodbe pursued Islamic reform with a passion as they sought to establish a society in which the members would be related not by blood but by the profession of a common creed, Islam, and sharing a common Fulbe culture.

The Torodbe had a number of achievements to their credit which inspired the nineteenth-century reformers. There were successful Torodbe *djihāds* in the seventeenth and eighteenth centuries which led to the formation of Torodbe imamates in Bundu, Futa Toro and Futa Jallon. The Torodbe also produced learned families such as the Toronkawa of 'Uthman dan Fodio, the Bari of Seku Ahmadu, and al-Hadjdj 'Umar's family. The nineteenth-century reformers drew a lot of encouragement from the Torodbe heritage which they used to mobilize support for their *djihāds*.

West African reformers

Apart from the Torodbe heritage, another source of inspiration to the reformers was the example of non-violent reform by Shaykh al-Mukhtār al-Kunti (1729–1811). Al-Kunti was the leader of the Ḳādiriyya brotherhood in the *bilād al-Sūdān* from about 1750–1811. From this position he wrote a lot on religious matters and exercised tremendous influence in the Western Sudan. Both 'Uthman dan Fodio and Seku Ahmadu regarded him as their spiritual guide in the Ḳādiriyya way. Even al-Hadjdj 'Umar who belonged to the Tijāniyya also held al-Kunti in high esteem. These three nineteenth-century reformers used the latter's views on religious matters to support and legitimize revolutionary action.

The ideas of Muhammad ibn 'Abd al-Karīm al-Maghīlī, the sixteenth-century itinerant Maghribian scholar, also influenced the West African reformers. Al-Maghīlī distinguished between the abode of Islam and that of war, defined the state of unbelief, and identified compromising rulers and *'ulamā'* (scholars) 'who have covered the truth with falsehood in a way that makes a number of ignorant Muslims go astray'. He ruled that *djihād* against such syncretic rulers and *'ulamā'* was obligatory on Muslims.

Just as the reformers were influenced by developments from within West Africa, they were also exposed to external influences. This was because political and religious developments in the Middle East, the birthplace of Islam, affected the entire Islamic world. One of such events was the capture of Mecca and Medina at the beginning of the nineteenth century by Wahhābī extremists and the reaction of Eastern brotherhoods to the take-over. Not only did the Wahhābī revolution catalyse militant action in the Islamic world, it also provoked a vigorous revival of religious brotherhoods. Part of that revival was the birth of the Tijāniyya order led in the Western Sudan by al-Hadjdj 'Umar. The *djihād* of 'Uthman dan Fodio is also said to have gained some impetus from the upsurge of such Eastern brotherhoods.

Finally, the *djihād* of 'Uthman dan Fodio provided a precedent for the other two prominent nineteenth-century reformers. In the first place, dan Fodio's *djihād* unleashed the revolutionary fervour that had been accumulated in the Western Sudan. The literature of the Sokoto *djihād* also encouraged militant reformism and it inspired subsequent leaders of *djihāds*. Al-Hadjdj ʿUmar and Seku Aḥmadu were personally exposed to the Sokoto Caliphate from where they drew some inspiration for their own reform movements.

Syncretism

The reform movements were propelled by certain forces which came together under the banner of Islam to unseat some local rulers in the Western Sudan. But before we analyse the composition of such 'forces', let us examine what they were fighting against.

Islam, as it was practised in nineteenth-century Western Sudan did not meet up to the ideals of the reformers. Western Sudanese converts did not totally abandon their traditional religious practices. They mixed Islam with traditional African beliefs. This syncretic Islam was practised both by the rulers of the Western Sudan and their Muslim subjects. The *'ulamā'* in the region tolerated this syncretism because they wished to continue to enjoy the patronage and protection of the ruling dynasties. They also served as political and administrative officials in the royal courts. Muslim traders, because of their international connections, attracted a lot of wealth to the Western Sudanese states. There was thus an intimate relationship between West African rulers and the Muslim trading and scholarly communities which prevented the latter from raising their eyebrows at the un-Islamic practices of the rulers.

However, the reformers frowned at this compromise and they strove to eradicate all the traditional religious practices that had been introduced into Islam. They started by preaching against all such practices and calling Muslims to return to pure Islam as enjoined by the *sharīʿa* (Islamic law). They also preached against the oppressive acts and corruption of the rulers, their abuse of power, their worldliness and their imposition of harsh taxation on their subjects.

The reaction of the rulers to this attempt to undermine their authority was to try and extinguish the revolution at the early stage. But the reformers regarded such attempts as acts of unbelief and declared the territories of such rulers as 'abodes of war' which had to be conquered and incorporated into the Muslim community. The result of this was the sweeping away of the authority of the rulers. Three caliphates thus sprang up in place of these local authorities: one in Sokoto, another in Massina and the third in the Senegambia.

Widespread support

The *djihād* forces that conquered the local rulers of the Western Sudan were of different ethnic and social backgrounds. They were led by the *shaykhs* who through their preaching and teaching rallied other Muslims, while spreading the influence of their respective brotherhoods. The nucleus of the movement was the *djamaʿa* (Community of the Faithful) made up of initiates and followers of the different brotherhoods, students of the s̲h̲ayk̲h̲s and other independent scholars. But the *djamaʿa* were not powerful enough to defeat the armies of the West African rulers. Therefore, they admitted other people into their ranks. These new recruits formed the majority of the fighting forces. They were Muslims who were attracted by the charisma of the leaders of the reform movements. They were Muslims who could have been accused of mixing Islam with traditional practices, but their participation in the *djihād* erased whatever would have marked them out of the *djamaʿa* as syncretics.

An important aspect of the *djihāds* was the Fulbe factor. The majority of the *djamaʿa* were Fulbe in origin and the leadership of the caliphates was also Fulbe dominated. This Fulbe influence has led many to conclude that the *djihāds* represented Fulbe insurrection against their host countries. However, this view cannot stand because while some Fulbe joined the *djihād* for the sake of ethnic solidarity, others fought on the side of the anti-*djihād* forces. Also, the *djihāds* of Seku Aḥmadu and al-Hadjdj ʿUmar were directed partly against Fulbe (Torodbe) political leadership in the Senegambia and Massina.

Nevertheless, the Fulbe had ample reasons to support the reformers' cause. There was a series of clashes between pastoral Fulbe and agricultural communities in the south, on the one hand, and between Fulbe and Tuareg in the north, on the other. While the problem with the agricultural communities always centred around the payment of taxes and fines for damages caused by Fulbe cattle on crops, the Tuareg problem was caused by the latter raiding Fulbe cattle. The *djihād* thus offered the Fulbe freedom from the burden of taxes and fines, and security from Tuareg raids.

In addition, the Fulbe of Massina and the Senegambia had other specific reasons to support the *djihād*. The Fulbe in Massina had been suffering from the oppressive rule of the Bambara of Segu since the middle of the eighteenth century. The Bambara frequently raided them, exacted very harsh tributes from them and enslaved them. Thus, the Massina Fulbe did not hesitate to throw in their lot with Seku Aḥmadu and his *djihād* against the Bambara overlords of Massina. The Fulbe of the Senegambia also suffered a similar fate from the hands of their Torodbe rulers. Coupled with this was the alliance of the Torodbe rulers of Senegambia and the French who refused to pay tribute to the Fulbe. The Fulbe of Futa Toro were thus enthusiastic in their support of al-Hadjdj ʿUmar's *djihād* against the corrupt local rulers and the 'infidel' French.

Lastly, the reformers drew a lot of support from the slave population and caste groups of the Western Sudan. The increase in slave raiding drove a lot of the prospective victims to join the leaders of the *djihād* while slaves were promised freedom if they fought on the side of the reformers. Thus Muslims and non-Muslims alike sought redemption and security by joining the *djihād*. Slaves consequently constituted the bulk of the fighting forces of the *djihād* and they were abundantly rewarded after the war.

It is thus clear that the fighting force of the reformers had different backgrounds. They came from the Fulbe, the Hausa, the Mande, the Wolof, and the Tuareg; from nomadic pastoralists, and settled agricultural communities; from the ranks of the literate *'ulamā'* and their disciples, and illiterate people; and from caste groups and slaves. Each group had its particular grievances, and all shared the dream of great advantages accruing to them if the prevailing situation was changed.

The faithful in dār al-Hidjra

An important episode in the reform movement was the *hidjra* (emigration) of the reformers and their followers from the territories of the local rulers who were threatened by their movements. 'Uthman dan Fodio and his followers fled Degel and settled in Gudu in 1804; Seku Ahmadu left Kuby in Massina for Nukuma in 1816–17 and al-Hadjdj 'Umar left Jugunku in Futa Jallon for Dinguiraye in 1849. These emigrations were not voluntary but were forced on them by the local authorities who expelled the revolutionaries for collecting arms, recruiting followers and for increasing their agitation for reforms.

From their new bases, the reformers now prepared for the inevitable clash with the local leadership. There was a massive collection of arms, erection of defences and 'Uthman dan Fodio and Seku Ahmadu assumed the title of *amir al-mu'minīn* (commander of the faithful). Many refugees, either fleeing from persecution or responding to the appeals of the *shaykhs* trooped into the new settlements. There was a lot of religious fervour in those bases. Many students were initiated into the religious brotherhoods. There were endless discussions of events that led to the *hidjra* and of preparations for war. Thus the *hidjra* not only removed the *djamaʿa* from immediate danger, it also gave them the opportunity to prepare for the *djihād*.

The reformers, however, had a tremendous advantage over their enemies, namely, that they enjoyed greater popular support. Because they saw their mission as having been ordained by God, they put all their heart into it and also championed the cause of the frustrated masses. They had the unflinching loyalty of the *djamaʿa*. The reformers were also seen as possessing supernatural powers, and the failure of several attempts to assassinate them further proved their invincibility and divine protection. All these, together with intellectual superiority and disciplined life-style, boosted their public image and drew a large following to them.

It is also important to note the manner of the reformer's assault on the local authorities. Their conquest of such large areas, despite the strength of their opponents, was a testimony to their careful planning. This also determined the extent of their conquests. While 'Uthman dan Fodio and Seku Ahmadu restricted their *djihāds* to their home regions in Hausaland and Massina respectively, al-Hadjdj 'Umar aimed at the conquest of the whole of the Western Sudan. He could embark on this grandiose scheme because his forces were more broadly based than those of 'Uthman dan Fodio and Seku Ahmadu, and they were well equipped and well trained. It was only his death in 1864 that brought his dreams to an end.

Some consequences of the djihāds

The immediate result of the *djihāds* was the establishment of Islamic theocracies called caliphates. These political entities were very huge but the degree of centralization achieved by each differed. Perhaps the highest degree of centralization was achieved at Ḥamdollahi (1818–62) because of its small, homogeneous population and good communications. Seku Aḥmadu and his successors were thus able to apply the *Sharīʿa* to a very large extent in their caliphate.

Secondly, political offices were shared among the reformers. The highest office of *amīr al-muʿminīn* was vested in the descendants of the reformers who resided in the capital cities. The emirates into which the caliphates were divided were governed by top-ranking officers of the *djihād* most of whom were scholars. Some slaves who were loyal to the *djihād* were also rewarded with high office. Because the Fulbe formed the bulk of the fighting forces during the *djihāds*, they became the rulers of the Western Sudan as traditional power and social standing were transferred to them. They filled most of the administrative positions and formed an elite group. Slaves who had participated in the *djihād* were freed; those who did not were re-enslaved, while more slaves were captured in raids across frontiers and in suppressing rebellions.

All individuals and groups within the caliphates were afforded protection and security. *Sharīʿa* courts were established and many un-Islamic practices were banned but they were replaced in some cases by equally imperfect acts. Moreover, because of the large size of the caliphates, some of the old practices resurfaced, and many compromises were made after the initial religious zeal had died down. Perhaps, the greatest success of the revolutions was in the field of education and conversion. Many schools were founded throughout the caliphates, and the *djihāds* resulted in the entrenchment of Islam and the two major religious brotherhoods, the Ḳādirīyya and the Tijāniyya, in West Africa.

22

The Sokoto caliphate and Borno

Introduction

In this chapter we shall outline the political structures and general developments in the Sokoto caliphate and Borno. These developments concerned not only the internal structures of the two states, but also the general direction of the history of Central Sudan. It is not possible here to attempt a comprehensive study of all the possible themes: the intention is, rather, to provide a framework for understanding the history of the region between 1820 and 1880. To begin with, it is necessary to review the main developments in the preceding forty-five years.

The Muslim reformers were very successful in their campaigns in the Hausa states and Nupe. Their aim initially was, through their preaching, to persuade the rulers to carry out reforms; and a number of rulers in the region, such as those of Kano, Zaria, Gobir, Katsina and Zamfara appeared ready to cooperate by initiating religious reforms. However, after 1788, the reform movement took another step, namely that of establishing autonomous Muslim communities within or outside the Hausa states in which Muslims would have rights as an independent group. This was because the reformers realized that reforms spearheaded by local rulers could only be temporary, given the political fragmentation of the region. This new strategy of *dār al-hidjra*, from the experience of the Prophet himself, was a necessary prelude to military confrontation.

The privileged status claimed by the Muslim community created tensions within the Hausa states. Their refusal to subject themselves to the control of the state, and the encouragement they gave to slaves who fled from their masters created a crisis. To reimpose their authority over the Muslim community, the rulers resorted to the use of force. They launched an offensive against the pastoral Fulbe as a way of putting pressure on the reformers, but this backfired because it drove the harassed Fulbe en masse into the reformers' camp. This gave the pastoralist military faction an unintended influence in the Sokoto caliphate.

After Shaykh ʿUthmān made the *hidjra* with his community from Degel to Gudu, formal war was declared in 1804. This was followed by the regional

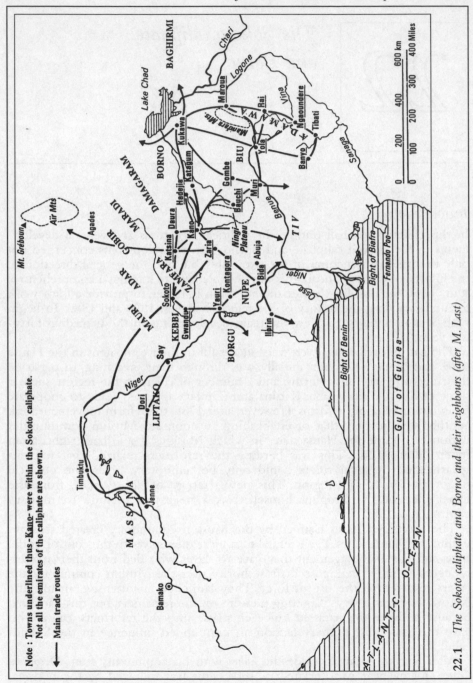

Note : Towns underlined thus - <u>Kano</u>- were within the Sokoto caliphate.
Not all the emirates of the caliphate are shown.

→ Main trade routes

22.1 *The Sokoto caliphate and Borno and their neighbours (after M. Last)*

distribution of flags and the formal appointment of commanders for each region in 1806 thus giving the movement a decentralized command. Although the reformers were outnumbered and out-equipped by the official forces, they were still able to win the war in the end due to their superior morale and good planning. By 1809, the main Hausa states had been taken by the *djihād* forces with their rulers fleeing into exile. It was only in Borno that the authority of the *mai* (as a king) was strong enough to survive the loss of his capital, Birni Ngazargamu.

The aftermath of war

The main issue after the *djihād* was reconstruction and this meant different things to each of the parties involved in the war. For the toppled rulers of the Hausa states, the task before them was to mobilize substantial support and reclaim their territories from the reformers. For the victorious Muslim reformers, reconstruction was complicated by the need to keep precisely to Islamic law. This was because there was a shortage of qualified personnel to man the different levels of the caliphate's administration since many scholars and students who could have done so died during the war.

Many steps were taken to solve the problem of the shortage of personnel. Relatives of the Shaykh were appointed into administrative office and supervised directly from the centre. Former officials of the previous regime were also employed but they were not trusted wholly by the caliphal government. This distrust, coupled with the inexperience of the administration, made the task of governing the caliphate very burdensome. Many complaints and disputes from all over the caliphate came to the Shaykh for arbitration. In 1812 the task of arbitrating disputes was divided between 'Abdullāh dan Fodio and the Shaykh's son, Muḥammad Bello. Thus, when the Shaykh died in 1817, there was no dramatic shift in the caliphate's policy. Despite the fact that the territories under the full control of the reformers were restricted, there was no other popular government that could rival their new administration. The task was therefore to extend the administration of the caliphate to the countryside and incorporate rural areas into it. But in Borno, the *mai* were struggling to use their control over the countryside to facilitate the reorganization of the state and the preservation of its autonomy despite the new caliphate.

The establishment and operation of the Sokoto caliphate and the emirates that constituted it meant dramatic changes in the old political system. Instead of the pre-*djihād* king with his sacred personality there was now the *amīr* whose person was not sacred. Allah, and not the state personified by the king, was the source of authority. Unlike the previous king who was more or less above politics, the *amīr* was the first among equals; his companions as a group were to share power under his leadership. Consequently, the role of former palace slave officials was reduced from that of administrative personnel to that of personal servants, and the formal office of queen mother or sister was eliminated. While the office of the former kings was hereditary, that of the *amīr* was theoretically open to any suitably pious candidate. The bureaucracy was streamlined and the *sharīʿa* law as interpreted by the Māliki school was to order relations in the new state.

The purposes of these changes were: to limit and formalize the operation of state affairs; to prevent the manipulation of previously unwritten rules; to remove the seat of government from the palace, and to establish a leadership whose authority was derived solely from Allah and accountable to the Muslim community. On the whole, the political experiment was dedicated to the realization of the reformers' ideas of a Muslim state. However, as much as they tried to rule according to the above plans and the *sharīʿa*, they recognized the necessity of exercising some flexibility especially in relation to differing local circumstances and certain exigencies. On the economic level, the experiment involved the integration of the rural economies of the region and their closer linkage with first the Mediterranean, and later the Atlantic economies.

The caliphal administration

The seat of the caliph was at Sokoto and authority to govern in different emirates emanated from him. The office of the caliph was formally above any local or ethnic identity as it was rooted in Islamic constitutional practice. The rule of the caliph was also void of any ceremony, ritualization or display of wealth.

When Shaykh ʿUthmān died in 1817, the division of the lands of the caliph into two main blocks was maintained: the eastern emirates under Muḥammad Bello who succeeded to the office of caliph with his base at Sokoto, and the western emirates under ʿAbdullāh with his seat at Gwandu. Bello delegated full responsibility for the western emirates as before to his uncle ʿAbdullāh but he kept for himself full responsibility for the eastern emirates, delegating only executive duties to Gidado, the vizier. The eastern emirates were very rich and the revenue from them went a long way to help in the early development of the caliphate.

The relationship between Sokoto and Gwandu was complex and depended in part on the nature of the personalities in charge. But it is clear that Gwandu represented ritual authority because the *amīrs* of Gwandu were noted for their piety while the Sokoto caliph was in charge of affairs with ultimate political authority. The relationship between other *amīrs* and the caliph during the period 1820–45 was characterized by equality as they were former fellow students. There was also a considerable degree of autonomy as each *amīr* consolidated his territorial position.

The major tasks of the caliphal administration was the supervision of the eastern emirates and the maintenance of the revenue on which the caliphate depended. To carry out these duties, the caliph depended on five groups: his household staff; his former fellow fighters who now acted as advisers and special messengers; the immediate family and relatives of the late Shaykh ʿUthmān who held major territorial responsibilities within Sokoto; the leaders of local Fulbe clans who also held major territorial posts, and finally, the families who comprised his father's old community and formed the scholar class in the capital. These last were given judicial and religious responsibilities in the new administration or allotted minor territorial posts.

The caliph's advisers among whom the *waziri* was the most notable were the links between the emirates and the caliph. In fact, the majority of the emirates came under the *waziri*'s office. Through these advisers, the caliph appointed or sanctioned the appointment of the *amīrs* and resolved any dispute over succession. Apart from these functions, the caliph and his delegates were the last court of appeal. Also the caliphal administration collected the revenue meant for the Sokoto treasury. These came in the form of gifts, taxes and tributes from the emirates. However, the relative poverty of the Sokoto hinterland and the fact that most of its population were scholars and pastoralists, with very few farmers, all of whom paid no tax, made the caliph dependent on the goodwill (revenue) of the other emirates. Some of the problems of the administration included the enormous size of the caliphate which created difficulties in communication, and the relative lack of military coercion.

Military and diplomatic activities

The military activities of the Sokoto caliphate were not extensive because the caliphate did not maintain a standing army. Expansion of the caliphate was through the activities of individual *amīrs* and not coordinated centrally. Its army was not a professional force and it was recruited on an ad hoc basis. Armed with spears, bows and swords, with some mounted on horses and camels, this army raided the Hausa and others in the regions. For much of the century, the caliphate was plagued by guerrilla warfare due to the dislocation of people caused by the *djihād*, food shortages caused by the dislocation of agriculture, or simply by the profits to be made from the sale of captives. This led to insecurity but trade was not disrupted because trading expeditions were always armed.

As a result of the military limitations of the caliphate, diplomacy became an important aspect of its policy. Diplomatic correspondence was handled personally by the caliphs. However, no state visits by the caliph took place, neither did he send any of his staff on embassies abroad. Rather, passing scholars, pilgrims and traders acted as bearers of messages and brought news of political developments abroad. Correspondence was exchanged with Morocco, Tripoli and Britain. Muḥammad Bello's interest in external relations had not only an intellectual twist, it also had deep political and economic considerations. These therefore determined his relations with the Muslim world and with other groups like the Tuareg, Timbuktu, Massina and Borno. Relations between Sokoto and the latter two were tense, those with Timbuktu were cordial, and relations with the Tuareg were ambiguous and uncertain. There were cases where the caliphate mixed diplomacy with warfare in dealing with smaller neighbouring communities. But apart from diplomacy and warfare, the commonest tool in inter-state relations were economic policies such as trade embargoes or blockades and these in fact proved more effective than warfare.

The emirates: political structure

There were some basic differences in the political structure of the emirates although the appointment of *amīrs* was generally based on hereditary and seniority principles. In Zaria, the office of *amīr* rotated round three distinct lineages while in all the other emirates it was restricted to a single lineage, but in some cases the lineage could recognize two or more 'branches'. The role and distribution of offices under the *amīr* did not follow a single pattern. In emirates with a homogeneous population such as Zaria, Kano, Sokoto and Katagum, some of the major offices and territories were distributed among the members of the population and such offices were retained by the descendants of the initial holders. However, in emirates with a heterogeneous population, no office-holding dynasties developed and official property and offices were not permanent. Rather, power was either concentrated in the *amīr* at the capital with a large slave element in the administration as in Borno, Nupe and Ilọrin in which the traditional ruler wielded some authority simultaneously with the Muslim reformers. The traditional rulers in such diarchies were eventually eliminated giving way to the paramouncy of the *amīr*.

In emirates with office-holding dynasties, the residence of office holders at the capital was crucial and in the course of the century, offices at the capital became more powerful than most of those based in the provinces. Powerful territorial office-holders posed the danger that they could seek complete autonomy and appeal to Sokoto for recognition as an independent emirate. Such cases always led to armed conflict.

Furthermore, the economic strength of rich emirates like Kano and Zaria made them indispensable to the caliphate's finances. There was also the possibility that if the *amīr* of such emirates gained sole control, it might tempt him to rival the caliph. It thus became the aim of the caliphal administration and that of the groups excluded from the office of *amīr* to prevent an excessive concentration of power in the hands of the *amīr*.

Administration at the grassroots was more uniform in the emirates than the upper level administration discussed above. Pastoralists were organized through their own leaders and they had strong kingship links which gave them a high degree of internal cohesion. Agricultural communities were also ruled through their local leaders. The links between the representatives of the local population and the emirate administration were the servants or agents of the office holder to whom was allocated the responsibility for that section of the population. The primary function of this local administration was that of tax collection, and it was only as part of this that it was involved in other aspects of the local life.

Social structure

There were two broad divisions in caliphate society. The first was the office-oriented group which comprised title-holders, their relatives, supporters and household slaves. The second group consisted of those who were not office-holders but were occupied in farming, trading and other crafts, along with their slaves. There was no rigidity in these divisions and this made for some overlap and considerable mobility both ways. Scholars and slaves, for instance, could be associated with either category.

The office-oriented category had other distinctive features apart from holding state offices. One was their relative immobility. Unlike ordinary people, they could not move freely from one emirate to another because once they left the emirate where they had rights to office, they automatically lost such rights which were not transferable. Furthermore, they had a high concern for genealogies, dynastic marriage alliances, and relatively strict rules of patrilineal inheritance whereas the common people ignored the minute details of genealogy and maintained a generalized identity with a particular area or ethnic group by facial marks and distinctive traditions. Again, the wives of major office-holders were kept in purdah while those of the others were not so restricted and they participated in trade, crafts and agriculture.

The position of slaves in the caliphate is also worth examining. A lot of slaves were kept in the caliphate. They were allowed to own property and they also had time to work for themselves, and could expect to have the chance of redeeming themselves. Women slaves could marry other slaves and their children were part of their owner's household, though still of slave status. But women slaves could also have children by free men, in which case their children were free and they themselves would be free on their owner's death. Muslim slaves were regarded as members of the Muslim society and so were not allowed to be exported especially to Christian states. Slaves did not pay tax, rather they worked for their owners.

The amount of tax paid by the free men in whatever form was low while office-holders paid much of their tax in the form of inheritance levies, in taxes on their accession to office, and in a series of gifts due on the appointment of an *amīr* or caliph. Indices of wealth for the office-oriented segment of society included horses, clothes and a large following; while, among the commoners, ownership of large numbers of slaves was a major indicator of wealth. However, the religious ideal on which the caliphate was based was sceptical about the ultimate value of great wealth and its consumption.

During the second half of the century, the caliphate witnessed an expansion in agriculture due to the availability of a large labour force comprising slaves, the encouragement of private production, the introduction of irrigation and the availability of iron for the making of tools for specific tasks. This increased agricultural output and expanded the economic activities of the caliphate.

Changes in the Sokoto caliphate, 1820–80

We can summarize the changes that took place in the Sokoto caliphate between 1820 and 1880 in three phases: the first, 1820–45 was a period of establishment; the second, 1845–55 was a decade of transition and disquiet; while the third, 1855–80 was a period of economic expansion.

1820–45

This period not only witnessed the need for military security against attacks by people defeated or displaced during the *djihād*, it also saw the need to build a new agrarian society. These tasks called for charismatic leaders, and officials were recruited for their Fulbe background and common Islamic faith. Although this period was characterized by external wars and campaigns to expand the frontiers of the caliphate, it was also a period of internal political stability with new administrative structures and posts allocated to new men. However, Kano, Katsina, and Zaria were exceptions because they carried over the administrative structures of the former Hausa states.

By the end of this period (1845) most emirates were securely established except Nupe. Capitals had been built everywhere except in Hadejia, and trade was well established. Intellectually, the caliphate flourished during this period as evidenced by the stream of books, poetry and letters written by the caliph Muḥammad Bello and other scholars. There was also the expansion of education in the towns and villages of the caliphate facilitated by the availability of textbooks and by the contribution of women teachers in the large households to the primary stages of kuranic education.

1845–55

This decade witnessed great changes that represented a questioning of the Islamic principles on which the caliphate was built. A major explanation for these changes was the old age of the reformers, i.e. leaders of the emirates, by the 1840s. This rendered them feeble and ineffective, and also created succession problems. Another issue in the decade was centred round the military. There were serious revolts and uprisings notably in western Katsina in 1843–44, Zaberma, Kebbi and Gobir in 1849–54, and Hadejia in 1848. All these revolts threatened Sokoto and Gwandu which were the nerve centres of the caliphate.

Finally, the decade also saw intellectual and religious movements which sparked off a series of migrations from the caliphate. The Tijāniyya controversy led by al-Ḥadjdj ʿUmar brought about ideological divisions among the scholars in the caliphate as a result of which some began to emigrate in protest.

However, despite the military, intellectual and religious upheavals, the caliphate was able to maintain a considerable degree of internal stability. Throughout the decade the caliph and the *amir* of Gwandu remained in office. While the other changes could be described as representing a handing over of power from one generation to the next, not only within the caliphate but also in the states opposed to it, it should be noted that the phenomenon was not peculiar to the Sokoto caliphate and its immediate environment. Other states that were dramatically reformed at the turn of the century such as France, Egypt, Austria and Germany were also experiencing a critical period. The most important feature of the upheaval in the caliphate was, however, the intellectual controversy which seemed to question the very essence of the state's existence, namely the Ḳādirīyya ideology.

22.2 *Hausa craft goods collected by Gustav Nachtigal in 1870*

1855–80

Two significant features of this period which stand out in the histories of the emirates were the relative peace and stability of the region, and the economic expansion of the caliphate which, in a sense, could be said to have been partly facilitated by the stable atmosphere. There were still numerous raids and attacks in different parts of the caliphate but these were not invasions that could seriously endanger it. Both trade and production was expanded in the Sokoto caliphate with vacant land within its frontiers being settled, and the caliphate traders pushing into areas far beyond. This economic expansion was accompanied by inflation which not only affected the standard of living of the people but also fuelled competition for office and expectations of a brighter future. Intellectually, the period also witnessed the increasing use of Hausa rather than Arabic or Fulani in books and poetry. In government, more traditional Hausa values of governance and attitude to authority were gradually incorporated into the political system.

Borno, 1820–45: the dyarchy

The history of Borno in the above period reveals an interdependence between Borno and the caliphate; events in the one had great significance for the other. Borno opposed 'Uthmān dan Fodio's *djihād* and in order to repel the attack, the *mai* sought the help of Shaykh Muḥammad al-Amīn al-Kanēmi who was a renowned scholar with international connections and local links with both the Shuwa Arabs and the Kanēmbu.

Following his victories over the *djihād* forces, al-Kanēmi was appointed as a semi-autonomous chief by the *mai*. He had no formal title in the Borno political structure. Instead, he pre-occupied himself with taking charge of the territory allotted to him. He expanded this by absorbing other semi-autonomous chiefs in his neighbourhood. He maintained a standing army of Kanēmbu spearsmen and depended on trade and the export of captives for his economic strength. His administrative council comprised six of his friends. He did not maintain a large court but made use of slave officials. Meanwhile, the power of the *mai* was dwindling at this time. He could not boast of a powerful military force although he still possessed the traditional authority which made for continuity and ensured the stability of the state.

Thus, by 1820, Borno was divided into two political zones: one territory administered by the *mai* with his seat at Birni Kafela, while the other was under Shaykh al-Kanēmi with his base at Kukawa. In fact, the position of al-Kanēmi was greatly strengthened in 1820 by the death of *mai* Dunama and the accession of his young son, Ibrāhīm.

Al-Kanēmi gradually built up his power but not in open defiance of the *mai*. This was because the majority of the Kanuri aristocracy supported the *mai* and attended to him. Also, while al-Kanēmi was expanding south and west of Borno, the bulk of Borno proper, east of Lake Chad still owed their allegiance to the *mai* and followed the traditional Kanuri authorities. The *mai* thus

22.3 *Shaykh Muḥammad al-Amīn al-Kānemī*

commanded the majority of Kanuri Borno and drew revenue from it while al-Kanēmi commanded the frontier zones to the west and south employing Borno cavalry and sending a share of his revenue to the *mai*. This arrangement between the *mai* and al-Kanēmi worked because of the latter's notable lack of ambition and dogmatism. Al-Kanēmi neither had the urgent commitment that characterized the Sokoto leaders nor attracted round himself men with such a sense of mission. He therefore made no attempt to outshine the *mai*'s court. While al-Kanēmi could use the *mai*'s authority which was larger than mere sectional interests, and quite real as an institution around which to rally Borno, the *mai* could also use al-Kanēmi for his own ends because he did not possess the reformist zeal that could threaten to destroy traditional Borno.

However, the interdependence between *mai* Ibrāhīm and al-Kanēmi did not survive the latter's death. Al-Kanēmi's son and successor, 'Umar, attempted to undermine the authority of the *mai*. This bred antagonism between the two sides and put an end to the twenty years of cooperation which had existed between the *mai* and the late Shaykh.

Borno 1845–80: from dyarchy to Shaykhdom

The decade 1845–55 was a very difficult one for Borno, even more than it was for the Sokoto caliphate. Borno experienced fundamental changes in the political system in addition to civil wars and disorders. The office of *mai* was abolished and his court disbanded while Shaykh 'Umar became the supreme power in the land. What happened was that in a bid to salvage his dwindling authority, *mai* Ibrāhīm in 1846 invited the Sultan of Baghirmi to destroy Shaykh 'Umar, but he lost his own life instead at the hands of the Shaykh. The Shaykh also defeated and killed *mai* 'Alī, Ibrāhīm's successor. After that, 'Umar also got into trouble with his own brother 'Abd al-Rahmān who deposed him. He was eventually reinstated, had 'Abd al-Rahmān executed, and continued to rule till 1881.

An explanation for this civil strife in Borno was the absence of any external threat, which allowed internal rivalries to surface. While Borno was in turmoil, Sokoto was at precisely the same time bedevilled with revolts and uprisings. A remarkable aspect of these events was the failure of either state to take advantage of the other's disorders. There was a rapid return to normalcy after 1855 in both states.

Thereafter, Borno was united under Shaykh 'Umar as the head of state. All power was centralized in his hands and he delegated it to whomever he chose. This created a situation in which loyalty to the Shaykh was a basic requirement for advancement within the political structure. Competition for office was open, unrestricted by rights of birth or rank. The court therefore consisted not only of members of the royal family but also free notables and slave officials. This political structure was markedly different from the one operated by al-Kanēmi in which the important officials of state were not so much his clients as his partners.

22.4 *Embroidered Borno woman's blouse made in the 1870s*

There were also important changes in the economy: Borno was gradually drawn into the caliphate's economic orbit as a supplier of raw materials such as hides, skins, ivory, ostrich feathers, slaves and natron, and as a consumer of luxuries with less profit accruing to those in power than before. The productive base of Borno did not expand as rapidly as that of the Sokoto caliphate. Consequently, Borno's trade debts increased. While these economic problems could be traced to Shaykh 'Umar's inadequate leadership, a more fundamental cause could be Borno's relation to the caliphate's expanding economy which relegated Borno relatively to the background. The caliphate's eastern expansion, and that of Baghirmi and Wadai, to the east of Borno also limited opportunities for Borno expansion. Towards the end of this period, the stability under Shaykh 'Umar gave way increasingly to political violence and rancour.

Conclusion

There were a number of differences in the histories of the Sokoto caliphate and Borno. While al-Kanēmi shared power with a ritually important *mai*, there was no such alternative traditional ruler in Sokoto under Muḥammad Bello. Secondly, al-Kanēmi lacked widespread family and clan connections to give him the kind of powerful support which Muḥammad Bello enjoyed.

Al-Kanēmi therefore relied more on slaves and friends, thus centralizing control in his own hands. Meanwhile, Muḥammad Bello delegated authority to his *djihād* fellows, who formed lineages or local interest groups. Furthermore, al-Kanēmi's scheme for the unification of Borno after its defeat was to rely on traditional loyalty to the *mai*, his own charisma, as well as self-interest and shared opposition to the Fulbe, whereas Bello used the Islamic ideology to unite the scattered *amīrs*. Economically, Borno exported slaves while Sokoto imported them and used them to develop its economy. Consequently, by the end of the period (1880s) the greater natural wealth of the caliphate tended to drain Borno economically.

23

Massina and the Torodbe (Tukuloor) empire until 1878

Introduction

The history of West Africa in the late eighteenth and nineteenth centuries is marked by the growing influence of the nomadic Fulbe. Not only did their numbers increase during the period, their economic importance also grew tremendously. In Futa Jallon and Futa Toro, they gradually shook off the dominance of the settled agricultural communities. This movement spread to Hausaland and from there to Liptako and Massina in the early nineteenth century. But in Massina they faced strenuous opposition from the Bambara of Segu who continued to lord it over them.

In the eighteenth century, the power of Segu was extending rapidly over all the neighbouring countries, and they made harsh exactions on the Fulbe pastoralists in particular. At the same time, because of anti-Islamic practices, Muslim centres like Jenne lost their vitality. The success of Islamic revolutions in Futa Toro and Futa Jallon in the second half of the eighteenth century, and in Sokoto at the beginning of the nineteenth century helped to spread revolutionary ideas in Massina, and encouraged the desire to change the situation.

Several marabouts attempted to take advantage of the revolutionary atmosphere prevailing in the delta area to throw off the Bambara yoke. All of them claimed allegiance to ʿUthmān dan Fodio, and the leader of the most prominent resistance in Massina was one Ahmadu Hammadi Bubu Sangare. However, it was Seku Ahmadu that succeeded in mobilizing the movement that threw off the Bambara yoke and set Massina up as a strong Muslim state from where he began to launch into other areas.

Seku Ahmadu (Shaykh Aḥmad Lobbo)

Born in 1773 in Massina, Seku Ahmadu was noted for his piety, honesty, and humility. He studied under a leading mystic in Jenne and preached for a return to pure Islam. He attracted a large following and maintained links with ʿUthmān dan Fodio of Sokoto who gave him the title of Shaykh and sent him a flag. His movement broke out in the form of a revolt against the local rulers and their

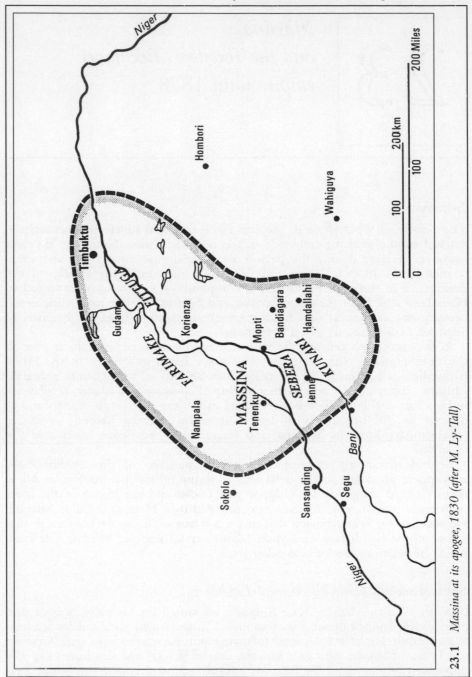

23.1 *Massina at its apogee, 1830 (after M. Ly-Tall)*

Segu allies. Segu was defeated in the encounter and this impressed many of the Fulbe who consequently rallied round him. Jenne was taken by the fighters in 1819 and Massina was thereafter organized as a powerful Islamic state.

But before Massina could consolidate its position in the region, it had to contend with a few enemies. The first was Segu. The Bambara of Segu refused to acknowledge the existence of Massina as an independent Muslim state. This led to prolonged wars which came to an end only when the Bambara were ready to come to terms with the presence of a Muslim state on their borders. Another resistance to Massina came from the Fulbe of Fittuga who wanted to launch their own *djihād* in the inland Niger delta area independent of Seku Ahmadu. They received the support of the Kunta, the rulers of Timbuktu, and Muḥammad Bello of the Sokoto caliphate. The caliphate supported Fittuga because Seku Ahmadu had used the opportunity of the death of 'Uthmān dan Fodio to renounce his allegiance to Sokoto. Despite all the support, the Fulbe of Fittuga were eventually defeated by Seku Ahmadu in 1823.

Seku Ahmadu then turned his attention to Timbuktu which at that time was ruled by the Kunta, a Moorish group that had imposed its authority there in the second half of the eighteenth century. Timbuktu also fell before Seku Ahmadu. Thus by 1845 the political power of Massina extended from Jenne to Timbuktu and from the region of Napala to Dogon country.

The institutions of the dina

Seku Ahmadu (1818–45) was able to provide firmly based religious and administrative structures for the new theocratic state called the *dina*. As in other Islamic states, the *sharīʿa* was applied to all areas of life in the state. There was a grand council of forty members appointed by Seku Ahmadu which assisted him in all areas of the exercise of power, although he sometimes went against the decision of the council. Apart from the grand council there was also a privy council which comprised Seku Ahmadu and two people from the grand council. This privy council considered all state business before submitting it to the grand council.

Justice, in the first instance, was dispensed by the *kādis*; punishment was usually very severe, and the public prosecutor was also extremely strict. Taxes and levies which included ordinary dues allowed by Islamic law and war contributions introduced by the grand council were collected by state officials. Captives taken during wars were made to cultivate large estates for the state. Thus, the provinces of Massina produced large quantities of rice, millet and various vegetables. However, trade suffered at this time because of the prolonged war with the Bambara.

For the purpose of efficient administration, the country was divided into five military provinces each headed by a relative or faithful disciple of Seku Ahmadu. The provinces were (a) the Niger and the border area between the Niger and the Bani, (b) the western border, (c) the right bank of the Bani, (d) the eastern border, and (e) the lake area. The capital, Ḥamdallahi, was

23.2   *Ruins of a defensive tower of the* tata *(fortress) at* Ḥamdallahi

established in 1820. Its most impressive structures were the mosque and the palace. It was efficiently policed and was very tidy. Life at the capital was very disciplined. For instance, there were strict rules about how the various classes of society spent their time.

The most important achievement of Seku Ahmadu was his attempt to get the nomadic Fulbe settled in communities. To this end, he established many farming and stockbreeding villages. And these all bore fruit under his son and successor, Ahmadu Seku.

Ahmadu Seku (1845–53) and after

The period of Ahmadu Seku is regarded as the most peaceful and prosperous in Massina during the century. This is not to deny that he encountered initial difficulties both at the domestic and external levels. The domestic problems arose from the succession disputes that followed the death of Seku Ahmadu. The external problems were posed by the Saro Bambara and the Tuareg of Timbuktu area who took the opportunity offered by the death of Seku Ahmadu to revolt against Massina authority. Both of them were repressed although the Tuareg were more violently dealt with. After this the Monimpe Bambara were also subjugated.

Despite these initial problems, the closing years of the reign of Ahmadu Seku were peaceful. He was able to preserve the frontiers of the kingdom from external aggression through a combination of diplomacy and force. He also succeeded in maintaining peace internally in the state. But after his death in 1853 both the domestic and foreign problems were again unleashed with greater intensity.

The succession crisis involved the various members of Seku Ahmadu's family, and it split Massina into hostile camps. Ahmadu mo Ahmadu who eventually succeeded to the throne lacked the political acumen and leadership qualities that could have healed the divisions. Instead, his reign deepened the crisis. He made radical changes in the very structures of the state by replacing the old and respected religious leaders and marabouts with young men of his own age with a liberalized outlook. The state, under him, was ridden with intrigues, rivalries and strife. This was the condition of Massina when al-Hadjdj 'Umar attacked it.

The rise of the Torodbe (Tukuloor) empire (1852–64)

By the beginning of the century, many states had sprung up in the Western and Central Sudan, the viability of whose political economy depended on a continuation of the slave trade. The Fulbe who were one of the most oppressed peoples of the age felt the situation very keenly. And it may be said that their reaction to the situation was the national movement within the context of Islamic reform which produced revolutionary states in Futa Toro, Futa Jallon and Sokoto, where there was already a considerable Muslim community. Slavery, however, was not abolished but was governed by kuranic laws. Some of the smaller states located between Massina, Futa Jallon and Futa Toro which still escaped Muslim law later fell before the Tijāniyya.

Al-Hadjdj 'Umar's *djihād* was a reaction to the situation prevailing in Futa Toro in the first half of the nineteenth century. There, as in other Islamic states in the Sudan at the period, Islam was threatened from within by succession crises, and from without by French expansion.

Al Hadjdj 'Umar's djihād

'Umar Saidu (al-Hadjdj 'Umar) was born in 1796 into a family of pious Muslims that had played an active part in the Muslim revolution of the late eighteenth century. He rejected the Ḳādirīyya sect which was one of the oldest Muslim brotherhoods in black Africa and joined the Tijāniyya after which he travelled to North Africa and the Middle East to master the principles of the new brotherhood. After twenty years of travelling (1826–47), during which he had acquired a great wealth of experience, he returned home with the title of Grand Caliph of the Tijāniyya with the mission of completing the Islamization of black Africa.

He stayed for some time (1830–8) in Sokoto where he learned about the organization of the holy war from Muḥammad Bello before proceeding homewards. He eventually settled in Futa Jallon, in preference to Futa Toro, making Jugunku his operational base. There he recruited supporters, purchased

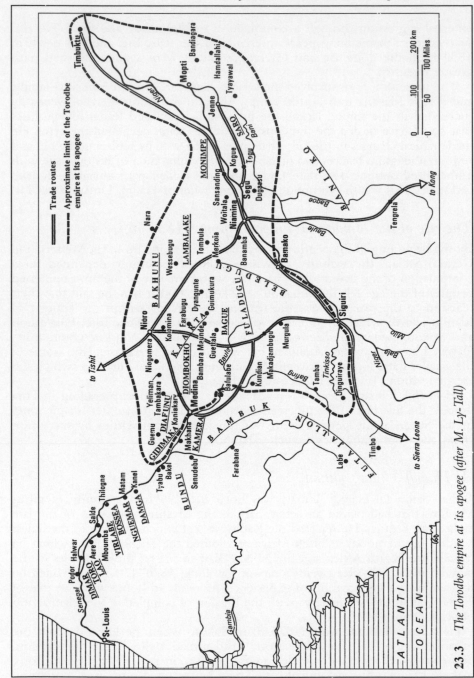

23.3 *The Torodbe empire at its apogee (after M. Ly-Tall)*

a lot of arms and campaigned extensively for the *djihād*. In 1847, he transferred his capital to Dinguiraye from where he fought against the ruler of the area, Gimba Sacko in 1852.

The Bambara of Segu and the neighbouring kingdom of Kaarta, as we have observed, were very resistant to Islam. They took pride in their states which had grown to be very powerful and which flourished from Mande to Timbuktu. Their strength depended both on a crack cavalry force and a professional army made up largely of crown slaves who were fiercely loyal to their masters and whose leader enjoyed special privileges in the state, especially during periods of succession. They also manufactured some of their own arms and ammunition. In this way, the Bambara had extended their power over many of their neighbours, and did a flourishing trade in slaves for export and for developing crown estates.

The Bambara, however, failed to unite in the face of the threat from the Tijāniyya. Segu pulled one way, and Kaarta the other. Even Kaarta was plunged into a civil war between the ruling Massassi and the Jawara from whom they had taken over power. 'Umar decided to attack piecemeal. He launched his attack first against Koniakary, then Nioro the capital of Kaarta. From there he turned his attention in 1857 on the French in the fortified city of Medina on the borders of Futa Toro. In spite of much courage and bravery shown by the Muslims, General Faidherbe succeeded in relieving the beleaguered French. The French became 'Umar's implacable foe as the Tijāniyya turned their attention eastwards.

Al-Hadjdj 'Umar returned from Futa in 1859, and he decided that it was time to march on Segu, the Bambara capital. This was at a time when Segu was already in a state of decline. Al-Hadjdj 'Umar entered Segu territory from the rear and seized some of the tributary areas controlled by Segu. With the advance of the *djihād* forces, the ruler of Segu sought an alliance with Massina whose leaders were also afraid of the Tijāniyya forces. But because of deep-seated internal problems, neither Segu nor Massina could offer an effective resistance to 'Umar's army. The Tijāniyya army entered Segu in 1861 and the ruler fled to Massina for refuge.

The war with Massina

Before the *djihād* of Al-Hadjdj 'Umar, Massina, like other Muslim states in the area was already facing problems emanating from its intractable neighbours. When Al-Hadjdj 'Umar's *djihād* began to advance, Massina felt really threatened that another power would usurp its religious and political dominance in the area. While 'Umar extended an arm of fellowship to Ahmadu mo Ahmadu of Massina – that they should combine to fight against the infidels – the latter refused, maintaining that the whole area from Segu to Karta came under his influence. This is interesting because, not only had Massina failed to convert Segu and some of the other areas located in this alleged sphere of influence, it also had virtually no political authority over them.

In 1860, following an alliance between Massina and Segu to resist Al-Hadjdj 'Umar's advance, the combined forces of the two states pitched camp against Sansanding which had already been conquered by 'Umar. Reluctant at first to fight against Massina, a fellow-Muslim state, 'Umar eventually used the alliance between Massina and Segu, an un-Islamic state, as the *casus belli* to justify the declaration of war against Ahmadu mo Ahmadu. 'Umar marched upon Massina in 1862 and occupied Hamdallahi, the capital. He placed it under his son Ahmadu and dealt severely with the treacherous Massina chiefs. He was then faced by a Timbuktu–Massina coalition.

The Kunta chief of Timbuktu, al-Bekkai, adopted the policy of supporting 'Umar's enemies in order to frustrate him. First in 1860, al-Bekkai made contact with the Bambara and offered them his moral support. Later in 1862, after the conquest of Massina, he also supported the revolt that was simmering at Hamallahi against the forces of 'Umar. This revolt tied down substantial forces of 'Umar's army and inflicted serious defeats upon them. It was this revolt that eventually led to the death of Al-Hadjdj 'Umar in 1864. But despite their initial victories, the rebels could not completely rout the *djihād* forces. Reinforcements led by Tijāni Alfa, 'Umar's nephew, brought relief to the Muslim forces and they were able to rout all the rebels and their allies.

Organization of the Torodbe (Tukuloor) empire

The Tukuloor empire founded by Al-Hadjdj 'Umar was vast, with its territories extending from Gidimaka to Timbuktu and from Dinguiraye to the Sahara. The government of this empire was however not centralized. Authority devolved upon individual centres of political-cum-religious administration headed by disciples called *talibs*. Al-Hadjdj 'Umar did not concern himself much with organization and administration; rather, he delegated such duties to his disciples. He saw himself first and foremost as a mystic whose primary mission was to complete the Islamization of the blacks.

His close aides were Alfa 'Umar Thierno Bayla Wan and Abdulaye Hausa, both of whom played critical roles in the *djihād*. He allowed the *talibs* a lot of influence in all major decisions by submitting his own plans to the council of the *talibs* for approval. And because of his generosity, he was able to attract a large following.

The *djihād* forces were a multi-ethnic army with contingents from Futa Toro, Hausaland, Futa Jallon, Khasso, Kaarta and Segu. The Futa Toro contingents were however the most numerous. This army, which comprised four battalions, each organized around a contingent from Futa Toro, was armed with trade rifles, swords and a few double-barrelled rifles. Local blacksmiths manufactured the ball fired from the guns. In addition to these were two cannons which were captured from the French. The main strength of the *djihād* forces however came not from physical arms but from their faith and well thought-out strategy. 'Umar encouraged his forces by regularly preaching to them about paradise and the rewards of the next world. This boosted the morale of the fighters and they took the *djihād* as a religious duty.

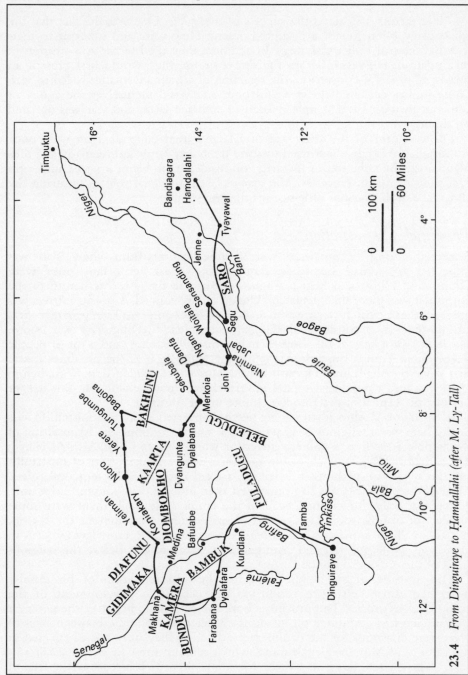

23.4 *From Dinguiraye to Ḥamdallāhi (after M. Ly-Tall)*

Other factors also aided the success of the *djihād*. One was the fact that the *djihād* army often fought a disunited enemy. They were also superior to their foes in terms of military strategy. In addition, they used terror as a weapon of intimidation. However, before fighting a group, they would first present an option of peaceful conversion, the rejection of which automatically led to war. Some groups accepted the peaceful offer and saved themselves the agony of war. But in most cases, people refused to embrace Islam and war was declared on them.

The economy of the army was to a large extent dependent on war booty. Although Al-Hadjdj ʿUmar tried to share the booty fairly and regularly and thus maintained the cohesion of the army till his death, problems erupted under his successor, Ahmadu. Neverless, the army played a crucial role in ensuring the allegiance of the various provinces of the empire.

Provincial administration

Scattered among the provinces were fortified centres from where Islam was expected to spread outwards. Among the most important ones were Dinguiraye, Nioro and Segu. Dinguiraye was the first historic centre of the empire. It was there that al-Hadjdj ʿUmar's family resided. A strong fortress was erected there which secured that side of the empire. The province was administered by a cousin of al-Hadjdj ʿUmar. Next to Dinguiraye was Nioro, the largest province of the empire. It had many fortresses, and a lot of people fleeing from French oppression swelled the population of the province. It was first ruled by Alfa ʿUmar Thierno before Mustafa succeeded him. Segu, before 1864 was just a provincial capital governed by ʿUmar's eldest son. But it later became the capital of the Torodbe empire under Ahmadu.

In all these Muslim fortresses in newly converted areas, administration was dual. There was a religious head whose task was to continue the Islamization of the people as well as a military governor who protected him. Also, Al-Hadjdj ʿUmar had a house in each of the provinces where he kept part of his family. He did not think of himself as having a fixed residence like temporal rulers. Each of the provinces was also organized as an independent administrative unit. ʿUmar was only the spiritual head of the empire. Although there were some pockets of trouble locally, order and security reigned throughout the region. Justice, in all the provinces was dispensed according to kuranic law by *ķādīs* in civil cases while political and criminal cases were brought before the religious head of the provincial capital.

The attitude of al-Hadjdj ʿUmar to the administration of his empire described above left little room for the economic development of the conquered territories. The provinces bore the economic brunt of the constant warfare and this continued till his death. While the economic consequences of wars were disastrous for the conquered territories, they were not all affected in the same way. Moreover, agriculture, which suffered most from the *djihād*, was revived in 1863–4. For instance, the Mandinka were rich in cotton, the Kita in tobacco, vegetables, watermelons and shea trees. Other areas like Kaarta, Dyangunke and Segu were also prosperous in terms of agriculture.

Trade also survived in some parts of Central Sudan despite the wars. The main routes linking the Sudan to the north and south remained busy. Apart from trade and agriculture, war booty also helped to enrich the state. From the wealth accumulated from all these sources, Al-Hadjdj 'Umar periodically carried out a substantial distribution of wealth to his *talïbs*. Revenue also came to the state from various levies such as: the *zakāt* which was levied on Muslims; the *mudu* which was annual alms given on the feast of Ramadān by Muslims, and the *usuru* paid by caravans and stocktraders. Under Al-Hadjdj 'Umar's successor, Ahmadu, these levies were increased substantially and became frequent causes of revolts. The *talïbs* also accused him of being less generous than his father.

Society in the Tukuloor empire was dominated by the *talïbs*. These were individuals from all races and countries, and from different social backgrounds who had been elevated by 'Umar in his bid to resist the domination of the traditional rulers. The *talïbs* were recruited on the basis of their knowledge and practice of Islam and they were present in all provincial capitals and large villages to help the newly converted inhabitants understand the ways of Islam. They monopolized all the senior posts in the empire and constituted a new political-cum-religious elite.

Ahmadu, who lacked the religious and military qualities of his father, al-Hadjdj 'Umar, found it difficult to assert his authority over the *talïbs*. He consequently relied on the *sofas* who were more purely a military class and who possessed little knowledge of Islam to counteract the influence of the *talïbs*. This led to rivalry between the *talïbs* and the *sofas* which became a prominent feature of Ahmadu's reign.

A difficult succession: Ahmadu (1862–78)

The first problem faced by Ahmadu on his accession were plots against him at Segu and at Hamdallahi. In dealing with the situation, he committed an error which cost him Sansanding, an important commercial centre. There was also the more fundamental problem of divisions among the *talïbs*. Ahmadu found himself at the head of two camps of *talïbs*. Instead of looking for ways to bring the two together, Ahmadu created a third faction, the *sofas* which was made up of conquered peoples who had enrolled in the army of the *djihād*. Thus, despite his outstanding intelligence and great piety, Ahmadu never succeeded in asserting his authority as his father had done.

Furthermore, he was faced with revolts throughout the region, the most serious of which came from Beledugu. Agriculture and trade suffered greatly as a result of these revolts. The revolts also distracted him from effectively overseeing the rest of the empire. This gave the provincial rulers the opportunity to act independently and refuse to report to him or send resources to assist him. Although Mustafa who ruled Nioro accounted to Ahmadu fairly regularly for his stewardship, Tijāni Alfa ruled the Massina region independently

23.5 *Entrance of Ahmadu's palace in Segu-Sikoro*

23.6 *Ahmadu receiving visitors in the palace court*

and carved out Bandiagara as his own capital. As if this was not enough, Ahmadu faced a fierce opposition from his brother, Muhammadu Habibu, who was embittered because he was allotted no significant authority in the empire. Habibu and another brother, Mukhtār, mobilized many *talībs* against Ahmadu and undermined his authority.

In 1869 Ahmadu started a process of strengthening his authority against the above threats from his brothers. For four years he carried on a bitter struggle against them and all those who supported them in their demand for the sharing of their fathers inheritance. At the same time, he suppressed some Bambara and Soninke centres of rebellion. He emerged victorious from the contest with his brothers. By 1874, Ahmadu was at the height of his power. At the instance of the *talībs* he made some territorial concessions to his brothers though care was taken to ensure that they were all to be under his authority. He also strengthened his administration at his capital in Segu.

Trade was resumed with the French trading posts of Upper Senegal and those of the English in Sierra Leone. The economy of the empire was consequently diversified. The Hausa trade and kola nut trade also expanded and the economic atmosphere in the Sudan remained stable for some time.

Conclusion

By 1878, Ahmadu had overcome all the obstacles that had faced him after his father's death. The Bambara still remained intractable but they no longer constituted a serious danger to the empire. The spread of Islam and the policy of cooperation with all races and social categories initiated by Al-Hadjdj 'Umar was continued by his successor and this produced a high degree of cultural integration in the region. The reality of this cohesion could be attested to by the fact that during the colonial period in the twentieth century, the Sudan which covered the former Torodbe empire had very few problems of ethnic rivalries. Moreover, the religious legacy bequeathed by al-Hadjdj 'Umar to his successors has contributed in no small measure to the cultural integration of the area.

24

States and peoples
of Senegambia
and Upper Guinea

This chapter examines the history of the peoples of the west coast of Africa from Senegal to the Bandama in the nineteenth century. There is a certain homogeneity in the history of this region during the nineteenth century though the same cannot be said of the previous centuries. This homogeneity was a function of the presence of Europeans and the formation of their strongholds all over the coast. But rather than approach the history of this region from the standpoint of the European presence, we shall look at it from that of the African peoples. Because the region covers different cultural areas, we shall look at each of them in turn, namely, the Senegambia, Upper Guinea and the Futa Jallon, the Kru Country, and the Southern Mande.

Senegambia

The Senegambian region is linked in the west with the Atlantic coast where it was exposed to European influences through the slave trade. Senegambian society was Sudanese and Muslim in character and this made it more stable than that of the Gulf of Guinea. However, despite this stability, the region was affected by many economic changes. One of such had to do with changes in the external demand for its products and slaves. Although the slave trade transacted in the region was reduced because of the abolitionist movement, it never really died down until the middle of the nineteenth century. The more important economic change in the region was the enormous increase in the prices offered for Senegambian products such as gum, gold, hides, ivory, bees' wax and groundnuts.

These changes in foreign trade affected the local economies. There was a shift of income from the slave merchants to groups of people who were in charge of the new production. A newly aggressive Islam also gained prominence in Senegambian society by the end of the eighteenth century. This aggression was a form of protest by the peasantry – who began to convert in large numbers – against the ruling class that was seeking to benefit from the new production by raiding rather than protecting them. This led to disorder and confusion which was especially prominent in the Wolof and Sereer kingdoms in the north, some of which we shall examine presently. This situation was to

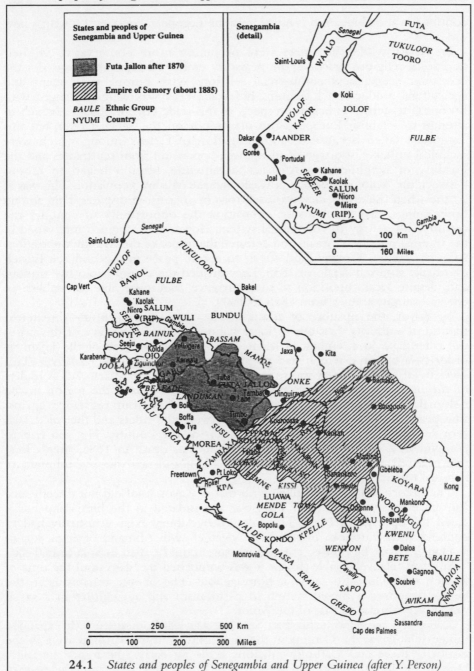

Key — States and peoples of Senegambia and Upper Guinea

Futa Jallon after 1870

Empire of Samory (about 1885)

BAULE Ethnic Group

NYUMI Country

Senegambia (detail)

FUTA

Senegal

WAALO

TUKULOOR TOORO

Saint-Louis

Koki

JOLOF

WOLOF

KAYOR

FULBE

Dakar JAANDER

Gorée

Portudal

Kahane

Joal

Kaolak

SALUM

Nioro

Miere

NYUMI (RIP)

Gambia

SEREER

0   100 Km

0   160 Miles

Main map labels:

Senegal

Saint-Louis

WOLOF

TUKULOOR

BAWOL

FULBE

Cap Vert

Kahane

Bakel

Kaolak

SALUM

Nioro (RIP)

WULI

BUNDU

Gambia

SEREER

FONYI BAINUK

BASSAM

Seeju

Kolda Veingara

MANDE

Jaxa

Kita

OIO

Karabane

Kamala

Ziguinchor

JOOLA

Juba

FUTA JALLON

ONKE

Bamako

BE

LANDUMAN

Tamba

Dinguiray

Bougouni

Boke

Labe

Niger

Boffa

Timbo

Koubossa

Tya

BAGA

SUSU

NALU

MOREA

SOLIMANA

Kankan

MOREA

TAMBAXA

Madina

Freetown Pt Loko

Gbeleba

Kong

Rokel

KISSI

Banankoro

KOYARA

KPA

LUAWA

Nafa

Mankono

MENDE TOMA

Odienne

WORODUGU

GOLA

Seguela

Bopolu

KONDO

DAN

MAU

KWENU

VAI DE

KPELLE

Monrovia

BASSA

WENYON

Daloa

BETE

BAULE

Cavally

SAPO

Gagnoa

DIOA

KRAWI

Soubre

NNOJAN

GREBO

AVIKAM

Bandama

Cap des Palmes

Sassandra

0   250   500 Km

0   100   200   300 Miles

24.1 *States and peoples of Senegambia and Upper Guinea (after Y. Person)*

continue in the nineteenth century until the European conquest brought a new order.

In Waalo, while the rulers were becoming more conservative in their traditional religious practices, the peasantry embraced Islam en masse. On the economic scene, new commercial relations with Europe took shape and agricultural products such as gums, hides, and bees' wax were exchanged with European traders. The bright prospects of this trade encouraged the French to attempt to establish European-run plantations on the Senegal river, but this enterprise failed because of a combination of factors among which were technical mistakes, shortage of manpower, opposition from the traders and the hostility of neighbouring Africans. Meanwhile, tension began to mount between the Wolof aristocracy in Waalo and the Muslim population. This was at a time when the aristocracy was itself torn by succession disputes. This, among other things, gave the Muslim opposition the opportunity to conquer the country and destroy the traditional system. However, the French intervened in the internal politics of Waalo and defeated the leader of the Muslim opposition. After the failure of many local efforts to restore peace in the land, the French eventually annexed Waalo in 1855. They divided the country into five cantons and, despite local opposition to their presence, they were able to establish an effective administration from 1855 to 1880.

In Kayor, the upsurge of Islam in the nineteenth century threatened traditional authority. Anxious to forge national unity in the face of this crisis, the ruler, Laat Joor, embraced Islam. This led to the spread of the Tijāniyya order in a country which had previously known only the Ḳādirīyya. This diversity of Islamic orders was to lead to the prevalence of marabouts as leaders of the brotherhoods, a phenomenon which characterized the region in the colonial period, and later became a feature of African resistance against European rule. In order to restore unity between the rulers and the ruled, Laat Joor set out to complete the Islamization of the country. He also had to contend with advancing French imperialism. His death in 1886, after a long guerrilla war, marked the end of the kingdom and saw the establishment of colonial rule in Kayor.

The history of Jolof was linked with that of Kayor. Jolof did not directly face European pressure because it was poor and isolated in the hinterland but it faced the upsurge of Islam. The Jolof ruler, Albury Njay eventually had to contend with European imperialism. Together with Ahmadu of Segu, son of al-Ḥadjdj 'Umar, he resisted colonial pressures until he died in Sokoto in 1900.

Siin was relatively stable in that it was untouched by Islam until the time of French rule. This also made it homogenous. The people inhabiting it, the Sereer, practised a mixed system of pastoralism and agriculture in a social system very similar to that of the Wolof.

Salum was more powerful than Siin but was less homogenous. It expanded militarily as far as the Gambia in the eighteenth century. Muslims were in the minority there and Catholic missions made an early appearance in 1849. Despite the fact that Muslims were few in Salum they were nonetheless very aggressive. The traditional aristocracy was consequently in a difficult situation, caught between the demands of the Europeans and a rebellious Islam which organized the peasants and minorities against them. The dynamism of the Tijāniyya also increased the tension. Eventually, Salum was attacked by a Tukuloor marabout, Maba (a disciple of al-Ḥadjdj ʿUmar of the Tijāniyya) who overthrew the old order and established his own rule. He was however killed in 1871 during a struggle with the Sereer of Siin. His empire consequently became weak because of quarrels among his successors. Thus it was easy for the French to occupy the region in 1887.

Upper Guinea and Futa Jallon

The Upper Guinea, embracing Guinea-Bissau, Sierra-Leone and Liberia, was one of the earliest centres of European influence in the region. This was because of the importance of the slave trade in the sixteenth century though it witnessed a decline in the eighteenth century. Apart from the coastal area which was peopled by the Juula (Dyula), the two most important groups in the Upper Guinea area were the Malinke and the Fulbe.

At the beginning of the nineteenth century, while Portuguese influence was declining in the area, the slave trade which had now become illegal continued for some time. During this period, the Malinke empire of Kaabu was having problems controlling its vassals such as the Bainuk. Meanwhile, the Fulbe minority in Kaabu was growing impatient with its subordinate position in the society. In the east, the Fulbe of Futa Jallon dominated the Mandinka as far as the Gambia in Kantora. Also at this time, the French were setting up trading posts in the region as a result of which the groundnut trade grew rapidly.

The above political order was overthrown in a series of events which could be dated to 1859 when the Fulbe of Futa Jallon began a decisive struggle against Kaabu. The result of this encounter was the death of the king of Kaabu and the collapse of the empire. The fall of Kaabu had major results – the Fulbe minority in the empire rebelled against their Mandinka rulers as far as the banks of the Gambia and they organized the kingdom of Fuladugu which continued to threaten the Mandinka. The next few years saw the Mandinka trying to regroup under new leaders.

They first tried to recoup their losses under one Sunkari Kamara. His opposition to trade soon set the French against him, and after some futile struggles, his career came to an end in 1882. Another leader, Fode Kaba Dumbuya, attempted to reorganize the Mandinka around the banks of the Gambia in 1875, but he was driven back by the Fulbe in the area. However, under these two leaders, Sunkari and Dumbuya, the Mandinka were able not only to resist the French and the Fulbe in the Casamance but also to preserve their ethnic identity through large-scale conversion to Islam.

The history of the area stretching from the Gambia to Sierra-Leone had been dominated from the eighteenth century by the development of the great Fulbe state of Futa Jallon. The rise of this state helped expand long-distance trade from the Sudanese interior to the coast where it was linked with the Europeans. At the beginning of the nineteenth century, the slave trade on the coast was carried on secretly around European trading posts until the middle of the century. The persistence of the slave trade in this area was due to its anchorages and deep indentations, and the proximity of Futa Jallon which raided widely for slaves and offered them for export.

In Futa Jallon, the society appeared relatively stable at the beginning of the nineteenth century. After the holy war of the previous century, the victors had established a new aristocracy over an extremely rigid and stratified society. The independent provinces and parishes which made up the state were ruled from the capital in Timbo by a class of aristocrats who occupied the top of the social hierarchy. Under them were their Jallonke subjects who were heavily oppressed to the point of losing their language. These people, who constituted three-quarters of the entire population, were harshly exploited and their activities closely supervised.

Between the upper and the lower classes was another group of individuals. These were poor Fulbe lineages that were unable to seize any estate or substantial booty during the war. However, despite the social rigidity and oppression which characterized Futa society there was a high level of Islamic culture in Futa Jallon. This was accompanied by a frequent use of Fulani in written form. In the realm of religion, the Fulbe of Futa Jallon did not monopolize the ultimate authority. They entrusted a prestigious role to outsiders such as the Jaxaanke whom they preferred because of their political neutrality. The Jaxaanke were first and foremost men of religion but they were also long-distance traders.

The power of the Fulbe of Futa Jallon rested on the military whose strength depended on the unity of the state which was undermined by the civil conflicts at the end of the eighteenth century. Despite this, the kingdom was kept intact by a set of rules which limited the amount of political violence in the state. These rules allowed for the rotation of the leadership of the state between the two rival families/parties – the Alfaya and the Soriya – at the capital, Timbo. Because of these internal divisions, the Fulbe of Futa Jallon could not pursue any aggressive policy of expansion. The result was that their neighbours such as the Jallonke were able to establish relatively strong states like Tamba and Solimana which blocked some of the trade routes used by the Fulbe. It was only in Labe, one of the provinces of Futa Jallon, that there was some degree of expansion northwards at the expense of the Mandinka empire of Kaabu.

But while Labe was developing in the north, a serious civil war was going on at Futa Jallon. This was in full swing in 1844 when al-Hadjdj 'Umar came to live at Jugunku on the borders of Futa Jallon after his return from pilgrimage. Peace was later restored when, faced with the revolt of the Hubbu, Futa rulers decided to resolve their differences and act in concert against the common foe.

The Hubbu were an extremist minority group of the Ķādiriyya who violently opposed the Tijāniyya and the Fulbe aristocracy. They consisted of Fulbe peasants, serfs of Jallonke origin, and newly imported slaves. At first their movement was mostly suppressed when it broke out all over Futa in 1849. But the rebels took refuge in the outlying areas and entrenched themselves in Fitaba under the leadership of one Jue and his son Abal, from where they constituted a serious threat to the rulers of Futa. The Hubbu were formidable fighters and Boketto, their fortress, was impregnable to Futa rulers. Twice, the Hubbu burnt Timbo, the Futa capital. The Fulbe eventually had to seek the assistance of Samori against them. The alliance with Samori, apart from diminishing the Hubbu threat, also proved profitable for the Fulbe of Futa Jallon who sold him cattle in exchange for slaves. Meanwhile, Futa Jallon remained torn by internal wranglings.

As noted earlier, the rise of Futa Jallon opened up a wide area for Sudanic trade to reach the sea coast. In other words, Sudanic influences infiltrated down to the coast and radically changed the culture of the coastal peoples especially as many of them had to accept the political authority of Futa Jallon. The area now known as Guinea-Bissau was under the Fulbe of Futa Jallon. Likewise were the Susu and the Landuman of Boke who unsuccessfully resisted Fulbe authority. Islam came to the Susu along with the political domination of Futa Jallon, and their culture was Sudanized at a high rate down to the colonial period. However, the Beafade in Guinea-Bissau and the Nalu of Rio Nunez escaped Fulbe influence because of their swampy habitat and their lack of interest in long-distance trade. Thus, the political authority of Futa did not extend as far as the sea but Sudanic influences nevertheless became profound in the area as a result of commercial contacts.

The arrival of Sudanic traders on the coast radically changed the cultures of the coastal peoples in the southern Susu country and in the domains of the Limba, Loko and Temne. Mandinka and Fulbe lineage groups settled widely on the coast, became politically dominant and introduced new ideas of politics to the area. Consequently, hitherto unstratified egalitarian societies now became organized into warrior chiefdoms and semi-centralized states. However, these coastal peoples retained their cultural identities by assimilating the numerically few newcomers linguistically. One of the social effects of the Sudanic presence on the coast was to create socio-political organizations which transcended existing political systems and extended into the forest lands of the south, beyond the borders of Sudanic trade in the areas previously mentioned. For instance, initiation societies like the *Poro*, spread widely among the coastal peoples from the Temne to the Kpelle of Liberia.

The history of the forest lands of the south in the nineteenth century is characterized by the expansion of peoples in different directions and by the growth of trade. During the first half of the century, the Temne were struggling to protect their territory from the incursions of the Susu and the Kpa Mende who were expanding in their direction. In the middle of the century, a trading network run by Sierra-Leone Creoles made its way to the interior thus integrating the region into the world market. Meanwhile the Mende who were located to the south of the Temne were also expanding. They formed great warrior chiefdoms in which their women played important leadership roles.

Their expansion separated two other closely related southern Mande peoples, the Kono and the Vai.

The Vai maintained quite sizeable chiefdoms and played an active part in the growth of the slave trade that characterized the area in the eighteenth and nineteenth centuries. These external contacts caused Vai culture to change considerably and brought out their creative initiative. In about 1818, the Vai invented their own script. The Gola was another group from the interior which started vigorous expansion in the eighteenth century. They pushed against others like the Vai, the De and the Kpelle in their advance towards the sea. Further south was the Saint Paul river which links the coast of Monrovia to the Konyan kingdoms and marked the boundary of the Sudanic world of the Mandinka. On the banks of this river was an isolated route between the savanna and the sea which determined the location of the Vai and the subsequent siting of Monrovia.

The Kru bloc

The Kru inhabited the coastal strip which stretched from Monrovia to the Bandama. They were forest farmers and hunters but were best known as seamen. In the nineteenth century, there was no link between the seas and the savanna immediately to the west of the Bandama. This was because the valley between the sea and the savanna had been closed by the Baule since the beginning of the eighteenth century and also because the rivers were hardly navigable. Consequently, there was no centralized polity and no long-distance trade in the area. There was however a relay trade which passed goods from one group to another. Thus the history of the area is that of small groups and their interaction on the one hand, and of their relation with the outside world on the other. Despite the notable linguistic homogeneity of the Kru, they could still be divided into several closely related communities, which in turn could be divided broadly into two groups: the Bete-Dida to the east of the Sassandra river and the better known Bakwe to the west.

A number of important changes took place in the area during the course of the nineteenth century. An east-west movement of some Kru lineages which had been going on for centuries in the interior was stopped about the middle of the century when they came up against more powerful groups. Another significant development was the integration of 'peasants' and 'sailors' in some of the Kru communities. Before the nineteenth century, there had been an age-long distinction between the sailors and the peasants. But the increasing role played by the peasants in the slave trade brought them into closer contact with the sailors thus leading to the integration of the two groups.

Special links were also forged between some Kru groups and Sierra Leone. This was due to the fact that European traders who patronized the Gulf of Guinea for both the clandestine slave trade and the legitimate trade made use of the Kru sailors as interpreters. As a result, the Kru soon established themselves in large numbers in Freetown and later in Monrovia as labourers and

24.2 *Kru canoemen*   **24.3** *Kru houses*

woodcutters. They remained cohesive, but adopted aspects of Creole culture as well. Protestant influence on the Kru, both from Sierra Leone and Liberia, was obviously an important factor in the rise of the 'Kingdom of the Grebo', modelled after the Fante Confederation of 1871 on the Gold Coast, and achieving a measure of national consciousness and a written language. This Grebo nationalism provided the background to the later career of Prophet Harris in Côte d'Ivoire.

As time went on, the ancient community of coastal fishermen came increasingly under the impact of European activities. After 1821, the coastal fringe came more or less under the authority of the government of Liberia. The line of the Sassandra remained firmly within Kru territory, but beyond it concentrations of other people were to be found in Kru territory among the Bete of Gagnoa and some of the Dida. The influence of European trade was spreading and it affected the culture of some of the groups at the mouth of the Sassandra river. However, throughout this period, the coastal regions remained unstable and subject to violent outbursts.

The world of the southern Mande

The southern Mande peoples inhabited the territory between the Guinea savannas and the coastal peoples. The main groups of the southern Mande were the Mende, Toma, Kpelle, Dan and Kwenu. They had many traits in common with the coastal riverine peoples. For example, they had no centralized state structure but widespread secret initiation societies. Thus, while the history of the southern Mande is inseparable from that of the coastal peoples with whom they always mixed, it was also inextricably linked with that of the southern

Mandinka, Sudanic peoples whose influence in the area went back to the decline of the ancient empire of Mali.

The southern Mandinka inhabited the upper Niger from the borders of Futa Jallon to the Bandama river. By the beginning of the nineteenth century, they had established a long-distance trading network which conveyed the kolanuts of the southern forests towards the Niger. The southern Mandinka was a traditional society dominated by a warrior aristocracy. Islam was practised by only a minority connected with the trading network. However, this trading network did not link with the sea. The country of the southern Mandinka was thus relatively a dead end as it traditionally looked towards the Niger and the Sudan from where their ancestors originated.

In the far west of this region was the village of Kankan which had developed into an important commercial centre in the eighteenth century, taking advantage of the Futa Jallon outlet to the sea. It was the centre for the famous Muslim Mandinka whose culture permeated the world of the Juula (Dyula) who were long-distance traders. Kankan was ruled by the Kaba who were at the same time a political, religious and commercial family. With the conversion of the Kaba by al-Hadjdj 'Umar between 1845 and 1850, they launched an unsuccessful campaign to impose their authority over their traditionalist neighbours. This created a chain of events which culminated in the eventual disruption of the old order among the southern Mandinka.

This disruption could be explained in terms of the increasing importance of Muslim traders due to the opening of many new routes since the eighteenth century. Moreover, this Muslim minority became increasingly aware of the holy wars and Muslim theocracies in the north. Therefore a time came when the Juula and Muslim elements could no longer accept the inferior position assigned to them by the rulers who clung to tradition and were unwilling to reform. This led to a series of localized conflicts in the region, beginning with the revolt of Moriule Sise in 1835. These conflicts were all connected in various ways with Islam and the world of trade, but they did not achieve the desired result of emancipating the Juula Muslims. Nevertheless, they demonstrated the fact that the Juula no longer accepted the place they had traditionally occupied in the society and that they were capable of disrupting the society as a whole.

This was the situation when Samori Ture came to the scene in the middle of the nineteenth century. Born about 1830 among largely traditionalist people, Samori took early to trade so as to escape from his father's authority. He became a warrior in 1848 in order to help rescue his mother who had been captured in war. The remarkable ability which he showed won him both friends and foes until he decided in 1861 to organize an army and embark on a military career on his own. He first won the support of the traditionalists of lower Toron, his mother's people, before proceeding to conquer other areas. Between 1871 and 1881 he brought the vast area occupied by the Mandinka under his control. His style of leadership and the changes he imposed on Mandinka society by ending the internal conflicts, opening trade routes which had been blocked during previous revolts and emancipating the Juula Muslims without enslaving the traditionalists brought him a lot of supporters from all sides.

Samori's first empire was a military hegemony which changed Mandinka society without destroying it. The Muslim traders were given a more important place while the traditionalists kept their freedom. However, Samori's empire cannot be called a Muslim state although it was ruled by an Islamized military class. This is because Samori was not a <u>shaykh</u> learned in Arabic or even deeply versed in Islamic culture. He often borrowed from the examples of the Fulbe and Tukuloor but he did not emphasize the primacy of religion in his statecraft. He was down-to-earth in his approach to the Mandinka problem. In twenty years he managed to give his society a new balance which favoured the Juula thus solving the crisis it had been going through for half a century. This was the situation of the southern Mande when the French struck in the 1880s.

Conclusion

The advance of European influence was the only factor common to the whole region under discussion. European influence was very strong on the coast where the slave trade continued illegally until the middle of the nineteenth century. The exchange of new African products like palm oil and groundnuts for European goods brought the coastal area more into the world market. Although these influences were much weaker in the interior where the Sudanic tradition and Islam persisted, the Juula revolution could largely be explained in terms of this growth of trade with the outside world. Samori's empire could thus be called, at least in part, a reaction to the impact of the outside world on his society. At the same time, he was clearly also influenced by the example of the Muslim revolutionaries of the Sudan.

25

States and peoples of the Niger Bend and the Volta

Introduction

The countries of the Volta basin and the Niger Bend were centres of a political system which extended beyond the region in the eighteenth century, filling the vacuum created by the fall of Gao in the sixteenth century, and exploiting the new economic and political conditions produced on the Gold Coast by the slave trade and the rise of the Asante empire. During the nineteenth century, however, new forces led to the fall of the great kingdoms and gave rise to migrations among the non-centralized groups. For the region, therefore, the nineteenth century was a period of major changes.

In the first place, there were major political and institutional upheavals. Large empires such as Asante and Kong, and the Mossi and Bambara kingdoms broke down due to a combination of internal tensions and external pressures. This triggered off movements of peoples especially from the non-centralized groups, some of whom migrated over wide areas. There were also notable changes in the flow, the articles and terms of trade which were often the cause and sometimes the result of the political changes. These changes marked the end of one era and heralded the beginning of another, namely, the slave trade and the colonial periods respectively. Christianity and Islam also spread widely. The spread of the former was facilitated by the advance of European influence, while the latter was fostered by Islamic hegemony at work in the Sahel. All these developments weakened the region and facilitated European conquest and the establishment of colonial rule.

The Asante system: its rise and decline

The Asante empire which was founded in the eighteenth century with its nucleus around Kumasi evolved a highly integrated political system whose political and spiritual unity was symbolized by the institution of the Golden Stool. It came to wield a tremendous economic and political power over not only the dependent kingdoms to the north but also the autonomous Fante chiefdoms and other states on the coast. At the centre of the empire were the groups associated with the Oyoko clan of Kumasi who evolved a centralized

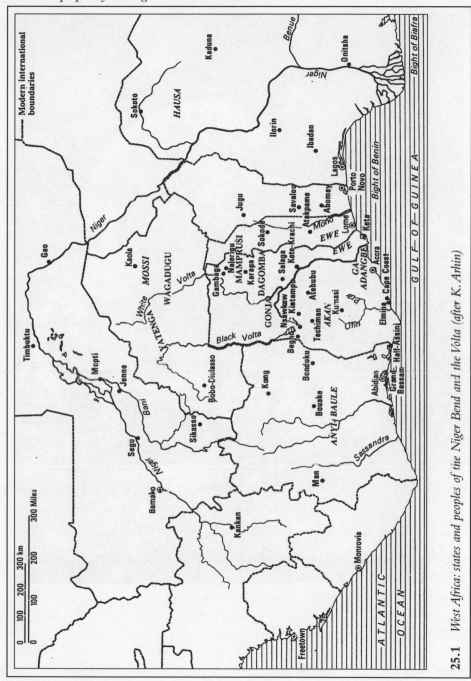

25.1 *West Africa: states and peoples of the Niger Bend and the Volta (after K. Arhin)*

25.2   *The Golden Stool of Asante*

monarchical system. Neighbouring Akan kingdoms such as Mampong, Nsuta, Dwaben, Bekwai, etc. as well as the northern kingdoms of Gyaman, Gonja, Dagomba and Mamprusi were incorporated into the empire. The king of Kumasi became the Asantehene and it was from there that he exercised authority over the whole empire.

Under Asantehene Osei Bonsu (1801–24), Asante embarked on a vigorous push to the coast in a determined effort to consolidate its control over the economy against the resistance of the peoples of the coastal regions. However, in 1826 the Asante were defeated by a coalition of the Fante states formed under the patronage and with the assistance of the British. This was to mark the beginning of the decline of the Asante empire.

At the height of its power during the early nineteenth century, the Asante empire comprised three different types of territories. The first was the central group of Asante chiefdoms, united under the authority of the Asantehene by the same language and culture, a network of kinship ties, a century of common military activities and pride in their spectacular achievements. The Golden Stool served as the focus of the unity of the people. The second category comprised neighbouring Akan states who accepted the primacy of the Golden Stool and other Asante institutions, and lived as Asante under the authority of the Asantehene. The third category of states were geographically and culturally distant peoples such as the Dagomba, the Mamprusi and the Gonja. Their main contribution to the empire was in the economic development of Kumasi, largely by the supply of tribute both in cash and in kind.

However, we should observe that this classification should not be made too rigid. The nature of Asante influence in these regions was fluid and was largely determined by the circumstances prevailing locally at the time. For instance, Asante preoccupations within the central Akan states were not only political but also economic. In the same vein, the non-Akan states to the north were subjected to military and political control largely because of the need to exploit their economic resources.

From 1826 until 1874, three significant trends were discernible in the Gold Coast region. First was the effort of the British to establish an informal British jurisdiction over the coastal peoples. The second was the effort of the coastal peoples to re-organize themselves and preserve their autonomy in the face of the dual threat from both the British and the Asante. The third was the continued and increasingly unsuccessful effort of the Asante to enforce their dominance of the early nineteenth century.

The effort of the British to establish an informal administration on the Gold Coast was most successful under Governor George Maclean (1830–43). His objectives were to check the expansion of the Asante and to use the Asante threat to force the coastal peoples to accept British control. To these ends, he introduced a three-party treaty between the Fante, Asante and the British in which all of them recognized the autonomy of the coastal communities south of the Pra river, undertook to keep trade routes open and agreed to refer any disputes to the British for arbitration. This treaty system became institutionalized in 1843 when the British government took over direct control of the coastal forts from the trading companies, and stationed a Governor to administer them with authority to establish an executive and a legislative council over the neighbouring peoples.

The Fante and other coastal peoples made many moves to free themselves not only from these European incursions but also from the threats of Asante domination. They protested to the British against the encroachments on their sovereignty, and embarked on various experiments to organize more centralized political institutions that would better ensure their autonomy. In particular, Fante chiefs and delegates from Denkyira, Wassa, Twifu and Assin in the western part of the coast formed the Fante Confederation in 1868 with the support of a rising educated elite. The Confederation was given a written constitution with modern administrative, judicial and financial institutions. The Ga and others to the east responded with a similar but more informal confederation. However, by 1872, even the Fante Confederacy was already fading out especially because of the hostility of the British who did their best to divide the chiefs and to repress and frustrate the African intellectuals who were behind the movement for confederation, and who depended on trading with Europeans for their livelihood.

Nevertheless, the Fante Confederation was of great significance although it was short-lived. It represented the last attempt of the coastal peoples to resist colonial incursions. It tried to revive the Fante unity that had been destroyed by the European presence. It also anticipated the role which the educated elite would play in the future history of the Gold Coast, namely, that of guiding the traditional chiefs within the nationalist movement. It thus demonstrated the way in which the colonial enterprise was digging its own grave by providing western education, the major weapon of Africans in the struggle against colonialism.

Meanwhile, Asante was also trying to assert its authority on the coast. Its attack on Elmina in 1872 provoked the British to mount a major military expedition to attack Kumasi in 1874. Kumasi was captured and burnt and Asante was made to renounce all its rights on the Gold Coast which was then placed formally under British administration. This only hastened the disintegration of the Asante empire. The revolt of Dwaben, one of the most valiant of the central Asante towns, in 1875 led to anarchy in Kumasi and in the vassal states to the north. The British soon took advantage of the disintegration when they invaded Kumasi in 1896, arrested the Asantehene, and lured him into exile.

The Mossi states

The Mossi kingdoms which rose gradually to prominence in the sixteenth century, and which reached the peak of their growth in the eighteenth century, entered a period of decay in the nineteenth century. This decay was a result of both internal and external problems in the territory. The kingdoms of

25.3 *The Exchequer Court, Kumasi, 1817*

25.4 *Mossi masked figures – probably 'earth priests' representing aboriginal authority, early 20th century*

Wagadugu and Yatenga were the most affected by these problems while the kingdom of Busuma thrived at the expense of its neighbours.

The powerful kingdom of Wagadugu was destroyed in wars with the Busuma and the Lallé. The Busuma war which spanned several years considerably weakened Wagadugu while Busuma used the opportunity to expand at the expense of both Wagadugu and the other smaller polities in the region. The Lallé war was sparked off by a trivial incident and this indicates the extent of the decay of the Mossi system at the time. The war dragged on for over fifty years and attracted an increasing number of belligerents until the French conquest.

Although Yatenga was not as powerful as Wagadugu, the kingdom also suffered decay during the nineteenth century. The first problem came from Yatenga's bid to extend its frontiers and integrate other elements such as the kingdoms of Yako and Riziam. The battles fought by Yatenga in these areas were very costly in terms of the toll they took on human life and resources. Secondly, external threats from the Jelgoji provoked a series of attacks from Yatenga which were equally costly. Chronic civil wars in the Yatenga kingdom also made matters worse. Rivals frequently replaced each other in quick succession, ruling alternately or sometimes even simultaneously. In fact, the fratricidal wars between the two main groups in the kingdom provided the occasion for French intervention at the end of the century.

The western and southern Volta plateaux

In this region, non-centralized communities of lineage groups and clans tried to cope with the upheavals of the time. These peoples with little in the way of political hierarchies were able to weather the turmoil of the nineteenth century better than the centralized states. They made up for their lack of centralized power through the existence of non-political institutions such as the *Poro* society of the Senufo. Thus, the experience of the Voltaic groups in the century was of invasions, preventive attacks, resistance, adaptation and intermarriage. While they resisted the attempts by successive groups of Mande, Mossi, Zerma, Marka and Fulbe to dominate them, they also readily adapted to the presence and economic opportunities provided by such groups, migrating only when the pressure became unbearable.

The Gwiriko, Kenedugu and other peoples to the south-west of what is now Burkina Faso experienced a similar climate of pressure, instability and conflict in the nineteenth century. Their major reaction was migration. Different groups such as the Pwa, Sissala, Gan and Dyan fought one another, intermarried and migrated in different directions especially during the early decades of the century. While these Voltaic groups migrated, they nevertheless retained their individual cultural identities despite some general similarities in their overall culture. They were obliged to spend most of their time establishing or defending themselves, not so much from their immediate neighbours as from Juula groups which continually harassed them without succeeding in subjugating them.

Other non-centralized Voltaic peoples such as the Gurunsi, the Bisa and the Samo also experienced an unstable political climate in the nineteenth century. While the Gurunsi were plundered by neighbouring groups, the reverse was the case with the Bisa who expanded at the expense of their neighbours. The country of the Samo was not conquered by any group but was used repeatedly as a withdrawal base by different warring groups. On the whole, the achievement of these non-centralized peoples at the end of the nineteenth century was quite substantial. Endowed with remarkable vitality and resilience, these groups which also remained attached to the traditional religions, showed brilliance in the way they resisted the colonial forces at the end of the century.

The eastern regions of the Volta plateaux

In these regions were Jelgoji and Liptako located between Massina and Sokoto on one side and Yatenga on the other. This geographical location made for remarkable intersections in the nineteenth-century history of these peoples. Early in the century, different Fulbe groups and camps were to be found there. In Jelgoji were the Jelgobe Fulbe who were subjects of the Jallube, whom they served as herdsmen. In the course of the century the Fulbe revolted against their overlords, obtained their independence and founded two new chiefdoms, Jiibo and Barbulle. The Ferrobe were another Fulbe group which inhabited this region. They were under the Gulmanceba in Liptako. Inspired by the Sokoto *djihād,* this Fulbe group rose up against their traditionalist masters under the leadership of one Brahima Saidu who later became the *amīr* of the new emirate of Liptako.

The political organization of Liptako under the Fulbe was very similar to that of Jelgoji and it was aimed at maintaining a balance between the different groups in the state. Power was transmitted among the ruling Ferroba through patrilineal descent from Saidu, the father of the Brahima who had led the *djihād.* The Torodbe, who were another Fulbe group in the state, constituted the electoral College that vetted and selected new *amīrs.* This system served to integrate the Torodbe into the society despite the fact that they were denied the direct exercise of power. The ceremony of installation of the *amīr* was also an occasion in which Islam and traditional religious practices met for the sake of societal equilibrium and to ensure the material prosperity of the new reign. Older Fulbe clans which could not aspire to the office of *amīr* were compensated with some subordinate political offices.

Another interesting feature of the history of the region to the east of the Volta pleataux in the nineteenth century was the changing pattern of alliances among the different communities. Threatened by Massina in 1858, the Fulbe of Jiibo and Barbulle sought the help of Yatenga and Datenga in the Mossi country to crush their enemies. After the defeat of Massina, the Fulbe turned against their Mossi allies, massacred them and went back to being on good terms with Massina. Meanwhile, rival groups in Jiibo and Barbulle sought the support of either Massina or Yatenga in their internal struggle for power.

25.5 *Mogho Naaba Sanem being greeted by his subjects, 1888*

25.6 *Bambara house types, 1887*

However, by the end of the century, the Kurumba, who were the indigenous inhabitants of Jelgoji before the immigration of the Fulbe, had become enough of a threat to provoke a coalition between Jelgoji and Liptako. The Tuareg also played an important role in the politics of the region.

The Bambara kingdoms of Segu and Kaarta

The history of Segu and Kaarta in the nineteenth century featured various acts of aggression that were regarded as acts of bravery, raids carried out with no attempt at organization and bitter warfare between kingdoms and within individual kingdoms, all portraying the most negative aspects of a major political system in a state of disintegration. Relations between Segu and Kaarta were strained especially as the rulers of Kaarta treated the kings of Segu with contempt. This situation would explain the persistent assaults carried out by Segu against Kaarta. Segu, which was stronger and more populous, always defeated Kaarta but never conquered it. This period was also characterized by the increasing prominence of the *tonjons,* notable warriors and entrepreneurs who exploited their reputation for militarism to rise to prominence. This was the situation of the Bambara kingdoms before the *djihād* of al-Hadjdj 'Umar swept them away.

Thus, in the nineteenth century, existing political structures in the centre and the north of the region covered in this chapter went into rapid decline and in some cases were dominated by new forces unleashed by the Sokoto *djihād.* The new forces exploited the internal problems caused by the ongoing decline of the existing polities, thus accelerating the pace of decline, and ensuring that they would in turn be swept away by foreign powers.

As indicated above, there are several explanations for this decline. While there were external influences such as new commercial pressures from the coast and the European push, there were also internal problems such as political instability and population movements. In these circumstances, social divisions increased which transformed the relatively egalitarian structures that had characterized the societies of the Sahel during their period of ascendency. Also important was the evolution of religious movements which became militant and intolerant of traditional cults. However, despite the disruptions and dislocations of the nineteenth century, many people continued to work for the survival of their communities. The ordinary people were not passive nor resigned to their fate; rather, despite the convulsions in the region, they showed remarkable adaptability in responding to the major challenges of the period such as the intrusion of colonialism.

Socio-economic tensions

Agriculture was the basis of the economic life of the peoples of the Niger Bend and the Volta. While the majority of the population went into agricultural production, the rest were engaged in trade, mostly in agricultural produce.

Some groups, like the Juula even combined the two activities. The coastal regions imported gold and slaves and supplied European products to their hinterland neighbours, while the Sahel imported kolanuts from the hinterland and weapons from the coast in exchange for salt, livestock and slaves. Between the Sahel and the coast were the savannah regions which supplied slaves, livestock, cereals and gold.

This situation was only slightly affected by the abolition of the slave trade by Britain in 1807. On the coast, the ban on commercial slavery was enforced while domestic slavery was tolerated. However, slavery expanded in the interior in the second half of the nineteenth century. This was due to a substantial rise in the cost of weapons which meant that greater numbers of slaves had to be offered in exchange for the same quantities of ammunition. Consequently, certain groups, such as the Zamberma specialized as slavers. Their main sources of supply were the *djihāds* conducted by the Muslim leaders of the north, the conflicts in the Mossi country, raids on the Tuareg and on areas bordering the trading posts on the coast, and other wars within the region. These captives were largely from agricultural communities which did not always succeed in defending themselves.

On the Gold Coast itself where slaves had constituted 90 per cent of the exports at the beginning of the century, abolition of the slave trade altered the economic situation to a considerable extent. Palm oil and rubber came to succeed slaves as the coast's leading export commodities. Gold was mined in the hinterland and moved southward while kolanut, another hinterland product, moved northward. In addition, luxury goods from Europe also moved down through North Africa, the Fezzān and the Hausa country to the Niger Bend. Silks and carpets from Turkey and Tripoli, natron from Borno and Hausa textiles were exchanged for kolanuts, gold, and cotton material from Dagomba, Mossi and Mande, as well as sheabutter and livestock from the Sudanese Sahel.

This commercial exchange led to the rise of Salaga, a town in the state of Gonja, as an important entrepot. It grew to become a very large city and its prosperity was to continue until the collapse of Asente power, when the trade routes shifted elsewhere. Commercial transactions in Salaga were largely carried out through barter, though gold dust and cowries were sometimes used as currencies.

Apart from Asante and Lobi, gold was also available on the left bank of the upper Black Volta. This gold was mined by men of various origins and women were also involved in its production. Slave labour was utilized extensively. It is, however, important to note here that the production of gold in this area was not supervized by an centralized state; rather the producers were individual entrepreneurs. Some of the gold-diggers involved themselves in slave-hunting because slaves were more profitable and because they could also be used in washing the gold.

While gold for Lobi was carried to the Gold Coast and Liberia, that from the left bank of the upper Black Volta went to the Sahara and Morocco. It was carried via local and regional trade routes, some of which passed through Salaga.

25.7 *A Mossi merchant, 1888*

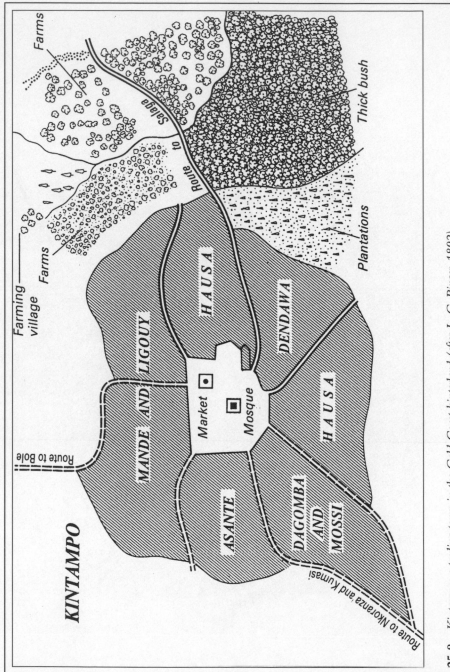

25.8 *Kintampo: a trading town in the Gold Coast hinterland (after L. G. Binger, 1892)*

In local trade it was used to purchase salt, kolanuts, slaves, livestock, grain and boubous (loose ankle-length robes). Salt was another important item of trade and it occurred in many forms. Of all the items of trade described above, the trade in slaves alone rose considerably in value in the second half of the century.

A network of routes spread out from Dori which shows that the Sahel was open to trade from all sides. This trade was carried by the Juula, the Hausa, the Mossi, Moors and Tuareg. Goods imported into Dori included tobacco, matting, livestock and salt from the north, which were exchanged for lengths of cotton, Hausa turbans and European manufactured products. Other items that were exchanged were slaves, worked copper, Guinea cloth, hardware and kolanuts. On the whole, despite the fact that the activity of traders was only a tiny fraction of the region's economy, it had a strong influence on the lives of all. Border communities developed which became centres for different peoples and ideas, thus becoming heterogeneous societies. The importance of such societies lay in the clear division of labour and specialist activities that were practised: there were landowners, tenants, brokers and a host of other craftsmen.

Social change

It is not surprising that there were major social changes in the lands lying on the Niger Bend and in the Volta basin in the nineteenth century, given the upheavals of the time. These changes were more pronounced in centralized states than in the non-centralized ones, more pronounced in the coastal regions than in the hinterland, and more in Islamized areas than elsewhere.

In centralized states, the condition of slaves and caste members was worsened: they were discriminated against, and they were oppressed and exploited by their Fulbe overlords. This led, for instance, to a slave uprising in Liptako in 1861. The indigenous peoples of Gulmanceba were reduced to servile status. Even artisans were denied the rights enjoyed by freemen and nobles; yet some of them, such as blacksmiths, were feared because of the creativity and magical nature of their work. In the Mossi kingdom of Wagadugu, slaves were made into eunuchs in large numbers. Meanwhile, individuals at the helm of societal affairs not only lived in opulence, they were also attended by large retinues of dependants. In addition to gifts, tributes on harvests and taxes levied on traders, these chiefs also received a certain percentage of plunder taken in raids.

However, in non-centralized societies, relations between slaves and their owners remained much more cordial. In Pura and Lobi, for instance, slaves were treated well and the institution of slavery was in fact used as a means of strengthening clan and territorial groups. This was because slaves were well integrated into the society and given certain rights of their own.

Within the centralized states, another source of tension was rivalry between the rulers and the nobility. In states such as Asante, the Bambara kingdoms, Yatenga, the kingdom of Wagadugu and Gwiriko, there were bitter struggles between the nobles and the rulers.

In the coastal lands, trade and education also produced some notable changes in the society. The shift from the slave trade to that of palm-oil, rubber, ivory and gold led to the rise of a new merchant class who also operated as agents of European companies. These great merchants supported a number of other African traders and controlled the supply of products from the interior.

The spread of western education on the coast also led to the rise of new social classes. These included the descendants of the great merchant families who had been educated in Europe since the beginning of the century or at Fourah Bay College in Sierra Leone. These people rose to positions of responsibility in their society. There were also those with rudimentary education who served as clerks to English and African merchants and lived as parasites on illiterate chiefs and their people. Between these two groups of educated people were those with a sufficiently good education to be able to become independent merchants and managers in the coastal towns. Despite the differences between them, the different groups often interacted and cooperated as evidenced by their joint action in the Fante Confederation discussed earlier.

Religious change

The nineteenth century in this region was a period of rapid advance for Islam in the north and centre, and the revival of Christianity in the south. Both religions emphasized the prestige of education and also presented a wider horizon to the people. In the northern part of the region, the inspiration derived from the previous *djihāds* of 'Uthmān dan Fodio of Sokoto, Seku Ahmadu of Massina and al-Hadjdj 'Umar led to the local *djihād* that resulted in the emirate of Liptako. Despite the celebrated resistance of the Mossi and Bambara to Islam, they were infiltrated by Islamic influences in the nineteenth century. The Bambara rulers of Segu not only consulted marabouts, they also welcomed them into their royal courts. A number of Mossi kingdoms also embraced Islam in the course of the century because they were exposed to Islamic influences through their commercial activities. Islam also became the leading religion of Dagomba, Mamprusi and Sansanne Mango, and in such areas, *imāms* became important political figures. Asante rulers also became sympathetic to the cause of Islam. Muslim traders from the Arab world flocked to the Asante capital and devotional items prepared by marabouts were sold for high prices. While Islam could not displace traditional religion which had become the basis of the political structure in the Asante empire, it nevertheless kept Asante princes from embracing Christianity.

While Islam was making headway in the north, Christianity was also being reintroduced in the south of the region under discussion. By 1828, the Evangelical Basel Mission and the Bremen Mission had been established on the south-eastern part of the Gold Coast. These missions opened model farms and technical schools. Methodist missionaries were also active on the western coast with Cape Coast as a base. They too established model farms in the Cape Coast district, opened many schools, and translated the basic works of Christianity

25.9   *Salaga in 1888*

25.10   *A Basel mission carpentry workshop in Christiansborg (Accra).*
Engraving from a photographic original, probably c. 1870

into Ga. The Reverend J. G. Christaller published a Twi grammar in 1874, and a dictionary of the Akan language in 1881. However, despite the efforts of Christianity and Islam, traditional religion managed to survive in the region.

Conclusion

The peoples of the land of the Niger Bend and the Volta basin invited aggression from without in the nineteenth century through their internecine conflicts. But the roots of this problem could be traced to previous centuries when the slave trade introduced certain economic contradictions into the region. Therefore, the migrations, settlement of new population groups, social tensions and even political and religious expansion of the nineteenth century were largely the results of this major phenomenon that had dominated the preceding centuries. Thus, in a sense, the nineteenth century marked the end of a very long period, not only in the history of this region, but also in Africa as a whole.

26

Dahomey, Yorubaland, Borgu and Benin in the nineteenth century

Introduction

The area covered by this chapter is bounded in the west by the Mono river, in the east and north by the Niger, and in the south by the Atlantic Ocean. It is mostly an undulating plain, rising and falling with the highest points in the Atacora and Kukuru hills. The vegetation is largely open although there are dense rain forests in the south-east which was the area of the ancient Benin kingdom.

There are four distinct though interrelated cultural areas in the region, viz., the Aja in the west, the Yoruba in the centre, the Borgu in the north and the Edo in the east. Each of these main cultural areas can be subdivided in terms of dialects of the main languages, ecology, and specific occupations of the inhabitants. The Aja-speaking peoples are in three principal sub-groups namely the Fon who dominated the ancient kingdom of Dahomey; the Gun of the Wẹmẹ river valley and the Porto Novo-Badagry region; and the Ewe now found in the south-western parts of the Benin Republic, southern Togo, and south-eastern Ghana.

The Yoruba cultural area is the most extensive in the Mono–Niger region. It embraces the greater part of south-western Nigeria. There are numerous subgroups among the Yoruba such as the Ọyọ, Ibarapa, Ifẹ, Ijẹbu, Ijẹṣa, Egba, Egbado, Ondo, Ikale, Ekiti, Owo, Akoko and Awori. Also on the present day Nigeria–Benin boundary are, from north to south, other Yoruba sub-groups such as the Ketu, Ọhọri, Ifọnyin and Anago.

The Borgu cultural area is made up of three main traditional power centres, namely Busa, Illo and Nikki. Busa and Illo were situated in the Borgu local government area of the old Kwara state and adjacent parts of the Sokoto state of Nigeria. Nikki, territorially the largest traditional state, was split by the present Nigeria–Benin border with the result that some parts of it were on the Nigerian side of the border while the rest were on the Benin side. Two major languages were spoken in Borgu: Batonu (or Bariba) and Boko, each of which is further sub-divided into several distinct dialects.

The fourth major cultural area in the region is that of the Edo-speaking people of the ancient Benin kingdom. These included not only the Edo of

26.1   *Carving of a warrior on the shoulders of a* babalawo *(medicine man) from north-eastern Yorubaland (probably) carved between 1850 and 1875*

Benin city, but also linguistically and historically related groups such as the Eṣan, Ivbiosakon, Akoko Edo, Itsekiri, Urhobo and Isoko.

These four major cultural areas were not isolated zones since they interacted widely. This is shown in the traditions of common origin preserved by the people which emphasized the idea of unity and tried to link the rulers in these four cultural sub-units. Apart from this, linguistic, cultural, economic and political factors also point to intergroup relations in the region. These linkages point to series of migrations, population movements and counter movements which continued well into the nineteenth century until they were discouraged by the establishment of colonial borders at the end of the century.

The history of the mono-Niger region, therefore, is one which gives an account of the interactions between the Aja, Yoruba, Edo and Bariba; and which also reflects the interpenetration between the cultural areas of the region and their other neighbours.

The Collapse of Old Ọyọ

At the beginning of the nineteenth century, the Old Ọyọ empire was the most important single power in the Mono-Niger region because it held sway over most of the lands and peoples in the region. While the nucleus of the empire did not extend beyond the Ogun and Ọṣun river basins, its tributary states covered approximately the western half of the Mono-Niger area. Within the Old Ọyọ empire was Dahomey which became a vassal in 1748 and remained so until the 1820s. Porto Novo was also secured as Ọyọ's main port for the export of slaves. Egba and Egbado countries were conquered because the routes linking Porto Novo with Ọyọ passed through their territories. Not only was Ọyọ's political influence very strong among the Egba and Egbado as shown by the presence of its *ajẹlẹ* (resident officials) in their midst, its cultural and economic influence was also made very real by the presence of Ọyọ settler colonies. Although Ketu and Ṣabẹ claimed to be autonomous, they maintained cordial links with Ọyọ. Eastern Borgu and the south-western part of Nupe also acknowledged the authority of the *alafin* of Ọyọ. The spread of Oyo influence in the above area was facilitated by the open nature of the terrain which made for easy communication and favoured the use of the Ọyọ cavalry force.

The eastern half of the Mono-Niger region which comprised the remainder of the Yoruba culture area, namely Ifẹ, Ijẹṣa, Ekiti, Ondo, Ijẹbu, Akoko, Ọwọ, Ikale, Okiti-pupa, Awori, and the Benin kingdom were not under the direct influence of Ọyọ. However, there was a continuous involvement of Ọyọ in the history of some of these other Yoruba kingdoms. There were also considerable links between Ọyọ and Benin. In fact, the ruling dynasties of both claimed a common origin from Ifẹ and from the same founder Ọranyan. This fraternal feeling was probably sustained by the fact that there was little or no opportunity for friction between the two states since each operated in a different area with different commercial potentials – Ọyọ in the savannah area, and Benin in the rain forests.

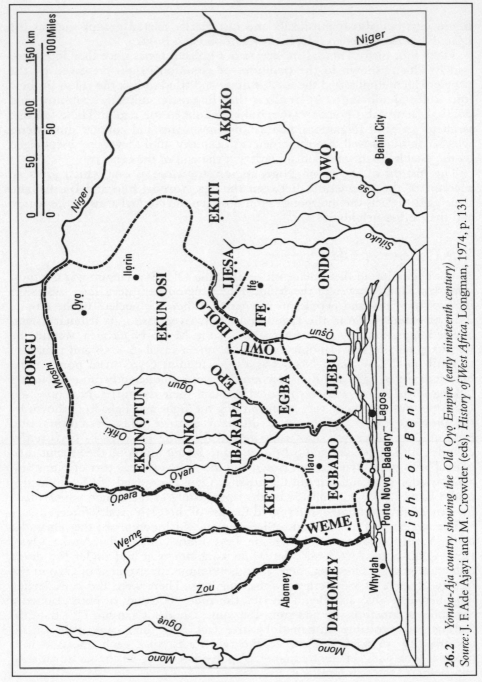

26.2 *Yoruba–Aja country showing the Old Ọyọ Empire (early nineteenth century)*
Source: J. F. Ade Ajayi and M. Crowder (eds), *History of West Africa*, Longman, 1974, p. 131

From the above, it can be seen that Old Ọyọ was at the centre of the history of the entire region, from the Mono to the Niger, such that its collapse in the third decade of the nineteenth century produced far-flung socio-political changes that were felt not only in Yorubaland but also in Dahomey, Borgu and Benin. The fall of the Old Ọyọ empire was caused by factors which had their roots in the eighteenth century but which became intensified in the first two decades of the nineteenth century. These included internal factors which manifested themselves in the power struggle between successive *alafin* and the lineage chiefs in the second half of the eighteenth century. These were in turn aggravated by external forces such as the southward extension of the *djihād* of 'Uthmān dan Fodio and the decline of the overseas slave trade. Coupled with these problems was the fact that the structure of the empire was deteriorating and that it had become militarily weak. This would account for the defeats inflicted on it by the Ẹgba in 1774, Borgu in 1783, and the Nupe in 1791. By the beginning of the nineteenth century, there was a complete breakdown of the international political situation as portrayed by shortlived and unsuccessful *alafin* such as Aole and Maku, and a protracted interregnum which lasted for almost two decades. Given this fragile situation, the revolt of Afonja as the professional head of the Ọyọ Army triggered off the chain of events that led eventually to the demise of the empire.

The effects of the collapse of Ọyọ were felt most in the western side of the region where the influence of the empire had been greatest and most direct. A major effect of the fall of the empire was the creation of a situation of general warfare and insecurity. This disturbed agriculture and local trade, disrupted coastal trade, and encouraged the intervention of Europeans in the politics of the interior. The wars engendered by the collapse of Ọyọ were of two categories. There were the *djihād* wars and the wars among the Yoruba states. In the category of *djihād* wars may be included the depredations of the supporters of the Fulbe in Ẹgbado territory; the Eleduwẹ war of 1836 between the Fulbe on one side and Borgu and Ọyọ on the other; and the 1840 war in which the Fulbe were defeated at Oṣogbo. The wars among the Yoruba states proved more devastating and they could be divided into three phases in which the highlights were the Owu war 1820–5, the Ijaye war 1860–5, and the Ekitiparapọ or Kiriji war 1877–93.

The Owu war was between the Ifẹ and their Ijẹbu allies assisted by Ọyọ warriors on one side, and the Owu, supported by the Ẹgba on the other. The aftermath of the war was the establishment of new settlements such as Ibadan, Abẹokuta, and Ijaye. There was also the re-establishment of the Ọyọ capital at Agọ-Ọja in the 1830s. These settlements became new centres of power in Yorubaland, each competing for recognition and succession to the political vacuum created by the fall of Ọyọ. The Ijaye war was a contest between Ijaye and Ibadan, with the Ẹgba of Abẹokuta assisting Ijaye to no advantage. It was indeed a struggle for leadership. It reached its climax with the destruction of Ijaye in 1862 though the war dragged on in different phases until the battle outside Ikorodu in 1865. The Ekitiparapọ was a grand alliance of the Ekiti,

26.3   *The Gateway of the Ijebu Yoruba town of Ipara, c. 1855.*
(Church mission of Gleaver 1855)

Ijẹṣa, and Igbomina, with the support of the Ifẹ and others, fighting to resist the
domination of the Ibadan. The war dragged on until the British came to make
peace in 1886, and even then did not finally end till 1893.

Another significant effect of the fall of Old Ọyọ was the rise of Dahomey as
an autonomous kingdom in 1820 and its frequent incursions into Yorubaland
until it was conquered by the French in 1892. The political stability of
Dahomey in the nineteenth century was a function of the long reigns of its
kings, the establishment of a centralized system of administration which was
successfully operated, and its economic strength. It was a combination of these
factors that encouraged Gezo, the king of Dahomey, to seize the opportunity
offered by the internal decline of Ọyọ to declare the independence of Dahomey
in the early 1820s. This was followed by a series of Dahomey invasions of
Yorubland, especially the territories of the Ẹgbado, Ketu, Ṣabẹ, Oke-Ọdan and
the Ẹgba of Abẹokuta. However, Dahomey was defeated twice by the Ẹgba in
1851 and 1864. Despite this, Dahomey raids in the Upper Ogun area continued
until the French conquest of 1892.

These Dahomey–Yoruba wars of the nineteenth century should, however,
not be seen in isolation and interpreted as inter-ethnic wars. They should
be seen alongside the various intra-Yoruba wars mentioned above, and the

intra-Aja wars of the same period, for example, the Dahomey wars in the Wẹmẹ river valley and Porto Novo in the late 1880s and early 1890s. At the least the pattern of alliances and definition of interests and priorities in these wars should lead us to see the cultural inter-relationship of the whole region, and to question the concept of tribalism and ethnicity as it developed during the colonial period.

The wars in the aftermath of the fall of Old Ọyọ had significant effects particularly on the western half of the Mono-Niger region. In the first place, there were far-reaching demographic changes and population movements in the region, and, as mentioned above, these did not respect the lines of 'ethnicity' that later came to be drawn in the colonial period. The large-scale destruction of major pre-nineteenth century towns such as Old Ọyọ itself, Igboho, Ikoyi, Igbọn, Irẹsa, Oje, Ketu and Ṣabẹ produced massive movements of peoples into new areas. New towns were established in new locations such as Ibadan, Abẹokuta, Ṣagamu and Aiyede, welcoming refugees from far and wide. The refugees also swelled the population of many older towns such as Ogbomoso, Oshogbo and Offa. There was massive enslavement of people and a substantial increase in the use of domestic slaves. The result was a significant ethnic interpenetration as Yoruba slaves ended up in Aja country and Aja refugees moved into related Yoruba communities.

The social effects of these population movements were many and varied. There was a significant increase in the level of urbanization as the walled town and armed guard seemed to offer the necessary requirement of security. The new towns experimented with new systems of government such as the military dictatorship in Ijaye under Kurumi, federalism in Abẹokuta under Ṣodẹkẹ, and constitutional monarchy in Ẹpẹ under Kosọkọ. In particular, there was the emergence of warriors as the dominant class in the politics of many of the new towns, and they soon overshadowed the pre-existing monarchical class. Thus many *ọbas* in Yorubaland seemed to have lost control of their towns to the *baloguns* or warlords. This adaptation process could also be found among some Aja communities settled within the Yoruba area who later adopted Yoruba-style *ọba*-ship institutions, a gradual process that continued into the twentieth century.

The decline of the Benin kingdom

The kingdom of Benin, like the Old Ọyọ empire, did not escape the destructive influences of the nineteenth century. But unlike Ọyọ, it was spared the actual experience of total collapse before the era of European conquest because of the durability of its political institutions. By 1800, the kingdom comprised nearly the whole of the eastern half of the Mono–Niger region. It embraced the eastern Yoruba states of Ẹkiti, Ondo and Ọwọ; western Igbo communities; as well as the Urhobo, Itsekiri and Ijọ in the south. While the Bini Edo in and around Benin city constituted the metropolitan area, the kingdom embraced other Edo-speaking peoples such as the Esan, the northern Edo, Urhobo and Isoko. In addition to these territories, Benin's authority was acknowledged all along the Atlantic coast as far as Lagos in the west. Benin also maintained a dynastic relationship with the Itsekiri, Awori-Yoruba and other related Anago chiefdoms.

Many factors were responsible for the fall of the Benin kingdom. Right from the eighteenth century up till the nineteenth, the kingdom experienced a gradual decline punctuated by periods of revival and territorial expansion. In the three or four decades before the European conquest at the end of the nineteenth century, the kingdom began to shrink due to a three-pronged assault on its territory. The first came from the Fulbe rulers of Nupe who spread the influence of the *djihād* to penetrate the northern and north-eastern parts of the Benin kingdom. Secondly, the expansion of Ibadan affected Benin domains in eastern Yorubaland, and Benin was so weak at this period that it could not send any assistance to its threatened vassals. The last push came from the Europeans who were penetrating the Benin kingdom from Lagos, and the Niger delta in the south-east. Consequently, Benin's trading privileges in the coastal trade were challenged by British traders and African middlemen such as the Itsekiri and the Ijọ. As a result of all these, the Benin port of Ughoton declined and Benin's near-monopoly of the coastal trade was brought rather abruptly to an end.

Meanwhile the prosperity and power derived from the coastal trade made some of the dependencies such as the Itsekiri and Agbor flout Benin's authority and rival its power. While the new wealth produced much tension and political conflicts in the Itsekiri kingdom of Warri for the rest of the century, Benin was already so weak that it could not as in the past take advantage of the situation to reassert its authority.

While the Benin kingdom faced such assaults from outside, it also faced grave internal problems. These were largely in the form of succession disputes which began around the middle of the nineteenth century and continued till the collapse of the kingdom. It is in the context of these internal tensions and divisions that an anti-European mood developed in Benin in the 1890s.

The growth of European interest

There were two phases in the growth of European interest in the region in the nineteenth century. In the first phase up to 1861 when the British annexed Lagos, there was relative freedom of movement and cooperation among the different Europeans. The second phase was a period of growing intensity in international rivalry, especially between Britain and France, with Germany entering the competition in the 1880s. This latter phase ended with the partition of the area between Britain and France in 1889. It should be noted, however, that the pattern of European activities in the two phases was determined to a large extent not only by the demands of the European governments but also by the changing nature of the local situation.

Thus, in the first phase of the growth of European interest in the Mono–Niger region, there was a certain flexibility in the composition and

26.4   *Shrine altar in the king's compound, Benin*

26.5   *A view of Benin city at the time of the British invasion, 1897*

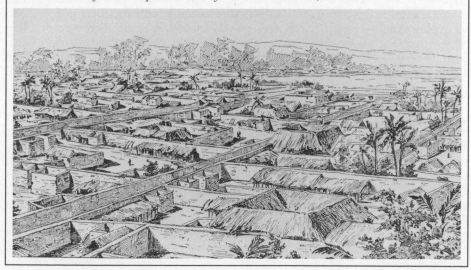

activities of the different categories of Europeans such as traders, explorers, travellers and missionaries who operated in Africa. They acted without much concern for their individual nationalities. As we have noted above, there was a similar disregard of ethnicity in the pattern of alliances of the African peoples. But while the activities of the Europeans were dictated largely by their commitment or lack of it to the abolitionist movement, the African rulers and communities had no such pre-occupation with the issue of abolition.

The Europeans of course had to reckon with the local African situation in which they operated. The explorers, missionaries and traders were obliged to operate within the pre-existing transportation and communication systems, and the pattern of geographical and intergroup relationships. In fact, the Europeans soon found out that developments in one part of the region always affected other parts because of the pre-existing inter-relationships of the peoples and cultures, as well as the religious and economic systems. For example, European abolitionists discovered that the wars in the interior had a great impact on the coast and that it was not enough to sign treaties with the coastal rulers. In order to stop the slave trade, the abolitionists had to deal with peoples in the interior also, and find ways of trying to stop the wars. The European approach to this situation was however piece-meal and divisive. For example, by focusing attention on Lagos and the eastern delta of the Niger, the Europeans destroyed the trade and influence of Benin along the coast. This was unforeseen, but it had wide implications for the distribution of power within the region.

The British annexation of Lagos and the naval attack on Porto Novo, both in 1861, marked a turning-point and ushered in the second phase of the growth of European activities in the region. The British action on Porto Novo alarmed the French who had considerable commercial interests there. This led to serious rivalry between the two powers in the Yoruba and Aja interior. The major theatre was however in western Yorubaland where the local people tried to exploit Anglo-French rivalry as a possible solution to the endemic problem of the frequent invasion of their territory by their more powerful neighbours. This rivalry eventually culminated in the French conquest of Dahomey in 1892, the Anglo-French partition of Borgu in 1895, the extension of British rule over the rest of Yorubaland and their conquest of Benin in 1897.

Socio-economic change

While the nineteenth century wars were going on and Europeans were seizing the opportunity to intervene in the affairs of the Mono–Niger region, many far-reaching changes were also taking place within the local societies themselves. To start with, the massive population movements both within and without the region produced important results. Migrations within the region facilitated the interaction and mixing of different ethnic groups. They also led to the growth of new settlements and an increased influx of slaves from the region into the New World. The scale of enslavement in the nineteenth century was an important factor in the remarkable survival of aspects of Yoruba and Aja culture in the New World. The reverse migration of emancipated slaves from Cuba, Brazil and other places back to their original home along the coast of the Mono-Niger region became an important factor in the spread of Christianity, western education and skills, and the modernization process generally.

The local population movements also had important consequences. The west-east migration of Aja-speaking peoples from Dahomey led to an increase in the size of existing eastern Aja settlements such as Badagry, Ajido and Koga, and the creation of numerous new settlements in the adjacent areas. The Ọyọ also migrated southwards. By 1830, the main centres in which Ọyọ migrants settled included Ibadan, Ijaye and the new Ọyọ town. Some Ọyọ elements also settled among the Igbomina, Ijẹṣa, Ẹkiti, Akoko, Ondo, Ikalẹ and Ilajẹ. At the same time, significant numbers of other eastern Yoruba groups such as the Ẹkiti and Ijẹṣa came as captives or freemen to Ibadan and other settlements in Osun, Ijẹbu and Ẹgba areas of Yorubaland. In Borgu the Fulbe *djihād* brought about great population movement southwards, which also had its impact on western Yorubaland.

This mixing of different ethnic and sub-ethnic groups led to considerable mutual exchange of ideas and material culture or intensified such tendencies as existed before. The Aja in Badagry adopted the Yoruba Ọba-ship institution. Ọyọ cultural influences such as the worship of Ṣango, and the spread of the men's loom and shoulder sling drums into eastern Yorubaland. Similarly, Benin influence can be seen on the court ceremonials, regalia, and chieftaincy titles in Ọwọ, Ẹkiti, Akoko, Ondo, Ijẹṣa, and among the Awori. Benin political and cultural influences also extended to the Itsekiri, Urhobo, Isoko and other Edo-speaking peoples.

Another significant change in the nineteenth century was the extension of settlements into the hitherto sparsely populated coastal areas. This was due to a number of factors. First, the nineteenth century wars rendered the more swampy coastal areas relatively safe and attractive to migration from the theatres of war in the more open hinterland. Secondly, the European trade from across the sea gradually became more important than the overland trade because of the transition from slave to 'legitimate' trade, thus conferring a definite economic advantage on the coastal regions. Lastly, there was a steady growth of European interest on the coast and this enlarged the traditional role of some coastal towns such as Lagos, Porto Novo and Cotonou to take on new and increasing responsibilities not only as ports but also as major centres of European activities and future capitals of the emerging colonial states and their independent African successors.

However, the economic factors played a very crucial role in all these changes especially with reference to the European presence. While trade brought the Europeans to the region it also justified their continued stay there. Thus the change from the slave trade to 'legitimate' trade required major structural adjustments from the European traders. However, for the Africans, in spite of the emphasis on the reluctance of many African states to give up the slave trade, and their confrontations with the abolitionists over the matter, the transition

 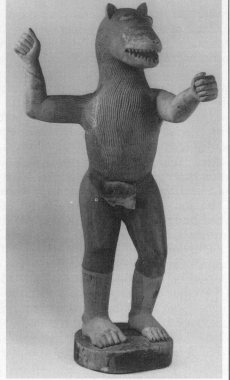

26.6 *Statue of a standing man probably representing King Gezo 1818–58*

26.7 *King Glélé (1858–89) symbolically represented as a lion*

was remarkably smooth. The case of Dahomey illustrates this very well. Dahomey had been a major exporter of slaves from the West African coast and it remained so till 1888 when slavery was abolished in Brazil. But while exporting slaves, it also began to increase its trade in palm oil as from the middle of the nineteenth century, first as a supplement to the export of slaves and eventually as the dominant factor in the state's economy. This transition from slaves to 'legitimate' trade meant that more slaves were needed for the production of palm oil and, as in other parts of the Mono–Niger region, war captives who otherwise would have been sold for export overseas were used extensively in agricultural production.

The most significant consequences of the abolitionist movement in this region were those linked with the modernization process and, of these, the return of liberated slaves from Sierra Leone, Cuba and Brazil was probably the most important. It was these 'Saros' and Brazilians who originally attracted

European Christian missionaries and played a crucial role as the first-generation middle class in the period. Among them were people like Bishop Samuel Ajayi Crowther, Reverend James Johnson, and hundreds of other less famous individuals who went into various occupations such as carpentry, design and construction of buildings, tailoring, and printing.

At first they settled along the coast in such areas as Whydah, Agwe, Porto Novo, Badagry and Lagos from where their influence spread far into the Aja and Yoruba interior. While the impact of the Saro was felt more in the area of British colonial influence, the Brazilians concentrated in what later became areas of French rule. However, despite this difference, both the Saros and the Brazilians contributed immensely to the overall development of the Mono–Niger region as an integral whole. Moreover, the Brazilians in either Lagos or Porto Novo shared familial ties not only among themselves, but also with their other homes in the New World. This made the Brazilian connection an example not only of the unity of African history but also of the link between the African continent and the black diaspora.

27

The Niger delta and the Cameroon region

Introduction

The area covered in this chapter is the coastal strip in the Atlantic Ocean which stretches from the mouth of the Benin river on the west to that of the Ogowe basin in the east. This region can be divided into five sub-units. The first comprises the creeks and swamplands of the Niger delta inhabited by the Ijọ and the Itsekiri in the western extreme. To the western hinterland of this area was the Benin kingdom. The second sub-region is that of the Igbo hinterland which lies to the north of the Niger delta and is most extensive to the east of the Niger. The Cross river basin which lies to the east of the Niger delta is the third unit. This region comprises Efik, Ibibio and other Bantu-related groups. The fourth sub-region is that of the Cameroon coast and its hinterland to the east of the Cross river valley, while the fifth sub-region is the basin of the Ogowe and the surrounding regions of Equatorial Guinea and Gabon.

The inhabitants of these areas were all members of the same language family, the Niger–Congo. Early ties among them were also reinforced by commercial contacts in the nineteenth century. Trade routes ran from the west to the east of the region, and from the coast to the hinterland, linking different groups. Rivers were also important in this respect because they served as the main channels of trade which brought diverse elements together.

Another common factor in the history of the region was the presence of Europeans on the coast which provoked similar reactions from the local peoples. The coastal communities thus experienced changes in their socio-political institutions in response to external stimuli. These stimuli came in the form of the slave trade and the effect of its abolition in the nineteenth century; the change to trade in local produce in place of slaves ('legitimate trade'); the entry of Christian missionaries into the region, and the onset of European imperialism and colonial conquest. We shall proceed to analyse these developments as we look at each of the sub-regions in order to get a clear picture of the nineteenth-century history of the Niger delta and Cameroon region.

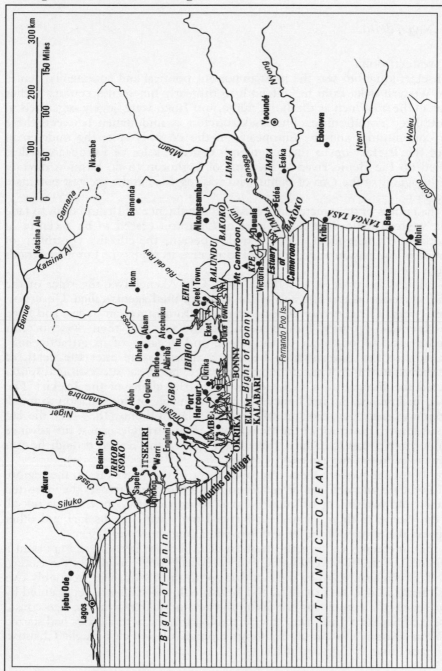

27.1 *Niger delta and the Cameroons in the nineteenth century (after E. J. Alagoa)*

The Niger delta

The western delta

The Itsekiri kingdom was the most important political and commercial centre in the Western delta from the fifteenth to the early nineteenth century. Other groups in the area such as the Ijọ, Urhobo, and Isoko were largely organized in decentralized communities. The Itsekiri acted as middlemen between these other communities and the Europeans on the coast. Despite the middleman role of the Itsekiri up to the nineteenth century, a lot of European traders travelled up the Benin river to the port of Ughoton to do business directly with the agents of the Ọba of Benin who was regarded as the greatest potentate in the area.

In the course of the nineteenth century, the influence of Benin began to fade in the western delta. The Benin port of Ughoton ceased to be a centre of overseas trade. Consequently, Itsekiri traders became the effective controllers of the trade of the region and Benin had to receive its supply of European goods through them.

To control the trade of the Benin river, Olu Akengbuwa, the ruler of the Itsekiri kingdom in the first half of the century, used agents called 'Governors of the Rivers'. The governor collected tributes from European traders and fixed prices for local produce. However, due to the fact that there was no clear procedure for appointment to this office and because of its attractiveness, succession to the governorship became a thorny issue after the death of Akengbuwa in 1848. The conflicts generated by these succession disputes attracted the intervention of Europeans into the affairs of the Itsekiri. The British, for instance, did not hesitate to take advantage of this situation to install and remove many governors at will. In fact, Nana Olomu (1884–94), the last and best known governor of the Benin river, in his struggle against the advance of colonial rule, had to fight a violent war against the British though he was eventually captured and exiled to Calabar.

The Ijọ of the western delta controlled most of the waterways in the region. Because they could not gain direct access to the European traders they resorted to piracy and harassment of Itsekiri and European vessels. But this was not all they did. Some of them carried on internal trade with the Itsekiri and other groups on the fringes of the Niger delta and along the lower Niger.

In the nineteenth century, the western delta did not become as important a commercial centre for overseas trade in slaves and palm produce as the eastern delta. This was attested to by the fact that up till the 1840s there were only two British firms in the western delta, and British colonial influence represented by the presence of a consul was not felt in the area until 1891 when a vice-consul was sent to Sapele. By this time, the scramble for African territories had started and Nana Olomu was already resisting colonial rule which brought Christian missionaries into the western delta.

27.2 *Nana Olomu of Itsekiri*

The eastern delta

The eastern delta comprised a number of city-states such as Bonny, Nembe, Okrika and Elem-Kalabari in the nineteenth century. Three important factors were responsible for the development of these states. They were the different ecological conditions of the mangrove swamps of the eastern delta, the long-distance trade with the Igbo hinterland and trade with the western delta. In these states, both internal and external trade were in the hands of the rulers: the kings called *amanyanabo* and the lineage heads called house heads.

The abolition of the slave trade by Britain in 1807 brought many changes to the eastern delta. In the first place, efforts to stop the slave trade led to new relationships between British officers and the delta states. It introduced the era of gunboat diplomacy in which British consuls used naval power to negotiate favourable conditions for British traders, missionaries and explorers. A lot of treaties were signed with the local chiefs which stipulated the stoppage of the slave trade by the chiefs and the adoption of trade in other produce. Such treaties also laid down rules for the conduct of the legitimate trade, specified the amount of custom duties to be paid by the traders, and the subsidies the British government would pay the local chiefs for agreeing to stop the slave trade.

In addition, some of the activities of the British on the coast gradually reduced the power of the local rulers. A case in point was the setting up of independent judicial systems called Courts of Equity by British traders with the participation of a few local house heads or chiefs but under the control of the latter. Meanwhile, British missionaries and traders tried to get into the hinterland, for example, by sponsoring voyages of exploration. The discovery of the mouth of the river Niger was one of the results of such voyages and it increased the interest of British traders and missionaries in the interior of Nigeria.

In the eastern delta, Christian missionaries, especially the CMS, began to establish a firm foothold. Under the leadership of Bishop Samuel Ajayi Crowther, the CMS established missions at Bonny in 1864, at Nembre in 1868, at Elem Kalabari in 1874 and Okrika in 1880. The rulers of Bonny and Nembe invited the missionaries for a number of reasons: to establish schools in which their children could learn how to read, write and speak English in order to carry on commercial relations with British firms, and this was to lead to better relations with the British government represented by the consuls and naval officers which could strengthen them against their neighbouring enemies in their power struggles. However, missionaries were not always welcomed in these areas. Powerful interests within each of the delta states resisted the establishment of Christian missions in those areas and Christianity thus constituted a factor of social instability in the nineteenth century.

The delta states experienced some socio-political upheavals in the nineteenth century, the roots of which could be traced to the difficulties created by the change from an economy based on the slave trade to one based on palm-produce. This switch led not only to changes in old trade habits and methods but also to the rise of new enterprising leaders at the expense of the old ones. Three major developments were also produced by this switch. First, the new trade led to an increase in the internal slave trade to supply the labour requirements of the delta states; second, the growth of new houses and heads resulted in the disturbance of the internal political balance, and third, competition for the hinterland markets led to several wars between the delta states.

Slaves had been a feature of the delta states long before the nineteenth century and each of the communities had ways of assimilating them. The number of slaves required to be integrated into the communities, however, increased considerably in the nineteenth century and each of the delta states had to devise new methods of acculturation to meet the situation. Slaves acquired the full rights of membership of their masters' lineage (house) and could rise in the heriarchy according to their ability, even to become house heads. Secret societies like the *Ekine* or *Sekiapu* were also used to acculturate such slaves and in Elem Kalabazri, slaves who did not learn the culture quickly were punished by another organization called the *Koronogbo*.

However, as the number of slave intakes into the societies increased to meet the demands of the palm oil trade, the households of many minor chiefs

27.3   *King Jaja of Opobo*

27.4   *King Bell's house in the 1840s*

became large and they consequently broke away from their parent houses to form their own. This decreased the prestige and wealth of the older houses because some of their members moved over to the more prosperous new houses through debts and other means. This competition for trade and slaves led to changes in the political leadership of the states. In Bonny, for instance, the struggle for power between two royal factions in the 1860s eventually led to the breaking away of one of the factions, led by Jaja of Opobo to found his state of Opobo in 1869. A similar crisis erupted in Elem Kalabari in 1882–4 which resulted in the breakdown of the state and the foundation of new ones such as Bakama, Buguma, and Abonema. No major disruption of the political system occurred in Nembe and Okrika. This was probably because they had experienced their own political turmoil earlier in the eighteenth century and they did not participate in the overseas trade at the same high level as Bonny and Elem Kalabari.

Apart from internal dislocations in some of the delta states there were also intergroup wars between them as they competed for the hinterland markets in the nineteenth century. Elem Kalabari was at the centre of all the wars. It fought Nembe to its west, Bonny to its south-east and Okrika to the east. These other states tended to form alliances from time to time. The only ally Elem Kalabari had was the new state of Opobo in the last quarter of the century.

Meanwhile, the British consuls on the coast tried to use the opportunity of the distraction provided by these interstate wars to get an opening for their traders and missionaries to move into the hinterland. To this end, the consuls served as peacemakers between the delta states but the wars did not weaken the resolve of each of the states to keep European traders from penetrating their territories. This led to many clashes between the British and the delta states which resulted in the eventual imposition of colonial rule on the area by the end of the century.

The Igbo hinterland

Igboland was characterized by a dense population and small states. This meant it suffered at the hands of slavers because there were no large states to protect the people. Different Igbo groups engaged in wars to capture slaves which they sold to the delta states and the Efik of Calabar who were the middlemen. Because Igboland was in the interior it did not come into direct contact with the Europeans before the nineteenth century despite the fact that it provided most of the slaves sold on the coast. Even the parts of Igbo country known to European visitors by the end of the century were those on the routes of rivers like the Niger, Imo and the Cross rivers. Such communities included Akwette, Ohombele on the Imo river, Aboh, Osomari, Oguta, Asaba and Onitsha on the Niger. The Aro, who controlled the internal trade routes and some of the markets were also well known both as traders and as operators of a popular oracle.

Despite the fact that the slave trade was abolished in 1807 by the British and that it lingered on the coast till about 1850, it continued in Igboland throughout the century where it constituted an important factor for social change. The slave trade in Igboland was disruptive. First, the manner in which slaves were obtained largely through kidnapping, raiding and wars tended to destroy social and political structures. Second, it also disrupted normal agricultural activities. Moreover, what the Igbo obtained in return for slaves was not equal to the total loss sustained as a result of the slave trade. Examples of items exchanged for slaves were spirits, firearms, hats, beads, cloth, iron, copper and bars, most of which replaced local products and stifled local industries.

Explorers were the first set of Europeans to penetrate the Igbo hinterland after which traders and missionaries followed suit. The first trading station was established by Macgregor Laird at Onitsha in 1856. In 1886, the Royal Niger Company established one of its main depots in Igboland at Asaba. Missionary activities were also started among the Niger Igbo with the CMS as the pioneers.

The Igbo, however, resisted all these intrusions into their land. The *ekumeku* secret societies of the western Igbo organized violent outbreaks between 1898 and 1911. But the British crushed this resistance brutally. The Aro Expedition of 1900 organized by the British to subdue Igboland represented the formal conquest of the people. It is however instructive to note that during this expedition, no military force came out to oppose the British because the Aro challenge to British authority was not a military one, rather it was commercial and indirect. After the British conquest of Igboland, the society was left open to foreign influences. Some of the people embraced Christianity but a large number still clung to their traditional culture and religion.

The Cross river basin

The Efik state of Calabar dominated trade on the Cross river basin. Curiously, the Ibibio who were the largest ethnic group in the area constituted the majority of slaves exported from that region. Other produce exported by the Efik came to them from the Igbo interior and the upper Cross river valley through the Aro traders. While certain groups in the Cross river valley such as the Itu, Umon and Akunakuna also tried to share in the proceeds of the trade with the Efik by changing tolls and by some other means, others carried on direct trade contacts with peoples in the northern Cameroon region.

The social structure and history of Calabar was different from that of the delta states. For instance, slaves in the two major communities of Duke Town and Creek Town which comprised the Efik state were not properly integrated into the society. The *Ekpe* secret cult of Calabar unlike the *Ekine* or *Sekiapu* society of the delta states kept them out of political power.

However, European traders, consuls and missionaries exercised greater influence in Calabar. Although traders were not at first permitted to establish stations on land, they wielded considerable economic influence from their ships on the river, granting credits to Efik traders and applying economic sanctions on any defaulting merchant. Later they seized the opportunity offered by the internal quarrels among the Efik to intervene in their affairs. Missionaries of the Church of Scotland Mission got to Calabar in 1846. While their mission station was open to converts and refugees from the community, it was also an intelligence centre: the missionaries watched the local scene and reported developments there to the British Consul. They also intervened in other ways in local affairs.

In 1842, an abolition treaty was signed with the rulers of Calabar in order to stop the slave trade and an annual subsidy was to be paid to them. From then on, British influence in Calabar gradually increased until 1891 when a Protectorate administration was established there.

The *obong* of Calabar

The monarchical institution in Calabar had a number of problems in the nineteenth century. The first was the weakness of the *obong*, king of Calabar. This was due to the relative newness of the kingship office. The position of king of *obong* only came to be established in the nineteenth century. Before this time, Calabar was probably ruled by lineage heads or *Ekpe* titleholders. Secondly, the presence of two competing kings in Calabar also made for problems: there was one king for Duke Town and another for Creek Town. Both established their positions over others of similar lineage connections because of the superior wealth they had acquired from the slave trade. Thirdly, there was fierce competition for office between several political leaders and members of the *Ekpe* society. At times, such competition attracted the intervention of the British. The last and perhaps the most serious political problem of Calabar was that the office of *obong* became identified in the nineteenth century with external trade with few traditional functions or authority. Legislative and executive powers lay with the leaders of the *Ekpe* society. The main function of the *obong* was to stand between the local communities and the whitemen.

The relative powers of the kings of Duke Town and Creek Town fluctuated throughout the first half of the nineteenth century. Duke Ephraim of Duke Town was the richest chief on the river between 1800–34 while Eyo Honesty II of Creek Town became the most influential trader between 1836–58. In addition, the king of Duke Town monopolized the most important *Ekpe* title of *Eyamba* while the leader of Creek Town only held the second highest title of *Obunko*.

Throughout the century, succession disputes for the kingship of Duke Town and Creek Town became a prominent feature of the politics of the Cross river and these gave the British an opportunity to interfere in the local affairs of the people.

The *Ekpe* society of the Bloodmen

The *Ekpe* society of Calabar was a secret organization which discussed social issues. It was the effective law-making and enforcing authority in Calabar in the nineteenth century. It was a highly stratified organization with eleven grades in

1858. Slaves were admitted into the lower grades, the highest grades were monopolized by the rich free nobility while the highest two grades were the exclusive preserve of the political heads of Duke Town and Creek Town. The *Ekpe* society thus discriminated against slaves and the poor because advancement in it was only possible through the payment of very exorbitant rates and this plus other forms of discrimination led to the social disturbances of the mid-nineteenth century. On the other hand, *Ekpe* may be seen as a positive force in the political system of Calabar in that it united all the freemen of wealth and influence in a common organization.

An association of plantation slaves known as the Bloodmen had come into being to protest at the sacrifice of slaves at the death of kings and lineage heads. The association neither pressed for the emancipation of slaves nor aimed at the seizure of political power from the *Ekpe*. All the Bloodmen did was to come into Calabar from the plantations in large numbers whenever there was a danger of slaves being sacrificed on the death of an important man, or being made to take the poison ordeal. Their agitation led the *Ekpe* to make a law in 1850–1 against human sacrifice.

From the foregoing it is clear that there is a similarity in the socio-political history of Calabar and the delta states in terms of the external pressures to which they were exposed. The difference is in the way they reacted internally to these external problems.

The Cameroon coast and its hinterland

The Cameroon coast was inhabited by north-western Bantu communities who were agriculturists, hunters and fishermen. This coast was characterized by mangrove swamps, creeks and inlets, and immediately behind it was the tropical rain forest. The inhabitants of this coast were generally organized into autonomous villages but sometimes some of these villages had petty paramount chiefs. Among some of the coastal peoples such as the Duala, Isuwu and others, the most important secret society was the *Jengu* which was based on the worship of water spirits. Just like the peoples of the Niger delta, the inhabitants of the Cameroon coast were faced with external pressures from European missionaries, traders and imperialists. The greatest pressure, of course, came from the abolitionists because of the important position of the institution of slavery in local communities.

The Duala were one of the groups on the Cameroon coast that established themselves as a centralized state in the eighteenth century with a paramount chief. However, due to succession disputes British traders interfered in their affairs in the nineteenth century and this led to divisions in Duala politics. In order to preserve their ethnic unity, the Duala established a council of notables called *Ngondo* which comprised representatives from the various Duala villages.

The Isuwu were another coastal group. They established a trading settlement called Bimbia which comprised three villages ruled by lineage heads. The power of these men was derived from their middleman position in the overseas trade. The richest and best known of the Bimbia merchant princes was Bile, and during his time concrete links were established with Duala. Culturally, their common membership of the *Jengu* society served to bring them together, and commercially, Bimbia and Duala traders cooperated in developing the trade of the area as well as establishing common links with the Bamenda grasslands in the interior. Most of the slaves reaching the coast between the 1820s and the 1840s came from the Bamenda interior and passed through the hands of Duala and Bimbia traders.

The abolition of the slave trade created some problems for the inhabitants of the Cameroon coast as stated earlier. However, slaves were still a crucial element in the transition from the slave trade to the legitimate state. This was because slave labour was used to produce palm-oil, palm kernels and other agricultural commodities. In fact, the kings on the Cameroon river even hired out some of their slaves to the Europeans at Fernando Poo and this proved to be an additional source of wealth for them. In the bid to abolish the slave trade and establish legitimate trade a number of treaties were signed between the British and the local rulers and this, among other things, gave the British opportunities to intervene in local politics, and led to the gradual loss of the sovereignty of the local rulers. The British also used the excuse of disputes between European and local traders over the repayment of trade debts to intervene in local affairs.

Missionaries were another important instrument of British influence on the Cameroon coast. The British Baptist Mission society were the first to make any impact in the region. They established churches, schools, workshops and a printing press. However, local opposition against them began to mount as they embarked on a massive conversion of the people.

There was a decline in trade on the Cameroon coast in the 1860s and 1870s which generated feelings of insecurity among the rulers of the area. It was in these circumstances that the Germans annexed Cameroon in July 1884. Resistance to German annexation broke out almost immediately and it continued until the outbreak of the First World War. This however did not stop the Germans from moving up into the Bamenda interior to secure control of hinterland trade.

The Ogowe basin and surrounding regions

The Ogowe basin and its surrounding regions are located to the south of Cameroon and they correspond more or less to the modern territories of Equatorial Guinea and Gabon. The region was inhabited by Bantu-speaking peoples who engaged in nomadic agriculture, hunting, fishing and crafts. These peoples had by the nineteenth century formed a large number of political entities which ranged in size from village-states to kingdoms. The products of their economic activities engendered extensive trading among the different communities. Moreover the arrival of the Portuguese on the coast in the fifteenth century gave a further boost to coastal trade.

27.5 *The Ogowe River Trader, Ouassengo, with ivory tusks and female members of his household*

27.6 *Antchuwe Kowe Rapontchombo ('King Denis'), an Ogowe river ruler, with his senior wife*

This development of commercial activity on the coast had major consequences. First, it led to a series of migrations by peoples such as the Fang and Kele who left their original settlements to seek greener pastures towards the coast. Second, it led to a change in the indigenous social structures. In addition to the old stratification of the society into three social classes, viz., the pure-bloods, half-castes and slaves, there was also a new merchant class based on wealth which exercised a monopoly on big business.

There was also a great deal of European influence in the region. Treaties were signed as from 1839 which led to the establishment of the French trading post of Gabon. A large number of voyages of exploration set off from this station extending French territorial claims far into the interior of the country. Meanwhile, European traders and missionaries settled in the region. For instance, there were about ninety European commercial companies in the Ogowe basin and surrounding region by 1882. In addition, there were numerous missionary stations and schools.

Despite these Western influences, the local communities were able to retain their cultural identity. They struggled very hard against European ideas to preserve their cultural heritage.

Conclusion

Although the nineteenth century saw the gradual spread of European influence over much of the region under review, the hinterland was not under the direct influence of Europe. Even in the coastal areas, internal history was determined by local factors and not by external factors. That was why the various communities on the coast responded to the challenges of the overseas slave trade in different ways depending on their peculiar cultures and histories. Thus the *Ekine* or *Sekiapu* society of the delta state was different from the *Ekpe* society of the Efik and the *Jengu* of the Cameroon coastal groups.

Despite the importance of the overseas trade to these communities, internal trade routes and exchange of local produce remained the basic economic livelihood of the majority of the people throughout the nineteenth century. In other words, one should not overlook the role played by internal factors in the history of the peoples of the Niger delta and the Cameroon region in the nineteenth century. This is not to deny the presence of external factors but to point out the continued existence of elements of local culture and institutions despite the Western influence in the area.

28

The African diaspora

Introduction

One of the major events in African and world history is the migration of Africans to the outside world under the auspices of the trans-Atlantic and other forms of slave trade. This movement lasted for many centuries and led to the establishment of African communities of varying sizes not only in Europe but also in the Middle East and the Americas.

The movement of Africans into Asia Minor and the Mediterranean world was the earliest of such migrations. It began several centuries before the Christian era, reaching its height after the seventh century. A lot of the Africans in question got to the Mediterranean world via the trans-Saharan trade routes while others migrated as free individuals such as scholars, pilgrims and traders to Mecca and Medina. Many of them were also to be found in other Muslim states such as the Ottoman empire where they enjoyed important status in the society.

The spread of Islam into India and the Far East also brought a lot of Africans into the region as soldiers and bureaucrats in the service of the Muslim sultans. Also the commercial activities of the Mediterranean introduced a number of Africans into Europe so that by the fifteenth century, substantial numbers of Africans were found in Sicily, Cyprus, Crete and on the southern Iberian Coast. The black population in England and France also increased considerably in the late eighteenth century due to direct maritime links between Europe and Africa.

The African diaspora was most pronounced in the Americas where they played important parts in the development of the societies in the New World. They helped subdue the vast wilderness in the New World and participated actively in the forging of new communities. Between the sixteenth and nineteenth centuries these Africans performed every type of task in the Americas and fulfilled every social role except those of the highest social status. Thus before the final abolition of the slave trade in the Americas, the majority of the Africans there were slaves who performed most of the menial tasks in those societies. This enabled them to make an important impact on the languages, cultures, economies and ethnic composition of most of the communities in the New World.

28.1   *Figure of a negroid man with an Indonesian kris at his back waistband, probably from what is now Vietnam and probably dating from the seventeenth century*

The Middle East and South East Asia

There were various reasons for the movement of Africans to the Middle East and South-East Asia in the nineteenth century. The most important reason was the slave trade. The major source of supply of slaves to Asia was East Africa. The trade from Zanzibar supplied slaves to the Persian Gulf from where they were resold to important markets in South-East Asia. A large number of slaves also came from Ethiopia. These Ethiopian slaves were caught in various local wars and raids and transported to the coast from where they were shipped by Arab traders to Arabian and Indian markets. Ethiopian slaves were highly prized in these places because of their intelligence and appearance. The island of Madagascar was another source of slaves to India. This traffic was handled by British and Dutch slavers, and a large number of the slaves bought were imported into British colonies in India. Africans were, however, not the only race moving in the Indian Ocean area in the nineteenth century. Others, such as Malays, Indians and Chinese, migrated either as slaves or indentured labourers.

The pilgrimage to Mecca was also another reason for the movement of Africans although it was an annual event. Many pilgrims from West Africa reached Mecca via the Cairo caravan or by way of some Red Sea ports. Wealthy African pilgrims travelled with numerous slaves with which they settled travelling expenses along the way. This means that slaves were used as a means of exchange. Consequently, there were many African as well as Asian slaves in Mecca and these were distributed by individual buyers throughout the Muslim world. Slaves were, however, not the only Africans in Arabia. Some free Africans stayed after their pilgrimage to pursue higher religious studies in the holy cities of Western Arabia.

Let us now examine the use to which these Africans were put in some Middle Eastern and Asian societies. In India, African slaves undertook menial tasks. They were used as plantation labourers but they served primarily in domestic roles such as concubines, eunuchs, water carriers, barbers, personal guards and stable boys in the princely states. In British settlements in India, African slaves worked as soldiers, sailors and dockers while others built fortifications. Also in the Malay Archipelago African slaves worked as plantation workers, trained mechanics, soldiers and miners. In the Middle East, African slaves were engaged in domestic activities as househelps, and also as sailors, soldiers, administrators and shop assistants in the cities. In the rural areas they served as water carriers, agricultural labourers, camel drivers, and shepherds. Poor pilgrims or stranded ones also worked as porters, streetsweepers, firewood fetchers, brewers, dockers and potters.

African slaves, either in the Middle East or Asia, held a very low status in the society. They were in the servile class. For instance, they were not integrated into the local Asian populations but were kept apart and discriminated against. They consequently constituted a separate ethnic group in the society. In South-west Arabia, they even lived in separate quarters because they were regarded as outcasts and no true Arab would marry a freed slave woman. However, one remarkable thing about these scattered African diaspora communities was that they were well organized and kept alive their own national traditions.

The diaspora in Europe

Africans had been present in Western Europe from ancient times but in very insignificant numbers. Their numbers only rose from about the fifteenth century when black Africans, first as slaves and then as freedmen, began to appear in southern Spain and Portugal. There, even free Africans occupied the bottom of the social ladder. Their legal status was uncertain because while slavery was not countenanced in French and British law as from the seventeenth and eighteenth centuries respectively it was practised in their overseas colonies until the nineteenth century. These free Africans in Europe were treated like their fellow Africans who were slaves in the tropical colonies.

Nevertheless, free Africans were present in Western Europe in considerable numbers from the mid-eighteenth century on. Although their numbers were quite small when compared with total populations in any of the European countries, their presence was more visible and real than their numbers would suggest because they were concentrated in the cities. In fact before the 1840s there were far more tropical Africans in Europe than Europeans in tropical Africa.

These clusters of Africans in Europe were concentrated in certain occupations. One was domestic service in which most of them worked as servants. They were also engaged in the merchant service where they served as sailors especially in Portugal. Another smaller group was made up of students who began to arrive in Europe in significant numbers by the middle of the eighteenth century. Many of them were wards of wealthy African chiefs who came to Europe via the good offices of European slave traders operating in Africa and under whose care they studied in Europe. A remarkable feature of the African communities in Europe was the fact that they were overwhelmingly male. To sustain the community, new sets of Africans had to be constantly brought in from overseas.

Africans were also to be found in Eastern Europe. They got there through the Ottoman slave trade which drew slaves from both sub-Saharan Africa and North Africa. In a few instances, small groups of Africans in certain parts of the Ottoman empire retained their culture into the twentieth century. An example is a small Hausa-speaking community in what was until recently Yugoslavia.

The Western diaspora: background to the nineteenth century

The African diaspora in the Americas was far greater than in Europe or Asia. At the beginning of the nineteenth century, the African-American population including the free and enslaved in the New World was about 8.5 million. The experience of this black population throughout the Americas varied considerably depending on a number of factors such as the proportion of the

28.2   *Black servant and eunuch with the child of their master in East India in the nineteenth century*

non-white population in the societies, the ratio of slaves to free, the magnitude of the slave trade, the way each colony developed and socio-economic changes in the regions. For example, in the Americas, slaves and free Africans who resided in the cities had more opportunities for upward social mobility and liberty than their counterparts in the rural plantations. However, the mortality rate was generally high among all the Africans in the New World. A lot of them died in slavery and it was almost certain that the overall population of about 8.5 million Africans and African-Americans existing in the Americas at the beginning of the nineteenth century represented less than the number of Africans imported into the continent after 1600.

Furthermore, there was not much difference in the nature of slavery in the different regions in the Americas. Despite the fact that Latin America, for instance, had a longer social experience with the institution of slavery than other colonies of British and French in the Americas, there was no fundamental difference in the slave system in the Americas. The only difference was in terms of degrees of participation of the different regions in the slave trade.

The single largest American importer of African slaves was Brazil. During the course of the slave trade Brazil received approximately 38 per cent of all Africans imported into the New World. However, in order to fully appreciate the experience of the African in the New World we would have to look at the relative participation of the various regions in the slave trade century by century. This procedure is necessary because differences in the date of entry into the trans-Atlantic trade and the fluctuations in the volume of imports by each region influenced not only the population spread but also the attitudes of the societies which emerged in the Americas by the late nineteenth century.

In the period before 1600, Spanish and Portuguese colonists in the New World received all of the African slaves coming into the continent at that time. These Africans not only served as cheap labour, they also helped maintain social viability because most of the indigenous Indian population were being killed by new diseases introduced into the Americas by both Europeans and Africans. By the end of the sixteenth century Africans in the New World considered themselves superior to the local Indians.

The seventeenth century saw the beginning of the well-organized Atlantic slave trade. In the course of the century the annual average rate of importation of slaves rose tremendously. This period also witnessed a considerable decline in the participation of Spanish colonies in the slave trade. Brazil however became the highest single importer of slaves in the New World for use in its sugar plantations.

The peak of the African diaspora to the New World was reached in the eighteenth century. Both the plantation societies in the Americas and the slave trade reached their fullest maturity. This phenomenal growth in the slave trade could be attested to by the fact that more than half of all the Africans imported into the New World arrived during the eighteenth century. In other words, over 6 million Africans were imported by the New World in the course of the eighteenth century. Furthermore, the century was also a period of intensive commercial relations between Africa and the outside world. Brazil also received more slaves than any other region in the Americas during the century. The eighteenth century therefore witnessed clearly the growth of the plantation slave society in the New World. As different plantations flourished the local export economies also expanded and stabilized. Lastly, the century was also a period of the most brutal exploitation and oppression of Africans in the New World. While the American colonies of the Europeans were pressing for their own freedom, they were busy reducing the liberty and legal privileges of their non-white population.

The abolitionist period

The nineteenth century witnessed the abolition of the slave trade. The American slave system crumbled in the face of internal and external attacks. The abolition of the British slave trade in 1808 affected slavery and the African in profound ways. The British anti-slavery campaign greatly reduced the number of Africans taken to the Americas during the century although the total still remained high. By 1870, the pattern of the slave trade had reverted to what it was before 1600 when Spanish and Portuguese colonies were the major importers. The rest of the slaves went to French colonies with a very small number entering the USA.

Most of the Africans in the Americas operated within the plantation system. But since the plantation system varied throughout the Americas, the Africans were exposed to different forces which moulded their own American culture no matter how great their numbers were. For example, a lot of modifications took place in the worship of Shango, a Yoruba God, and even the forms of Shango varied considerably from Cuba to Trinidad, to Haiti, to Brazil. What was true for the worship of Shango was also true for other aspects of the social life of the people. This was due to the fact that they had to adapt to the new social conditions they met in the New World.

Moreover, the situation in the African population in the Americas varied from one part of the continent to another. In the Carribean the Africans formed the majority of the population. In the USA on the other hand, blacks were in the minority. In some parts of Latin America such as Ecuador, Chile, and Argentina there was a great intermixture among Africans, American Indians and European groups resulting not only in mixed blood but also in a virtual genetic disappearance of the blacks.

Also, the development of the population of the different regions in the New World did not follow the pattern of their individual participation in the trans-Atlantic slave trade. In other words, regions which imported a large number of slaves during the course of the trade did not have a corresponding increase in the number of black elements in their population at the end of slavery. Except in the USA, there was a drastic decline in the American slave populations towards the end of the nineteenth century. This shows that the American system of slavery failed to create an inherently viable and self-reproducing society or to produce an efficient and reliable labour supply. Worse still, part of the lasting impact of slavery was that of permanently retarding the ability of the black population in the Americas to compete effectively in societies where they were in the minority.

The impact of Africa

By the time the American slave systems crumbled in the nineteenth century, American societies were generally hostile to Africans and African culture. However, Africans made a considerable impact on many aspects of American society such as language, music, religion, food, art, agriculture and architecture. In some cases the African influence was strong enough to create a distinct African–American culture which competed with, and sometimes complemented the European-derived culture.

The positon of Africans in the political structures in the Americas varied widely. In the USA there was a rigid division between black and white in the population. In fact, any individual with any degree of African ancestry was relegated to the category of black. Thus African-Americans in the USA formed a small minority which was relatively powerless in political terms. By contrast, throughout the rest of the hemisphere, society was divided into three groups of black, mixed and white. This meant that blacks constituted a recognized social category with their own set of legal rights and social privileges. The chances of social mobility for blacks in the rest of the hemisphere also varied from place to place.

During the era of slavery, a majority of Africans and African-Americans served either as agricultural labourers, or in domestic service. They were engaged in various other tasks which ranged from shopkeeping to mining. By the end of the eighteenth century, both the overland and coastal transportation systems in Jamaica were monopolized by them. This situation did not change very much after slavery was abolished. However, internal social mobility and the general quality of life of the blacks depended on the immediate circumstances of each of the communities. In the relatively unstable societies, the Africans and African-Americans influenced the structure to their own advantage.

Furthermore, Africans contributed almost as much to the rest of the society as they accepted from it. The creativity of Africans was particularly evident in colonies where they were in the majority and had to build a cohesive society from different groups of individuals who, though black, had different backgrounds. This shows that they were not just passive and without initiative.

By the time African slavery was abolished in the Americas, the position of Africans there had deteriorated sharply from what it was a century before. In the USA, for instance, there was legal discrimination and socio-economic denial of the non-white sector. Elsewhere, in places like Cuba, Jamaica, Barbados and Brazil, a small number of African-Americans attained positions of social prestige and political power. In Haiti, they controlled the state after the revolution of 1789.

28.3   *Toussaint L'Ouverture, leader of the Saint-Domingue revolution and father of independent Haiti*

During the nineteenth century, African–American achievements both at the individual and at the collective level were outstanding. Despite the antagonism of white Americans and their socio–economic disabilities, Africans were able to create successful communities throughout the Americas. They established educational institutions such as Codrington College in Barbados and a number of colleges in the USA. The African–Americans also played a significant role in American technological innovation by inventing many invaluable machines.

Despite the fact that the diaspora was cruel and difficult for the African slaves, they exercised a lot of patience and made the best of the opportunities available to them. Through years of hardship, toil and struggle, they eventually emerged as an important part of most American societies.

The diaspora and Africa

The issue of the African diaspora in the Americas continued to receive constant attention albeit, with varying degrees of seriousness from both white and black Americans. In the USA the idea of repatriation of Africans was embarked upon. Repatriation began in earnest after 1815 and by 1830 Liberia had become a colony of repatriated Africans. Ex–slaves, sponsored by the American colonization society with the financial support of the federal and many state governments constituted the majority of the African returnees. Some were Africans taken from confiscated slave ships during the nineteenth century and shipped back to Africa by the British. The rest were missionaries recruited in the Caribbean and southern states of the USA to assist in the spread of the Christian gospel in West Africa.

However, only a few thousand Africans returned home compared to the millions who got to the New World. There were a number of reasons for this. First, there was a lack of support to establish a transportation system comparable to the one that previously brought the slaves to the Americas for the purpose of taking them back to Africa. Second, repatriation during the nineteenth century offered few material rewards for either Europeans or non–Europeans.

Thus by the end of the nineteenth century the idea of repatriation had died down. African–Americans became pre–occupied with developments within their immediate environment. They set out to establish a good life for themselves and to make the most of the opportunities before them.

The return–to–Africa scheme thus faded out gradually but it did not die. Individual promoters such as Henry Sylvester Williams and later Marcus Garvey rose up in 1897 and the 1920s respectively and infused the repatriation movement with new appeal. Thus by the time Garvey's organization, the Universal Negro Improvement Association, collapsed in 1927, Africa had begun to come into the limelight in world affairs.

29

Conclusion:
Africa on the eve
of the European conquest

Introduction

This concluding chapter will look at the main developments in African history at the end of the third quarter of the nineteenth century. Special attention will be focused on the decade 1875–85 which witnessed a phenomenal growth of European interests and led to the European scramble for African territories and the eventual conquest of Africa. There were other common trends in African development on the eve of the European conquest, one of which was the attempt by various African leaders to strengthen themselves and their states. Such attempts were, however, frustrated by the European presence.

The chapters in this volume have demonstrated that the nineteenth century was a period of rapid change in Africa. We have also noted that most of the far-reaching and widespread changes which took place in the course of the century were a result of internal factors. Other changes were influenced or even initiated by European activities on the coast which began to penetrate into the interior after 1850. These changes led to varying and sometimes contradictory results and tendencies. For instance, while the general tendency was towards the strengthening of the state systems, the initial impact of state formation often destabilized wide areas, causing the sudden rise and collapse of some states. The efforts of some leaders to unify Ethiopia and reform its institutions may be cited as an example of movements that had only a local impact. Other reform efforts, like those of Egyptian rulers, had effects that spread throughout a whole region. Still, other changes such as the Mfecane and the *djihāds* of Western and Central Sudan, had a lasting impact on wider regions.

The European demand for agricultural produce, and their commercial activities generally, constituted a major factor of change among various African communities. This was because trade affected access to firearms and the acquisition of wealth, both of which were instrumental to the rise and fall of states in many parts of Africa. Western ideas of socio-political organization introduced by missionaries and foreign traders also led to important changes

315

in various parts of the coastal areas stretching from Sierra Leone to Southern Africa, and to Madagascar.

These different changes must be seen in the context of the deliberate efforts which various African leaders were making to reform their societies. Some of them derived their inspiration for reform from Islamic ideas, some from the ideas of European missionaries and traders, while others continued along pre-nineteenth-century lines, adapting traditional institutions and values to new state formations. However inspired, the various leaders tried to take advantage of the European commercial presence to acquire new technologies in their research projects, but found that their resources were rather being exploited to further strengthen European technologies to their disadvantage. Thus the European presence subverted the African effort at self-development.

Political structures

This effort at self-development was perhaps most prominent in the political sphere. This is because the different regions that participated in the slave trade had learnt that the best way to survive and even profit from the slave trade was to strengthen their states and the military basis of their power. At the beginning of the nineteenth century political and economic structures were generally unstable in most parts of Africa. While some states were rising, others were falling. Some of the old state structures were fragile, with a weak hold on the people. It was only in the Maghrib and Egypt that there existed strong states with durable political structures due to their long experimentation with Islamic law. In other places in Africa, efforts to build strong states in the nineteenth century generated intense political rivalries which in turn devastated existing political systems as was the case in the Volta region. Other examples of such political disintegration were the initial impact of the Mfecane, and the spread of European trade and the expansion of the Chokwe and Ovimbumdu on the Luba and Lunda state systems. Several states and empires disappeared as a result of these developments. At the same time, there was the rise of stronger states with more effective administrative structures.

Most of the states that survived from the eighteenth century did so through major internal reform. This was because the nineteenth century presented such new challenges that each state was faced with the option of either trying to reform and expand at the expense of its neighbours or falling a victim of the expansion of others. While a few states like Benin merely shrank and survived, others underwent a much more complex but fruitful ordeal. Such states as Asante, Dahomey and Buganda completely overhauled, albeit subtly, their political structures by making significant changes and strengthening their institutions of government. Others, like Borno, experienced a change of dynasty without appearing to have made too radical a transformation of the traditional political system.

The Mfecane, apart from the initial devastation which it caused, succeeded in establishing several larger, more efficient and stronger states, with more durable structures than had hitherto existed. It spread a new model of the revolutionized northern Nguni state which involved the creation of a standing army from age-grades, the integration of conquered peoples into the dominant culture, and an entirely new conception of the relationship between the ruler and the ruled. While the ruler was more of an administrative and executive head of the state he also exploited his headship of different religious cults to weld the people together and legitimize his authority.

The purpose of the Ethiopian reform was to revive the ancient Coptic state which had broken into several feuding chiefdoms under ambitious chieftains who remained obdurate and recalcitrant. Although two emperors, Téwodros II and Yohannes IV, succeeded to a certain extent in reviving national conscious-ness, they lacked the wherewithal sufficient to curb the ambitions of the subordinate chieftains effectively and permanently.

The rulers of Egypt wanted to revive the ancient glories of the pharaohs. To this end, Muḥammad ʿAlī set out to undermine the Mamluks, establish a new hierarchy of officials, strengthen his control over land and agriculture, build a more industrial economy, support a reformed army, and win autonomy from the Ottomans. Khedive Ismāʿīl continued this spirit of reform by employing Europeans to supervise abolitionist and commercial ventures in the Sudan and by building the Suez canal, other canals and irrigation works, and communic-ation systems. His aim was to buy European technology to modernize Egyptian structures and institutions.

In the Sudan belt, the *djihād* movements sought to create Islamic societies by installing pious rulers who would rule according to the *Ḳuʾrān*. In Sokoto, this was successful to a large extent. The Islamic empire in Massina also united several people within the framework of a centralized state, with durable administrative structures and legal principles, in spite of its internal dynastic rivalries and the hostility of the French. Moreover, under al-Hadjdj ʿUmar, the Tijaniyya brotherhood provided a wide range of peoples spread over an immense area with a bond of unity and the basis of loyalty to the ruler. In this way, Islam helped to facilitate the expansion of Muslim states into non-Muslim areas as was the case in Ilorin and Nupeland of Nigeria. Samori Ture also sought to use Islam to unify his peoples irrespective of whether they were previously Muslims or traditionalists.

Christianity served a similar purpose. It provided a cultural framework for the Creole society created in Freetown, Libreville, Freretown, and other freed slave settlements. Many Africans welcomed the missionaries, not for evangelism per se, but for the European education which they offered. The rulers of Madagascar, for instance, tried to use Western ideas acquired through Christian missionaries in their political re-organization. They tried to balance the influence of French Catholics with that of English Protestants. When they felt threatened, they tried to expel both, but succeeded only in driving them underground. They ended up with entrenched Protestantism at court,

Catholicism in the rural areas, and an aggressive France determined to establish colonial rule. In the same vein, some new states in southern Africa accepted missionaries as their advisers and external champions, but found that inevitably their loyalties were divided. In some other important missionary centres like Ab'okuta and the Fante states, a few Western-educated leaders used their literary skills and European ideas of government to get reforms carried out within the traditional governmental systems.

Military systems

The durability of political structures depended on the military and this was never more so than in the nineteenth century. Hitherto, the strength of the political system depended more on the network of cults and kinship relationships. As long as the army consisted largely of occasional mass levies of farmers who provided their own weapons and provisions, the army was more important in relationship to neighbouring peoples than in the internal structure of power within the state. The emergence of a cavalry force created not only an elite within the army but also a high-powered class whose members had to share with the ruler access to the resources to obtain horses and recruit horsemen.

Up to the middle of the nineteenth century, neither imported nor locally manufactured firearms had made much difference to the structure of the state of Africa. While it could succeed for a while in the hands of disciplined troops against people unfamiliar with firearms, it was no match for a disciplined cavalry force armed with spears or poisoned arrows. The Egba of Abeokuta, for instance, used firearms to resist Dahomean invasions but they could not stand before the better-disciplined Ibadan soldiers in the 1860s who fought mostly with locally manufactured weapons. Similarly, the relative success of Téwodros in Ethiopia depended more on his strategy of surprise attacks and forced marches of troops travelling light than on fire power.

The nineteenth century, however, saw the rise of professional warriors, and this was ultimately to change the relative importance of the military in the structure of power within the states. These were people more or less permanently under arms due to the frequency of wars and political rivalries. Some men took war as a sort of enterprise which could eventually lead to the acquisition of political power and the control of economic resources. Thus a successful warrior would acquire title to an office which he used to integrate himself into strategic positions in the political system. In a few cases, the ruler was the war leader. Shaka turned the age-grades into professional warriors by training, equipping and disciplining them. His army became the core of the state. Even those generals that broke away from him used their troops to impose their rule over different groups thus creating several new kingdoms. Their discipline, training and provisioning kept them loyal to their commanders even under harsh conditions. The most successful of such standing armies in the nineteenth century were those which depended mostly on local resources for their armaments and upkeep.

The importation of European guns by African rulers spread widely in the nineteenth century. This is not to say that European guns were not imported before the nineteenth century, but it was in the third quarter of the century when the more effective guns began to be imported that European firearms could be said to be making a significant impact on warfare and political systems in Africa. As the importation of such guns became more important in war, they also became an essential feature of commerce, diplomacy and statecraft. African rulers obtained the bulk of the supply of their guns initially from North Africa and later also from the coastal trade of West and East Africa.

This growing importance of European firearms led to the decline of the cavalry in areas where it had hitherto been important. In its place was an infantry armed in the European style which rose to become the elite of the army. The cavalry was thus relegated to the second line of defence and reserve. This had important social and economic implications that eventually strengthened the ruler and helped him to emerge as the highest executive authority in the state.

Social and economic transformation

The nineteenth century witnessed major social transformations in Africa. We have already noted the rise of the warrior class. We need also to discuss briefly the transformations in the nature of slavery and the rise of a politically significant merchant class.

There was growing demand for labour in the nineteenth century which led to the expansion of the scale of slave labour, an increase in the areas in which enforced labour was used, and a greater use of migrant labour. In the third quarter of the century, the general trend was towards increased slaveholding within the household for production. Intensification of political rivalries in the nineteenth century, as we have seen, led to a significant increase in the frequency of wars and raids. These were engaged in for a multiplicity of reasons, but the ultimate result was a vast increase in the number of war captives. Such captives were used to satisfy labour requirements in agriculture, craft production, mining, and as warriors in the emerging professional armies. Thus, the ruling elites in the different societies began to depend not on large kinship groups as before, but on large households of followers and slaves who worked on large farms with which they maintained the households and the warriors at the battlefront. Surpluses were also exchanged at local markets and made available for long-distance trade. The proceeds from such commercial activities were used to buy imported arms and attract more followers.

Following the end of the Atlantic slave trade, there was an increased demand for slaves to produce and transport products like palm-oil, palm-kernels, gold, peanuts, sugarcane, ivory and cloves, by headloads or by canoes down to the coast. This led, among other things, to the rise of plantation slavery. Also, there was a tremendous increase in the population of slaves in the various communities. Although there were instances of slave revolts, usually, these slaves did not form a distinct class. This was because of the wide variations in their fortunes and lifestyles which made it difficult for them to combine as a class. Moreover, they were generally acculturated and integrated, albeit to a limited degree, into the society through individual households, except in a few cases like old Calabar where they were rather more permanently alienated.

The expanding scope of commercial activities also led to an increase in the number and importance of merchants. Long-distance trade, caravan centres and other auxilliary facilities became established in North, West, East and Central Africa by the middle of the nineteenth century. There were also other forms of enforced labour besides slave labour, such as 'debt hostages' whose labour served partly as interest on a loan taken earlier, and partly as a guarantee that the loan would eventually be repaid. By the 1870s, this system was particularly prominent on the Gold Coast where it began to rival slave labour in significance. It has been said that while slavery was a way of recruiting forced labour from outside, 'debt hostages' were enforced labourers recruited from within the community. Meanwhile, a distinct merchant class was evolving in North Africa but it was slow to emerge in other parts of the continent. Even in places influenced by Christianity and European ideas, the merchants did not usually operate as a distinct capitalist class. Rather, they tended to acquire chieftaincy titles within their states in their search for political influence. In parts of the Western Sudan and Senegambia, the most influential merchants were often the religious leaders. In other places, merchants also doubled as warriors, thus making them part of the ruling class.

The class of Southern Africa in the nineteenth century was rather peculiar. By the 1870s, there was an increasing demand for labour by Boers and Britons, especially on the diamond fields of Griqualand West. The solution to this was found not just in the refugees who fled from the Mfecane but even more in rendering Africans landless, and giving them the sole option of working for white farmers and entrepreneurs under very harsh conditions. The white colonists in Southern Africa thus arrogated to themselves the right to extract labour virtually by force from Africans.

The changing balance of power

Thus, in various ways, the most important transformation of the 1870s in Africa were significant changes in the roles and capabilities of Europeans in Africa. These changes were themselves reflections of changes in Europe. The industrial revolution was affecting European states in different ways and resulting in a shifting balance of power. Thus the defeat of France by Germany, for instance, led to a new policy of imperial expansion by France in Algeria and Senegambia as a way of compensating herself. This further intensified colonial competition among the European powers.

Explorers, missionaries and traders all became pathfinders for European imperialists in Africa. Meanwhile, the efforts made by African rulers to employ European ideas and technologies in reforming and modernizing their societies were frustrated. Consequently, the African rulers who, on the whole, had collaborated with European traders and missionaries in the substitution of 'legitimate' trade for the Atlantic slave trade could not but notice changes in the attitude of the Europeans in the 1870s. They became impatient of being tied down only to the coastal trade. They were anxious to penetrate into the interior and to undermine the basis of the coastal economies by emancipating domestic slaves and recruiting them into pioneer colonial armies to spearhead penetration by force.

Missionaries also played a crucial role in the weakening of African states on the eve of the colonial conquest. As part of the strategy of reform of many of the rulers, the missionaries were able to penetrate into several African communities. They promoted literacy and accustomed their congregations to many European goods. But they were in no position to protect the people from the new aggressive imperialism. Rather, some of them began to advocate that the establishment of European rule was a necessary condition for successful evangelization and development. The information that they had gathered about African communities became important sources of military intelligence for the Europeans in the wars of conquest. Missionary activities also became a factor of division by encouraging an atmosphere of rivalry in which some African states supported particular European nationals to secure advantages over their neighbours.

Of all European activities in Africa, however, it was trade that brought the most serious problems upon the Africans. While Africans sought to control trade and obtain maximum gain from it, Europeans also wanted to derive as much advantage as possible from the trade between them and the Africans. Europeans, however, outplayed Africans in this bid. In North Africa they secured excessive privileges for European nationals by treaty agreements with the Ottoman court, thus weakening the ability of the local rulers to control trade in their own land. This was not all. Under the pretext of seeking to establish free trade, the Europeans encouraged African rulers to borrow heavily from European banks at exorbitant rates of interest. They thus weakened the economies of the African states and the control of the rulers over them. On the whole, these subversive activities greatly undermined the autonomy of the rulers and led to their loss of independence.

When agreements broke down, the Europeans sought to enforce their will with a new confidence and aggressiveness that was observable from the 1870s onwards. This was the result of the growing realization that they had a superiority in the quality and quantity of their arms and ammunition. New guns that began to be imported in the 1870s tilted the balance of power in favour of the European-led armies. This, coupled with a good knowledge of the terrain afforded them by the use of Africans, either allies and collaborators or emancipated slaves, in the rank and file of their armies, gave them much confidence. This did not mean that the conquest was easy: the European commanders rarely underestimated their African opponents, and neither should we.

The legacy of wars

By 1870, efforts at reform in African societies had produced changes which on the whole strengthened the capacity of Africans to defend themselves. At the same time, the European presence constituted a great threat to African security, especially since the success of African leaders had been achieved through very violent wars, and at the expense of traditional solidarities among neighbours, an attitude that developed from the era of the slave trade. The larger and stronger states that had emerged with more effective concentration of executive power did so at the expense of weaker states. This process, as we have noted, engendered many wars, and wars became more ruthless and more total than before. Several communities lost their corporate identities. The states that emerged during this period had more durable political institutions and more clearly defined frontiers. Thus, while the nineteenth-century wars strengthened state power, they may also be said to have disregarded traditional solidarities in general and the ethnic factor in particular. There are many examples of this in the nineteenth century, such as in the Yoruba and Maasai wars, and the Mfecane.

Europeans were able to exploit this legacy of nineteenth-century wars in their determination to frustrate the growth of African state power. Their first tactic was to emphasize strong national interests, thus reversing earlier trends of multinational cooperation. European traders, explorers and missionaries in Africa began to identify themselves either as Britons, French or Germans. This was not very effective as African rulers soon discovered that all European nationals were agents of imperialism, and they quickly learnt how to play one European power against the other.

This led the Europeans to develop new tactics, the most effective of which were international agreements to regulate the 'Scramble' and limit the flow of arms and ammunition into Africa, and especially to prevent its flow into hostile African hands. While in Africa, Europeans dealt with individual African rulers and states, and concluded several treaties with them. In Europe they decided to exclude African states from recognition in international law. Thus, they took steps to partition Africa, without the participation of African rulers, and as if Africa were a no-man's-land. Africans, on the other hand, could not forge a pan-African solidarity similar to that pursued by the Europeans. Each African state acted in its own individual interest. Several explanations may be offered for this, but the most significant would seem to be the legacy of wars, the rivalries and enmities which were like the cracking of the wall precisely at the time that the lizard intruder was pushing to enter.

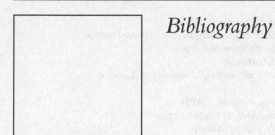

Bibliography

Abbreviations and list of periodicals and publishers

AHS	*African Historical Studies* (became *IJAHS* in 1972); Boston University, African Studies Center
BCEHSAOF	*Bulletin du Comité d'études historiques et scientifiques de l'Afrique Occidentale française*, Dakar
BIFAN	*Bulletin de l'Institut française* (later *fondamental*) *de l'Afrique Noire*, Dakar
BSOAS	*Bulletin of the School of Oriental and African Studies*, London
CEA	*Cahiers d'études africaines*, Paris: Mouton
CJAS	*Canadian Journal of African Studies*, Canadian Association of African Studies, Department of Geography, Carleton University, Ottawa
CUP	Cambridge University Press
EALB	East African Literature Bureau, Nairobi
EAPH	East African Publishing House, Nairobi
HA	*History in Africa: A Journal of Method*, Waltham, Massachusetts
HMSO	Her (His) Majesty's Stationery Office, London
HUP	Harvard University Press
IAI	International African Institute, London
IFAN	Institut français (later fondamental) de l'Afrique Noire, Dakar
IJAHS	*International Journal of African Historical Studies*, Boston University, African Studies Center
IRSH	Institut de recherches en sciences humaines, Niamey
IUP	Ibadan University Press
JAH	*Journal of African History*, Cambridge: CUP
JHSN	*Journal of the Historical Society of Nigeria,* Ibadan
JHUP	Johns Hopkins University Press, Baltimore
JICH	*Journal of Imperial and Commonwealth History*, Institute of Commonwealth Studies, London
JRAI	*Journal of the Royal Anthropological Institute*, London.
JSAS	*Journal of Southern African Studies*, London: OUP
KUP	Khartoum University Press
MUP	Manchester University Press
NEA	Nouvelles Editions Africaines, Dakar
NUP	Northwestern University Press
OUP	Oxford University Press
PUF	Presses Universitaires de France, Paris
PUP	Princeton University Press

RFHOM	Revue française d'histoire d'Outre-mer, Paris
ROMM	*Revue de l'Occident Musulman et de la Méditerranée, Aix-en-Provence*
SFHOM	Société française d'histoire d'Outre-mer, Paris
SNR	*Sudan Notes and Records*, Khartoum
SOAS	School of Oriental and African Studies, University of London
SUP	Stanford University Press
TAJH	*Transafrican Journal of History*, Nairobi: EAPH
THSG	*Transactions of the Historical Society of Ghana*, Legon
TNR	*Tanzania Notes and Records*, Dar es Salaam
UCP	University of California Press
UJ	*Uganda Journal*, Kampala
UPP	University of Pennsylvania Press
UWP	University of Wisconsin Press
YUP	Yale University Press

Bibliography

Abdel-Malek, A. (1969) *Idéologie et renaissance nationale: l'Egypte moderne* (Paris: Anthropos)

Abir, M. (1977) 'Modernisation, reaction and Muhammad Ali's 'Empire' ', *Middle Eastern Studies*, 13, 3, pp.295–313

Abitbol, M. (1979) *Tombouctou et les Arma de las conquête marocaine du Soudan nigérien en 1591 à l'hégémonie de l'Empire du Macina en 1833* (Paris: Maisonneuve a Larose)

Abubakar, S. (1970) *The Lamibe of Fombina: A Political History of Adamawa 1809–1901* (Zaria; Ahmadu Bello University Press)

Abun-Nasr, J.M. (1962) 'Some aspects of the Umari branch of the Tijanniyya', *JAH*, 3, 2, pp.329–31

Abun-Nasr, J.M. (1975) *A History of the Maghrib* (2nd edn. Cambridge: CUP)

Adamu, M. (1978) *The Hausa Factor in West African History* (Zaria: Ahmadu Bello University Press)

Ageron, C.R. (1968) *Les Algériens musulmans et la France, 1871–1919*, (2 vols, Paris: Faculté des Lettres et Sciences Humaines, Sorbonne)

Ageron, C.R. (1972) *Politiques coloniales au Maghreb* (Paris: PUF)

Ageron, C.R. (197) *De l'insurrection de 1871 au déclenchement de la guerre de libérations* (1954), *Histoire de l'Algérie contemporaine*, 2 (Paris: PUP)

Ahmed, J.M. (1966) *The Intellectual Origins of Egyptian Nationalism* (London: OUP)

Ajayi, J.F.A. (1969) *Christian Missions in Nigeria, 1841–1891: The Making of a New Elite* (Evanston: NUP)

Ajayi, J.F.A. and Crowder, M. (eds) (1988) *History of West Africa*, Vol. 2 (2nd edn, London: Longman)

Ajayi, J.F.A. and Crowder, M. (eds) (1985) *Historical Atlas of Africa*, (London: Longman)

Ajayi, J.F.A. and Peel, J.D.Y. (eds) (1992) *People and Empires in African History: Essays in Memory of Michael Crowder* (London: Longman)

Ajayi, J.F.A. and Smith, R.S. (1964) *Yoruba Warfare in the Nineteenth Century* (Cambride: CUP).

Akinjogbin, I.A. (1965) 'The prelude to the Yoruba civil wars of the nineteenth century', *Odu*, 2, 2, pp.81–6

Akinjogbin, I.A. (1967) *Dahomey and Its Neighbours, 1708–1818* (Cambridge: CUP)

Akinjogbin, I.A. and Ekemode, G.O. (eds) (1976) *Proceedings of the Conference on Yoruba Civilization held at the University of Ife, Nigeria, 26–31 July 1976*

Akintoye, S.A. (1969) 'The north-eastern districts of the Yoruba country and the Benin kingdom', *JHSN*, 4, 4, pp.539–53

Akintoye, S.A. (1971) *Revolution and Power Politics in Yorubaland, 1840–1893* (London: Longman)

Alagoa, E.J. (1964) *The Small Brave City State: A History of Nembe-Brass in the Niger Delta* (Madison: University of Winconsin Press)

Alagoa, E.J. (1970) 'Long-distance trade and states in the Niger Delta', *JAH*, 11, 3, pp.319–29

Alagoa, E.J. (1971a) 'The development of institutions in the states of the Eastern Nigeria Delta', *JAH*, 12, 2, pp.269–78

Alagoa, E.J. (1971b) 'Nineteenth-century revolutions in the states of the eastern Niger Delta and Calabar', *JHSN*, 5, pp.565–73

Alagoa, E.J. and Fombo, A. (1972) *A Chronicle of Grand Bonny* (Ibadan: IUP)

Ali, A.I.M. (1972) *The British, the Slave Trade and Slavery in the Sudan, 1820–1881* (Khartoum: KUP)

Allen, J. de. Vere (ed.) (1977) *Al-Inkishafi. Catechism of a Soul* (Nairobi, Kampala and Dar es Salaam: EALB)

Alpers, E.A. (1969) 'Trade, state and society among the Yao in the nineteenth century', *JAH*, 10, 3, pp.405–20

Alpers, E.A. (1975) *Ivory and Slaves in East Central Africa* (London: Heinemann)

Alpers, E.A. (1976) 'Gujarat and the trade of East Africa, c.1500–1800', *IJAHS*, 9, 1, pp.22–44

Andrews, G.R. (1980) *The Afro-Argentines of Buenos Aires 1800–1900* (Madison: UWP)

Anstey, R. (1975) *The Atlantic Slave Trade and British Abolition, 1760–1810* (London: Macmillan)

Ardener, E. (1956) *Coastal Bantu of the Cameroons* (London, IAI)

Arhin, K. (1967) 'The structure of Greater Ashanti (1700–1824)' *JAH*, 8, 1, pp.65–85

Arhin, K. (1970) 'Aspects of the Ashanti northern trade in the nineteenth century', *Africa*, 40, 4, pp.363–73

Arhin, K. (1979) *West African Traders in Ghana in the Nineteenth and Twentieth Centuries* (London: Longman)

Asad, T. (1966) 'A note on the history of the Kababish tribe', *SNR*, 47, pp.79–87

Asiegbu, J.U.J. (1969) *Slavery and the Politics of Liberation, 1787–1861: A Study of Liberated African Emigration and British Anti-Slavery Policy* (London: Longmans Green)

Asiwaju, A.I. (1973) 'A note on the history of Sabe: an ancient Yoruba Kingdom', *Lagos Notes and Records*, 4, pp.17–29

Asiwaju, A.I. (1976) *Western Yorubaland Under European Rule, 1889–1945: A Comparative Analysis of French and British Colonialism* (London: Longman)

Asiwaju, A.I. (1979), 'The Aja-speaking peoples of Nigeria: a note on their origins, settlement and cultural adaptation up to 1945' *Africa*, 49, 1, pp.15–28

Atmore, A. and Marks, S. (1974) 'The imperial factor in South Africa in the nineteenth century: towards a reassessment', *JICH*, 3, 1, pp.105–39

Austen, R.A. (1970) 'The abolition of the overseas slave trade: a distorted theme in West African history', *JHSN*, 5, 2, pp.257–74

Awe, B. (1964) 'The rise of Ibadan as a Yoruba power, 1851–1893' (DPhil thesis, Oxford University)

Awe, B. (1973) 'Militarism and economic development in nineteenth-century Yoruba country: the Ibadan example', *JAH*, 14, 1, pp.65–78

Ayache, G. (1979) *Etudes d'historie marocaine* (Rabat: SMER)

Ayache, S. (1963) *l'accession au trône (1828) de Ranavalona I: à travers le témoignage de Raombana (1854)* (Tananarive: Imprimerie Nationale)

Ayache, S. (1975) Esquisse pour le portrait d'une reine: Ranavalona Ière', *Omaly sy Anio*, 1–2, pp.251–70

Ayache, S. (1977) 'Jean Laborde vu par les témoins malgaches, *Omaly sy Anio*, 5–6, pp.191–222

Ayandele, E.A. (1966) *The Missionary Impact on Modern Nigeria 1842–1914: A Political and Social Analysis* (London: Longmans Green)

Ayliff, J. and Whiteside, J. (1962) *History of the Abambo, Generally known as Fingos*, (1st edn, 1912, Cape Town)

d'Azevedo, W.L. (1969–71) 'A tribal reaction to nationalism', *Liberian Studies Journal*, 1, 2

Ba, A.H. and Daget, J. (1962) *L'Empire peul du Macina (1818–1853)* (Paris: Mouton)

Ba, O. (1976) *La pénétration française au Cayor, 1854–1861* (Dakar: Oumar Ba)

Baer, G. (1961) 'The village shaykh in modern Egypt', in U. Heyd (ed.) *Studies in Islamic History and Civilization* (Jerusalem: Hebrew University)

Baer, G. (1962) *A History of Landownership in Modern Egypt 1800–1950* (London: OUP)

Baeta, C. G. (ed.) (1968) *Christianity in Tropical Africa* (London: OUP)

Bagodo, O. (1979) 'Le royaume Borgu Wassangari de Nikki dans la première moitié du XIXe siècle: essai d'histoire politique' (Mémoire de Maitrise d'Histoire, Université Nationale du Bénin, Abomey-Calavi)

Baier, S. (1977) 'Trans-Saharan trade and the Sahel: Damergu 1870–1930', *JAH*, 18, 1, pp.37–60

Baier, S. (1980) *An Economic History of Central Niger* (Oxford: Clarendon Press)

Baier, S. and Lovejoy, P.E. (1977) 'The Tuareg of the Central Sudan: gradations of servility at the desert edge (Niger and Nigeria)', in S. Miers and I. Kopytoff (eds), pp.391–411

Barkindo, B.M. (ed.) (1978) *Studies in the History of Kano* (Ibadan: Heinemann)

Barry, B. (1972) *Le royaume du Waalo. Le Sénégal avant la conquête* (Paris: Maspero)

Bartels, F.L. (1965) *The Roots of Ghana Methodism* (Cambridge: CUP)

Barth, H. (1857) *Travels and Discoveries in North and Central Africa* (5 vols, London: Longman, Brown, Green, Longmans and Roberts)

Barth, H. (1963) *Voyages et découvertes dans l'Afrique septentrionale et centrale pendant les années 1849 à 1855 (4 vols. Paris: Bohné)*.

Bascom, W.R. (1972) *Shango in the New World* (Austin: University of Texas Press)

Batran, A.A. (1983) *Islam and Revolution in Africa: A Study in Arab-Islamic Affairs* (Brattleboro: Center for Arab and Islamic Studies)

Bazin, J. and Terray, E. (1982) *Guerres de lignages et guerres d'Etats en Afrique* (Paris: Archives contemporaines)

Bdira, M. (1978) *Relations internationales et sous-développement: La Tunisie, 1857–1864)* (Uppsala: Acta Univers)

Beach, D. (1980) *The Shona and Zimbabwe, 900–1850* (New York: Macmillan)

Beachey, R.W. (1967) 'The East African ivory trade in the nineteenth century,' *JAH*, 8, 2, pp.269–90

Beemer, H. (1937) 'The development of the military organisation in Swaziland', *Africa*, 10, pp.55–74

Behrens, C. (1974) *Les Kroumen de la côte occidentale d'Afrique* (Bordeaux CNRS, centre d'études de géographie tropicale, Talence)

Bello, M. (1951) *Infaq al-Maisur*, ed. C.E.J. Whitting, (London: Luzac)

Belrose-Huyghes, V. (1975) 'Un exemple de syncrétisme esthétique au XIXe siècle: le Rova de Tananarive d'Andrianjaka à Radama ler', *Omaly sy Anio*, 1–2, pp.273–307

Belrose-Huyghes, V. (1977) 'Considération sur l'introduction de l'imprimerie à Madagascar', *Omaly sy Anio*, 5–6, pp.89–105

Belrose-Huyghes, V. (1978a) 'Le contact missionnaire au féminin: Madagascar et la LMS, 1795–1835', *Omaly sy Anio*, 7–8, pp.83–131

Belrose-Huyghes, V. (1978b) 'Historique de la pénétration protestante à Madagascar jusqu'en 1829' (Thèse de 3ème cycle, Paris-Antananarivo)

Benachenhour, A. (1966) *L'Etat algérien en 1830. Ses institutions sous l'émir Abd-el-Kader* (Algiers)

Benedict, B. (1965) *Mauritius; Problems of a Plural Society* (New York; Praeger)

Bennett, N.R. (1978) *A History of the Arab State of Zanzibar* (London: Methuen)

Bennett, N.R. (1981) *Mirambo of Tanganyika, 1840–1884* (New York: OUP)

Berger, I. (1981) *Religion and Resistance in East African Kingdoms in the Precolonial Period* (Tervuren: Musée Royale d l'Afrique Centrale)

Berntsen, J.L. (1979) 'Pastoralism, raiding and prophets: Maasailand in the nineteenth century' (PhD thesis, University of Wisconsin, Madison)

Berque, J. (1978) *L'intérieur du Maghreb, XVe–XIXe siècle* (Paris: Gallimard)

Bertho, J. (1949) 'La parenté des Yoruba aux peuplades du Dahomey et du Togo', *Africa*, 19, pp.121–32

Bethell, L. (1970) *The Abolition of the Brazilian Slave Trade. Britain, Brazil and the Slave Trade Question, 1807–1869* (Cambridge: CUP)

Binger, L.-G. (1892) *Du Niger au golfe de Guinée par le pays de Kong et le pays Mossi (1887–1889)* (2 vols, Paris: Hachette)

Biobaku, S.O. (1957) *The Egba and Their Neighbours* (Oxford: Clarendon Press)

Birks, J.S. (1978) *Across the Savannahs to Mecca: The Overland Pilgrimage Route from West Africa* (London: Hurst)

Birmingham, D. (1976) 'The forest and the savannah of Central Africa', in J.E. Flint (ed.), pp.222–69

Boahen, A.A. (1964) *Britain, the Sahara, and the Western Sudan, 1788–1861* (Oxford: Clarendon Press)

Boahen, A.A. (1966) *Topics in West African History* (London: Longman)

Boahen, A.A. (1975) *Ghana: Evolution and Change in the Nineteenth and Twentieth Centuries* (London: Longman)

Bonner, P. (1983) *Kings, Commoners and Concessionaires: The Evolution and Dissolution of the Nineteenth-Century Swazi State* (Cambridge: CUP)

Bontinck, F. (1974) 'La double traversée de l'Afrique par trois Arabes de Zanzibar (1845–1860)', *Etudes d'histoire africaine*, 6, pp.5–53

Bosworth, C.E. Van Donzel, E., Lewis, B., Pellat, C. (eds) (1978) *The Encyclopedia of Islam*, new edn, Vol. 4 (Leiden/London: Brill/Luzac)

Botte, R. (1982) 'La guerre interne au Burundi', in J. Bazin and E. Terray (eds), pp.269–317

Boudou, A. (1940–2) *Les jésuites à Madagascar aux XIXe siècle* (Paris: Beauchesne)

Boudou, A. (1943) 'Le complot de 1857', in *Collection de Documents concernant Madagascar et les pays voisins* (Paris: Académie Malgache)

Bourdieu, P. (1970) *Sociologie de l'Algérie* (3rd edn, Paris: PUF)

Boyd, J. (1982) 'The contribution of Nana Asma'u Fodio to the jihadist movement of Shehu Dan Fodio from 1820 to 1865' (MPhil thesis, North London Polytechnic)

Boyer, P. (1970) 'Le problème kouloughli dans la Régence d'Alger', *ROMM*, numéro spécial, pp.79–94

Boyer, P. (1971) 'L'Odyssée d'une tribu saharienne; les Djerama, 1881–1929', *ROMM*, 10, pp.27–54

Brenner, L. (1973) *The Shehus of Kukawa* (Oxford: Clarendon Press)

Brookes, E.H. and Webb, C. de B. (1965) *A History of Natal* (Pietermaritzburg: University of Natal Press)

Brooks, G.E. (1972) *The Kru Mariner in the Nineteenth Century* (Newark, Delaware: University of Delaware)

Brooks, G.E. (1975) 'Peanuts and colonialism: consequences of the commercialization of peanuts in West Africa, 1830–70', *JAH*, 16, 1, pp.29–54

Brown, K. (1976) *People of Salé: Tradition and Change in a Moroccan City, 1830–1930* (Cambridge, Mass: HUP)

Brown, L.C. (1974) *The Tunisia of Ahmad Bey, 1837–1855* (Princeton: PUP)

Brown, M. (1978) *Madagascar Rediscovered: A History from Early Times to Independence* (London: Damien Tunnacliffe)

Brown, W.A. (1968) 'Towards a chronology of the caliphate of Hamdullahi (Māsina)', *CEA*, 7, 31, pp.428–43

Brown, W.A. (1969) 'The caliphate of Hamdullahi, c.1818–1864: A study in African history and traditions' (PhD thesis, University of Wisconsin, Madison)

Bryant, A.T. (1964) *A History of the Zulu and Neighbouring Tribes* (Cape Town: C. Struik)

Bugner, L. (ed.) (1980) *The Image of the Black in Western Art* (New York: William Morrow)

Bull, M.M. (1972) 'Lewanika's achievement', *JAH*, 13, 4, pp.463–72

Bundy, C. (1979) *The Rise and Fall of the South African Peasantry* (Berkeley: UCP)

Burke III, E. (1976) *Prelude to the Protectorate in Morocco: Precolonial Protest and Resistance 1860–1912* (Chicago: Chicago University Press)

Burman, S. (1981) *Chiefdom Politics and Alien Law: Basutoland under Cape Rule, 1871–1884* (New York: Africana Publishing)

Burton, R.F. (1860) *The Lake Regions of Central Africa* (2 vols. London: Longman, Green, Longman & Roberts)

Burton, R.F. (1872) *Zanzibar; City, Island and Coast* (2 vols. London: Tinsley Brothers)

Burton, R.F. (1894) *First Footsteps in East Africa* (London: Tylston & Arnold)

Butler, G. (1974) *The 1820 Settlers. An Illustrated Commentary* (Cape Town: Human & Rousseau)

Cachia, A.J. (1975) *Libya Under the Second Ottoman Occupation, 1835–1911* (Tripoli)

Caillon-Fillet, O. (1978) 'Jean Laborde et l'Océan Indien' (thèse de 3ᵉ cycle, Université de Aix-en-Provence)

Campbell, G. (1981) 'Madagascar and the slave trade, 1850–1895', *JAH*, 22, 2, pp.203–28

Campbell, Mavis (eds) (1992) *Back to Africa: George Ross and the Maroons from Nova Scotia to Sierra Leone* (Trenton, N.J.: Africa World Press)

Caplan, G.L. (1970) *The Elites of Barotseland 1878–1969* (Berkeley: UCP)

Carreira, A. (1947) *Mandingas da Guiné Portuguesa* (Bissau: Centro do Estudos da Guiné Portuguesa. Memórias no.4)

Cassanelli, L.V. (1982) *The Shaping of Somali Society* (Philadelphia: UPP)

Caulk, R.A. (1972) 'Firearms and princely power in Ethiopia in the nineteenth century', *JAH*, 13, 4, pp.591–608

Chamberlain, C. (1979) 'Bulk exports, trade tiers, regulation and development: an economic approach to the study of West Africa's "Legitimate Trade" ', *Journal of Economic History*, 39, 2, pp.419–38

Chater, K. (1984) *Dépendance et mutations précoloniales. La Régence de Tunis de 1815 à 1857* (Tunis: Publications de l'Université de Tunis)

Chérif, M.H. (1970) 'Expansion européenne et difficultés tunisiennes de 1815 à 1830', *Annales ESC*, 25, 3, pp.714–45

Chérif, M.H. (1978) 'Hammuda Pacha Bey et l'affermissement de l'autonomie tunisienne', in *Les Africains* (Paris: Jeune Afrique), Vol. 7, pp.99–127

Chérif, M.H. (1979) 'Propriété des oliviers au Sahel des débuts du XIXe à ceux du XIXe siècle', in *Actes du Premier Congrès d'Histoire et de la Civilisation du Maghreb* (Tunis: Centre d'études et de recherches économiques et sociales) Vol. 2, pp.209–52

Chérif, M.H. (1980) 'Les mouvements paysans dans la Tunisie du XIXe siècle, *ROMM*, 30, pp.21–55

Childs, G.M. (1970) 'The chronology of the Ovimbundu Kingdom', *JAH*, 11, 2, pp.241–57

Chilver, E.M. (1961) 'Nineteenth-century trade in the Bamenda Grassfields, Southern Cameroons', *Afrika und Übersee* 14

Chittick, H.N. and Rotberg, R.L. (1975) *East Africa and the Orient: Cultural Synthesis in Precolonial Times* (New York: Africana Publishing)

Chrétien, J.P. (1981) 'Le commerce du sel de l'Uvinza au XIXe siècle: de la cueillette au monopole capitaliste' in *Le sol, la parole et l'écrit, Mélanges en hommage à Raymond Mauny* (2 vols, Paris: SPHOM), Vol. 2, pp.919–40

Christaller, J.G. (1933) *Dictionary of the Asante and Fante Language* (2nd edn, first edn, 1881, Basel: Basel Evangelical Missionary Society)

Clapperton, H. (1829) *Journal of a Second Expedition into the Interior of Africa* (London: Murray)

Clarence-Smith, W.G. (1979a) *Slaves, Peasants and Capitalists in Southern Angola, 1840–1926* (Cambridge CUP)

Clarence-Smith, W.G. (1979b) 'Slaves, commoners and landlords in Bulozi c.1875 to 1906', *JAH*, 20, 2, pp.219–34

Clarence-Smith, W.G. and Moorsom, R. (1975) 'Under-development and class formation in 1845–1915', *JAH*, 16, 3, pp.365–81.

Cohen, D.W. (1986) *Busoga, 1700–1900*

Cohen, D.W. and Greene, J.P. (eds) (1972) *Neither Slave nor Free: The Freedom of Peoples of African Descent in the Slave Societies of the New World* (Baltimore: JHUP)

Cohen, W.B. (1980) *The French Encounter with Africans: White Response to Blacks, 1530–1880.* (Bloomington: Indiana University Press)

Collins, R.O. (1975) *The Southern Sudan in Historical Perspective* (Tel Aviv, University of Tel Aviv Students Association)

Collins, R.O. and Tignor, R.L. (1967) *Egypt and the Sudan* (Eaglewood Cliffs, NJ: Prentice-Hall)

Colvin, L.G. (1974) 'Islam and the state of Kajoor: a case of successful resistance to jihad', *JAH*, 15, 4, pp.587–606

Colvin, L.G. (1982) *Kajor and the French. A Study of Diplomacy from the Slave Trade through the Conquest* (New York: Nok)

Cooper, F. (1977) *Plantation Slavery on the East Coast of Africa* (New Haven and London: YUP)

Coquery-Vidrovitch, C. (1971) 'De la traite des esclaves à l'exportation de palme et des palmistes au Dahomey: XIXe siècle' in C. Meillassoux (ed.), pp.107–23

Coquery-Vidrovitch, C. (1972) 'Research on an African mode of production' in M.A. Klein and G.W. Johnson (eds), pp.33–52

Coquery-Vidrovitch, C. (1976) 'La mise en dépendance de l'Afrique noire: essai de périodisation historique', *CEA*, 16, 1–2, pp.7–58

Coquery-Vidrovitch, C. and Moniot, H. (1974) *L'Afrique noire de 1800 à nos jours* (Paris: PUF)

Cordell, D.D. (1977) 'Eastern Libya, Wadai and the Sanusiya: A tariqa and a trade route', *JAH*, 18, 1, pp. 21–36

Cornevin, R. (1962) *Histoire du Dahomey* (Paris: Berger-Levrault)

Corwin, A.F. (1967) *Spain and the Abolition of Slavery in Cuba, 1817–1886* (Austin and London: University of Texas Press)

Coupland, R. (1933) *The British Anti-Slavery Movement* (Oxford: Clarendon Press)

Coupland, R. (1938) *East Africa and its Invaders* (Oxford: Clarendon Press)

Coupland, R. (1939) *The Exploitation of East Africa, 1856–1890* (London, Faber)

Crahan, M. and Knight, F.W. (eds) (1970) *Africa and the Caribbean, the Legacies of a Link* (Baltimore: JHUP)

Craton, M. (ed.) (1970) *Roots and Branches: Current Directions in Slave Studies* (Oxford: Pergamon)

Crummey, D. (1969) 'Téwodros as reformer and modernizer', *JAH*, 10, 3, pp.457–69

Crummey, D. (1971) 'The violence of Téwodros', *Journal of Ethiopian Studies*, 9, 2, pp.107–25

Crummey, D. (1972) *Priests and Politicians: Protestant and Catholic in Orthodox Ethiopia, 1830–1868* (Oxford: Clarendon Press)

Cunnison, Ian (1959) *The Luapula Peoples of Northern Rhodesia* (Manchester: MUP)

Cunnison, Ian (1966) 'Kazembe and the Arabs to 1870', in E. Stokes and R. Brown (eds), pp.226–37

Curtin, P.D. (ed.) (1967) *Africa Remembered* (Madison: UWP)

Curtin, P.D. (1969) *The Atlantic Slave Trade: A Census* (Madison: UWP)

Curtin, P.D. (1975) *Economic Change in Pre-Colonial Africa: Senegambia in the Era of the Slave Trade* (Madison: UWP)

Curtin, P.D., Feierman, S., Thompson, L. and Vansina, J. (1978) *African History* (Boston: Little, Brown)

Daget, S. (1973) 'Les mots esclave, nègre, Noir et les jugements de valeur sur la traite négrière dans la littérature abolitionniste française, de 1770 à 1845', *RFHOM*, 60, 4, pp.511–48

Daget, S. (1980) 'Rôle et contribution des états-côtiers dans l'évolution des rapports entre Africains et Européens du XVe au XIXe siècle', *Annales de l'Université d'Abidjan sér. D.* (Lettres), 13, pp.311–36

Daget, S. (1983) *Catalogue analytique des armements français soupçonnés de participation au trafic négrier illégal, 1814–1867* (Paris: SFHOM)

Daget, S. (1990) *La Traite des Noirs* (Edition Ouest-France)

Darkwah, R.H. (1975) *Shewa, Menelik and the Ethiopian Empire 1813–1889* (London: Heinemann)

Davenport, T.R.H. (1978) *South Africa: A Modern History* (2nd edn, London: Macmillan)

David, R. (1970) 'Negro contributions to the exploration of the globe', J.S. Roucek and T. Kiernan (eds) *The Negro Impact on Western Civilization* (New York: Philosophical Library)

Davis, R. (1973) *The Rise of the Atlantic Economies* (Ithaca: Cornell University Press)

Davis, R.W. (1976) *Ethnolinguistic Studies on the Kru Coast, Liberia* (Newark, Delaware: Liberian Studies Association)

De Kiewiet, C.W. (1937) *The Imperial Factor in South Africa* (Cambridge: CUP)

De Kiewiet, C.W. (1968) *A History of South Africa, Social and Economic* (London: OUP)

Dean, W. (1976) *Rio Claro: A Brazilian Plantation System, 1820–1920* (Stanford: SUP)

Debbasch, Y. (1961–2) 'Le marronage: essai sur la désertion de l'esclavage antillais', *L'Année sociologique*

Debrunner, H.W. (1967) *A History of Christianity in Ghana* (Accra: Waterville)

Decary, R. (1960) *L'ile Nosy Bé de Madagascar: histoire d'une colonisation* (Paris)

Degler, C. (1971) *Neither Black nor White: Slavery and Race Relations in Brazil and the United States* (New York: Macmillan)

Delafosse, M. (1972) *Haut-Sénégal-Niger* (2 vols, Paris: Maisonneuve & Larose)

Delivré, A. (1974) *L'Histoire des rois d'Imerina, Interprétation d'une tradition orale* (Paris: Klincksieck)

Delval, R. (1964) *Radama II: Prince de la Renaissance Malgache, 1861–1863* (Paris: Editions de l'Ecole)

Deng, F.M. (1978) *Africans of Two Worlds* (New Haven and London: YUP)

Denis, P. (1961) *Histoire des Mangbetu et des Matshaga jusqu'à l'arrivée des Belges* (Tervuren: Musée royal de l'Afrique centrale)

Denoon, D. (1973) *Southern Africa since 1800* (New York: Praeger)

Deschamps, H. (1960) *Histoire de Madagascar* (Paris: Berger-Levrault)

Dez, J. (1967) 'Le Vakinankaratra, esquisse d'une histoire regionale', *Bulletin de Madagascar*, 256, pp.657–702

Diallo, T. (1972) *Les institutions politiques du Fouta Djalon au XIXe siècle (Fifi Laamu Alsilaamaaku Fuuta Jallo)* (Dakar: IFAN, Initiations et Etudes africaines, 28)

Dias, J.R. (19881) 'Famine and disease in the history of Angola c.1830–1930', *JAH*, 22, 3, pp.349–79

Dickson, H.R. (1941) *The Arab of the Desert* (London: Allen & Unwin)

Dike, K.O. (1956) *Trade and Politics in the Niger Delta, 1830–1885: An Introduction to the Economic and Political History of Nigeria* (Oxford: Clarendon Press)

Dike, K.O. and Ekejiuba, F. (1990) *The Aro of Southeastern Nigera 1650–1980* (Ibadan; UPL)

Djeghloul, A. (1976) 'La formation sociale algérienne à la veille de la colonisation', *La Pensée*, 185, pp.61–81

Dodwell, H.H. (1931) *The Founder of Modern Egypt; a Study of Muhammad Ali* (Cambridge: CUP)

Douin, G. (1933–41) *Histoire du règne de Khédive Ismaïl* (3 vols, Rome: Société Royale de géographie d'Egypte)

Drachoussoff, V. (1947) 'Essai sur l'agriculture indigène au Bas-Congo', *Bulletin agricole du Congo belge et du Ruanda-Urundi*

Drescher, S. (1977) *Econocide, British Slavery in the Era of Abolition* (Pittsburgh: Pittsburgh University Press)

Dugmore, R.H. (1958) *The Reminiscences of an Albany Settler* (eds) E. Van der Riet and L.A. Hewson, (Cape Town: Grocott & Sherry)

Dumett, R.E. (1971) 'The rubber trade of the Gold Coast and Asante in the nineteenth century: African innovation and market responsiveness' *JAH*, 12, 1, pp.79–101

Duminy, A. and Ballard, C. (eds) (1981) *The Anglo-Zulu War: New Perspectives* (Pietermaritzburg: University of Natal Press)

Dumont, F. (1974) *L'Anti-Sultan ou Al-Hajj Omar Tal du Fouta, Combattant de la foi* (Dakar and Abidjan: NEA)

Dunn, R.E. (1977) *Resistance in the Desert: Moroccan Responses to French Imperialism, 1881–1912* (London: Croom Helm)

Ehrensaft, P. (1972) 'The political economy of informal empire in pre-colonial Nigeria, 1807–1884', *CJAS*, 6, 3, pp.451–90

Ekechi, F.K. (1972) *Missionary Enterprise and Rivalry in Igboland 1857–1914* (London: Frank Cass)

Ekejiuba, F.I. (1972) 'The Aro systems of trade in the nineteenth century', *Ikenga*, I, I, pp.II-26;I, 2, pp.10–21

Ekman, E. (1975) 'Sweden, the slave trade and slavery', *RFHOM*, 62, 226–7, pp.221–31

Elango, L.Z. (1974) 'Bimbia and British in the nineteenth century, 1833–1879. A study in Anglo-Bimbian trade and diplomatic relations' (unpublished PhD, Boston University)

Ellis, E. (1858) *Three Visits to Madagascar During the Years 1853–1854–1856* (London: Murray)

Ellis, W. (1867) *Madagascar Revisited: Describing the Events of a New Reign and the Revolution which followed* (London: Murray)

Ellis, W. (nd, preface 1869) *The Marty Church: A Narrative of the Introduction, Progress and Triumph of Christianity in Madagascar* (London: Snow)

Eltis, D. and Walvin, J. (eds) (1981) *The Abolition of the Atlantic Slave Trade. Origins and Effects in Europe, Africa and the Americas* (Madison: UWP)

Engerman, S.L. and Genovese, E.D. (eds) (1975) *Race and Slavery in the Western Hemisphere: Quantitative Studies* (Princeton: PUP)

Esoavelomandroso, M. (1978a) 'Notes sur l'enseignement sous Ranavalona 1ère: l'instruction réservée à l'élite Ambario, 2–3, pp.283–90

Esoavelomandroso, M. (1978b) 'Religion et politique; l'evangélisation du pays betsimisarka à la fin du XIXe siècle', *Omaly sy Anio*, 7–8, pp.7–42

Estermann, C. (1956–61) *Etnografia do sudoeste de Angola* (3 vols, Lisbon: Junta de Investigaçoẽs do Ultramar)

Etherington, N.A. (1979) 'Labour supply and the genesis of South African confederation in the 1870s', *JAH*, 20, pp.235–53

Evans-Pritchard, E.E. (1949) *The Sanusi of Cyrenaica* (London: OUP)

Fage, J.D. (1959) *An Introduction to the History of West Africa* (2nd edn, Cambridge: CUP)

Fage, J.D. (1975) 'The effect on the export slave trade on African population', in R.P. Moss and R.J. Rathbone (eds), *The Population Factor in African Studies* (London: University of London Press), pp.15–23

Fahmy, M. (1954) *La révolution de l'industrie en Egypte et ses conséquences sociales au XIXe siècle (1800–1850)*, (Leiden: Brill)

Faidherbe, L. (1863) *L'Avenir du Sahara et du Soudan* (Paris: Librairie Challamel Aine)

Feierman, S. (1974) *The Shambaa Kingdom: A History* (Madison: UWP)

Filliot, J.M. (1974) *La traite des esclaves vers les Mascareignes au XVIIIe siècle* (Paris: ORSTOM)

Fisher, H.J. and Rowland, V. (1971) 'Firearms in the Central Sudan', *JAH*, 12, 3, pp.215–39

Flint, E. (1970) 'Trade and politics in Barotseland during the Kololo period', *JAH*, 11, 1, pp.71–86

Flint, J.E. (ed.) (1976) *The Cambridge History of Africa Vol. 5, from c.1790 to c.1870* (Cambridge: CUP)

Florent, H. (1979) *Le gouvernement de Tamatave de 1864 à 1882. Développement économique* (Tananarive: TER, Département d'histoire)

Fogel, R.W. and Engerman, S.L. (1974) *Time on the Cross: The Economics of American Negro Slavery* (2 vols, Boston: Little, Brown)

Folayan, K. (1967) 'The Egbado and Yoruba–Aja power politics, 1832–1894' (MA thesis, University of Ibadan)

Folayan, K. (1972) 'Tripoli and the war with the USA, 1801–05', *JAH*, 13, 2, pp.261–70

Forde, D. (1951) *The Yoruba-speaking Peoples of South-Western Nigeria* (London: IAI)

Forde, D. (ed.) (1956) *Efik Traders of Old Calabar* (London: OUP)

Forde, D. (ed.) (1967) *West Africa, Kingdoms in the Nineteenth Century* (London: OUP)

Forde, D. and Jones, G.I. (1950) *The Ibo and Ibibio-speaking Peoples of South-Eastern Nigeria* (London: IAI)

Foster, P. (1965) *Education and Social Change in Ghana* (London: Routledge, Kegan Paul)

Franklin, J.H. (1969) *From Slavery to Freedom: A History of Negro-Americans* (3rd edn, New York: Knopf)

Freeman, T.B. (1843) *Journal of Two Visits to the Kingdom of Ashantee in Western Africa* (London: Mason)

Freeman-Grenville, G.S.P. (1962) *The East African Coast: Select Documents* (Oxford: Clarendon Press)

Freeman-Grenville, G.S.P. (1965) *The French at Kilwa Island* (Oxford: Clarendon Press)

Fulton, R.M. (1968) 'The Kpelle traditional political stystem', *Liberian Studies Journal*, 1, 1, pp.1–19

Fyfe, C. (1963) *Sierra Leone Inheritance* (London: OUP)

Fyfe, C. (1972) *Africanus Horton, 1835–1883* (New York: OUP)

Fyfe, C. (ed.) (1978) *African Studies since 1945: A Tribute to Basil Davidson* (London: Longman)

Fyfe, C.M. (1981) *The History of Sierra Leone: A Concise Introduction* (London: Evans)

Fynn, J.K. (1974) 'The structure of Greater Ashanti: another view', *THSG*, 15, 1, pp.1–22

Galbraith, J.S. (1970) 'Myth of the "Little England" era', in A.G.L. Shaw (ed.) *Great Britain and the Colonies, 1815–1865* (London: Methuen), pp.27–45

Gallagher, J. and Robinson, R. (1953) 'The imperialism of free trade', *Economic History Review*, 6, 1

Gallisot, R. (1965) 'Abdelkader et la nationalité algérienne', *Revue Historique*, 89, 2, pp.339–68

Ganiage, J. (1959) *Les origines du protectorat français en Tunisie* (1861–1881) (Paris: PUF)

Gann, L.H. and Duignan, P. (eds) (1969) *Colonialism in Africa, 1870–1960, Vol. 1: The History and Politics of Colonialism 1870–1914* (Cambridge: CUP)

Gann, L.H. and Duignan, P. (eds) (1970) *Colonialism in Africa, 1870–1960, Vol. 2: The History and Politics of Colonialism 1914–1960* (Cambridge: CUP)

Gardel, G. (1961) *Les Touareg Ajjer* (Algiers: Baconnier)

Gbadamosi, T.G. (1979) *The Growth of Islam among the Yoruba* (London: Longman)

Gellner, E. (1969) *Saints of the Atlas* (London: Weidenfield & Nicolson)

Gemery, H.A. and Hogendorn, J.S. (eds) (1979) *The Uncommon Market. Essays in the Economic History of the Atlantic Slave Trade* (New York: Academic Press)

Genovese, E.D. (1968) *Economie politique de l'esclavage* (Paris: Maspero)

Genovese, E.D. (1974) *Roll, Jordan, Roll: The world the Slaves Made* (New York: Pantheon)

Gibb, H.A.R. and Bowen, H. (1960) *Islamic Society and the West* (London: Hatchard and Son)

Godelier, M. (1975) 'Modes of production, kinship and demographic structure' in M. Bloch (ed.), *Marxist Analysis and Social Anthropology* (London: Malaby) pp.3–29

Goerg, O. (1960) 'La destruction d'un réseau d'échange précolonial: l'exemple de la Guinée'. *JAH*, 21, 4, pp.467–84

Good, C.M. (1972) 'Salt, trade and disease: aspects of development in Africa's northern great lakes region', *IJAHS*, 5, 4, pp.543–86

Goodfellow, C.F. (1966) *Great Britain and South African Confederation 1870–1881* (Cape Town: OUP)

Gourou, P. (1955) *La densité de la population rurale au Congo belge* (Brussels: ARSC)

Gourou, P. (1971) 'Favourable or hostile physical environments', in *Leçons de géographie tropicale*, (The Hague-Paris: Mouton) pp.89–90

Gow, B.A. (1979) *Madagascar and the Protestant Impact: The Work of the British Missions, 1818–95* (London: Longman)

Gran, P. (1979) *Islamic Roots of Capitalism: Egypt 1760–1840* (Austin & London: University of Texas Press)

Gray, J.M. (1962) *History of Zanzibar from the Middle Ages to 1856* (London: OUP)

Gray, R. (1970) *A History of the Southern Sudan, 1839–1889* (Oxford: Clarendon Press)

Gray, R. and Birmingham, D. (eds) (1970) *Pre-colonial African Trade: Essays on Trade in Central and Eastern Africa before 1900* (London: OUP)

Green, A.H. (1978) *The Tunisian Ulama, 1873–1915* (Leyden: Brill)

Green, W.A. (1974) 'The West Indies and British West African policy in the nineteenth century; a corrective comment', *JAH*, 15, 2, pp.247–59

Green-Pedersen, S.E. (1975) 'The history of the Danish slave trade, 1733–1807', *RFHOM*, 62, 226–7, pp.196–220

Greenfield, R. (1965) *Ethiopia: A New Political History* (London: Pall Mall)

Groves, C.P. (1954) *The Planting of Christianity in Africa* Vol. 2 (London: Lutterworth)

Guilhem, H. and Hebert, J. (1961) *Précis d'Histoire de la Haute-Volta* (Paris: Ligel)

Gulliver, P.H. (1955) 'A History of the Songea Ngoni', TNR, 41, pp.16–30

Gulliver, P.H. (1963) *Social Control in an African Society: A Study of the Arusha Agricultural Maasai of Northern Tanganyika* (London: Routledge, Kegan Paul)

Gutman, H.G. (1975) *Slavery and the Numbers Game. A Critique of Time on the Cross* (Urbana: University of Illinois Press)

Guy, J. (1980) *The Destruction of the Zulu Kingdom. The Civil War in Zululand 1879–1884* (London: Longman)

al-Hajj, M.A. (1964) 'The Fulani concept of jihad', *Odu*, 1, pp.45–58

al-Hajj, M.A. (1967) 'The 13th century in Muslim escatology: Mahdist expectations in the Sokoto caliphate', *Research Bulletin, Centre for Arabic Documentation* (Ibadan), 3, 2, pp.100–15

Hall, G.M. (1971) *Social Control in Slave Plantation Societies: A Comparison of St. Domingue and Cuba* (Baltimore: JHUP).

Hamani, D. (1975) Contribution à l'étude de l'histoire des états hausa: l'Adar précolonial (Niamey: IRSH)

Hammond, R.J. (1966) *Portugal and Africa, 1815–1910* (Stanford: SUP)

Hancock, W.K. (1942) *Survey of British Commonwealth Affairs, Vol. 2: Problems of Economic Policy. 1918–39* (London: OUP)

Hardyman, J.T. (1977) 'Malagasy refugees to Britain, 1838–41', *Omaly sy Anio*, 5–6, pp.141–89

Harries, L. (1961) *Swahili Poetry* (Oxford: Clarendon Press)

Harries, P. (1981) 'Slavery, social incorporation and surplus extraction: the nature of free and unfree labour in south-east Africa', *JAH*, 22, 3, pp.309–30

Harris, M. (1964) *Patterns of Race in the Americas* (New York: Walker)

Harris, R. (1972) 'The history of trade at Ikom, Eastern Nigeria', *Africa*, 63, 2, pp.122–39

Harris, R. (1982) 'The horse in West African history', *Africa*, 52, pp.81–5

Hart, D.M. (1966) 'Segmentary system and the role of "five-fifths" in tribal Morocco', *ROMM*, 3, pp.65–95

Hart, D.M. (1970) 'Conflicting models of Berber tribal structure in the Moroccan Rif: the segmentary alliance systems of the Aith Waryachar', *ROMM* 7, pp.93–100

Hartwig, G.W. (1970) 'The Victoria Nyanza as a trade route in the nineteenth century', *JAH*, 11, 4, pp.535–52

Hartwig, G.W. (1976) *The Art of Survival in East Africa: the Kerebe and Long-Distance Trade, 1800–1895* (New York: Africana Publishing)

Hartwig, G.W. and Patterson, K.D. (eds) (1978) *Disease in African History* (Durham, N.C.: Duke University Press)

Hasan, Y.F. (1967) *The Arabs and the Sudan* (Edinburgh: Edinburgh University Press)

Hassan, A. and Naibi, A.S. (1962) *A Chronicle of Abuja* (Lagos: African Universities Press)

Herskovits, M.J. (1938) *Dahomey, an Ancient West African Kingdom* (New York: J.J. Augustin)

Hertslet, E. (1894) *The Map of Africa by Treaty* (2 vols, London: Harrison)

Higman, B.W. (1976) *Slave Economy and Society in Jamaica 1807–1832* (New York: CUP)

Hill, R. (1966) *Egypt in the Sudan* (London: OUP)

Hiskett, M. (1973) *The Sword of Truth* (New York: OUP)

Hiskett, M. (1975) *A History of Hausa Islamic Verse* (London: SOAS)

Hitchcock, R. and Smith M.R. (eds) (1982) *Settlement in Botswana* (London: Heinemann)

Hobsbawm, E.J. (1977) *Industry and Empire* (new edn, Harmondsworth: Penguin)

Hoetink, H. (1973) *Slavery and Race Relations in the Americas: Comparative Notes on their Nature and Nexus* (New York: Harper & Row)

Hogendorn, J.S. (1977) 'The economics of slave use on two "plantations" in the Zaria emirate of the Sokoto caliphate', *IJAHS*, 10, 3, pp.369–83

Holsoe, S.E. (1967) 'The cassava-leaf people: an ethno-historical study of the Vai people with a particular emphasis on the Tewo chiefdom' (PhD thesis, Boston University)

Holt, P.M. (1970) *The Mahdist State in the Sudan 1881–1898* (2nd edn, Oxford: Clarendon Press)

Holt, P.M. (1973) *Studies in the History of the Near East* (London: OUP)

Hopkins, A.G. (1973) *An Economic History of West Africa* (London: Longman)

Hopkins, A.G. (1980) 'Africa's Age of Improvement', *HA*, 7, pp.141–60

Hopkins, T.K. and Wallerstein, I. et al, (1982) *World-Systems Analysis: Theory and Methodology* (Beverly Hills: Sage), pp.104–20

Horton, J.A. (1969) *West African Countries and Peoples*, ed. G. Shepperson (Edinburgh: Edinburgh University Press).

Horton, R. (1954) 'The ohu system of slavery in a northern Ibo village-group', *Africa*, 24, 4, pp.311–16

Horton, R. (1969) 'From fishing village to city-state: a social history of New Calabar' in M. Douglas and P. Kaberry (eds) *Man in Africa* (London: Tavistock), pp.37–58

Hourani, A. (1962) *Arabic Thought in the Liberal Age 1798–1939* (London: OUP)

Huntingford, G.W.B. (1955) *The Galla of Ethiopia: The Kingdoms of Kafa and Janjero* (London: IAI)

Ikime, O. (ed.) (1980) *Groundwork of Nigerian History* (Ibadan, Heinemann)

Inikori, J.E. (1977) 'The import of firearms into West Africa, 1750–1607: a quantitative analysis', *JAH*, 18, 3, pp.339–68

Inikori, J.E. (ed.) (1982) *Forced Migration: The Impact of the Export Slave Trade on African Societies* (London: Hutchinson)

Isaacman, A. (1972a) *The Africanization of a European Institution: the Zambezi Prazos, 1750–1902* (Madison: UWP)

Isaacman, A. (1972b) 'The origin, formation and early history of the Chikunda of South-Central Africa', *JAH*, 13, 3, pp.443–62

Isaacman, A. (1976) *The Tradition of Resistance in Mozambique: Anti-Colonial Activity in the Zambezi Valley 1850–1921* (Berkeley: UCP)

Isichei, E. (1973) *The Ibo people and the Europeans: The Genesis of a Relationship to 1906* (London: Faber)

Issawi, C.P. (1966) *Economic History of the Middle East 1800–1914; a Book of Readings* (Chicago: University of Chicago Press)

Izard, M. (1970) *Introduction à l'histoire des royaumes Mossi* (2 vols, Recherches Voltaiques, 12, Paris/Ouagadougou: CNRS/CVRS)

Jacobs, A.H. (1965) 'The traditional political organization of the pastoral Massai' (DPhil thesis, Oxford University)

Jacobs, C.J. (1960) 'Theodore II and British intervention in Ethiopia', *Canadian Journal of History*, 1, 2, pp.26–56

Jakobsson, S. (1972) *Am I not a Man and a Brother? British Missions and the Abolition of the Slavery in West Africa and the West Indies, 1756–1838* (Uppsala: Gleerup)

Jesman, C. (1966) 'The tragedy of Magdala: a historical study', *Ethiopia Observer*, 10

Johnson, M. (1970) 'The cowrie currencies of West Africa', *JAH*, 11, 1, pp.17–49, 3, pp.331–53

Johnson, M. (1976) 'The economic foundations of an Islamic theocracy – the case of Masina', *JAH*, 17, 4, pp.481–95

Johnson, S. (1921) *History of the Yorubas* (London: Routledge)

Johnson, H.A.S. (1967) *The Fulani Empire of Sokoto* (London: OUP)

Jones, A. (1981) 'Who were the Vai?', *JAH*, 22, 2, pp.159–78

Jones, G.I. (1963) *The Trading States of the Oil Rivers: a Study of Political Development in Eastern Nigeria* (London: OUP)

Julien, C.A. (1964) *Histoire de l'Algérie contemporaine, Vol. 1, La conquête et les débuts de la colonisation* (Paris: Presses Universitaire de France)

July, R. (1967) *The Origins of Modern African Thought* (New York: Praeger)

Kagame, A. (1961) *L'histoire des armées bovines dans l'ancien Rwanda* (Brussels: Académie royale des sciences d'Outre-Mer)

Kagame, A. (1963) *Les Milices du Rwanda précolonial* (Brussels: Académie Royale des Sciences d'Outre-Mer)

Kamara, M. (1975) *La vie d'El Hadji Omar* (trans. by Amar Samb, Dakar: Editions Hilal)

Kaplow, S.B. (1978) 'Primitive accumulation and traditional social relations on the nineteenth-century Gold Coast' *CJAS*, 12, 1, pp.19–36

Kasozi, A.B. (1974) 'The spread of Islam in Uganda, 1844–1945' (PhD thesis, University of California, Santa Cruz)

Keddie, N. (ed.) (1972) *Scholars, Saints and Sufis* (Berkeley: UCP)

Keenan, J. (1977) *The Tuareg: People of Ahaggar* (London: Allen Lane)

Kelly, J.B. (1968) *Britain and the Persian Gulf, 1795–1880* (Oxford: Clarendon Press)

Kent, R.K. (1962) *From Madagascar to the Malagasy Republic* (London: Thames and Hudson)

Kietegha, J.B. (1983) *L'or de la Volta Noire* (Paris: Karthala)

Kimambo, I.N. (1969) *A Political History of the Pare of Tanzania: c.1500–1900* (Nairobi: EAPH)

Kimambo, I.N. (1970) 'The economic history of the Kamba 1850–1950', *Hadith*, 2, pp.79–103

Kimambo, I.N. and Temu, C.W. (eds) (1969) *A History of Tanzania* (Nairobi: EAPH)

Kimble, D. (1963) *A Political History of the Gold Coast* (Oxford: Clarendon Press)

Kittler, G.D. (1961) *The White Fathers* (New York: Image Books)

Kiwanuka, M.S.N. (1967) *Mutesa of Uganda* (Nairobi: EAPH)

Kiwanuka, S.N. (1972) *A History of Buganda* (London: Longman)

Klein, H.S. (1976) 'The Cuban slave trade in a period of transition 1790–1843', *RFHOM*, 62, 226–7, pp.67–89

Klein, H.S. (ed.) (1978) *The Middle Passage. Comparative Studies in the Atlantic Slave Trade* (Princeton: PUP)

Klein, M.A. (1968) *Islam and Imperialism in Senegal Sine-Saloum, 1847–1914* (Stanford: SUP)

Klein, M.A. and Johnson, G.W. (eds) (1972) *Perspective on the African Past* (Boston: Boston University Press)

Knight, F.W. (1970) *Slave Society in Cuba during the Nineteenth Century* (Madison: UWP)

Knight, F.W. (1974) *The African Dimension in Latin America and the Caribbean: An Historical Dictionary and Bibliography* (Metuchen, NJ: Scarecrow Press)

Kraiem, A. (1983) 'Ali ben Khalifa', in *Réactions à l'occupation française de la Tunisie en 1881* (Tunis: CNUDST), pp.145–58

Krapf, J.L. (1860) *Travels, Researches and Missionary Labors during an Eighteen Years' Residence in Eastern Africa* (Boston: Ticknor & Fields)

Kuper, H. (1947) *An African Aristocracy: Rank among the Swazi of Bechuanaland* (London: OUP)

Lacheraf, M. (1978) *l'Algérie, nation et société* (2nd edn, Algiers: SNED)

Laitin, D.D. (1982) 'The international economy and state formation among the Yoruba in the nineteenth century' *International Organization*, 26, 4, pp.637–714

Lander, R. (1830) *Records of Captain Clapperton's Last Expedition* (London: Colburn & Bentley)

Landes, David S. (1958) *Bankers and Pashas: International Finance and Economic Imperialism in Egypt* (London: Heinemann)

Langworthy, H.W. (1972) *Zambia Before 1890* (London: Longman)

Laroui, A. (1975) *L'histoire du Maghreb*, Vol. 2 (Paris: Maspero)

Laroui, A. (1977) *Les origines sociales et culturelles du nationalisme marocain (1830–1912)* (Paris: Maspero)

Last, M. (1967a) *The Sokoto Caliphate* (London: Longman)

Last, M. and al-Hajj, M.A. (1965) 'Attempts at defining a Muslim in 19th-century Hausaland and Bornu', *JHSN*, 3, 2, pp.231–40

Latham, A.J.H. (1973) *Old Calabar, 1600–1891. The Impact of the International Economy upon a Traditional Society* (Oxford: Clarendon Press)

Law, R. (1977) *The Oyo Empire, c.1600–c.1836: A West African Imperialism in the Era of the Atlantic Slave Trade* (Oxford: Clarendon Press)

Law, R. (1980) *The Horse in West African History* (London: IAI)

Levine, D.N. (1965) *Wax and Gold: Tradition and Innovation in Ethiopian Culture* (Chicago and London: University of Chicago Press)

Levine, D.N. (1974) *Greater Ethiopia. The Evolution of a Multiethnic Society* (Chicago and London: University of Chicago Press)

Levine, R.M. (1980) *Race and Ethnic Relations in Latin America and the Caribbean: An Historical Dictionary and Bibliography* (Metuchen, NJ: Scarecrow Press)

Levtzion, N. (1968) *Muslims and Chiefs in West Africa* (Oxford: Clarendon Press)

Lewis, B., Ménage, V.L., Pellat, C. and Schacht, J. (eds) (1971) *The Encyclopaedia of Islam*, 3 Vols, 3 (new edn, Leiden/London: Brill/Luzac)

Lewis, H.S. (1965) *A Galla Monarchy: Jimma Abba Jifar, Ethiopia, 1830–1932* (Madison: UWP)

Lewis, I.M. (1955) *Peoples of the Horn of Africa* (London: IAI)

Little, K. (1965–6) 'The political function of the Poro', *Africa*, 35, 4, pp.349–65; 36, 1, pp.62–72

Little, K. (1970) *The Mende of Sierra Leone* (London: Routledge & Kegan Paul)

Livingstone, D. (1857) *Missionary Travels and Researches in South Africa* (London: Murray)

Lloyd, C. (1949) *The Navy and the Slave Trade. The Suppression of the African Slave Trade in the Nineteenth Century* (London: Longman) (2nd edn, 1968)

Lloyd, P.C. (1963) 'The Itsekiri in the nineteenth century: an outline social history', *JAH*, 4, 2, pp.207–31

Lovejoy, P.E. (1982) 'The volume of the Atlantic slave trade: a synthesis', *JAH*, 23, 3, pp.473–501

Lovejoy, P.E. (1983) *Transformations in Slavery: A History of Slavery in Africa* (Cambridge: CUP)

Lovejoy, P.E. and Baier, S. (1975) 'The desert-side economy of the Central Sudan', *IJAHS*, 8, 4, pp.553–83

Lye, W.F. (1967) 'The Difaqane: the Mfecane in the southern Sotho area, 1822–24', *JAH*, 8, 1, pp.107–31

Lye, W.F. (ed.) (1975) *Andrew Smith's Journal of his expedition into the interior of South Africa 1834–35* (Cape Town: Balkem)

Lynch, H. (1967) *Edward Wilmot Blyden, Pan-Negro Patriot, 1832–1912* (London: OUP)

Mainga, M. (1973) *Bulozi Under the Luyana Kings: Political Evolution and State Formation in Precolonial Zambia* (London: Longman)

Mandala, E. (1979) 'The Kololo interlude in Southern Africa, 1861–1891' (MA thesis, University of Malawi)

Mane, M. (1974–5) *Contribution à l'histoire du Kaabu, des origines au XIXe siècle* (Dakar: Mémoire de l'Université de Dakar)

Marcus, H.G. (1975) *The Life and Times of Menilek II, 1844–1913* (Oxford: Clarendon Press)

Marks, S. and Atmore, A. (eds) (1980) *Economy and Society in Pre-industrial South Africa* (London: Longman)

Martel, A. (1965) *Les confins saharo-tripolitains de la Tunisie, 1818–1911* (Paris: PUF)

Martin, B.G. (1976) *Muslim Brotherhoods in Nineteenth Century Africa* (Cambridge: CUP)

Mason, J.P. (1978) 'Desert strongmen in the East Libyan Sahara (c.1820): a reconstruction of local power in the region of the Augila oasis', *Revue d'histoire maghrébine*, 6, pp.180–8

Mason, M. (1970) 'The Nupe Kingdom in the nineteenth century; a political history' (PhD thesis, University of Birmingham)

al Masri, F.H. (1963) 'The life of Shehu Usman dan Fodio before the jihad', *JHSN*, 2, 4, pp.435–48

al Masri, F.H. (ed. and trans.) (1978) *Bōyan Wujūb al-Hijra 'ala' l-Ibed* by 'Uthman Ibn Fūdī̄ (Khartoum: KUP)

Matsebula, J.S.M. (1972) *A History of Swaziland* (Cape Town: Longman)

M'Bokolo, E. (1981) *Noirs et blancs en Afrique équatoriale: Les sociétés côtières et la pénétration française (vers 1820–1874)* (Paris: Mouton)

McCall, D.F. and Bennett, N.R. (eds) (1971) *Aspects of West African Islam* (Boston: Boston University African Studies Center)

McCarthy, M. (1983) *Social Change and the Growth of British Power in the Gold Coast: the Fante states 1807–1874* (Lanham, Md: University Press of America)

McCaskie, T.C. (1980) 'Office, land and subjects in the history of the Manwere *fekuo* of Kumase: an essay in the political economy of the Asante state', *JAH*, 21, 2, pp.189–208

McGaffey, W. (1970) *Custom and Government in the Lower Congo* (Berkeley and Los Angeles: UCP)

McKay, W.F. (1975) 'A precolonial history of the southern Kenya coast' (PhD thesis, Boston University)

McPherson, J.M., Holland, L.B. et al. (1971) *Blacks in America: Bibliographical Essays* (New York: Doubleday)

McSheffrey, G.M. (1983) 'Slavery, indentured servitude, legitimate trade and the impact of abolition in the Gold Coast, 1874–1901', *JAH*, 24, 3, pp.349–68

Mears, W.G.A. (1970) *Wesleyan Baralong Mission in Trans-Orangia, 1821–1884* (2nd edn, Cape Town: Struik)

Medeiros, F. de (1984) 'Peuples du golfe du Bénin Aja-ewe', in *Colloque de Cotonou* (Paris: Karthala)

Meek, C. K. (1925) *The Northern Tribes of Nigeria*, 2 vols. (London: OUP)

Meillassoux, C. (ed.) (1971) *The Development of Indigenous Trade and Markets in West Africa* (London: OUP)

Meillassoux, C. (1974) 'From reproduction to production. A Marxist approach to economic anthropology', *Economy and Society*, 3, pp.315–45

Meillassoux, C. (1975) *L'esclavage en Afrique précoloniale* (Paris: Maspero)

Meillassoux, C. (1981) *Maidens, Meal and Money* (Cambridge: CUP)

Memmi, A. (1963) *La poésie algérienne de 1830 à nos jours (Approches socio-historiques)* (Paris: Mouton)

Mendes Moreira, J. (1948) *Fulas do Cabu* (Bissau: Centro de Estudos da Guiné Portuguesa)

Mercer, P. (1971) 'Shilluk trade and politics from the mid-seventeenth century to 1861', *JAH*, 12, 3, pp.407–26

Mercier, P. (1950) 'Notice sur le peuplement Yoruba du Dahomey-Togo', *Etudes Dahoméennes*, 4, pp.29–40

Metcalfe, G.E. (1962) *Maclean of the Gold Coast* (London: OUP)

Metcalfe, G.E. (1964) *Great Britain and Ghana: Documents of Ghana History, 1807–1957* (London: Nelson)

Metegue N'Nah, N. (1979) *Economies et sociétés au Gabon dans la première moitié du XIXe siècle* (Paris: L'Harmattan)

Meyer-Heiselberg, R. (1967) *Notes from the Liberated African Department in the Archives at Fourah Bay College, Freetown, Sierra Leone* (Uppsala: Scandinavian Institute of African Studies)

Middleton, J. and Campbell, J. (1965) *Zanzibar: Its Society and Its Politics* (London: OUP)

Miège, J.L. (1961–3) *Le Maroc et l'Europe (1830–1894)*, 4 vols (Paris: PUF)

Miers, S. (1971) 'Notes on the arms trade and government policy in Southern Africa between 1870 and 1890', *JAH*, 12, 4, pp.571–8

Miers, S. (1975) *Britain and the Ending of the Slave Trade* (London: Longman)

Miers, S. and Kopytoff, I. (eds) (1977) *Slavery in Africa: Historical and Anthropological Perspectives* (Madison: UWP)

Miller, J.C. (1973) 'Slaves, slavers and social change in ninteenth century Kasanje', in F.W. Heimer (ed.) *Social Change in Angola* (Munich: Weltforum Verlag) pp.9–29

Minna, M. (1982) 'Sultan Muhammad Bello and his intellectual contribution to the Sokoto Caliphate', (PhD thesis, London University)

Moffat, R. (1945) *The Matebele Journals*, ed. J.P.R. Wallis, 2 vols (London: Chatto & Windus)

Moffat, R. and Moffat, M. (1951) *Apprenticeship at Kuruman*, ed. I. Schapera (London: Chatto & Windus)

Mantagne, R. (1930) *Les Berbères et le Makhzen dans le sud du Maroc* (Paris)

Monteil, C. (1932) *Une cité soudanaise, Djenne, métropole du Delta central du Niger* (Paris: Société d'éditions géographiques, maritimes et coloniales)

Monteil, V. (1966) *Esquisses Sénégalaises* (Dakar: IFAN)

Monteil, V. (1977) *Les Bambara de Segou et de Kaarta,* 1st edn, 1924 (Paris: Maisonneuve)

Moreno Fraginals, M. (ed.) (1977) *Africa en America Latina* (Mexico: UNESCO)

Morgan, M. (1969) 'Continuities and traditions in Ethiopian history. An investigation of the reign of Téwodros', *Ethiopia Observer*, 12

Morton-Williams, P. (1964) 'The Oyo Yoruba and the Atlantic trade, 1670–1830', *JHSN*, 3, 1

Moulero, T. (1964) 'Histoire et légende de Chabi', *Etudes dahoméennes*, 2, pp.51–93

Mudenge, S.I. (1974) 'The role of foreign trade in the Rozvi empire: a reappraisal', *JAH*, 15, 3, pp.373–91

Muller, C.F.J. (ed.) (1974) *Five Hundred Years: A History of South Africa* (2nd edn, Pretoria and Cape Town: University of South Africa)

Munthe, L. (1960) *La Bible à Madagascar, les deux premières traductions du Nouveau Testament malgache* (Oslo: Egede Instututtet)

Munthe, L., Ravoajanahary, C. and Ayache, S. (1976) 'Radama Ier et les Anglais: les négociations de 1817 d'après les sources malgaches', *Omaly sy Anio*, 3–4, pp.9–104

Murray, D.R. (1971) 'Statistics of the slave trade to Cuba, 1790–1867', *Journal of Latin American Studies*, 3, 2, pp.131–49

Mutibwa, P.M. (1974) *The Malagasy and the Europeans: Madagascar's Foreign Relations, 1861–1895* (London: Longman)

Mveng, E. (1963) *Histoire du Cameroun* (Paris: Présence Africaine)

Mworoha, E. (1977) *Peuples et rois de l'Afrique des lacs* (Dakar: NEA)

Myatt, F. (1970) *The March to Magdala* (London: Leo Cooper)

Nacanabo, D. (1982) 'Le royaume maagha de Yako' (doctoral thesis, Université de Paris)

Nachtigal, G. (1967) *Sahara und Sudan, Ergebnisse Sechsjahriger Reisen in Afrika* (Graz)

Nair, K.K. (1972) *Politics and Society in South Eastern Nigeria 1841–1906: A Study of Power, Diplomacy and Commerce in Old Calabar* (London: Frank Cass)

al-Naqar, U. (1972) *The Pilgrimage Tradition in West Africa: An Historical Study with Special Reference to the Nineteenth Century* (Khartoum: KUP)

Nardin, J.C. (1965) 'Le Libéria et l'opinion publique en France, 1821–1847', *CAE*, 6, 1, pp.96–144

Nayenga, F.P.B. (1976) 'An economic history of the lacustrine states of Busoga, Uganda, 1750–1939' (PhD thesis, University of Michigan)

Needham, D.E. (1974) *From Iron Age to Independence; History of Central Africa* (London: Longman)

Neumark, S.D. (1954) *Foreign Trade and Economic Development in Africa: A Historial Perspective* (Stanford: Food Research Institute)

Newbury, C.W. (1961) *The Western Slave Coast and Its Rulers: European Trade and Administration Among the Yoruba and Adja-Speaking Peoples of South-Western Nigeria, Southern Dahomey and Togo* (Oxford: Clarendon Press)

Newbury, C.W. (1966) 'North African and Western Sudan trade in the nineteenth century: a re-evaluation', *JAH*, 7, 2, pp.233–46

Newbury, C.W. (1972) 'Credit in early nineteenth-century West African trade', *JAH*, 13, 1, pp.81–95

Newbury, D.S. (1980) 'Lake Kivu regional trade during the nineteenth century', *Journal des Africanistes*, 50, 2, pp.6–30

Newbury, M.C. (1975) 'The cohesion of oppression: a century of clientship in Kinyaga, Rwanda' (PhD thesis, University of Wisconsin)

Newitt, M.D.D. (1973) *Portuguese Settlement on the Zambesi, Exploration, Land Tenure and Colonial Rule in East Africa,* (London: Longman)

Nicholls, C.S. (1971) *The Swahili Coast: Politics, Diplomacy and Trade on the East African Littoral, 1798–1856* (London: Allen & Unwin)

Norris, H.T. (1975) *The Tuaregs* (Warminster: Aris & Philips)

Northrup, D. (1976) 'The compatibility of the slave and palm oil trades in the Bight of Biafra', *JAH*, 17, 3, pp.352–64

Nuñez, B. (1980) *Dictionary of Afro-Latin American Civilization* (Westport, Conn: Greenwood Press)

Nwani, O.A. (1975) 'The quanitity theory in the early monetary system of West Africa with particular emphasis on Nigeria, 1850–1895', *Journal of Political Economy*, 83, 1, pp.185–93

Ochsenwald, W. (1980) 'Muslim–European conflict in the Hijaz: the slave trade controversy, 1840–1895', *Middle Eastern Studies*, 16, 1, pp.115–26

Oded, A. (1974) *Islam in Uganda* (New York: Halsted Press)

Ogot, B.A. (1967) *A History of the Southern Luo People, 1500–1900* (Nairobi: EAPH)

Ogot, B.A. (ed.) (1974) *Zamani: A Survey of East African History* (2nd edn, Nairobi: EAPH)

Ogot, B.A. (1976) *Kenya Before 1900* (Nairobi: EAPH)

Ogot, B.A. (1979) 'Population movements between East Africa, the Horn of Africa and the neighbouring countries', in *The African Slave Trade from the Fifteenth to the Nineteenth Century* (Unesco, General History of Africa, Studies and Documents, 2, Paris), pp.175–82

Ogot, B.A. and Kieran, J.A. (eds) (1968) *Zamani: A Survey of East African History* (Nairobi: EAPH)

Olaniyan, R. (1974) 'British desires for legitimate trade in West Africa, 1860–1874: 1, the Imperial dilemma', *Odu*, 9, pp.23–44

Oliveira Martins, F.A. (ed.) (1952) 'Hermenegildo Capelo e Roberto Ivens, vol. II', in *Diarios da viagem de Angola a contra-costa* (Lisbon), pp.366–83

Oliver, R. (1965) *The Missionary Factor in East Africa* (2nd edn, London: Longman)

Oliver, R. and Fage, J.D. (1962) *A Short History of Africa* (Harmondsworth: Penguin)

Oliver, R. and Mathew, G. (eds) (1963) *A History of East Africa*, Vol. 1 (Oxford: Clarendon Press)

Oloruntimehin, B.O. (1972a) *The Segu Tukulor Empire* (London: Longman)

Oloruntimehin, B.O. (1972b) 'The impact of the abolition movement on the social and political development of West Africa in the nineteenth and twentieth centures', *Ibadan*, 7, 1, pp.33–58

Omer-Cooper, J.D. (1966) *The Zulu Aftermath, A Nineteenth Century Revolution in Bantu Africa* (London: Longman)

Ottenberg, S. (1958) 'Ibo oracles and intergroup relations', *Southwestern Journal of Anthropology*, 14, 3, pp.295–317

Packard, R.M. (1981) *Chiefship and Cosmology: An Historical Study of Political Competition* (Bloomington: Indiana University Press)

Page, M.E. (1974) 'The Manyena hordes of Tippu Tip: a case study in social stratification and the slave trade in East Africa', *IJAHS*, 7, 1, pp.69–84

Pallinder-Law, A. (1974) 'Aborted modernization in West Africa: The case of Abeokuta', *JAH*, 15, 1, pp.65–82

Palmer, H.R. (1928) *Sudanese Memoirs* (Lagos: Government Printer)

Palmer, R. and Parsons, N. (eds) (1977) *The Roots of Rural Poverty in Central and Southern Africa* (London: Heinemann)

Pankhurst, R.K.P. (1964) 'Ethiopia and the Red Sea and Gulf of Aden ports in the nineteenth and twentieth centuries', *Ethiopia Observer*, 8

Pankhurst, R.K.P. (1966) 'The Emperor Theodore and the question of foreign artisans in Ethiopia' in *Boston University Papers in African History*, Vol. 2 (Boston: African Studies Centre, Boston University)

Pankhurst, R.K.P. (1968) *Economic History of Ethiopia 1800–1935* (Addis Ababa: Haile Sellasie I University, Institute of Ethiopian Studies)

Pankhurst, R.K.P. (1973) 'The library of Emperor Téwodros at Maqdala (Magdala)' *BSOAS*, 36, pp.17–42

Pankhurst, R.K.P. (1974) 'Téwodros. The question of a Greco-Romanian or Russian hermit or adventurer in nineteenth-century Ethiopia', *Abba Salama*, 5, pp.136–59

Parrinder, E.G. (1947) 'The Yoruba-speaking peoples of Dahomey', *Africa*, 17, pp.122–48

Parrinder, E.G. (1967) *Story of Ketu* (Ibadan: IUP)

Patterson, O. (1982) *Slavery and Social Death: A Comparative Study* (Cambridge, Mass: HUP)

Person, Y. (1968–75) *Samori, une Révolution Dyula* (3 vols, Dakar, IFAN)

Person, Y. (1972) 'Samori and resistance to the French', in R. Rotberg and A. Mazrui (eds), *Protest and Power in Black Africa* (New York: OUP), pp.80–112

Peterson, J. (1969) *Province of Freedom. A History of Sierra Leone, 1787–1870* (London: Faber)

Phiri, K.M. (1975) 'Chewa history in Central Malawi and the use of oral traditons, 1600–1920' (PhD thesis, University of Wisconsin)

Plowden, W.C. (1868) *Travels in Abyssinia and the Galla Country* (London: Longmans Green)

Porter, A. (1963) *Creoledom: A Study of the Development of Freetown Society* (London: OUP)

Price, R. (1973) *Maroon Societies* (New York: Doubleday-Anchor)

Priestley, M. (1969) *West African Trade and Coast Society, A Family Study* (London: OUP)

Quinn, C.A. (1972) *Mandingo Kingdoms of the Senegambia: Traditionalism, Islam and European Expansion* (London: OUP)

al-Rafe'i, A.R. (1948) *Asr Isma'il* (2nd edn, Cairo Maktabat al-Nahdah al-Misriyyah)
al-Rafe,i, A.R. (1951) '*Asr Mohammad-Ali* (3rd edn, Cairo: Maktabat al-Nahdah al-Misriyyah)
Raison, F. (1970) 'Un tournant dans l'histoire religieuse merina du XIXe siècle: la fondation des temples protestants à Tananarive entre 1861 et 1869, *Annales de l'Université de Madagascar* (série Lettres et Sciences humaines), 11, pp.11–56
Ralibera, D. (1977) 'Recherches sur la conversion de Ranavalona II', *Omaly sy Anio*, 7–8 pp.7–42
Ranger, T.O. (ed.) (1968) *Emerging Themes of African History* (Nairobi: EAPH)
Ranger, T.O. and Kimambo, I. (eds) (1972) *The Historical Study of African Religion* (Berkeley: UCP)
Rangley, W.H.J. (1959) 'The Makololo of Dr. Livingstone', *Nyasaland Journal*, 12, pp.59–98
Raombaha (1980) *Histoires I* (edn and French trans. by S. Ayache, Fianarantosa)
Rasmussen, R.K. (1977) *Mzilikazi of the Ndebele* (London: Heinemann)
Rasoamioraramanana, M. (1974) *Aspects économiques et sociaux de la vie à Majunga 1862–1881* (TER, Département d'histoire)
Rasoamioraramanana, M. (1981) 'Pouvoir merina et esclavage dans le Boina dans la deuxième moitié du XIXe siècle, 1862–1883' (Colloque sur l'histoire du nord-ouest, Majunga)
Renault, F. (1976) *Libération d'esclaves et nouvelle servitude* (Abidjan-Dakar: NEA)
Renault, F. and Daget, S. (1980) 'La traite des esclaves en Afrique', *Etudes scientifiques* (Cairo)
Reynolds, E. (1974a) *Trade and Economic Change on the Gold Coast, 1807–1874* (London: Longman)
Reynolds, E. (1974b) 'The rise and fall of an African merchant class on the Gold Coast, 1830–1874', *CEA*, 14, 2, pp.253–64
Reynolds, E. (1975) 'Economic imperialism: the case of the Gold Coast', *Journal of Economic History*, 35, 1, pp.94–116
Rivlin, H.A.B. (1961) *The Agricultural Policy of Muhammad 'Ali in Egypt* (Cambridge, Mass: HUP)
Roberts, A.D. (ed.) (1968) *Tanzania before 1900* (Nairobi: EAPH)
Roberts, A.D. (1973) *A History of the Bemba* (Madison: UWP)
Roberts, R. (1980) 'Long distance trade and production: Sinsani in the nineteenth century', *JAH*, 21, 2, pp.169–88
Robinson, R. (1985) 'The Berlin Conference of 1884–85 and the Scramble for Africa', in *Proceedings of the Conference on the Berlin West African Conference* (Berlin, February 1985, edited by the German Historical Institute, London)
Rodney, W. (1970) *A History of the Upper Guinea Coast 1545–1800* (Oxford: Clarendon Press)
Rodney, W. (1972) *How Europe Underdeveloped Africa* (London: Bogle l'Ouverture)
Roncek, J.S. and Kiernan, T. (eds) (1970) *The Negro Impact on Western Civilization* (New York: Philosophical Library)
Ronen, D. (1971) 'On the African role in the trans-Atlantic slave trade in Dahomey', *CEA*, 11, 1, pp.5–13
Ross, D. (1967) 'The rise of the autonomous kingdom of Dahomey, 1818–1894, (PhD thesis, University of London)
Rubenson, S. (1966) *King of Kings: Téwodros of Ethiopia* (Nairobi: OUP)

Sabry, M. (1930) *L'Empire égyptien sous Mohamed Ali et la question d'Orient (1811–1849)* (Paris: Paul Geuthner)

Sabry, M. (1933) *L'empire égyptien sous Ismail et l'ingérence anglo-française* (1863–1879) (Paris: Paul Geuthner)

Saint-Martin, Y. (1967) *L'empire toucouleur et la France, un demi-siècle de relations diplomatiques (1846–1893)* (Dakar: Publications de la Faculté de lettres et sciences humaines)

Sanders, P. (1975) *Moshoeshoe: Chief of the Sotho* (London: Heinemann)

Santi, P. and Hill, R. (eds) (1980) *The Europeans in the Sudan 1834–1878* (Oxford: Clarendon Press)

Sarbah, J.M. (1906) *Fanti National Constitution* (London: Clowes)

Saunders, C. and Derricourt, R. (eds) (1974) *Beyond the Cape Frontier, Studies in the History of the Transkei and Ciskei* (London: Longman)

Schnapper, B. (1961) *La politique et le commerce français dans le golfe de Guinée de 1838 à 1871* (Paris and the Hague: Mouton)

Schnapper, B. (1959) 'La fin du régime de l'exclusif: le commerce étranger dans les possessions franéaises d'Afrique tropicale (1817–1870)', *Annales Africaines*, pp.149–99

Schnerb, R. (1957) *Le XIXe siècle, L'apogée de l'expansion européenne (1815–1914)* (Paris: PUF)

Schuler, M. (1970) 'Ethnic slave rebellions in the Caribbean and the Guianas', *Journal of Social History* 3, 4

Serjeant, R.B. (1966) 'South Arabia and Ethiopia – African elements in the South Arabian population', *Proceedings of the 3rd International Conference of Ethiopian Studies*, Vol. 1, pp.25–33

Shea, P.J. (1974) 'Economies of scale and the dyeing industry of precolonial Kano', *Kano Studies*, no. 1, 2, pp.55–61

Shepperson, G. and Price, T. (1958) *Independent Africa: John Chilembwe and the Origins, Setting and Significance of the Nyasaland Native Uprising of 1915* (Edinburgh: Edinburgh University Press)

Sheriff, A.M.H. (1971) 'The rise of a commercial empire: an aspect of the economic history of Zanzibar, 1780–1873' (PhD thesis, University of London)

Shorter, A. (1972) *Chiefship in Western Tanzania: A Policital History of the Kimbu* (Oxford: Clarendon Press)

Simpson, G.E. (1978) *Black Religions in the New World* (New York: Columbia University Press)

Skinner, E.P. (1964) *The Mossi of Upper Volta: The Political Development of a Sudanese People* (Stanford: SUP)

Slama, B. (1967) *L'insurrection de 1864 en Tunisie* (Tunis: Maison tunisienne de l'édition)

Smaldone, J.P. (1972) 'Firearms in the Central Sudan: a revaluation', *JAH*, 13, 4, pp.591–608

Smaldone, J.P. (1977) *Warfare in the Sokoto Caliphate (Cambridge: CUP)*

Smith, A.K. (1973) 'The peoples of Southern Mozambique: an historical survey', *JAH*, 14, 4, pp.565–80

Smith, E.W. (1956) 'Sebetwane and the Makalolo', *African Studies*, 15, 2, pp.49–74

Smith, H.F.C. (1961) 'A neglected theme of West African history; the Islamic revolutions of the 19th century' *JHSN*, 2, 2, pp.169–85

Smith, M.G. (1960) *Government in Zazzau* (London: OUP)

Smith, M.G. (1978) *The Affairs of Daura* (Berkeley: UCP)

Soumoni, E. (1983) 'Trade and politics in Dahomey 1841–1892, with particular reference to the House of Regis' (PhD thesis, University of Ife)

Sow, A.I. (1968) *Chroniques et récits du Fuuta Jallon* (Paris: Klincksieck)

Spear, T. (1972) 'Zwangendaba's Ngoni 1821–1890: a political and social history of a migration' (Occasional Paper No. 4 of the African Studies Program, University of Wisconsin, Madison)

Spear, T. (1981) *Kenya's Past: An Introduction to Historical Method in Africa* (London: Longman)

Stamm, A. (1972) 'La société créole à Saint-Paul de Loanda dans les années 1838–1848', *RFHOM*, 217, pp.578–610

Stanley, H.M. (1874) *Coomassie and Magdala* (London: Sampson, Low, Marston, Low & Searle)

Stanley, H.M. (1878) *Through the Dark Continent* (2 vols, London: Low, Marston, Searle & Rivington)

Staudenraus, P.J. (1961) *The African Colonization Movement, 1816–1863* (New York: Columbia University Press)

Stefaniszyn, B. and de Santana, H. (1960) 'The rise of the Chikunda condottieri', *Northern Rhodesian Journal*, 4, pp.361–8

Stengers, J. (1962) 'L'impérialisme colonial de la fin du XIXe siècle; mythe ou réalité', *JAH*, 3, 3, pp.469–91

Stewart, C.C. and Stewart E.K. (1973) *Islam and the Social Order in Mauritania: A Case Study from the nineteenth century* (Oxford: Clarendon Press)

Stokes, E. and Brown, R. (eds) (1966) *The Zambezian Past: Studies in Central African History* (Manchester: MUP)

Swai, B. (1984) Precolonial states and European merchant capital in Eastern Africa', in A Salim (ed.), *State Formation in Eastern Africa* (London: Heinemann), pp.15–35

Szymanski, E. (1965) 'La guerre hispano-marocaine 1859–1860', *Rocznik orientalistyczny*, 2, pp.54–64

al-Tahtāwï, R.R. (1869) *Manāhedj al-albāb al-Miṣriyya fi mabāhedj al-ādā al-ʿaṣriyya*

Tal, Al-Hajj ʿUmar (1983) *Bayān Mawaḳa* (trans. S.M. Mahibou and J.L. Triaud) (Paris: Editioins du CNRS)

Tambo, D.C. (1976) 'The Sokoto caliphate slave trade in the nineteenth century', *IJAHS*, 9, 2, pp.187–217

Teixeira Da Mota, A. (1954) *Guiné Portuguesa* (2 vols, Lisbon: Agencia Geral do Ultramar)

Temini, A. (1978) *Le beylik de Constantine et Hadj Ahmed Bey (1830–1837)* (Tunis: Publications de la RHM)

Temperley, H. (1972) *British Anti-Slavery, 1823–1870* (London: Longman)

Terray, E. (1972) *Marxism and 'Primitive' Societies* (New York: Monthly Review Press)

Theal, G.M. (1891) *History of South Africa, 1795–1834* (London: Swan, Sonnenschein)

Theal, G.M. (1900) *History of South Africa: The Republics and Native Territories from 1854–1872* (London: Swan, Sonnenschein)

Thomas, R. and Bean, R. (1974) 'The fishers of men: the profits of the slave trade', *Journal of Economic History*, 34, 4, pp.885–914

Thompson, L. (ed.) (1969) *African Societies in Southern Africa* (London: Heinemann)

Thompson, L. (1975) *Survival in Two Worlds: Moshoeshoe of Lesotho 1786–1870* (Oxford: Clarendon Press)

Thompson, V. and Adloff, R. (1965) *The Malagasy Republic: Madagascar Today* (Stanford: SUP)

Tiendrebeogo, Y. (1964) *Histoire et coutumes royales des Mossi de Ouagadougou* (Ouagadougou: Naba)

Toledano, E. (1982) *The Ottoman Slave Trade and its Suppression, 1840–1890* (Princeton: PUP)

Toplin, R.B. (ed.) (1974) *Slavery and Race Relations in Latin America* (Westport, Conn.: Greenwood Press)

Toplin, R.B. (ed.) (1981) *Freedom and Prejudice: The Legacy of Slavery in the United States and Brazil* (Westport, Conn.: Greenwood Press)

Townsend, W.J. (1892) *Madagascar: Its Missionaries and Martyrs* (London: Partridge and Co.)

Trimingham, J.S. (1952) *Islam in Ethiopia* (London: OUP)

Trimingham, J.S. (1962) *A History of Islam in West Africa* (London: OUP)

Trimingham, J.S. and Fyfe, C. (1960) 'The early expansion of Islam in Sierra Leone', *Sierra Leone Bulletin of Religions*, 2

Tukur, M.M. (1977) 'Values and public affairs: the relevance of the Sokoto Caliphal experience to the transformation of the Nigeran polity' (PhD thesis, Ahmadu Bello University)

Twaddle, M. (1966) 'The founding of Mbale', *UJ*, 30, I, pp.25–38

Tyam, M.A. (1961) *La Vie d'El-Hadj Omar* (Qacida en Poular) (trans. H. Gaden, Paris)

Tylden, G. (1950) *Rise of the Basuto* (Cape Town: Juta and Co)

Tzadua, P. (1968) *The Petha Nagast, The Law of Kings* (Addis Ababa)

Ullendorff, E. (1960) *The Ethiopians* (London: OUP)

Usman, Y.B. (ed.) (1979) *Studies in the History of the Sokoto Caliphate* (Sokoto, State Historical Bureau)

Uzoigwe, G.N. (1973) 'The slave trade and African society', *THSG*, 14, 2, pp.187–212

Valensi, L. (1969a) *Le Maghreb avant la prise d'Alger 1790–1830* (Paris: Flammarion)

Valensi, L. (1969b) 'Islam et capitalisme: production et commerce des chéchias en Tunisie et en France aux 18e et 19e siècles', *Revue d'histoire moderne et contemporaine*, 17, pp.376–400

Valensi, L. (1977) *Fellahs tunisiens. L'économie rurale et la vie des campagnes aux 18e et 19e siècles* (Paris & The Hague: Mouton)

Valette, J. (1960) *Les Relations extérieures de Madagascar au XIXème siècle* (Tananarive: Imprimerie officielle)

Valette, J. (1962) *Etude sur le règne de Radama 1* (Tananarive: Imprimerie nationale)

Van Jaarsveld, F.A. (1961) *The Awakening of Afrikaner Nationalism 1868–1881* (Cape Town: Human & Rousseau)

Vansina, J. (1966) *Kingdoms of the Savanna* (Madison: University of Wisconsin Press)

Vatin, J.C. (1974) *L'Algérie politique, Histoire et société* (Paris: A. Colin)

Vellut, J.-L. (1972) 'Notes sur le Lunda et la frontière luso-africaine (1700–1900)' *Etudes d'histoire africaine*, 3, pp.61–166

Vellut, J.-L. (1975) 'Le royaume de Cassange et les réseaux luso-africains (ca.1750–1810)' *CAE*, 15, 1, pp.117–36

Verbeken, A. (1956) *Msiri, roi de Garenganze l'homme rouge du Katanga* (Brussels)

Verger, P. (1955) 'Yoruba influences in Brazil', *Odu* 1, 3

Verger, P. (1968) *Flux et reflux de la traite des nègres entre le golfe de Bénin et Bahia de Todos los Santos, du XVIIe au XIXe siècle* (Paris: Mouton)

Verger, P. (1976) *Trade Relations between the Bight of Benin and Bahia* (Ibadan: Ibadan University Press)

Voll, J.O. (1969) 'A history of the Khatmiyyah tariqa' (PhD thesis, Harvard University)

Waïgalo, N. (1977) 'Le Macina de 1853 à 1896' (dissertation, Bamako)

Walker, E.A. (1957) *A History of Southern Africa* (3rd edn, London: Longmans Green)

Walker, J.W. St. G. (1976) *The Black Loyalists: The Search for a Promised Land in Nova Scotia and Sierra Leone, 1783–1870* (New York, Africana Publishing Co.)

Wallerstein, I. (1976) 'The three stages of African involvement in the world-economy', in P.C.W. Gutkind and I. Wallerstein (eds), *The Political Economy of Contemporary Africa* (Beverly Hills: Sage), pp.30–57

Wallerstein, I. (1980) *The Modern World-System: Vol. 2 Mercantilism and the Consolidation of the European World Economy, 1600–1750* (New York: Academic Press)

Wallerstein, I. (1989) *The Modern World System III: The Second Era of Great Expansion of the Capitalist World-Economy, 1730–1840* (San Diego: Academic Press)

Were, G.S. (1967) *A History of the Abaluyia of Western Kenya: 1500–1930* (Nairobi: EAPH)

Wheeler, D.L. and Pélissier, R. (1971) *Angola* (New York: Praeger)

Wilks, I. (1975) *Asante in the Nineteenth Century: The Structure and Evolution of a Political Order* (Cambridge: CUP)
Williams, E. (1944) *Capitalism and Slavery* (London: Deutsch)
Willis, J.R. (1978) 'The Torodbe clerisy: a social view', *JAH*, 19, 2, pp. 195–212
Willis, J.R. (ed.) (1979) *Studies in West African Islamic History: The Cultivators of Islam* (London: Cass)
Willis, A.J. (1967) *An Introduction to the History of Central Africa* (2nd edn, London: OUP)
Wilson, A. (1972) 'Long-distance trade and the Luba Lomani empire', *JAH*, 13, 4, pp.575–89
Wilson, M. and Thompson, L. (eds) (1969) *The Oxford History of South Africa, Vol. I: South Africa to 1870* (Oxford: Clarendon Press)
Wylie, K.C. (1977) *The Political Kingdom of the Temne: Temne Government in Sierra Leone, 1825–1910* (New York: Africana Publishing)
Wyse, A.J.G. (1989) *The Krio of Sierra Leone, an Interpretative History* (London)

Ylvisaker, M. (1983) *Lamu in the Nineteenth Century: Land, Trade and Politics* (Boston: Boston University Press)
Yoder, J.C. (1974) 'Fly and elephant parties: political polarization in Dahomey, 1840–1870', *JAH*, 15, 3, pp.417–32

Zebadia, A. (1974) 'The career and correspondence of Ahmed al-Bakkāy of Tombuctu: an historical study of his political and religious role from 1847 to 1866' (PhD thesis, University of London)
Zewde Gabre-Sellassie (1975) *Yohannes IV of Ethiopia* (Oxford: Clarendon Press)
Ziadeh, N. (1958) *Sanūsīyah: A Study of a Revivalist Movement in Islam* (Leiden: Brill)

Index

al-Abbās, 133, 135, 137
'Abd al Ķādir, 4, 201–2, 212
'Abdallāh al-Nadīm (1843–96), 139
Abẹokuta, 15, 24, 35, 37, 283, 284, 285, 318
  see also Egba
Abonema, 298
Adare language, 155
Aden, 81, 154
Africa
  Anglo-French rivalry in, 4, 12
  balance of power, 320–1
  capitalist expansion, 11
  centralization, 23–4, 25
  changes in, 1–2, 8, 9, 13, 68, 70, 315
  commercial unification of, 25
  demography, 2–3, 15
  development of, 2, 8
  diaspora, 291, 305, 314
  economic trends, 25
  effects of slave trade, 3, 319–20
  European interest in, 3–5
  and external trade, 5, 321
  and foreign wives, 85
  impact of, 312–14
  impact of Egypt on, 139
  impact of Europe on, 1–2, 19, 320–1
  incorporation in world economy, 10–14, 25
  internal initiatives in, 7–8
  Islamic revolutions in, 15–16
  legacy of wars in, 322
  military systems, 318–19
  missionaries in, 4–5, 17–19, 33, 317–18, 321
  modernization, 24, 58
  patterns of authority in, 7
  political trends, 23–5, 316–18
  reactions to abolition of slavery, 30–5

  religions of, 16, 19, 23
  social and economic transformation, 319–20
  sources for, 1
  underdevelopment of, 176, 315, 316
  unification efforts in, 317
  Western-educated elite in, 19–21, 22, 24, 25
  Western education in, 5, 17–19, 25
  see also Central Africa; East Africa; North Africa; South Africa; Southern Africa; West Africa
Africans
  and 'African personality', 22, 23
  in Americas, 305, 308–11, 312, 314
  in Europe, 305, 308
  in Middle East and Asia, 305, 307–8
  participation in slave trade, 89
  relations with Boers, 64–5
  repatriation of, 314
  in South Africa, 61–3
  and white settlers, 50, 51
  see also traders, African
age-grades, 7, 41, 42, 44, 45–6, 48, 49, 76, 96, 318
agents, 1, 8
agriculture, 3, 5–7, 8, 10, 11, 12, 13, 18, 25, 35, 111, 126, 144, 174, 209, 210, 254
  in Cape Colony, 51, 53
  in Egypt, 134–5
  of northern Nguni, 40–1, 47
  and poor soils, 115, 117
  and population densities, 112–15
  in Sokoto, 230, 231
  in Tukuloor, 248–9
  in Volta region,

  see also food production; production
Agwe, 291
Ahaggar Tuareg, 212, 213
Aḥmad Bey (1837–55), 185, 200
Aḥmad Lobbo see Seku Aḥmadu
Ahmadu (1862–78), 248, 249–51, 254
Ahmadu mo Ahmadu, 243, 245, 246
Ahmadu Seku (1845–53), 242–3
Aja, 279, 281, 285, 288, 289
Akan, 265, 278
Akoko, 279, 281, 289
Albany, 50, 51, 53, 57
Alexandria, 4, 129, 134, 135, 138
Algeria, 24, 199, 211, 212, 214
  administration of, 201, 202, 205
  army in, 201, 202
  colonialism in, 207
  crisis (1866–89), 181–2
  foreign capital in, 205, 206
  French conquest of, 12, 178, 181, 183, 188, 200–6, 216
  Islam, 205
  resistance in, 201–2, 207, 208
  taxation, 181
Algiers, 4, 176, 178, 182, 199, 201
Ambo, 73
Ambongo, 165
Ambundu, 114
America see United States
  see also Americas
American crops, 114, 117, 126
Americas, 10, 11, 305, 308–11, 312, 14
Amhara, 150, 152
amir, 6, 7, 16, 227, 230, 231, 269
Andalusia, 190
Andrianampoinimerina (1792–1810), 164–5
Anglican Church, 19, 21
Angola, 2, 4, 13, 21

agriculture, 117
chiefdoms, 126
and Lunda state, 124, 126
population density in, 114
Portuguese in, 123
slave labour in, 120, 123
trade, 118
animal rearing, 115, 117, 210
Antananarivo, 165, 172
Arabs, 79, 81, 85–7, 88, 91, 128, 133,
140, 147, 154, 201, 212, 276
see also Omani Arabs; traders, Arab
Arkiko, 152, 154
armies, 138, 142, 148, 157, 165, 167,
174, 185, 190, 194, 196, 200,
201, 202, 229, 245, 246, 248,
318, 321
Aro, 7, 298, 299
Asante empire, 262–6, 275, 276, 316
Asia, 86, 139
Awori, 279, 281
Awsa, 154, 163

Badagry, 4, 35, 279, 289, 291
Bagabo, 109
Baganda, 86
Bagemder, 150, 152, 157
Bahr al-Ghazāl, 145, 147
Bajuni, 81
Bakama, 298
Baker, Samuel, 145
Bambara, 15, 222, 239, 241, 242,
245, 251, 262, 271, 275, 276
Bamenda, 302
Banjul, 4
Bantu, 19, 39, 114, 292, 301, 302
Barbados, 312, 314
Barbulle, 269
Bardera, 154–5
Bari, 144, 145
Bariba, 279, 281
Bashingo traders, 109
Bassa Cover, 34
Basuba traders, 107
beads, 10
Beduins, 134, 135, 214
al-Bekkai, 246
Bell, John, 157
Bemba kingdom, 72, 78
Benadir, 81, 85, 154–5
Benguela, 120, 128
Benin, 37, 279, 281, 283, 289, 294,
316
decline of, 285–6
European interest in, 286–8
Benue, 31
Berbera, 154
Berbers, 178, 219

Bete, 258, 259
Bezanozano, 165
Bimbia, 301–2
Bisa, 70, 84, 269
Black Volta, 272
Bloodmen, 300–1
Blyden, Edward Wilmot, 21, 22, 23
Boers, 39, 62, 65, 320
and British, 4–5, 47, 49, 51, 56,
59, 63, 64, 65, 66
in Cape Colony, 50, 51
and defeat of Zulus, 57
and Great Trek, 13, 49, 56–7, 58
independence of, 61
and Mfecane, 41, 47, 49, 53–4,
56–8
pre-1870 republics, 63–4
relations with Africans, 64–5
Bonny, 295, 296, 298
Borgu, 279, 281, 283, 288, 289
Borno, 16, 225, 227, 229, 230,
234–8, 272
Brahima, 269
Brazil, 28, 31, 71, 289, 290, 291, 310,
311, 312
brotherhoods, Islamic, 16, 85, 178,
82, 186, 187, 189, 192, 202,
207, 213, 214, 219, 220, 221–3,
224, 243, 245, 254, 256, 317
Buganda, 16, 17, 24, 84, 86, 91, 102,
104, 105, 109, 110, 145, 316
Bugerere, 105
Buguma, 298
Bukerebe state, 107, 109
Bulawayo, 45
Bunafu, 6, 7, 110
Bundu, 219, 220
Bunyoro, 24, 100, 104, 105, 109, 110,
145
Burundi, 24, 94, 100, 104, 115
Busa, 279
Busoga, 6, 104, 105, 107, 110
Busuma, 268
Buvuma, 107
Buzinza, 107

Cairo, 4, 8, 118, 129, 134, 135, 148
Calabar, 31, 35, 298, 299–301, 320
Caliphates, 218, 221, 224, 227–31
see also Sokoto Caliphate
camel nomads, 209, 210, 212–13,
216
Cameroon, 3, 35, 218, 299, 301–2
Europeans in, 304
missionaries in, 302, 304
slave trade, 31, 302, 304
Cape Coast, 4
Cape Colony, 4, 13, 18, 19, 47, 59, 65

African-white relations in, 50–1,
54
agriculture, 51, 53
before 1870, 61–2
British-Xhosa conflict in, 55, 56,
61
cheap labour in, 51, 53, 55, 57–8
defeat of Ngwane, 54–5
economic problems, 51
effects of Mfecane in, 57–8
influx of migrants to, 51–4
Mfengu-Xhosa relations, 55–6
war with Lesotho, 65, 67
see also South Africa
Cape Palmas (Maryland), 34
capitalism *see* world-economy
caravans, 118, 126, 186, 213
Caribbean, 10, 311, 312
Casamance, 255
cash crops, 12, 13
caste groups, 222, 223, 275
cattle, 7, 41, 47, 49, 96, 98, 111, 174,
210, 222
cavalry, 318, 319
Central Africa, 39, 91
abolition of slave trade, 73
acculturation in, 73, 77
changes in, 68, 70
conquest of poor soils, 115, 117
Christian missionaries in, 17, 18,
99
demography, 114–15
domestic slavery, 78
effect of Nguni and Kololo
invasions, 75–8
exploration of, 99
incorporation in world-economy,
70, 73, 78, 117–18
negative effects of slavery in, 73
new states in, 71–2, 77
political instability, 78
political systems, 124
population growth, 3, 115, 123
Portuguese in, 120, 123, 128
power in, 124, 126, 128
slave trade, 10, 70–3, 77, 117, 120,
123
sparse and dense populations,
112–15
trade, 25, 117–23, 124, 126, 128
Western-educated elite in, 19
centralization, 7, 23–4, 25, 39, 76, 86,
93, 124, 126, 148, 275
Cetshwayo, 65
Chamgamire empire, 48, 76
Chewa, 70
chiefs, 124, 126, 128, 157
see also rulers

Chokwe, 2, 25, 115, 124, 126, 316
Christianity, 17, 19, 22–3, 24, 25, 56, 58, 99, 165, 276, 278, 289, 296
  and abolition of slave trade, 27, 32, 33, 35, 37, 38
  in Ethiopia, 150, 151, 162, 163
  impact of, 317–18
  in Madagascar, 165, 167, 169, 171–2, 175
  in Sotho state, 47
  see also missionaries, Christian
Church Missionary Society (CMS), 17, 18, 23, 99, 296
circumcision, 42–3, 44
cities, 178, 180
  see also towns
Ciwere Ndhlou, 76
cloth *see* textile industries
cloves, 4, 13, 84, 86, 88, 98
colleges, 18, 19, 23, 276, 314
colonialism, 1, 3, 8, 11, 14, 24–5, 26, 1–3, 99, 123, 139, 175, 180, 183, 202–5, 207–8, 254, 271, 322
communities, 7
Congo Basin *see* Kongo region
Constantine, 178, 183, 201, 202
constitutional reform, 24
copper, 128, 275, 299
Copts, 17, 135, 160
Côte d'Ivoire, 37
Cotonou, 289
cotton, 12, 87, 135, 248
craftsmen, 2, 6
Creek Town, 299, 300, 301
Creoles, 4, 21, 34, 120, 257, 259
Cross river basin, 292, 299–301
Crowther, Bishop Samuel Ajayi, 21, 291, 296
Cuba, 28, 71, 289, 311, 312
cultural borrowing, 73, 77
cultural identification, 2
cultural interaction, 16, 85–6
Cyrenaica, 16, 212, 214

Dagomba, 265, 272, 276
Dahomey, 12, 31, 35, 37, 279, 281, 83, 284, 285, 288, 289, 290, 316
Dajazmach Sabagadis (1822–31), 152
Dan, 259
Darfur, 118, 140, 142, 145
Datenga, 269
death rates, 115
Delagoa Bay, 41, 42, 44, 45, 49, 76
demography, 2–3, 41–2, 114–15
  see also population
Denmark, 28

depopulation, 3, 73, 117
diamonds, 5, 65
diaspora, 291, 305, 314
Dida, 258, 259
dina, 241–2
Dingiswayo, 42, 43, 44
Dinguiraye, 223, 245, 246, 248
diseases, 73, 98, 115, 185
Divane, James M., 19
djihāds, 6–7, 15–16, 24, 154, 202, 207, 216, 232, 238, 243–8, 269, 271, 276, 283, 315, 317
  consequences of, 224
  and emigrations, 223, 225, 232
  and Fulbe, 222, 239, 241, 286, 289
  and Hausa states, 225, 227
  and Massina, 239, 241
  reconstruction after, 227
  sources of, 219–21
  support for, 221–3
Duala, 301, 302
Duke Town, 299, 300, 301
Dutch, 4, 5, 28, 29
Dyula (Juula), 16, 255, 260, 261, 268, 272, 275

East Africa, 6
  abolition of slave trade, 37, 98
  Christian missionaries in, 17, 18, 99
  coast-hinterland trade, 83–4, 88–93
  coastal peoples (c.1800), 79–81
  cultural interaction in, 85–6
  effects of trade expansion, 84–6, 93–4
  European interest in, 98–9
  exploration of, 98–9
  incorporation in world-economy, 13, 87, 88
  and international trade, 86–7
  Islam in, 87, 89
  Maasai wars, 96, 98
  migrations, 2
  Nguni invasion of, 94, 96
  Omani influence in, 81
  slave trade in, 84, 86, 87, 88, 89, 93, 307
  social structure, 85, 89
  state formation in, 93, 94
  trade in, 25, 84–7, 88–94
  trade with Great Lakes region, 107, 109, 110
  trade with Zambezi valley, 70, 71
  Western-educated elite in, 19
  see also Great Lakes region
Edo, 279, 281, 285

education, Western, 5, 18–19, 23, 25, 37, 58, 137, 165, 169, 172, 200, 276, 289, 317, 318
Efik, 292, 298, 299, 304
Egba, 279, 281, 283, 284, 289, 318
Egbado, 279, 281, 283
Egypt, 4, 8, 17, 118, 154, 206, 209, 315, 316, 317
  agriculture and land use, 134–5, 138
  Anglo-French rivalry, 12, 129, 131
  army in, 138, 142
  centralization, 24
  changes in, 2
  cultural development, 135–7
  education, 136–7
  and Ethiopia, 152, 154, 162–3
  expansion into Africa, 134
  foreign control of, 137–8
  incorporation in world economy, 11–12, 134, 137
  impact of, 139
  Islam in, 129, 138–9
  modernization of, 135, 142
  national movement in, 129–34
  Revolution (1881–2), 138–9
  and the Sudan, 139, 140, 142, 145, 149
Ekiti, 279, 281, 283, 285, 289
Ekitiparapo, 283–4
Ekpe society, 300–1, 304
Elem-Kalabari, 295, 296, 298
elites, 5, 19–21
Embu, 85
emirates, 224, 227, 228–9, 230, 232
Enarya kingdom, 155, 157
Equatoria, 145
Ethiopia, 8, 17, 22, 307, 315, 317
  abolition of slave trade, 159
  centralization, 24
  Christianity in, 150, 151, 159, 162, 163
  conflict with Britain, 160
  and Egypt, 139, 162–3
  Islam in, 150, 151, 162
  political disorganization of, 150–4
  reunification efforts, 157–60
  unity under Yohannes IV, 161–3
Ethiopianism, 22–3
Europe, 7, 8, 12, 14, 45, 252, 254, 255, 261, 272, 286, 302, 304, 315, 316
  and abolition of slave trade, 27–9, 35
  Africans in, 305, 308
  and African underdevelopment, 176
  and Benin, 286–8

and Central African trade, 118, 120
and East African trade, 86–7, 98–9
and Egypt, 137, 138
impact on Africa, 1–2, 9, 19,
    317–18, 320–1, 322
increased interest in Africa, 3–5
and Libya, 199–200, 207
and Madagascar, 167, 169–70,
    172, 175
and Maghrib, 180–1, 199, 205–6,
    207–8
and Morocco, 190, 192–7
and Niger delta, 292, 294, 296,
    298, 304
trade with Africa, 5, 321
and Tunisia, 185, 199–200
Europeans, 1, 10, 149, 160, 180–1,
    182, 183, 189, 292, 299, 320,
    321
Ewe, 279
exploration, 3, 98–9, 296, 299, 304
exports, 3, 10, 12, 13, 25, 35, 98
    see also trade, external

fallāhin, 134, 135, 139, 142
famine, 41, 48, 73, 91, 93, 98, 107,
    85, 186, 197
Fang, 2, 304
Fante Confederacy, 24, 25, 259, 262,
    265, 266, 276, 318
Far East, 27, 28, 139, 305
Fashoda, 144, 145
females, 41, 42
Ferrobe, 269
feudalism, 150, 157
firearms, 5, 27, 54, 91, 94, 105, 109,
    110, 124, 128, 147, 152, 216,
    299, 318, 319, 321, 322
Fittuga, 241
Fon, 279
food production, 105, 107, 109, 114,
    115, 117
forest areas, 3, 40, 112, 117, 120,
    257–8
Fourah Bay College, 18, 23, 276
France, 14, 81, 84, 86, 152, 154, 159,
    160, 163, 176, 180, 192, 196,
    198, 202, 211, 212–3, 222, 245,
    248, 251, 254, 255, 304, 308,
    318
    and abolition of slave trade, 27,
        28, 29, 30
    African exports to, 35
    and Benin, 286, 288
    Christian missionaries from, 17,
        19, 317
    conquest of Algeria, 178, 181,
        183, 200–6, 216

and Madagascar, 164, 167, 169,
    170, 171–2, 175
    rivalry with Britain, 4, 12, 129, 131
    and trans-Saharan trade, 214
    and Tunisia, 176, 180–1, 185, 186
    in West Africa, 4
freed slaves, 4, 5, 24, 30, 32–5, 99,
    224, 289, 290–1, 308, 310, 314
    see also Liberia; Sierra Leone
Freetown, 4, 33, 258, 317
Fuladugu kingdom, 255
Fulani, 7, 16
Fulbe, 218, 219, 220, 225, 228, 232,
    238, 242, 243, 255, 256, 257,
    261, 268, 269, 275
    djihāds of, 16, 222, 224, 239, 241,
        283, 286, 289
    influence of, 239
Fundj Sultanate, 140, 142
Fūr Sultanate, 140, 142
Futa Jallon, 219, 220, 223, 239, 243,
    46, 255–8, 260
Futa Toro, 218, 219, 220, 222, 239,
    243, 246

Ga, 266, 278
Gabon, 32, 35, 37, 302, 304
Gambia, 30, 33, 35, 255
Garvey, Marcus, 314
Gaza kingdom, 15, 45, 49
    Nguni of, 72, 75–6
Geledi, Sultan of, 154–5
Germany, 4, 14, 86, 96, 98, 99, 183,
    286, 302
Glasgow Missionary Society, 17,
    18–19
Goba, 70
Gobir, 225, 232
Gojam, 152, 155, 157, 159, 163
Gola, 258
gold, 5, 10, 65, 70, 142, 272
Gold Coast, 12, 18, 21, 24, 31, 37,
    259, 262, 265–6, 272, 320
Gondar, 150, 152, 157, 159, 160
Gonja, 265
Gordon, Charles George, 145
Gorée, 4, 37, 38
Great Britain, 24, 81, 134, 137, 138,
    152, 154, 163, 192, 200, 206,
    265–6, 284, 286, 302, 308
    and abolition of slave trade, 27,
        28, 29, 30, 98, 311
    African exports to, 35
    annexation of Transvaal, 65
    annexation of Xhosaland, 56, 59,
        61
    and Boers, 4 5, 47, 49, 50, 51, 56,
        59, 64, 65, 66

and Cape Colony, 61–2
    conflict with Ethiopia, 160
    expansion in South Africa
        (1870–80), 65
    and Lesotho, 65
    and Madagascar, 165, 167, 170,
        171, 172, 175
    and Natal, 63
    and Niger delta, 294, 295–6, 298,
        299
    rivalry with France, 4, 12, 129,
        131
    and Sierra Leone, 32, 33, 34
    supremacy of, 14
    and Xhosa, 55, 56
    and Zanzibar trade, 84, 86
Great Fish river, 50, 56
Great Lakes region, 2, 3, 86
    and coastal trade, 94
    centralization in, 24
    conflict in, 102, 104, 105, 110,
        111
    and Egypt, 139
    markets in, 105, 107
    migration in, 107
    political structure, 100–4, 111
    production and extraction, 104–5
    religious movements, 110
    trading networks, 107–10
Grebo, 259
Griqualand West, 65, 67, 320
groundnuts, 4, 12, 35
Gudu, 223, 225
Guinea-Bissau, 255, 257
Gulf of Guinea, 252, 258
Gun, 279
Guragé, 155, 163
Gurunsi, 269
Gwandu, 228
Gwangara, 76, 96
Gweno, 93

al-Hadjdj 'Umar, 15, 16, 218, 219,
    220, 221, 222, 223, 232, 243–6,
    249, 251, 256, 260, 271
Haiti, 311, 312
Hamdallahi Caliphate, 218, 224,
    241–2
Harar, 154, 155, 163
Hasan I (1873–94), 194, 196, 198
Hausa, 7, 219, 222, 225, 227, 229,
    232, 234, 251, 275, 308
Hausaland, 15, 16, 223, 239, 246, 272
Hehe, 96
Hlubi, 49
Holy Ghost Mission, 5
Horn of Africa, 139, 154–7
horses, 47

Horton, James Africanus, 21, 22–3
households, 6
Hubbu, 256–7
human reproduction, control of, 41, 46
human sacrifice, 301
hunters, 2, 41, 73, 112, 115

Ibadan, 15, 283, 284, 285, 286, 289, 318
Ibibio, 292, 299
Ibrāhīm, 131, 133
Ifẹ, 279, 281, 283, 284
Igbo, 3, 7, 285, 292, 295, 298–9
Ijaye, 283, 285, 289
Ijẹbu, 279, 281, 283, 289
Ijẹṣa, 279, 281, 284, 289
Ijọ, 285, 286, 292, 294
Ikale, 279, 281, 289
Illo, 279
Imbangala, 124
Imerina, 8
imports, 12, 94
India, 81, 88, 305, 307
Indian Ocean trade, 10, 79, 83–7, 88, 89, 91, 93
   see also slave trade, Indian Ocean
Indians, 81, 86, 88, 89, 91, 98
initiation ceremonies, 7, 41, 42–3, 48
   see also age-grades
International Financial Commission, 81, 815, 206
iron, 109, 111, 114, 174
irrigation, 3, 12, 117, 135, 144
Islam, 17, 25, 35, 208, 216, 224, 232, 248, 249, 269, 305, 316
   in Algeria, 205
   and desert nomads, 211–12
   in East Africa, 87, 89
   in Egypt, 129, 138–9
   in Ethiopia, 150, 151, 162
   and land tenure, 6–7
   law, 7, 189, 190, 192, 194, 198, 221, 224, 227–8, 241
   in Massina, 239, 241–2
   in Morocco, 189–92, 197
   in Senegambia, 252, 254–5
   and slavery, 243
   in Somalia, 155, 157
   spread of, 218
   in the Sudan, 147, 148–9
   and syncretism, 221
   in Upper Guinea, 255, 257, 260, 261
   in Volta basin, 276
   in West Africa, 218–19ff.
   see also brotherhoods, Islamic; djihāds

Ismāʿīl (1863–79), 133–4, 135, 137, 138, 145, 147, 162
Isoko, 281, 285, 289, 294
Isuwu, 301–2
Italy, 160–1, 163, 206
Itsekiri, 281, 285, 286, 289, 292
ivory, 3, 4, 13, 70, 71, 72, 79, 84, 86, 88, 93, 98, 109, 110, 117, 120, 128, 144

Jallāba, 145, 147
Jallonke, 256
Javabu, John Tengo, 19
Jawara, 245
Jaxaanke, 256
Jelgoji, 268, 269, 271
Jenne, 239, 241
Jews, 181, 182
Jieng, 145
Jiibo, 269
Jimma-Kakka, 157
Johnson, Rev. James, 21, 22, 23, 291
Jolof, 254
Juula *see* Dyula

Kaabu, 255, 256
Kaarta kingdom, 245, 246, 249, 271
Kaba, 260 ·
kabīlas, 190, 192
Ḳādirīyya brotherhood, 16, 219, 220, 224, 232, 243, 254, 256
Kaffa kingdom, 155
Kalagne, 124, 126
Kamba, 84–5, 91, 93
al-Kanēmi, Muḥammad, 16, 234, 236, 237–8
Kankan, 260
Kano, 6, 214, 216, 225, 230, 232
Karagwe, 91, 104
Kasongo, 118
Katsina, 225, 232
Kayor, 254
Kele, 304
Kenya, 19, 85, 91, 93, 98, 100, 107
Kenyane, Reverend, 19
Ketu, 281, 284, 285
Khasso, 246
Khoi Khoi, 67
Khoisan, 50, 53
Kikuyu, 85, 86, 93
Kilwa, 71, 79, 89–91
Kilwa Kisiwani, 79
Kilwa Kivinje, 79, 84
kingdoms, 7, 15, 16, 42–9
   see also states
Kipsigi, 98
Kiswahili language, 85
Kita, 248–9

Kivu, Lake, 107
Kivui, 85
Kololo state, 47–8, 49, 71, 76–7, 78
Kong, 262
Kongo, region, 114, 118, 123
Kono, 258
Kru, 258–9
Kuba, 120
Kumasi, 262, 265, 266
Kunta, 241, 246
al-Kunti (1729–1811), 219, 220
Kurumba, 271
Kyaggwe, 104

Laborde, Jean, 169, 174
labour, 51, 53, 55, 57–8, 86, 88, 120, 123, 319, 320
Lagos, 4, 18, 37, 286, 288, 289, 291
Lakes region, 107
Lamu island, 81, 85
land, 6, 7, 12, 40–1, 42, 48, 86, 134–5, 138, 205
Lango, 109
languages, 1, 18, 33, 48, 85, 155, 165, 234, 278, 279, 292
Latin America, 310, 311, 312
   see also Americas; Brazil; Cuba
leather, 10
Lesotho, 47, 49, 65, 67
Liberia, 4, 21, 23, 24, 30, 31, 32, 34–5, 37, 255, 257, 259, 272, 314
Libya, 186–7, 188, 209
   administration of, 205
   Europe and, 199–200
   foreign capital in, 206
   Islam in, 16, 182
   Sanūsiyya, 182, 187, 211
lineages, 7, 43, 76, 96, 100, 210, 216, 230, 257
Liptako, 269, 271, 275, 276
Livingstone, David, 5, 17, 37, 77, 99
Livingstone Mission, 17
Lobengula, King, 18
Lobi, 272, 275
Lokoja, 35
Lokoya, 144, 145
London Missionary Society, 17, 18, 99, 165, 169
Lozi, 47, 48, 70, 71, 77, 78, 120
Lualaba valley, 112, 120
Luanda, 120, 123
Luapula valley, 128
Luba, 115, 126, 128, 316
Lufuma, 126
Lunda, 68, 70, 78, 120, 124, 126, 316
Lundu, 77
luxury goods, 10, 11, 89, 94, 110, 272

Maasai, 85, 86, 93, 94, 96, 98, 322
Maba, 255
Madagascar, 8, 13, 19, 317–18
  administrative reforms, 172, 174
  and Britain, 165, 167, 170, 171,
    172, 175
  centralization, 24
  economic development, 174–5
  foreign policy, 167, 169, 170–1
  and France, 164, 167, 169,
    170,171–2, 175
  Merina consolidation in, 164–5
  military reforms, 174
  missionary schools in, 18, 165,
    172
  modernization of, 165–7, 169,
    171, 174, 175
  population movements, 2
  religion in, 165, 167, 169, 171–2,
    175
  social developments, 172
  standing army, 165, 167, 174
Magdala, 157, 160, 162
al-Maghīlī, 219, 220
Maghrib, 211, 316
  anti-European revolts in, 206–7
  economic crises in, 181–2
  European colonization of, 180–1,
    207–8
  factors of change in, 181
  incorporation in world-economy,
    12, 185, 205–6
  loss of independence, 176
  Makhzen (state), 176–80, 189,
    190, 192, 194, 197
  naval wars, 199
  revolts in, 182
  rural society, 178, 180
  urban society, 178, 180
  see also Algeria; Libya; Morocco;
    Tunisia
Mahdī, 16, 145, 149, 163
maize, 7, 41, 89, 114, 117, 126
Majerteyn Sultanate, 154
Makua, 71, 72, 84
Malawi, 68, 91, 96
males, 41, 42
Malindi, 79, 81
Malinke, 255
Mambari, 71, 124
Mamlūks, 129, 131, 134, 176
Mamprusi, 265, 276
Mande, 219, 222, 245, 258, 259–61,
    268, 272
Mandinka, 248, 257, 258, 260, 261
Manganja peoples, 48, 77
marabouts, 206, 239, 254
marriage customs, 85, 126

Maseko Nguni, 48
Massassi, 245
Massawa, 152, 154, 163
Massina, 15, 16, 24, 218, 221, 222,
    223, 229, 239–43, 245–6, 249,
    269, 317
Mauritius, 13, 29, 30, 89, 165, 167, 9,
    175
Mazrui, 79, 81
Mbundu, 126
Mbwela, 76
Mecca, 305, 307
Medani, 142
medicine, 115, 172
Mende, 257, 259
Menelik, 159–60, 163
Menelik II, 24
merchants, 12, 21, 24, 73, 86, 87, 98,
    180, 276, 320
Merina, 164–5 ff., 172
Merka, 81, 85
Methodists, 17, 18, 55, 276
Mfantsipim School, 18
Mfecane, 4, 7, 8, 24, 76, 315, 320,
    322
  effects of, 49, 57–8, 64, 77–8, 316,
    317
  explanations of, 2, 41–2, 48, 50
  geographical area of, 39
  impact on Cape Colony, 51–8
  meaning of, 39
  and northern Nguni, 48–9
  and Sotho kingdom, 46
Mfengu, 55–6, 57, 58, 61, 67
Middle East, 70, 139, 216, 220, 305,
    307
  see also Arabs; Islam
migrations, 2, 6, 15, 42, 48, 51, 58,
    68, 75–8, 94, 115, 155, 223,
    225, 262, 68, 281, 288–91, 305
  see also Mfecane
Miji Kenda, 84, 85
military class, 78
military regiments, 42, 43, 44, 45–6,
    96
  see also age-grades
military systems, 318–19
  see also armies
military techniques, 42, 44, 96
Mirambo, 94
missionaries, Christian, 1, 8, 9, ·
    17–19, 35, 37, 45, 102, 200,
    288, 291, 316
  in Calabar, 299–300
  in Cameroon, 302, 304
  in Cape Colony, 55–6
  in East Africa, 17, 18, 99
  in Great Lakes region, 109

  impact of, 317–18, 321, 322
  in Madagascar, 18, 165, 169–70,
    171, 172
  in Niger delta, 292, 294, 296, 299
  in Sierra Leone, 33
  in Sotho state, 47
  spread of, 4–5
  in Volta basin, 276
modernization, 24, 58, 135, 147–8,
    65–7, 169, 174, 175, 183,
    184–6, 289, 290
Moffatt, Rev. Robert, 18
Mogadishu, 81, 85
Mombasa, 79, 81, 83, 91
Mono-Niger region
  and Benin kingdom, 285–6
  coastal-interior relations, 288
  cultural intermixing in, 279, 281,
    289
  European interest in, 286–8, 289
  and Old Ọyọ, 281–5
  population movements, 285, 289
  and returned slaves, 289, 290–1
  socio-economic change, 288–91
  trade, 289–90
Monrovia, 258
Morija, 47
Morocco, 176, 200, 201, 202, 229,
    272
  army in, 190, 194, 196
  crisis (1878–81), 181, 182, 197
  and Europe, 190, 192–7, 199, 202,
    207–8
  foreign trade, 194, 196
  government reforms, 192–6, 198
  incorporation in world-economy,
    12, 206
  Islam, 190, 192, 197, 198
  political structure, 189–92
  and Sahara, 212
  special identity of, 189
  taxation, 181, 190, 192, 194, 197
Moshoeshoe, 46–7, 53, 59, 61, 63,
    64, 65
Mossi, 262, 266–8, 269, 272, 275, 276
Mozambique, 4, 21, 39, 68, 76, 128
  and Atlantic slave trade, 71
  and Central African slave trade, 72
Mpande, 44
Mpondo, 54, 55, 57
Msene Nguni, 48
Mshope kingdom, 96
Msiri kingdom, 126
Mswazi, 43–4
Mthethwa kingdom, 42, 44, 49
Mubārak, A., 138
Muḥammad III (1757 90), 189, 190,
    198

Muḥammad IV (1822–59), 190, 192, 194, 196
Muḥammad 'Alī, 8, 12, 131–3, 134–5, 137, 140, 142, 144
Muḥammad Bello, 227, 228, 229, 232, 237, 238, 241
Muhammadu Habibu, 251
Mulaj, 124, 126
Muslims, 16, 73, 218, 220, 221, 222, 231
    see also Arabs; Islam; traders, Arab
Muteba (1857–73), 126
Mutesa, 102, 145
Mwakikonge, 85
Mwenda, 128
Mwenemutapa, 78
Mzilikazi, 45–6, 49, 57

Nana Olumu (1884–94), 294
Nandi, 98
Napoleon Bonaparte, 2, 4, 8, 129
Napoleon III, 202, 205
Natal, 2, 13, 15, 47, 65,
    before 1870, 62–3
    missionary schools in, 18, 19
nationalism, 12, 129–34
Nawej (1820–52), 124
Ndebele, 15, 45–6, 47, 49, 57, 64, 76
Ndwandwe state, 42–3, 45, 48, 49, 50
Nembe, 295, 296, 298
Ngindu, 84
Ngonyo, 85
Nguni, 2, 15, 24
    Gaza, 72, 75–6
    social classes among, 77–8
    southern, 50, 55, 58
    of Zwangendaba, 76, 94, 96
    see also Nguni, northern
Nguni, northern, 2, 7, 39, 58, 94
    famine among, 41
    farming practices of, 40–1
    and Mfecane, 48–9, 55, 56, 87, 94
    and population pressures, 41–2
    social structure, 41, 49, 94, 96
    states, 42–9
Ngwane, 43, 49, 54–5, 57
Niger bend, 16, 288
    civil wars, 268
    religious change, 276, 278
    social change, 275–6
    socio-economic tensions in, 271–5
Niger delta, 12, 13, 35, 286 ·
    eastern delta, 295–8
    Europeans in, 292, 294, 296, 298, 304
    and Igbo hinterland, 298–9

slave trade, 31, 296, 298
    wars in, 298
    western delta, 294
    see also Mono-Niger region
Niger province, 241
Nigeria, 3, 7, 8, 23, 218, 279, 296, 317
Nikki, 279
Nioro, 248, 249
Njelu kingdom, 96
Nkore, 104
Noath, 145
nomads, 186, 192, 209, 210, 211, 212, 213–16, 218, 223, 242
North Africa, 201, 319, 320
    and abolition of slave trade, 30–1
    development of, 205–6
    population growth, 3
    religions, 17
    revolts in, 206–7
    slave trade, 216
    trade in, 25, 321
    see also Egypt; Maghrib; Morocco; Sahara; Sudan
Nsenga, 73
Nukama, 223
Nupe, 31, 225, 230, 232, 281, 283, 286, 317
Nyamwezi, 84, 91
Nyaneka kingdom, 126
Nyasa, Lake, 84, 89, 91
Nyungu ya Mawe, 94

Ogowe basin, 292, 302–4
Okrika, 295, 296, 298
Old Qyǫ, 2, 15
    collapse of, 8, 281–5
Omani Arabs, 71, 79, 81, 84, 85, 86–7, 88–9 ff.
Ondo, 279, 281, 285, 289
Opobo, 298
Orange Free State, 57, 63–4, 65, 67
Oromo, 85, 152, 155, 163
Ottoman empire, 8, 200, 305, 308
    abolition of slave trade, 30
    and desert nomads, 211
    economy of, 11–12
    and Egypt, 129, 131, 133, 137
    and Ethiopia, 152, 154
    and Libya, 186
    and Tunisia, 185
Ovambo, 117, 123
overpopulation, 2
Ovimbundu, 25, 114, 117, 120, 123, 124, 126, 316
Qwǫ, 279, 281, 285, 289
Owu, 283
Qyǫ, 279, 289

    see also Old Oyo
Oyoko, 262, 265

palm oil, 3, 4, 12, 35, 296, 319
Pan-Africanism, 22, 23, 26
Pangani valley, 91, 93, 94
Pare, 91, 93
Paris Evangelical Missionary Society, 17, 47
pastoralists, 2, 3, 93, 96, 98, 218, 223, 230, 254
pasture, 40, 41
Pate island, 81, 85
Pedi, 15, 64, 65, 67
Pemba, 86, 88
pirates, 199
plantations, 10, 13, 14, 28, 71, 86, 88, 98, 254, 311
Pokomo, 5
political structures, 11, 12, 13, 15, 16, 23–4, 70, 100–4, 124, 189–92, 230, 316–18
polygamy, 19, 23
Pongolo river, 40, 42, 43
population
    growth, 3, 15, 40, 41–2, 48, 115, 123
    movements, 2–3, 15, 88, 94, 107, 285, 289
    sparse and dense models, 112–15
    see also Mfecane
Poro, 268
Porte, 137, 186
    see also Ottoman empire
Porto Novo, 279, 281, 285, 288, 289, 291
Portuguese, 4, 10, 14, 17, 28, 30, 31, 45, 72, 76, 120, 123, 128, 302, 310
printing press, 24, 47
production, 11, 13, 41, 104–5, 112, 114, 117
Protestants, 17, 19, 35, 37, 99, 171–2, 317

Rabeh, 32
race, 22, 23, 58
Radama I (1810–28), 165–7, 174, 175
Radama II (1861–3), 169–70
Ranavalona I, Queen (1828–61), 167–9
Ranavalona II, Queen, 171, 172
Red Sea, 118, 152
re-exports, 98
reforms, 8, 12, 24, 172, 174, 183–6, 192–6, 219, 220–1, 225, 227, 317

see also djihāds
refugees, 54–4, 57
religion, 4–5, 17–19, 22, 110, 152,
    159, 161–2, 163, 167, 169,
    171–2, 175, 218–19, 221, 271,
    276, 278
    see also Christianity; Islam;
    traditional religions
resources, 40–1, 111
Réunion, 71, 89, 167, 169, 175
rice, 89, 126, 174, 241
Rift Valley, 100
Roman Catholics, 17, 19, 35, 99,
    159, 162, 169, 172, 200, 254,
    317, 318
royal families, 41, 43, 44, 100, 300
    see also lineages
Rozwi, 13, 48, 76, 77
rubber, 3, 4, 12
rulers, 6, 7, 32, 39, 41, 42, 94, 100,
    102, 104, 105, 124, 128, 220,
    318, 318
    see also amir; chiefs
Rwanda, 94, 102, 104, 105, 107, 110,
    115

Ṣabę, 281, 284, 285
Sahara, 16, 186
    economy and trade, 213–16
    French occupation of, 212–13
    Islam in, 216
    nomad-sedentary relations,
        210–11
    and outside world, 210–13
    research on, 216–17
    and slave trade, 30–1, 32, 214,
        216
    society and environment, 209–10,
        216
    trade routes, 25, 211, 212
Sahel, 210, 214, 271, 272, 275
Sahla Sellasé (1813–47), 152
Saʿīd (1854–63), 133, 135, 137
Saʿīd, Sultan Seyyid (1806–56), 81,
    83, 86, 87, 91
Saifawa dynasty, 16
Sakalova, 165, 167, 169
Salaga, 272
salt, 10, 104, 107, 109, 111, 275
Salum, 254–5
Samo, 269
Samori Ture, 15, 16, 260–1, 317
Sangu, 96
Sanūsī brotherhood, 16, 182, 186,
    187, 207, 211, 214
Saros, 290–1
Sassandra, 259
savannah, 3, 40

schools, 18, 19, 33, 165, 200, 224,
    296, 302, 304
    see also education, Western
Scramble for Africa, 13, 78, 175, 315,
    322
    see also colonialism
scripts, 1
Sebetwane, 47, 48, 49, 76–7
secret societies, 7, 296, 299, 300–1,
    302, 304
Segu, 222, 239, 241, 242, 245, 246,
    248, 249, 251, 271, 276
Seku Ahmadu, 15, 218, 219, 220,
    221, 222, 223, 224, 239–43
Sena, 70, 73
Senegal, 32, 35, 37
Senegal river, 254
Senegambia, 4, 12, 16, 218, 221, 222,
    252–5, 320
Sereer, 252, 255
Seychelles, 71
Shaka, 7, 24, 39, 42, 44–5, 48, 49, 54,
    57, 94, 318
Shambaa, 91, 93
Shango worship, 311
shaykhs, 8, 135, 221–3, 227
    Swahili, 79
Shi, 115
Shilluk, 144–5
Shirazi, 79, 88
Shire Valley, 48, 77
Shoa, 150, 152, 154, 155, 157, 159,
    160, 163
Shona, 46, 68, 70, 72, 76, 78
Sierra Leone, 18, 21, 22, 23, 24, 30,
    31, 32–4, 35, 251, 255, 257,
    258, 259, 276, 290
Siin, 254
Sinoe, 34
slave raids, 3, 84, 94, 98, 110, 142,
    145, 149
slave trade, 3, 9, 13, 14, 17, 37, 77,
    213, 255, 258, 316, 319–20
    and legitimate trade, 5, 11, 290,
        292, 296, 321
    see also slave trade, abolition of;
    slave trade, Atlantic; slave trade,
    Indian Ocean; slave trade,
    internal
slave trade, abolition of, 3, 4, 12, 14,
    25, 185, 200, 243, 272, 289–90,
    300, 311–12
    African reactions to, 30–5, 37
    in Central Africa, 73
    in East Africa, 86, 98
    in Ethiopia, 159
    impetus for, 27–9
    limitations of, 37–8

in Madagascar, 174
in Niger delta, 292, 295, 298–9
process of, 29–31
and protecting new trade, 35–7
resistance to, 28–9
    see also freed slaves
slave trade, Atlantic, 10–11, 27–38,
    120, 252, 255, 256, 258, 262,
    288, 289–90, 305, 310–11, 319,
    321
    numbers involved in, 27, 31–2
    persistence of, 31, 32, 37
    see also slave trade, abolition of
slave trade, Indian Ocean, 3, 13, 27,
    29, 32, 37, 84, 86, 87, 88, 89,
    93, 109, 110, 307
    and Kilwa, 79
    and Zambezi basin, 70–3
    see also slave trade, abolition of
slave trade, internal 3, 27, 37, 72, 78,
    85, 86, 88, 93, 107, 109, 110,
    216, 272, 275
    in Niger delta, 296, 299
    in Sudan, 142, 214
    trans-Saharan, 30–1, 32
slaves, role and treatment of, 51, 78,
    85, 86, 120, 123, 210, 222, 223,
    224, 227, 230–1, 238, 275, 285,
    296, 301, 304, 310, 319–20
    see also freed slaves
Smith, Sir Harry, 59, 61
Sobhuza, 42, 43, 49
social classes, 77–8, 276, 320
social structure, 6, 7, 41–2, 49, 85,
    89, 230–1
Soga, Tiyo, 19, 20
Sokoto Caliphate, 7, 16, 216, 218,
    219, 239, 241, 243, 269
    administration of, 227–9
    and Borno, 229, 234–8
    centralization, 24
    changes in, 232
    djihād in, 221, 232, 271
    economic expansion, 233
    military and diplomatic activities,
        229
    political structure, 230, 232
    slave trade, 31, 227, 230–1, 238
    social structure, 230–1
    taxation, 230, 231
Solimana, 256
Somalia, 81, 85, 154–7, 163
Soninke, 16
Soshangane, 45, 75–6
Sotho, 15, 43, 45, 46–7, 49, 53, 57,
    59, 61, 63, 64–5, 67, 76, 77
Sotho-Tswana, 7, 40, 41
South Africa, 4–5, 19, 22, 38

Boer republics in, 63–4
British expansion in, 65
British withdrawal from interior of, 59–61
colonial self-rule in, 61–3
see also Cape Colony; Natal; Southern Africa
Southern Africa, 2, 7, 8, 15, 40, 50, 320
Christian missionaries in, 18–19
effects of Mfecane in, 39, 49, 57–8, 64
frontier wars, 56
incorporation in world-economy, 11, 13
migrations to East and Central Africa, 75–5, 94, 96
population growth, 3
wars in, 51, 54, 56, 59, 65, 66, 67
see also Mfecane; South Africa
Spain, 28, 176, 192, 198, 206, 308, 310
states, 3, 39, 41, 42, 49, 176, 178, 315, 316
centralized, 7, 23–4, 25, 76, 86, 93, 124, 126, 148, 275
formation of, 13–14, 68, 70, 71–2, 75, 77, 93, 94
in Great Lakes region, 100–4, 111
non-centralized, 7, 93, 210, 275
Sudan, 12, 131, 160, 243, 261
agriculture, 144
and camel nomads, 216
and Central African trade, 118
centralization, 148
djihāds, 15–16, 218, 222, 225, 315, 317
economy, 251
and Egypt, 139, 140, 142, 145, 149
foreigners in, 149
Islam, 147, 148–9
modernization of, 147–8
religious reforms, 219–23
resistance in, 142, 144, 145
slave trade, 31, 142, 144, 149, 214, 222
trade routes, 25, 212, 249
and Turkey, 140, 142, 144–9
Suez Canal, 12, 134, 137
sugar, 63, 120
Sulaymān (1792–1822), 189, 190, 194
Susu, 257
Swahili, 79, 85, 126
language, 87, 89
Swahili traders, 16, 25, 71, 72, 85, 86, 87, 91, 93, 109, 118
Swazi, 15, 42, 43–4

Swaziland, 49
Sweden, 28
syncretism, 221

al-Ṭahṭāwā (1801–73), 136, 138
talībs, 249, 251
Tamatave, 165, 167
Tamba, 256
Tanganyika, Lake, 91, 118
Tanzania, 17, 39, 76, 89, 91, 94, 100, 118
Taung, 59, 61
taxation, 63, 109, 124, 142, 145, 181, 190, 192, 194, 211, 222, 230, 231, 241
technology, 72, 178, 180, 315, 316
Temne, 257
Téwodros II, Emperor of Ethiopia, 157–60, 317, 318
textile industries, 87, 89, 94, 120
Thaba Bosiu, 46
Thembu, 42, 54, 55, 57, 62
Tigré, 150, 152, 154, 157, 159, 160, 161, 163
Tijāni Alfa, 249, 251
Tijāniyya, 16, 192, 207, 218, 219, 220, 224, 232, 243, 245, 254, 255, 256, 317
Tile, Nehemiah, 19, 22
Timbo, 256
Timbuktu, 229, 241, 242, 245, 246
Tippu Tip, 32, 118
Tlemcen, 178
Tlokwa, 59
Tonga, 70, 73
Torodbe, 219–20, 269
see also Fulbe; Tukuloor empire
towns, 15, 178, 180, 285
trade, external, 5, 9, 12, 24, 41, 194, 196, 205–6, 213, 289–90
and abolition of slave trade, 35
and Central Africa, 117–18, 120, 124
and East Africa, 86–7
in Great Lakes region, 109–10
impact on Africa, 321
and luxury goods, 10, 11
and Madagascar, 174–5
in Maghrib, 181
and Senegambia, 252, 254
socio-economic effects of, 84–6
and Zambezi valley, 70
see also slave trade; Europe; Europeans
trade, internal, 5, 8, 9, 25, 32, 53–4, 70, 71, 79, 83–4, 88–93, 107–9, 117, 18–23, 211, 212, 213, 216, 249, 251, 260

in Cameroon, 292 ff., 302, 304
and Kilwa hinterland, 89–91
in Niger delta, 31, 296, 298
in Volta and Niger regions, 271–5
see also slave trade; traders, African; traders, Arab
traders, African, 2, 4, 16, 21, 25, 31, 32, 71, 72, 86, 87, 91, 107, 109, 110, 118, 120, 300
traders, Arab, 16, 32, 37, 71, 72, 73, 77, 84, 85, 86, 87, 91, 93, 109, 118, 144, 260, 276, 307
traders, European *see* Europe; Europeans
traditional religions, 16, 19, 172, 218, 221, 269, 276, 278
Trans-Zambezi Nguni states, 48
Transvaal, 40, 49, 57, 63, 64, 65, 66, 67
tribute payments, 7, 78, 104, 105, 124, 144, 145
Tripoli, 176, 178, 212, 214, 216, 229
see also Libya
Tripolitania *see* Libya
Tsonga, 43, 45
Tswana, 47, 53, 57, 64, 76
see also Sotho–Tswana
Tuareg, 212, 213, 214, 216, 222, 223, 229, 242, 271, 272, 275
Tukuloor empire (1852–64), 243–51
see also Torodbe
Tunis, 176, 178, 185, 199, 200, 201
Tunisia, 30, 188
colonialism in, 207
crisis (1866–89), 181–2, 185–6
foreign capital in, 206
French control of, 176, 180–1, 186, 200
incorporation in world-economy, 12, 181
land tenure, 6
modernization and reforms, 183–6, 200, 205
rebellion in, 207, 208
taxation, 181, 185
urban life, 178
Turkey, 131, 133, 134, 137, 139, 140, 142, 144–9, 176, 178, 183, 188
see also Ottoman empire

Uganda, 19, 100, 109, 110, 145
Ujiji, 91
'ulamā', 134, 135, 178, 190, 192, 194, 196, 197, 198, 220, 221, 223
underpopulation, 2
see also depopulation
Undi, 77
United Presbyterian Mission, 17

United States, 4, 14, 84, 86, 167, 174, 175
  and abolition of slave trade, 27, 28, 29, 30, 32
  Africans in, 311, 312, 314
  missionaries from, 17
Universities Mission to Central Africa (UMCA), 17, 19, 99
Unyamwezi, 84, 94
Unyanyembe, 91, 118
Upper Guinea, 12, 255–8, 261
Urabist Revolt (1881–2), 12, 135, 138–9
Urhobo, 281, 285, 289, 294
Usukama, 107
'Uthmān dan Fodio, 15, 218, 219, 220–1, 223, 225, 228, 239, 241, 283

Vai, 258
Valley Tonga, 73
Venda, 64
Victoria, Lake, 107, 109
Volta basin
  eastern regions, 269, 271
  political structures, 316
  religious change, 276, 278
  slave trade, 272, 275
  social change, 275–6
  socio-economic tensions in, 271–5
  western and southern groups, 268–9
Vumba Kuu, 79

Waalo, 254
Wagadugu, 268, 275
Walda Sellasé (1795–1816), 150, 152
Wallo, 159, 163
Wanga kingdom, 86, 93

warriors, 271, 285, 318, 320
wars, 3, 4, 31, 45, 49, 51, 54, 56, 59, 65, 66, 67, 283–4, 298, 318, 319, 321, 322
  see also Mfecane
weapons, 72
  see also firearms
Wesleyan Missionary Society, 17, 18, 55
West Africa, 7, 239, 276
  and abolition of slave trade, 29–30, 31, 32–5, 37
  centralization in, 24
  Christian missionaries in, 18, 276
  djihāds, 15, 218–24
  and Ethiopianism, 22–3
  French influence in, 4
  incorporation in world-economy, 12
  population growth, 3
  and slave trade, 10, 222
  Torodbe heritage, 219–20, 243–9
  Western-educated elite in, 21, 24
West Indies, 28, 29, 33
  see also Caribbean
Westernization, 19–21, 22, 24, 35, 37, 200
  see also education, Western; Europe; United States
White Fathers, 5, 17, 99
white settlers, 13, 50 ff., 62–3, 123, 182, 188, 206
  see also Boers
Whydah, 35, 37, 291
witchcraft, 73
Wolof, 219, 222, 252, 254
Womunafu, 110
world-economy, 10–14, 25, 70–3, 78, 87, 88, 117–18, 134, 137, 205–6

Xhosa, 50, 53–6, 58, 59, 61, 62, 67

Yao, 25, 71, 73, 77, 84, 89, 91
Yatenga, 268, 269, 275
Yohannes IV, Emperor of Ethiopia, 161–3, 317
Yoruba kingdom, 2, 15, 23, 31, 33, 79, 281, 283–5, 286, 288, 289, 322

Zaire, 91, 100, 114, 115
Zaire river trade, 118, 120, 128
Zamberma, 272
Zambezi basin, 10, 47
  Kololo in, 76–8
  migrations in, 75–8
  political changes, 68, 70
  slave trade, 70–3
  trade, 70
  and world-economy, 70
  see also Central Africa
Zambia, 68, 96
Zamfara, 225
Zande, 145
Zanzibar, 13, 79, 81, 88, 128, 154, 175
  and Central African trade, 118
  and hinterland trade, 83–4, 91
  and international trade, 86–7
  slave trade, 3, 37, 71, 98, 307
Zaria, 225, 230, 232
Zeila, 154
Zigula kingdom, 91, 94
Zimbabwe, 39, 57, 76
Zulu, 7, 19, 24, 39, 42, 44–5, 49, 51, 57, 65, 94
Zwangendaba, 48, 49, 76, 94, 96
Zwide, 42, 43, 44, 45